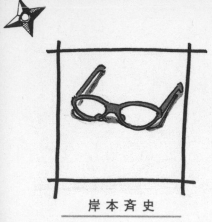

岸本斉史

This is a Naruto side story.
This story is completed in
one volume.
The main character is an 11-year-old
girl named Sarada.
And the person drawing the story is
a 40-year-old dude.
Enjoy...

—Masashi Kishimoto, 2015

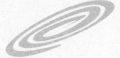

Author/artist Masashi Kishimoto was born in 1974 in rural
Okayama Prefecture, Japan. After spending time in art college,
he won the Hop Step Award for new manga artists with his
manga **Karakuri** (Mechanism). Kishimoto decided to base his
next story on traditional Japanese culture. His first version of
Naruto, drawn in 1997, was a one-shot story about fox spirits;
his final version, which debuted in **Weekly Shonen Jump** in
1999, quickly became the most popular ninja manga in Japan.

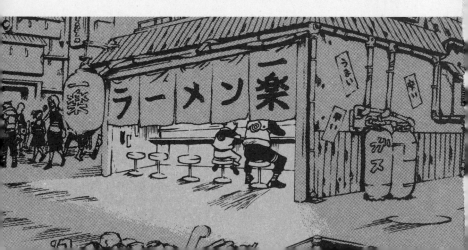

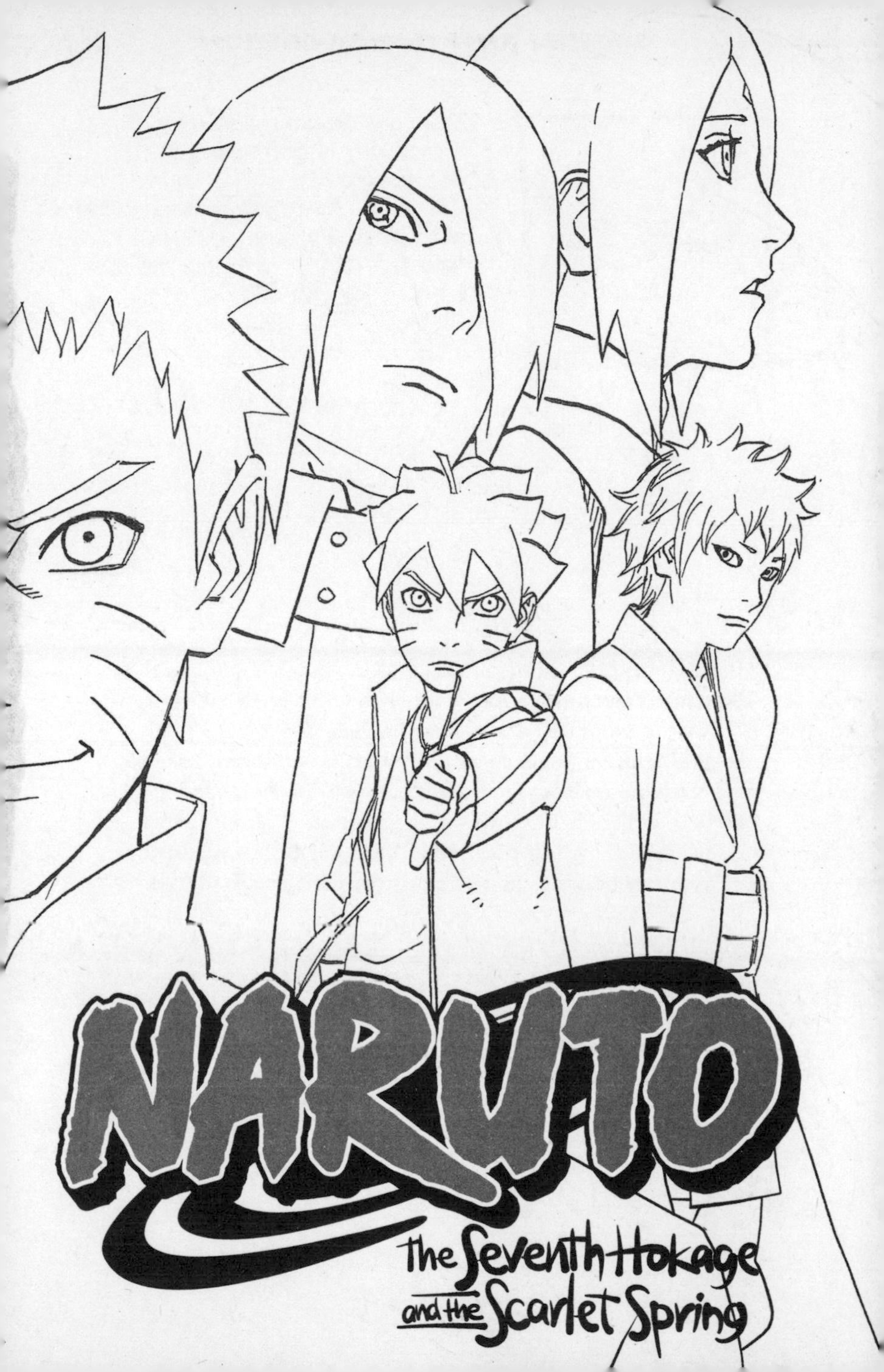
NARUTO
The Seventh Hokage
and the Scarlet Spring

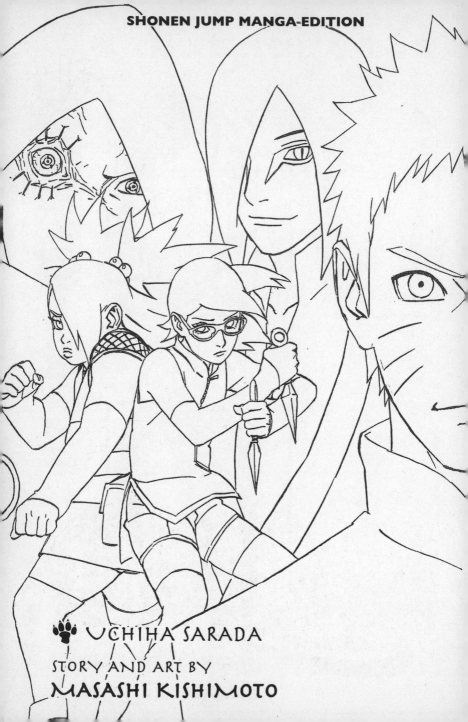

SHONEN JUMP MANGA-EDITION

UCHIHA SARADA

STORY AND ART BY

MASASHI KISHIMOTO

CHARACTERS

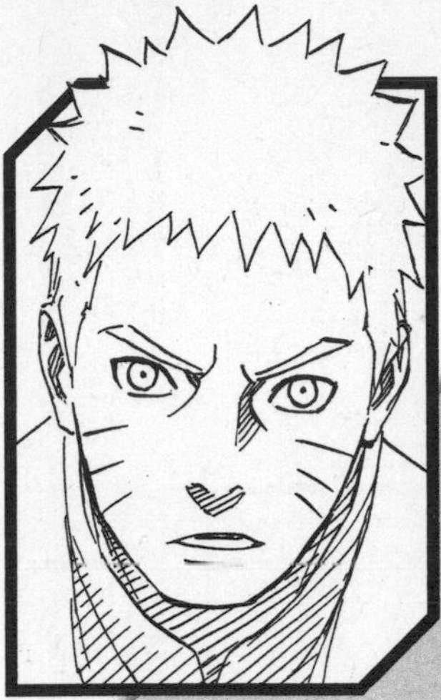

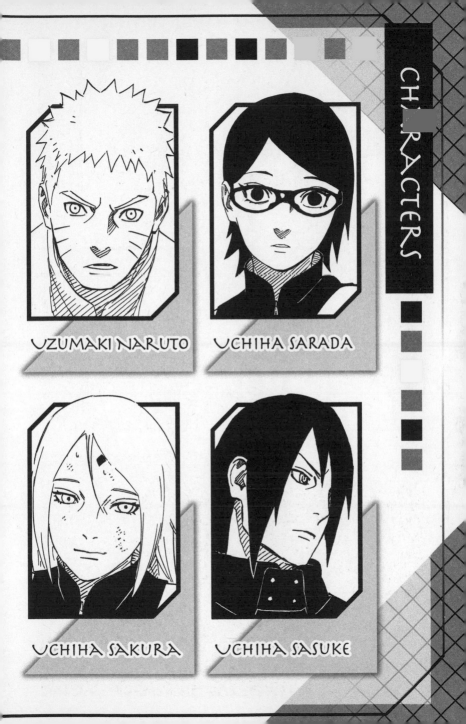

UZUMAKI NARUTO

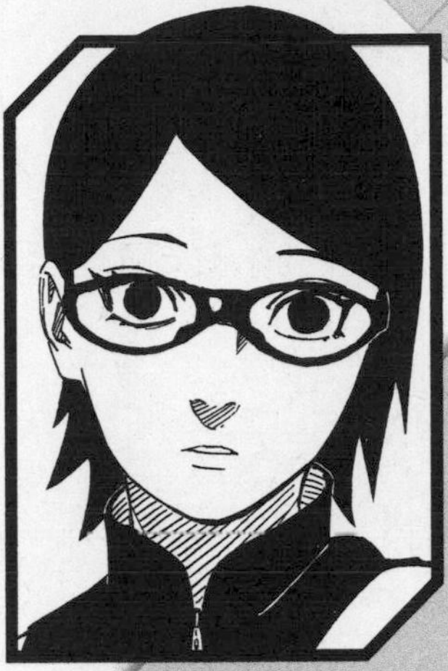

UCHIHA SARADA

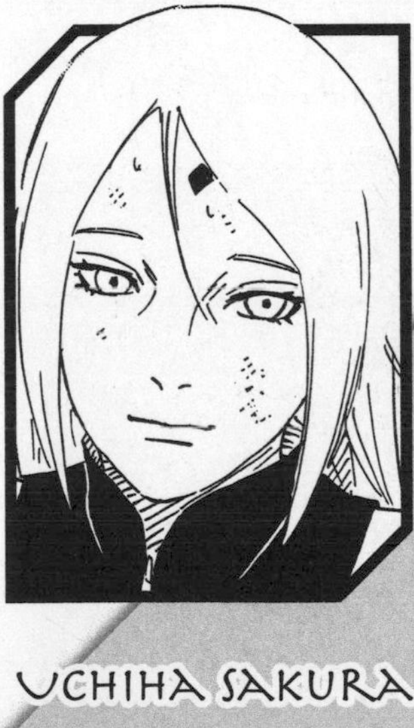

UCHIHA SAKURA

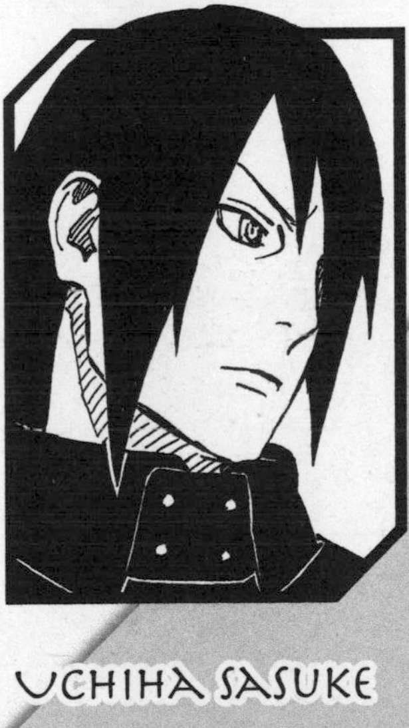

UCHIHA SASUKE

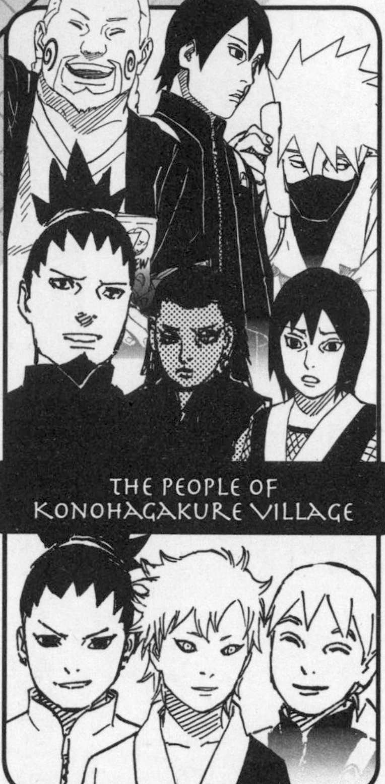
THE PEOPLE OF KONOHAGAKURE VILLAGE

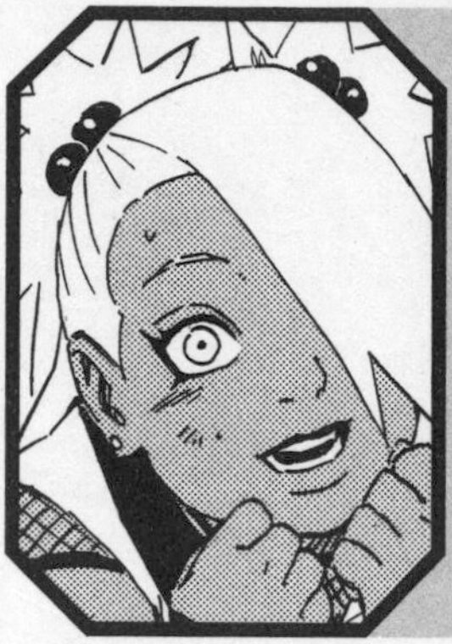

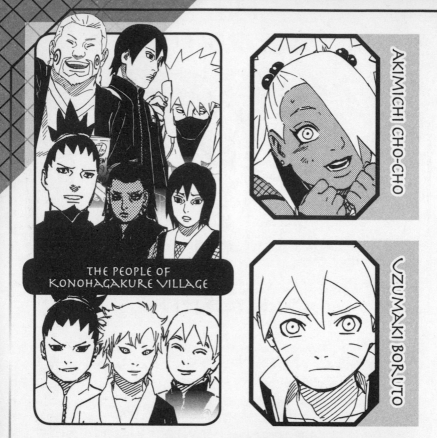

AKIMICHI CHO-CHO

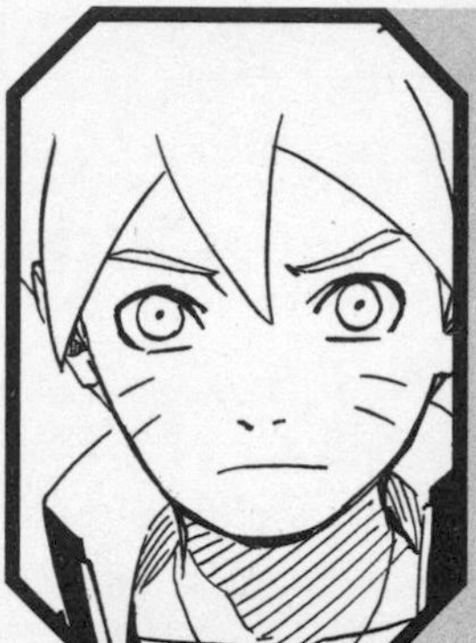

UZUMAKI BORUTO

THE STORY SO FAR...

Naruto, the biggest troublemaker at the Ninja Academy in the village of Konohagakure, becomes a ninja along with his classmates Sasuke and Sakura. They grow and mature through countless trials and battles. However, Sasuke, unable to give up his quest for vengeance, leaves Konohagakure to seek Orochimaru and his power.

Two years pass. Naruto grows up and engages in fierce battles against the Tailed Beast-targeting Akatsuki, and the Fourth Great Ninja War against them begins. At the end of the fierce battle, Naruto joins forces with Sasuke and succeeds in sealing away the resurrected rabbit goddess Kaguya.

Time passes, and the people rejoice in the peace that has come to be. While at a loss about his son Boruto's pranks, Naruto works hard for his village as the Seventh Hokage. Meanwhile, the Ninja Academy's graduation examination draws near...

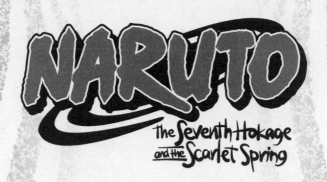

NARUTO

the Seventh Hokage and the Scarlet Spring

UCHIHA SARADA

CONTENTS

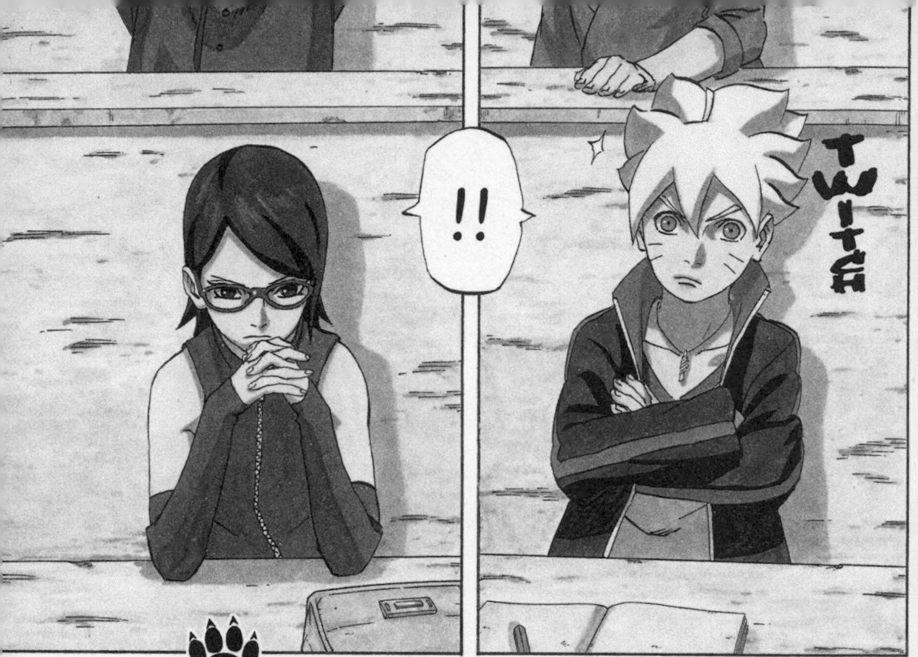
TWITCH
!!

Number 700+1: Uchiha Sarada

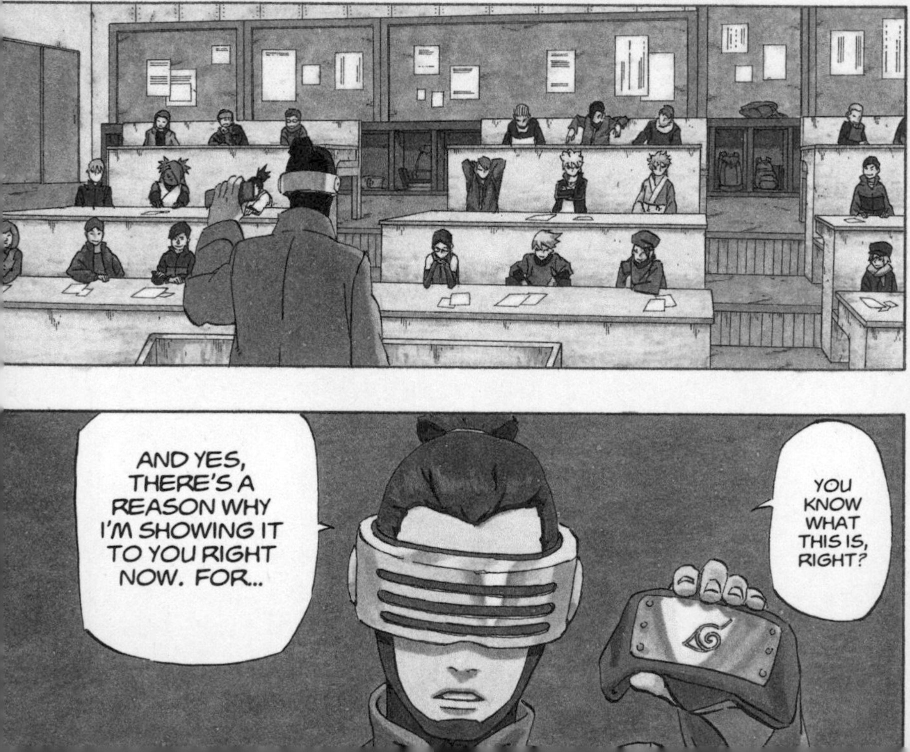
YOU KNOW WHAT THIS IS, RIGHT?
AND YES, THERE'S A REASON WHY I'M SHOWING IT TO YOU RIGHT NOW. FOR...

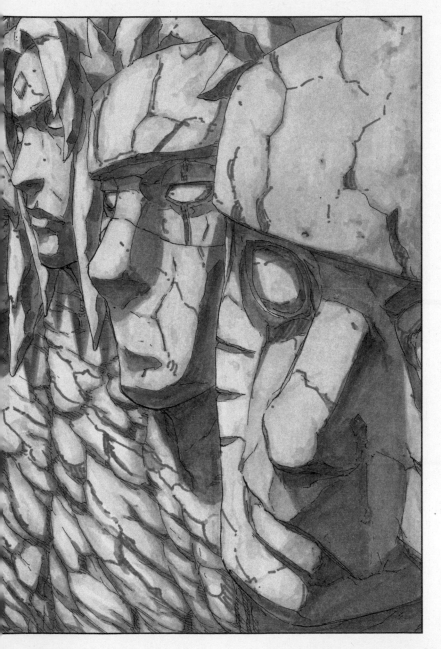

Number 700+1: Uchiha Sarada

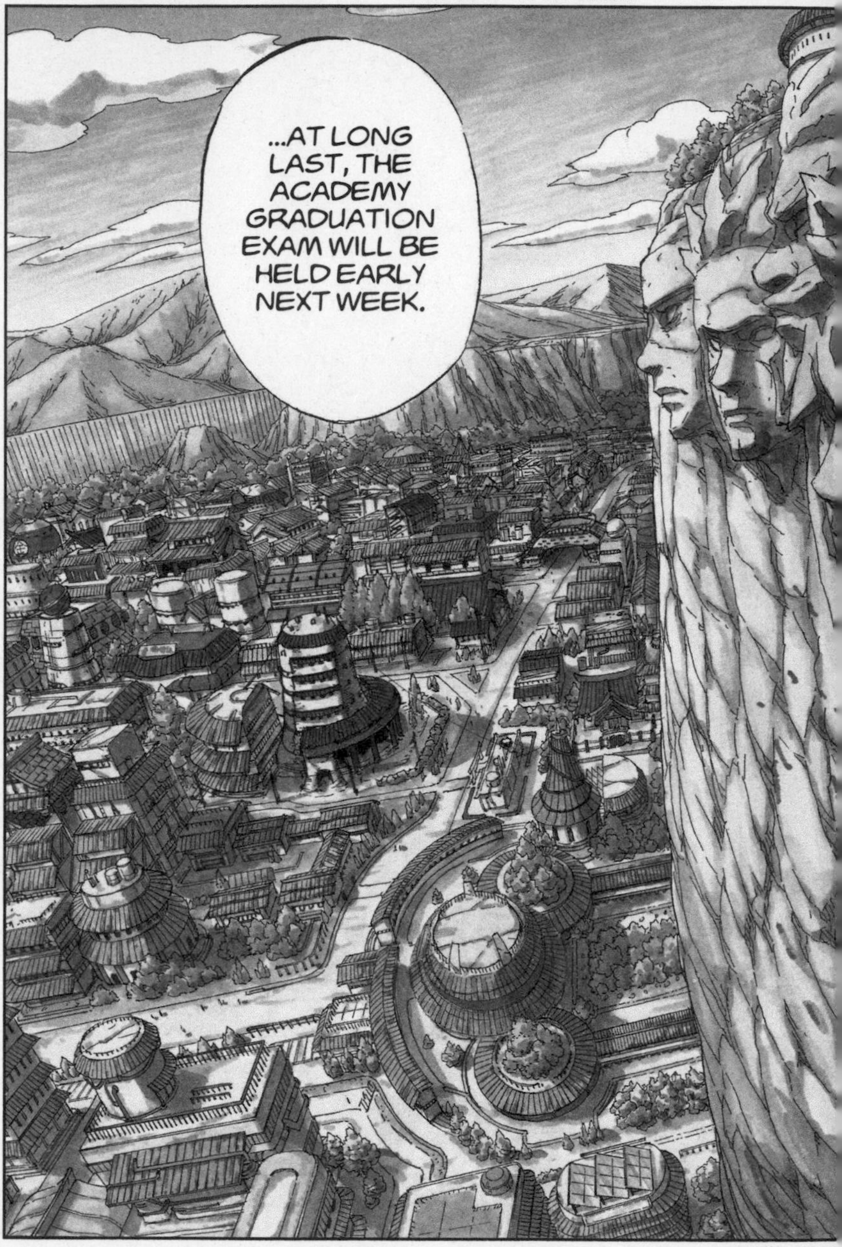
...AT LONG LAST, THE ACADEMY GRADUATION EXAM WILL BE HELD EARLY NEXT WEEK.

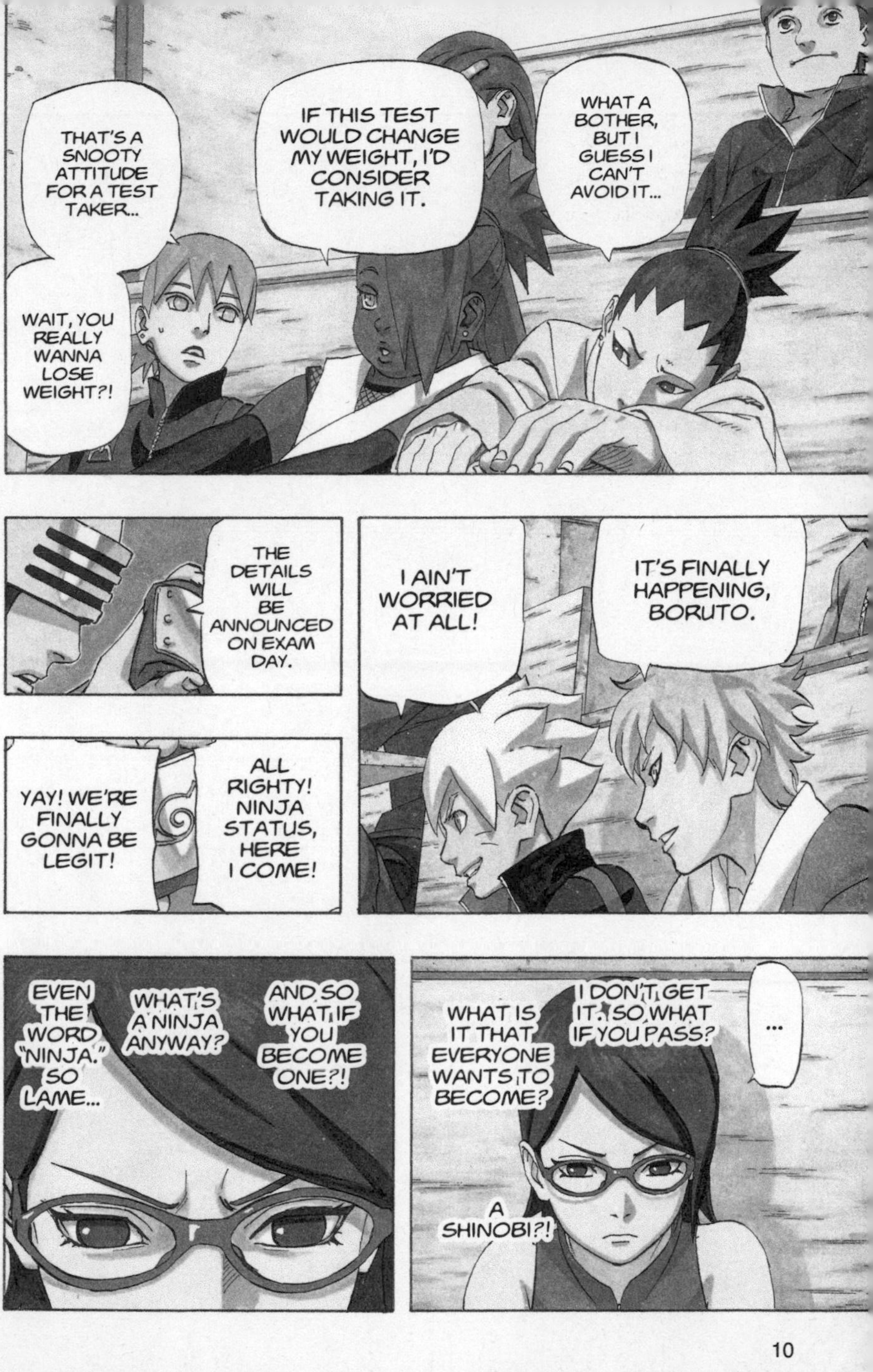
WHAT A BOTHER, BUT I GUESS I CAN'T AVOID IT...
IF THIS TEST WOULD CHANGE MY WEIGHT, I'D CONSIDER TAKING IT.
THAT'S A SNOOTY ATTITUDE FOR A TEST TAKER...
WAIT, YOU REALLY WANNA LOSE WEIGHT?!
IT'S FINALLY HAPPENING, BORUTO.
I AIN'T WORRIED AT ALL!
THE DETAILS WILL BE ANNOUNCED ON EXAM DAY.
ALL RIGHTY! NINJA STATUS, HERE I COME!
YAY! WE'RE FINALLY GONNA BE LEGIT!
...
I DON'T GET IT. SO WHAT IF YOU PASS?
WHAT IS IT THAT EVERYONE WANTS TO BECOME?
A SHINOBI?!
AND SO WHAT IF YOU BECOME ONE?!
WHAT'S A NINJA ANYWAY?
EVEN THE WORD "NINJA." SO LAME...

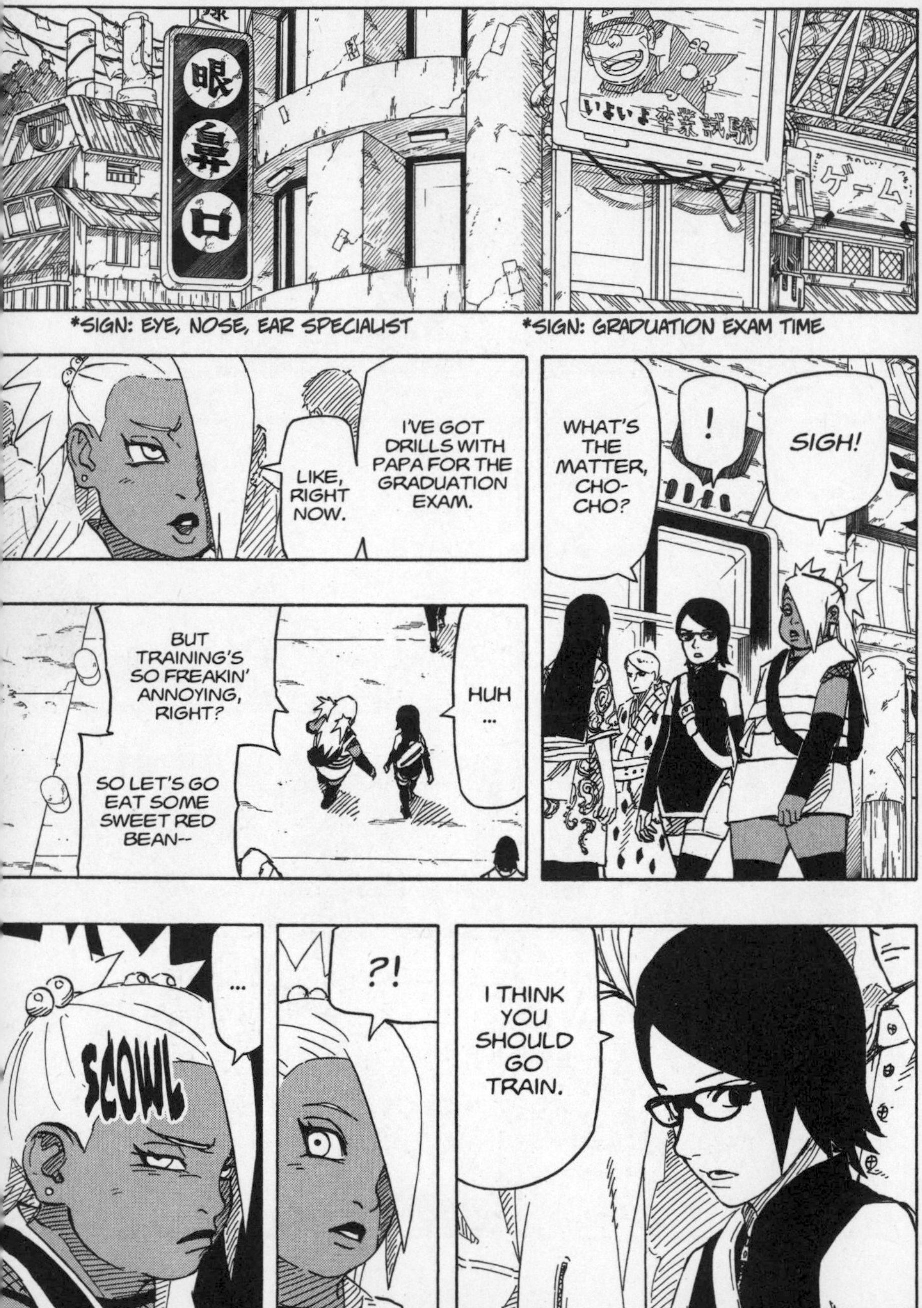

眼
鼻
口
いよいよ卒業試験
ゲーム
*SIGN: GRADUATION EXAM TIME
*SIGN: EYE, NOSE, EAR SPECIALIST
SIGH!
!
WHAT'S THE MATTER, CHO-CHO?
I'VE GOT DRILLS WITH PAPA FOR THE GRADUATION EXAM.
LIKE, RIGHT NOW.
HUH ...
BUT TRAINING'S SO FREAKIN' ANNOYING, RIGHT?
SO LET'S GO EAT SOME SWEET RED BEAN--
I THINK YOU SHOULD GO TRAIN.
?!
...
SCOWL

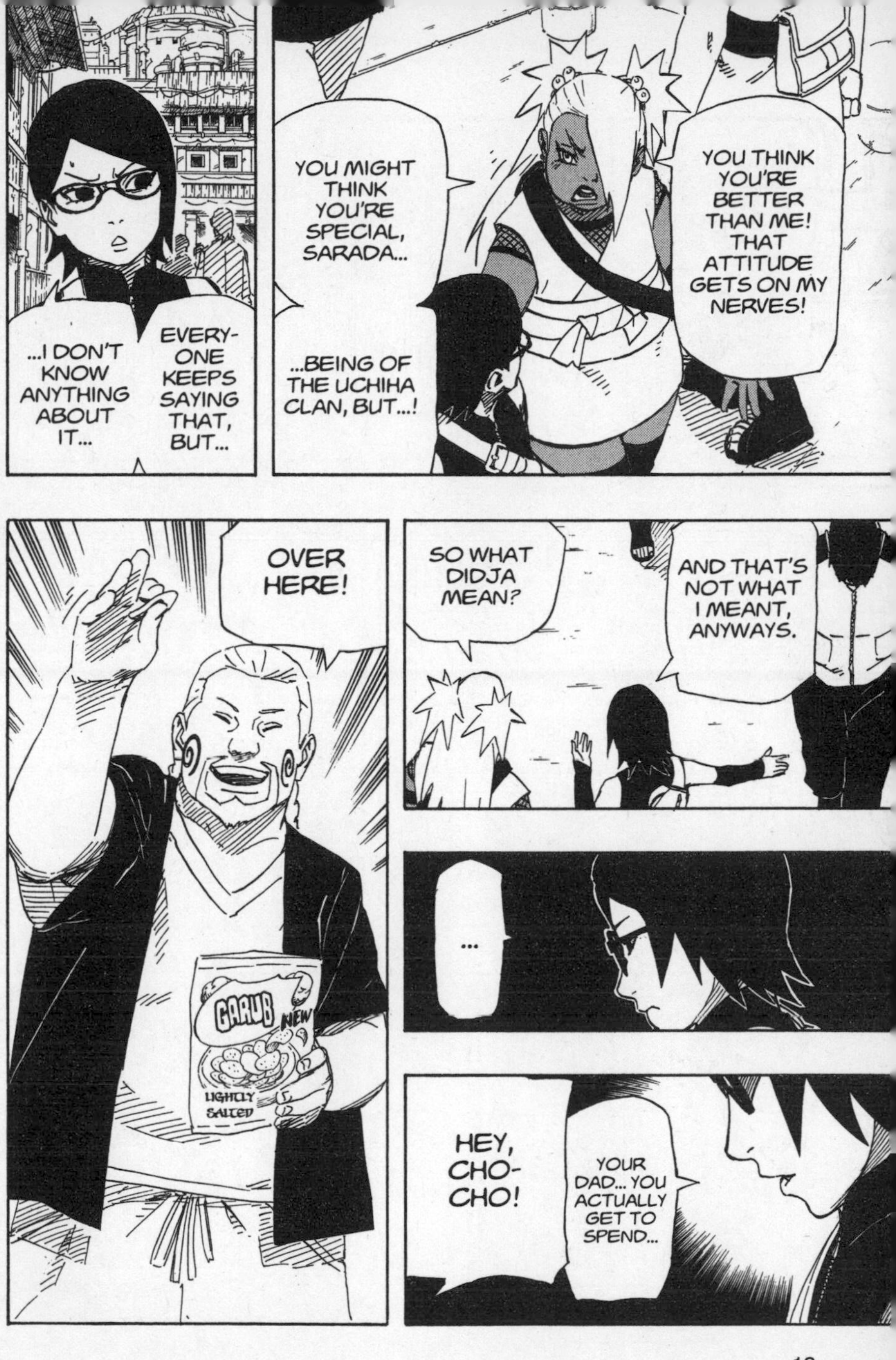
YOU MIGHT THINK YOU'RE SPECIAL, SARADA...
...BEING OF THE UCHIHA CLAN, BUT...!
YOU THINK YOU'RE BETTER THAN ME! THAT ATTITUDE GETS ON MY NERVES!
EVERY-ONE KEEPS SAYING THAT, BUT...
...I DON'T KNOW ANYTHING ABOUT IT...
AND THAT'S NOT WHAT I MEANT, ANYWAYS.
SO WHAT DIDJA MEAN?
...
YOUR DAD... YOU ACTUALLY GET TO SPEND...
HEY, CHO-CHO!
OVER HERE!
GARUB
NEW
LIGHTLY SALTED

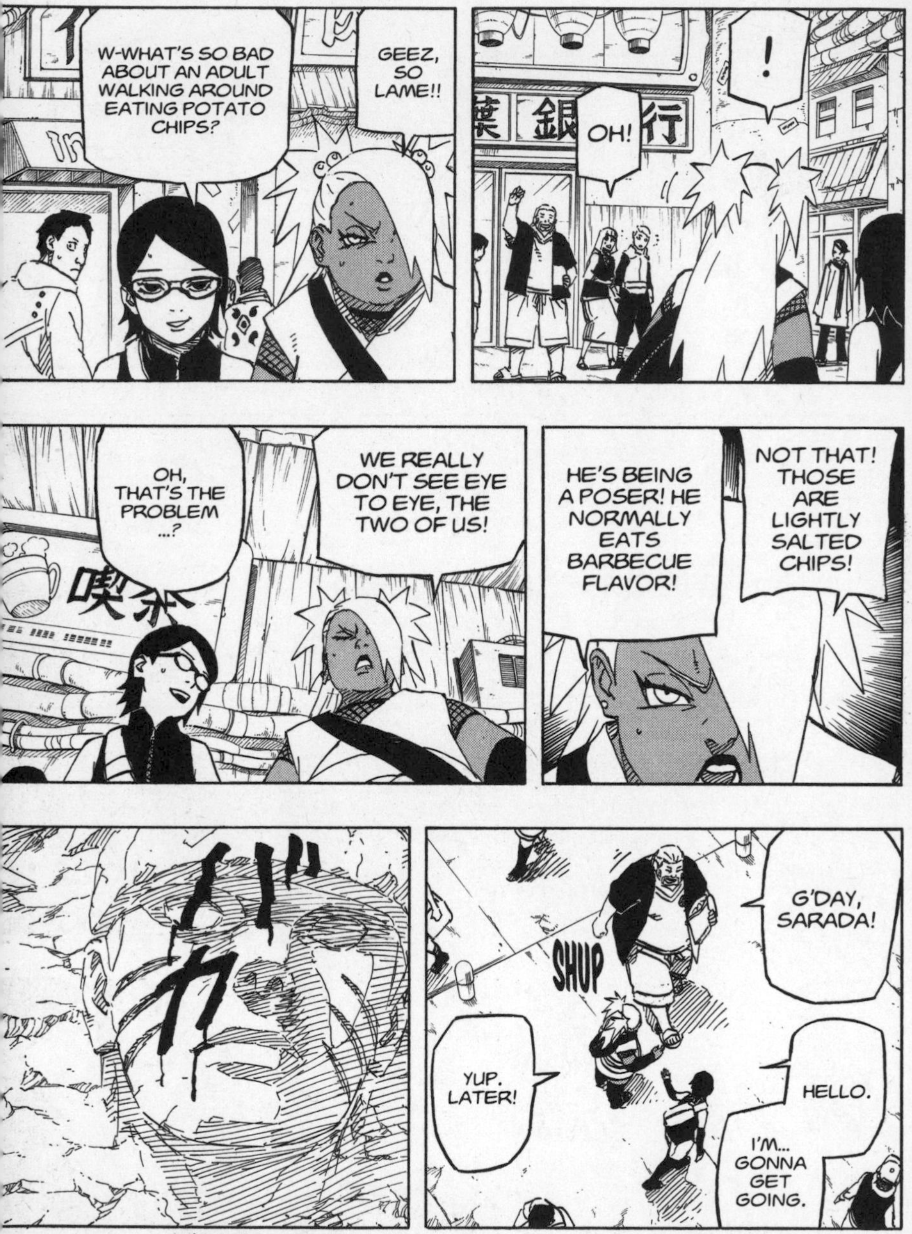
!
OH!
GEEZ, SO LAME!!
W-WHAT'S SO BAD ABOUT AN ADULT WALKING AROUND EATING POTATO CHIPS?
NOT THAT! THOSE ARE LIGHTLY SALTED CHIPS!
HE'S BEING A POSER! HE NORMALLY EATS BARBECUE FLAVOR!
WE REALLY DON'T SEE EYE TO EYE, THE TWO OF US!
OH, THAT'S THE PROBLEM ...?
G'DAY, SARADA!
SHUP
HELLO.
YUP. LATER!
I'M... GONNA GET GOING.

*WRITING: IDIOT

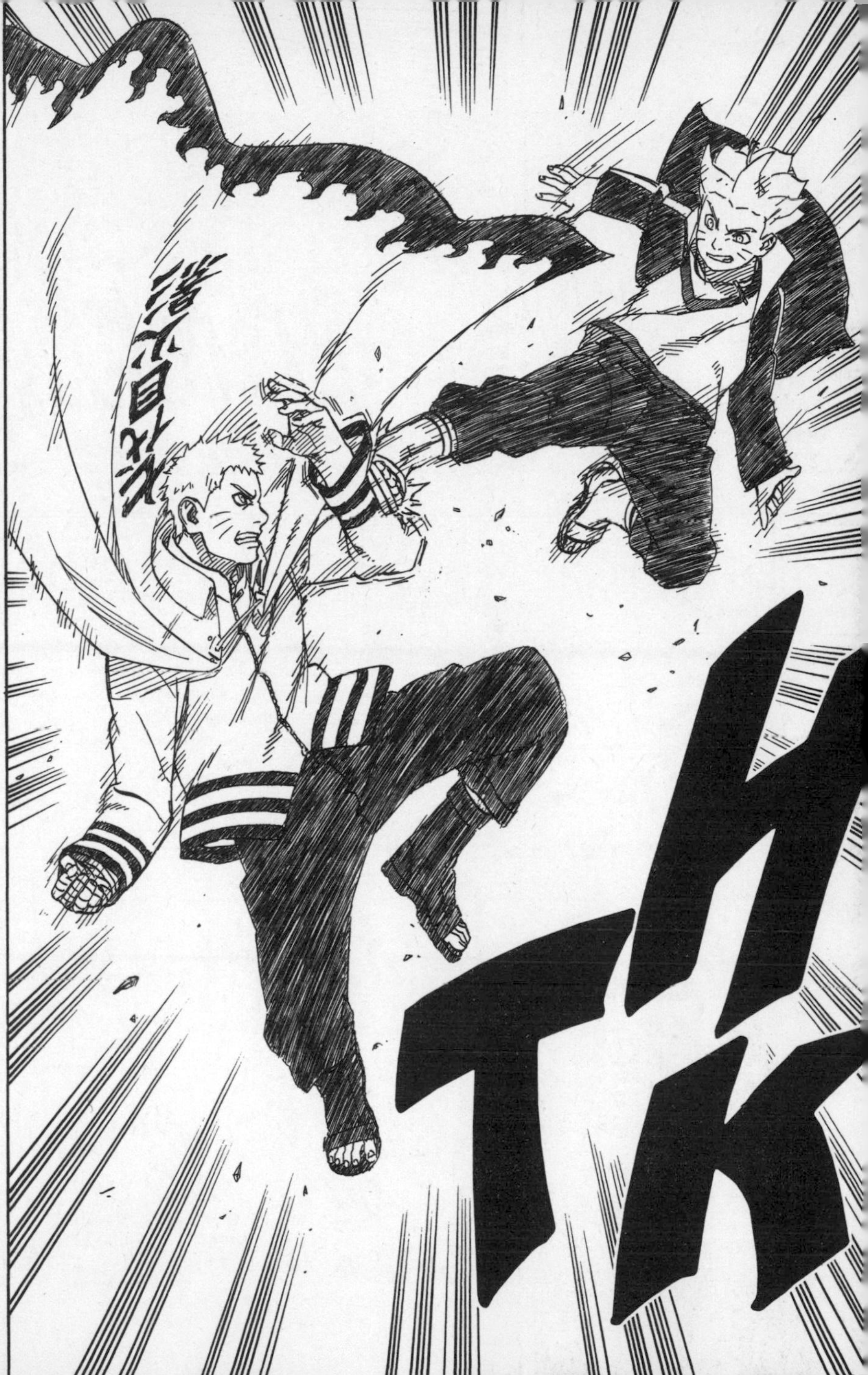

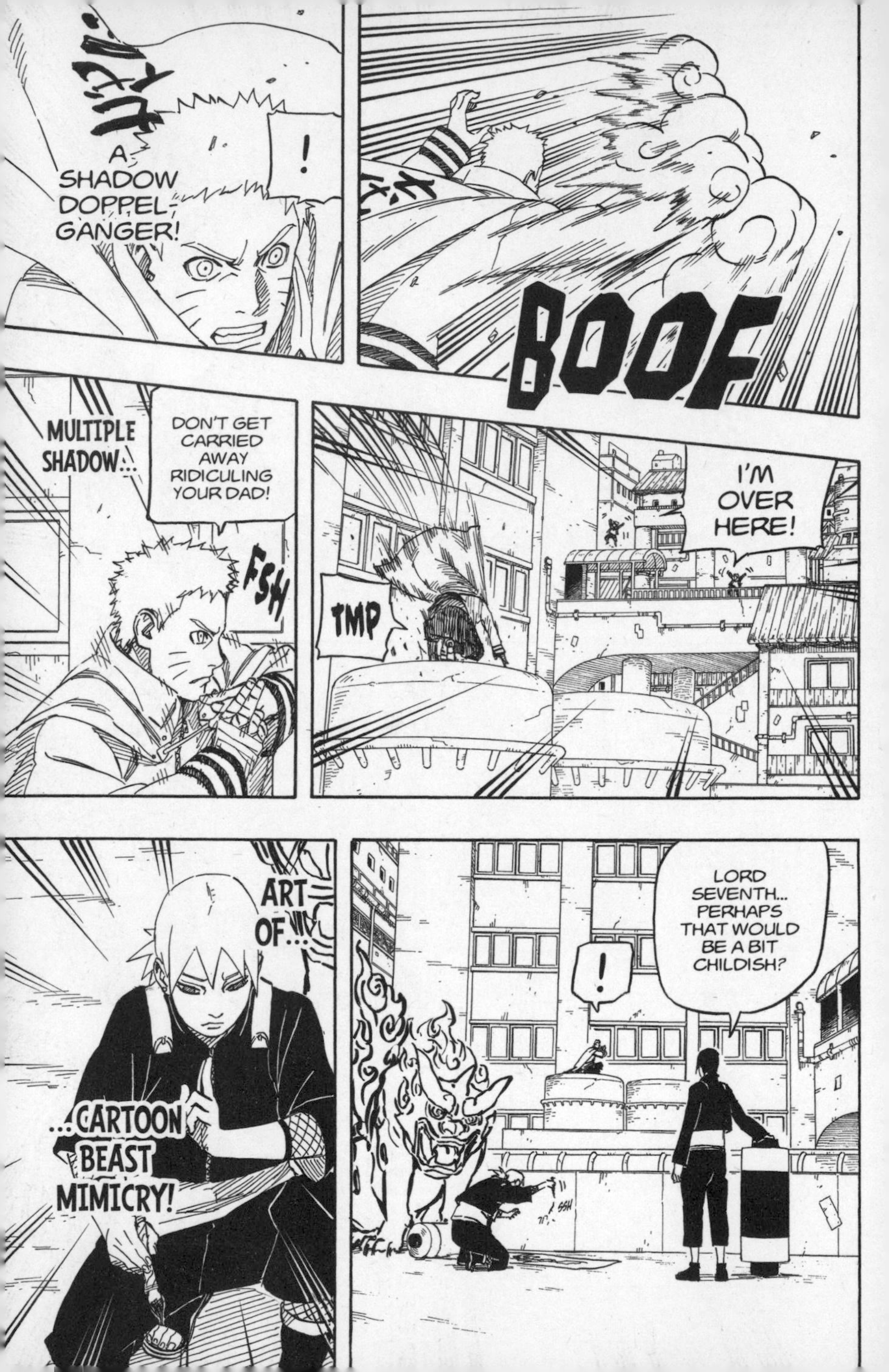
BOOF
!
A SHADOW DOPPELGANGER!
I'M OVER HERE!
TMP
DON'T GET CARRIED AWAY RIDICULING YOUR DAD!
FSH
MULTIPLE SHADOW...
LORD SEVENTH... PERHAPS THAT WOULD BE A BIT CHILDISH?
!
SSH
ART OF...
...CARTOON BEAST MIMICRY!

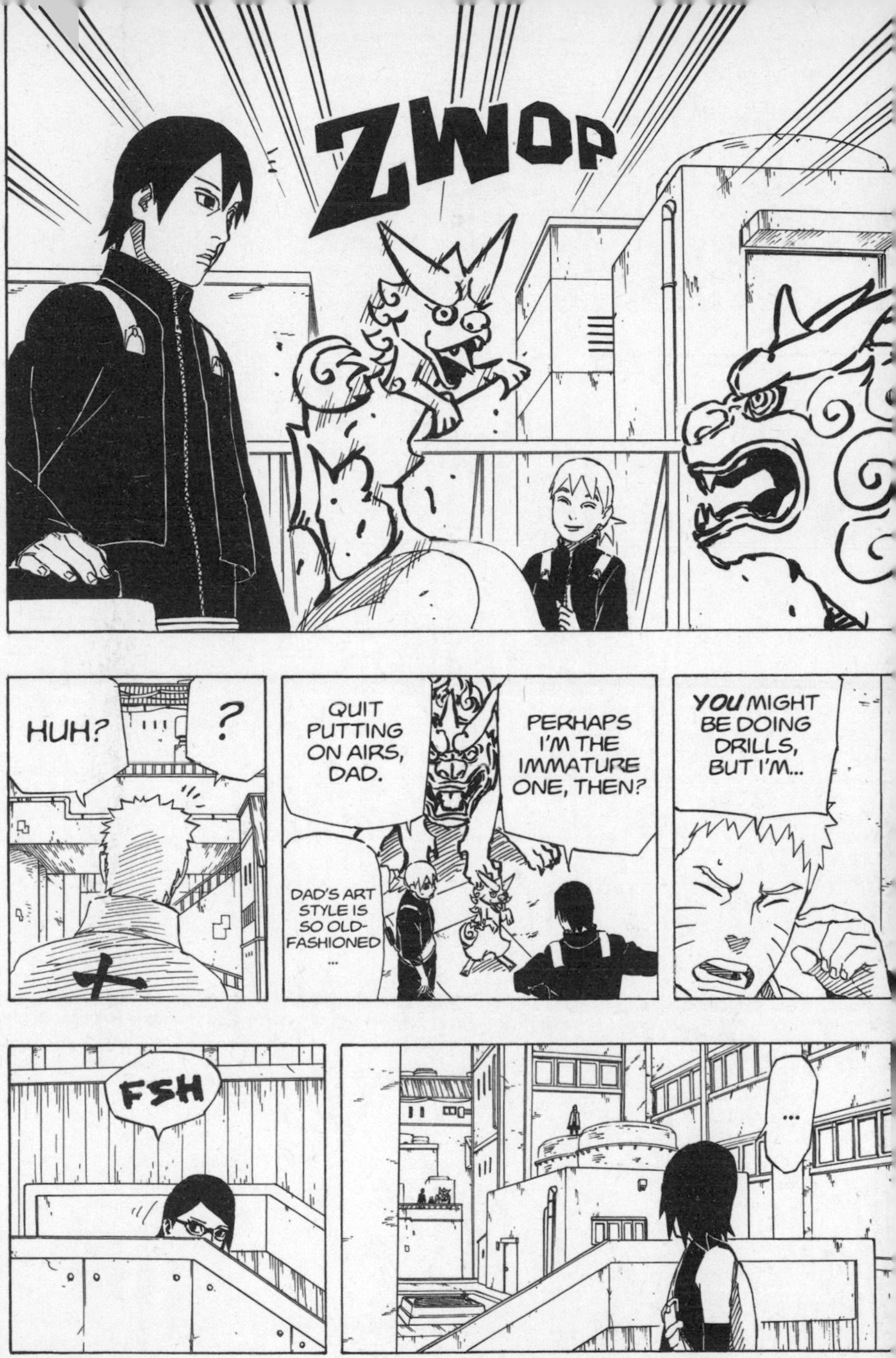
ZWOP
YOU MIGHT BE DOING DRILLS, BUT I'M...
PERHAPS I'M THE IMMATURE ONE, THEN?
QUIT PUTTING ON AIRS, DAD.
DAD'S ART STYLE IS SO OLD-FASHIONED ...
?
HUH?
...
FSH

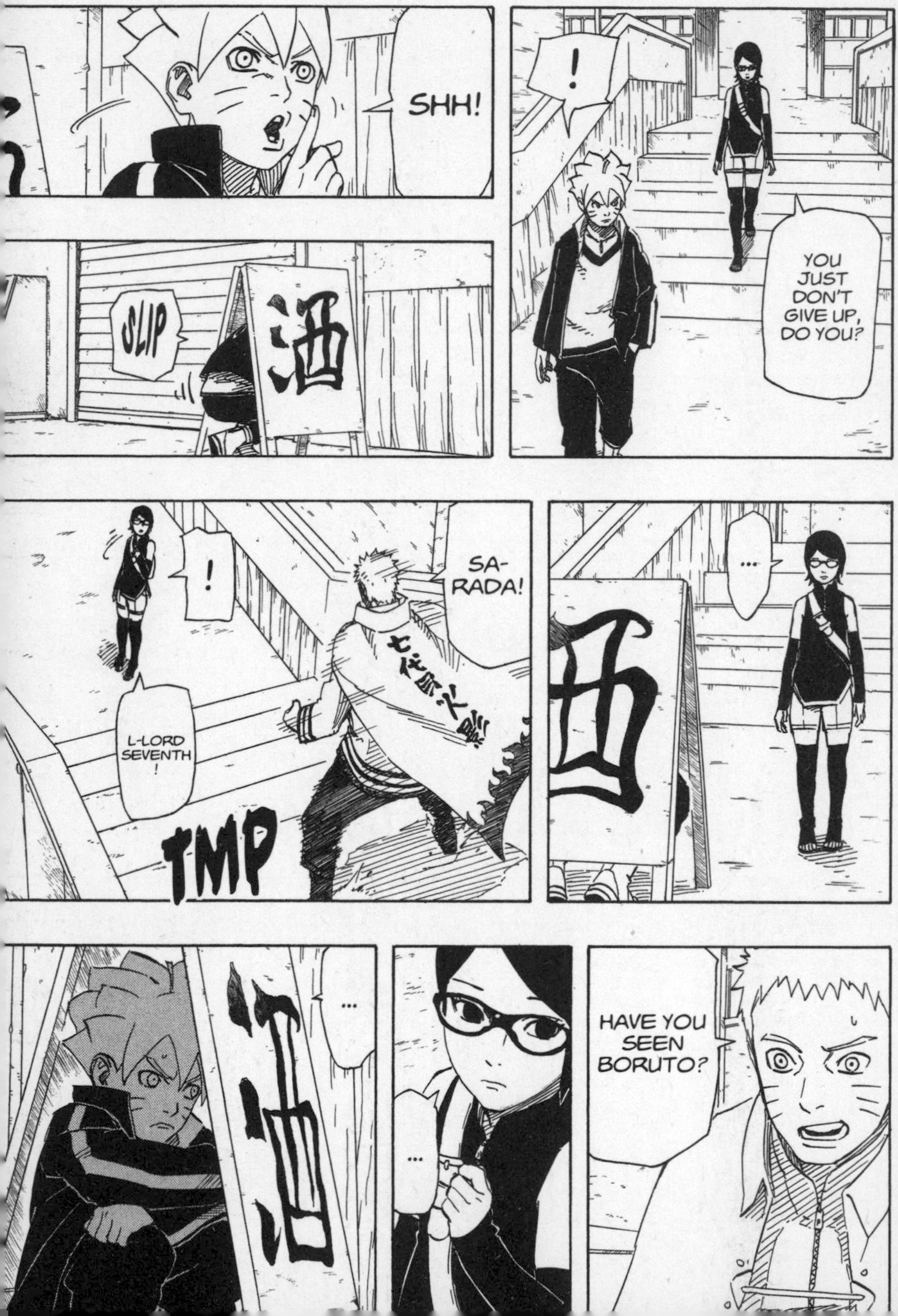
!
YOU JUST DON'T GIVE UP, DO YOU?
SHH!
SLIP
...
SA-RADA!
!
L-LORD SEVENTH!
TMP
HAVE YOU SEEN BORUTO?
...
...
...

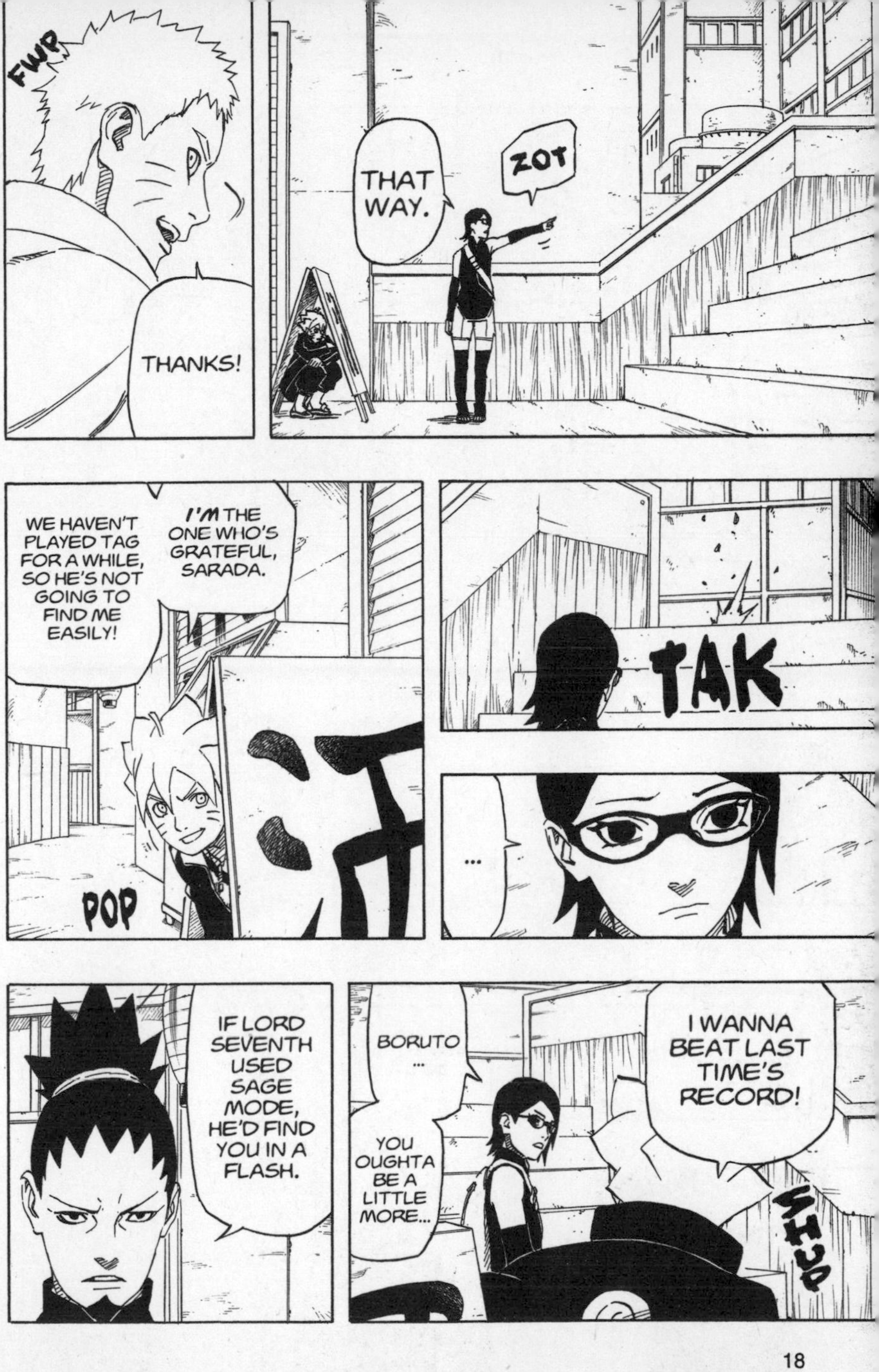

ZOT
THAT WAY.
FWP
THANKS!
TAK
...
I'M THE ONE WHO'S GRATEFUL, SARADA.
WE HAVEN'T PLAYED TAG FOR A WHILE, SO HE'S NOT GOING TO FIND ME EASILY!
POP
I WANNA BEAT LAST TIME'S RECORD!
SHUP
BORUTO ...
YOU OUGHTA BE A LITTLE MORE...
IF LORD SEVENTH USED SAGE MODE, HE'D FIND YOU IN A FLASH.

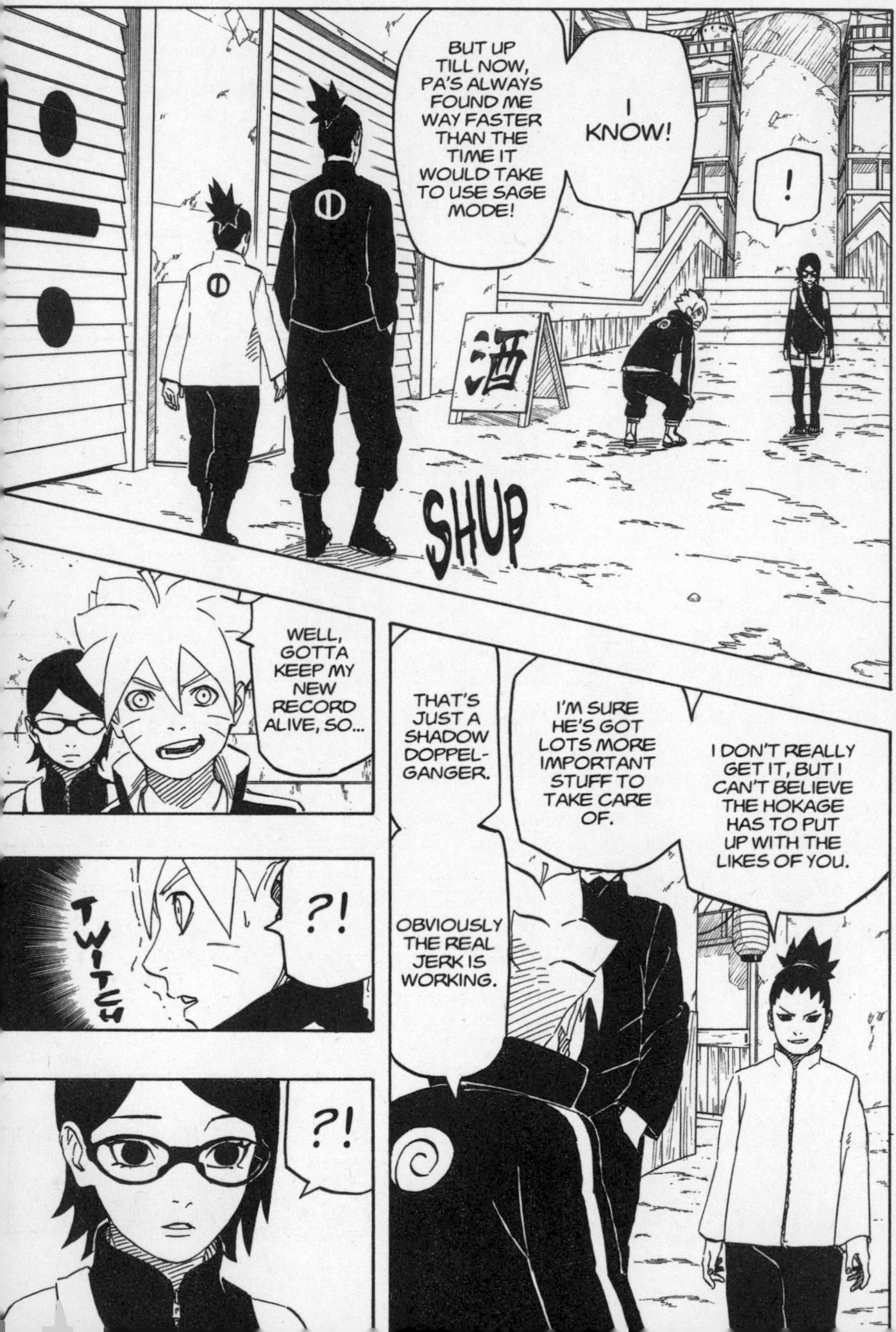
!
I KNOW!
BUT UP TILL NOW, PA'S ALWAYS FOUND ME WAY FASTER THAN THE TIME IT WOULD TAKE TO USE SAGE MODE!
SHUP
I DON'T REALLY GET IT, BUT I CAN'T BELIEVE THE HOKAGE HAS TO PUT UP WITH THE LIKES OF YOU.
I'M SURE HE'S GOT LOTS MORE IMPORTANT STUFF TO TAKE CARE OF.
THAT'S JUST A SHADOW DOPPEL-GANGER.
OBVIOUSLY THE REAL JERK IS WORKING.
WELL, GOTTA KEEP MY NEW RECORD ALIVE, SO...
?!
TWITCH
?!

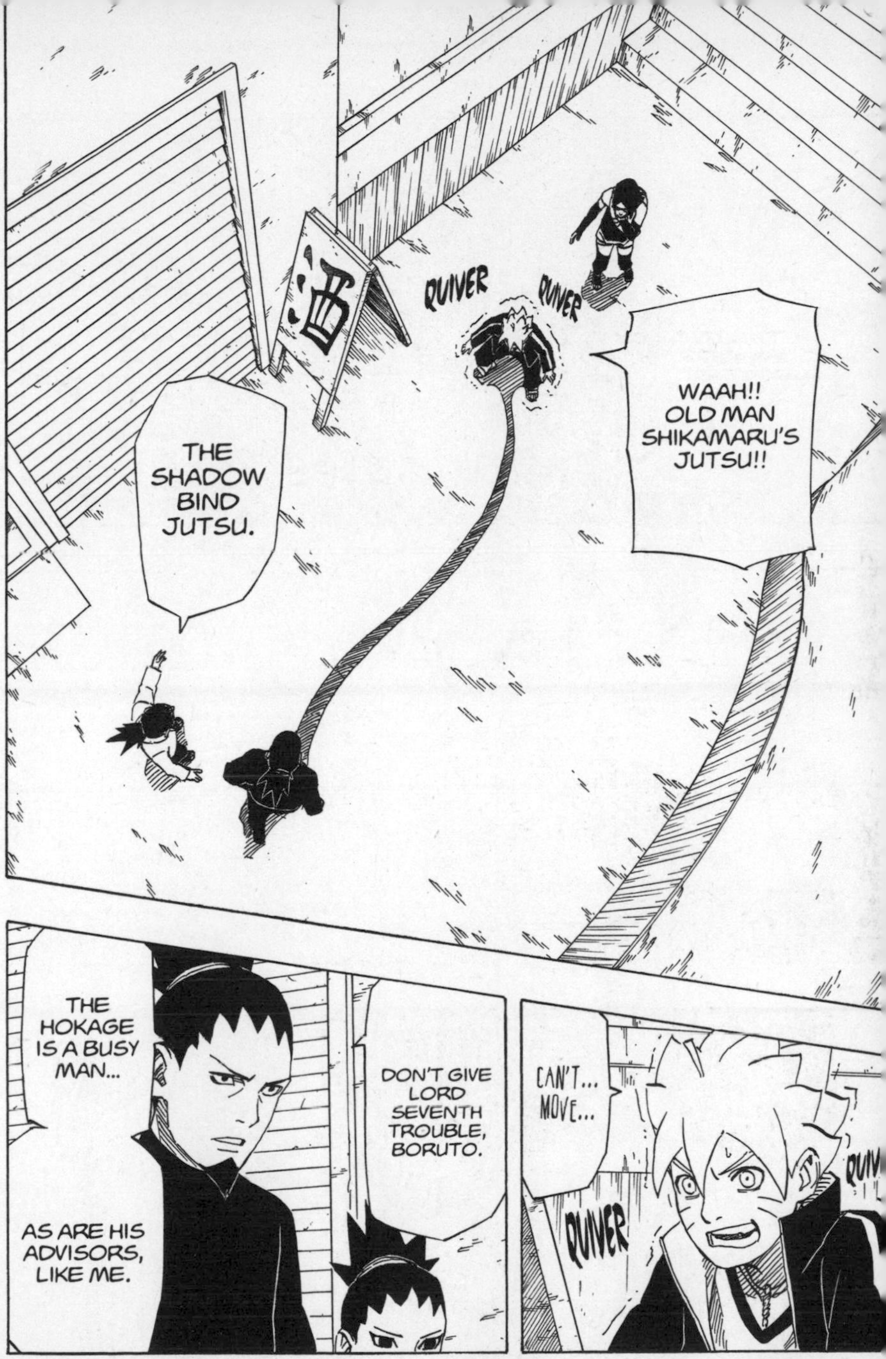
WAAH!! OLD MAN SHIKAMARU'S JUTSU!!
QUIVER
QUIVER
THE SHADOW BIND JUTSU.
CAN'T... MOVE...
QUIV
QUIVER
THE HOKAGE IS A BUSY MAN...
AS ARE HIS ADVISORS, LIKE ME.
DON'T GIVE LORD SEVENTH TROUBLE, BORUTO.

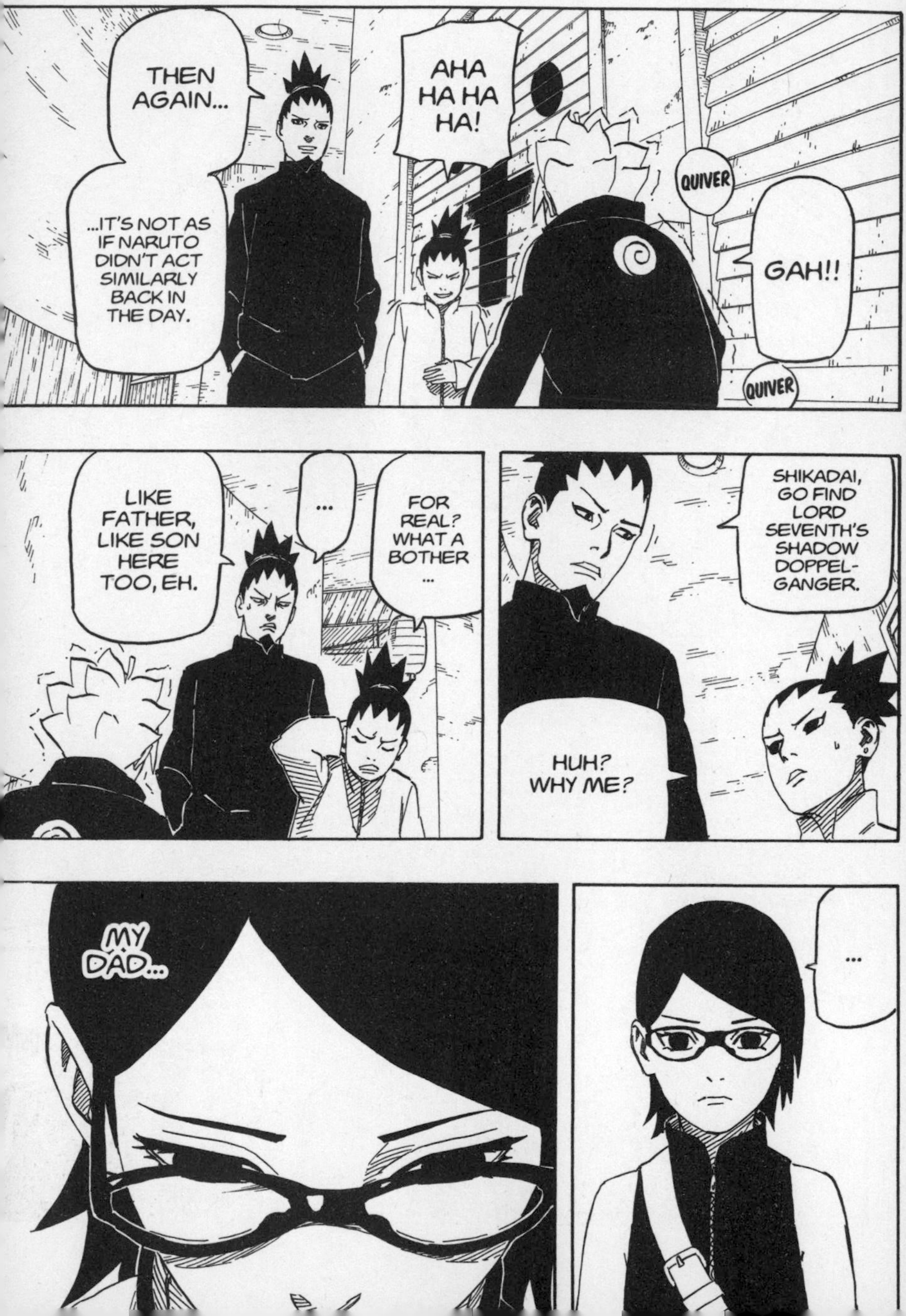
QUIVER
GAH!!
QUIVER
AHA HA HA HA!
THEN AGAIN...
...IT'S NOT AS IF NARUTO DIDN'T ACT SIMILARLY BACK IN THE DAY.
SHIKADAI, GO FIND LORD SEVENTH'S SHADOW DOPPEL-GANGER.
HUH? WHY ME?
FOR REAL? WHAT A BOTHER ...
...
LIKE FATHER, LIKE SON HERE TOO, EH.
...
MY DAD...

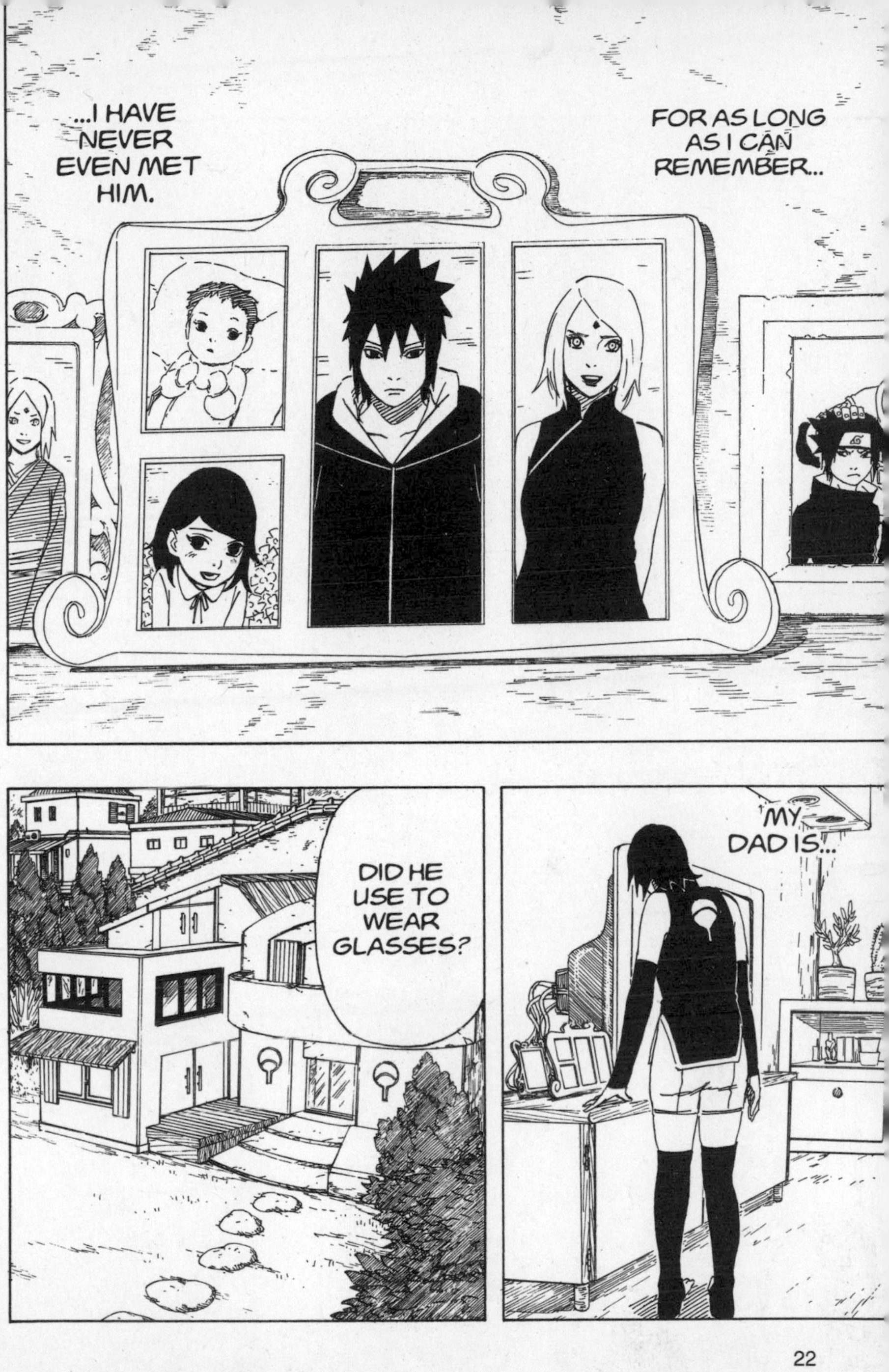
FOR AS LONG AS I CAN REMEMBER...
...I HAVE NEVER EVEN MET HIM.
MY DAD IS...
DID HE USE TO WEAR GLASSES?

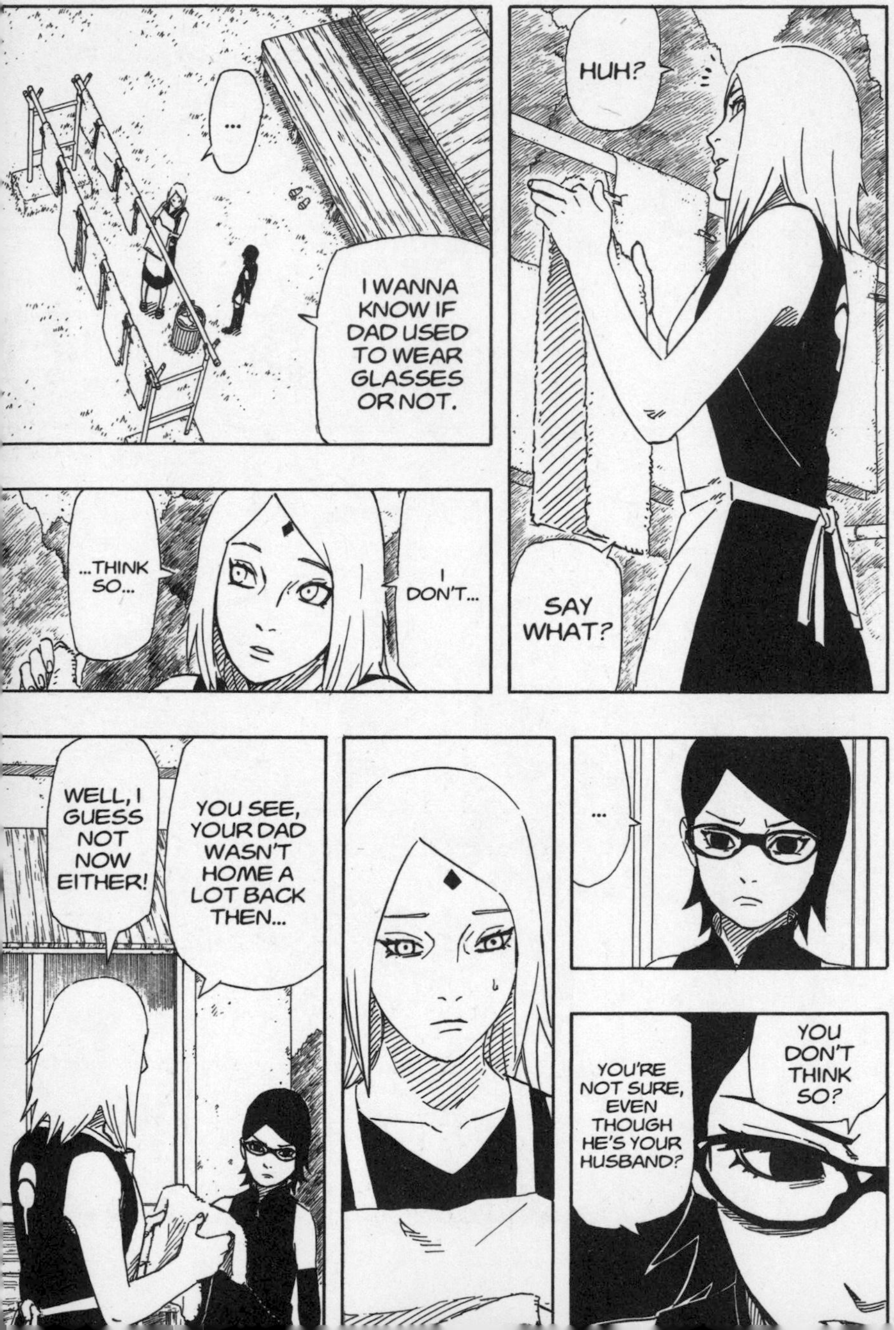
HUH?
SAY WHAT?
...
I WANNA KNOW IF DAD USED TO WEAR GLASSES OR NOT.
I DON'T...
...THINK SO...
...
YOU DON'T THINK SO?
YOU'RE NOT SURE, EVEN THOUGH HE'S YOUR HUSBAND?
YOU SEE, YOUR DAD WASN'T HOME A LOT BACK THEN...
WELL, I GUESS NOT NOW EITHER!

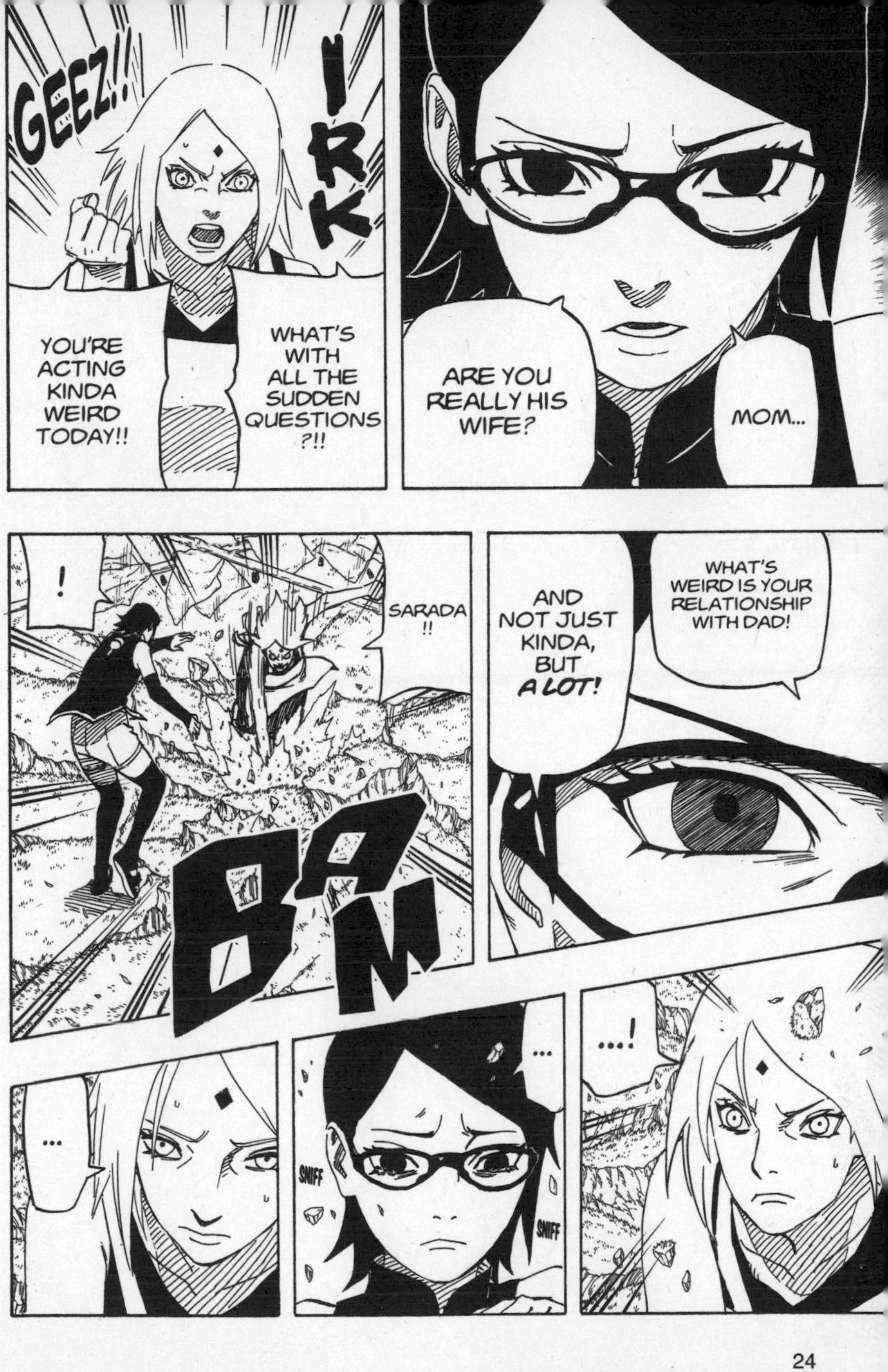
MOM...
ARE YOU REALLY HIS WIFE?
IRK
GEEZ!!
WHAT'S WITH ALL THE SUDDEN QUESTIONS?!!
YOU'RE ACTING KINDA WEIRD TODAY!!
WHAT'S WEIRD IS YOUR RELATIONSHIP WITH DAD!
AND NOT JUST KINDA, BUT *A LOT*!
SARADA!!
!
BAM
...!
...
SNIFF
SNIFF
...

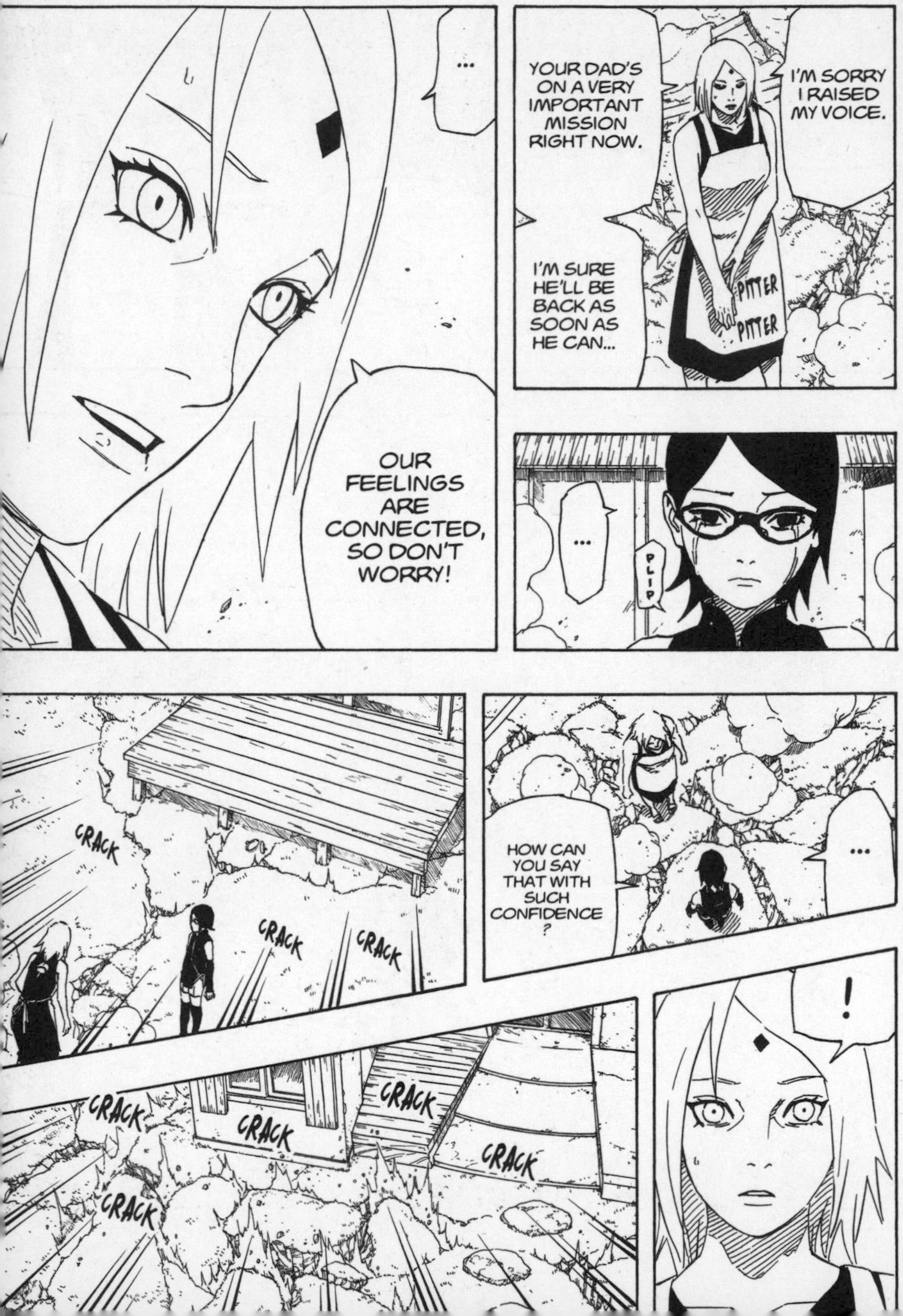
I'M SORRY I RAISED MY VOICE.
YOUR DAD'S ON A VERY IMPORTANT MISSION RIGHT NOW.
PITTER
PITTER
I'M SURE HE'LL BE BACK AS SOON AS HE CAN...
...
PLIP
...
OUR FEELINGS ARE CONNECTED, SO DON'T WORRY!
...
HOW CAN YOU SAY THAT WITH SUCH CONFIDENCE?
CRACK
CRACK
CRACK
!
CRACK
CRACK
CRACK
CRACK
CRACK

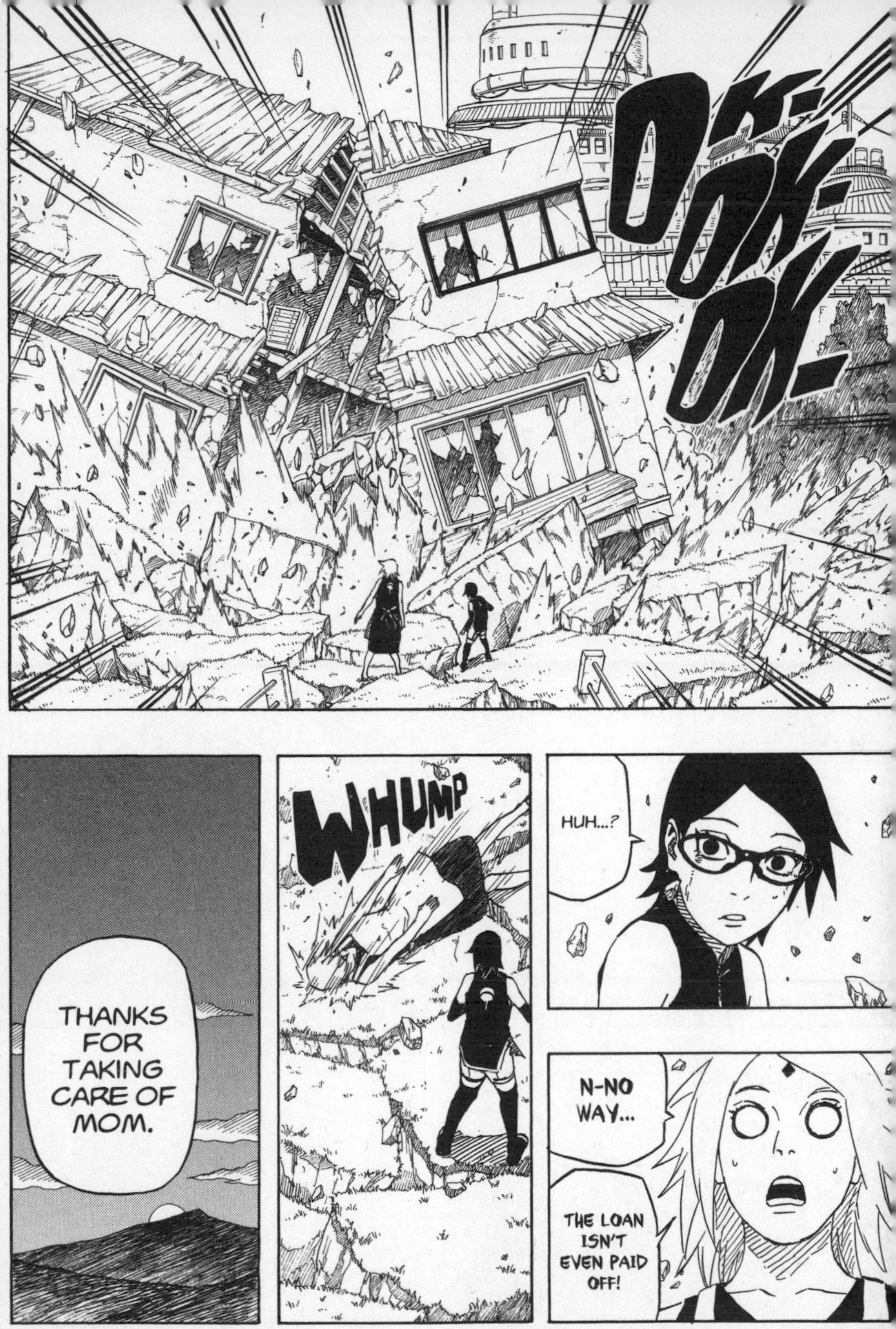
HUH...?
N-NO WAY...
THE LOAN ISN'T EVEN PAID OFF!
WHUMP
THANKS FOR TAKING CARE OF MOM.

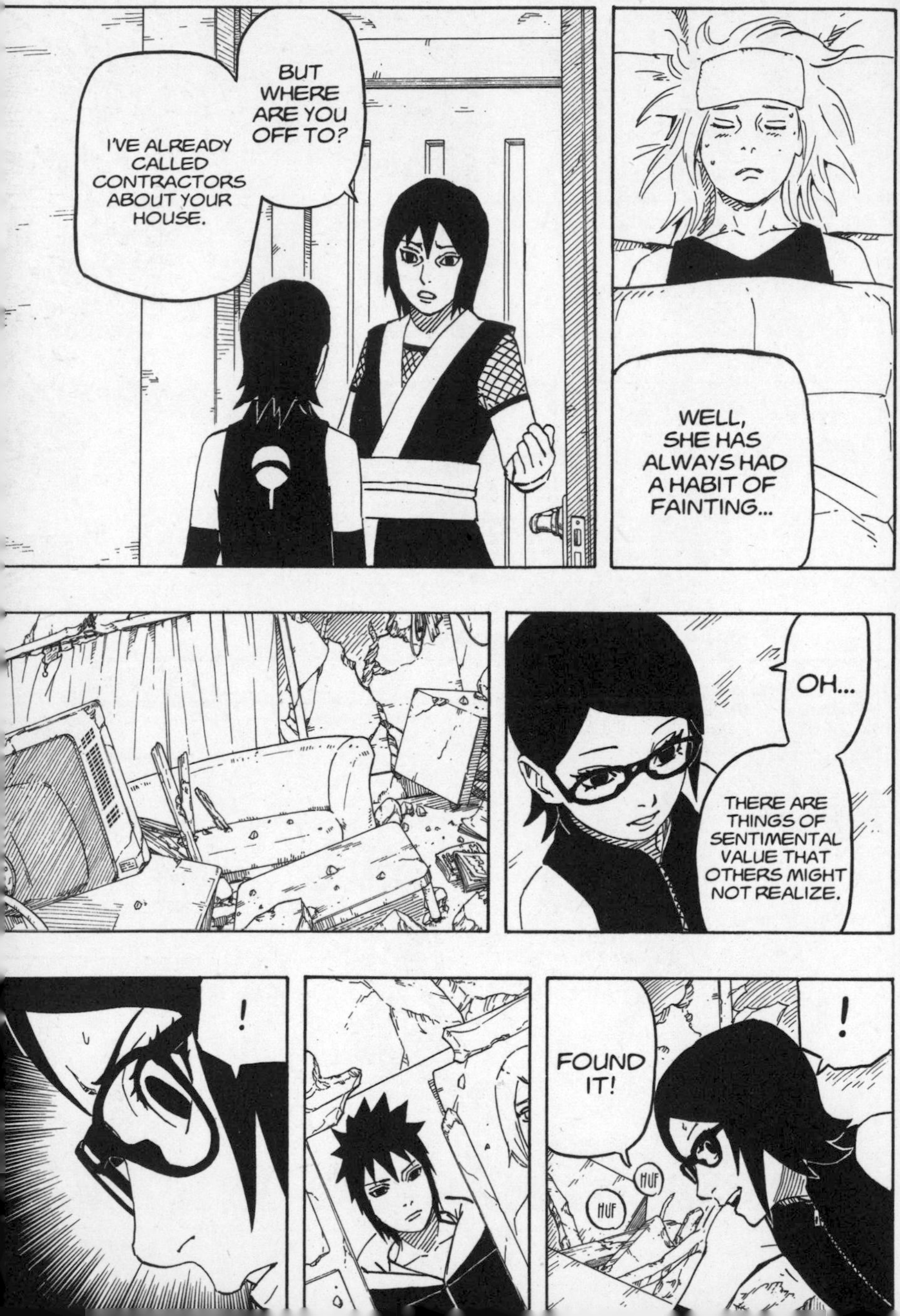
WELL, SHE HAS ALWAYS HAD A HABIT OF FAINTING...
I'VE ALREADY CALLED CONTRACTORS ABOUT YOUR HOUSE.
BUT WHERE ARE YOU OFF TO?
OH...
THERE ARE THINGS OF SENTIMENTAL VALUE THAT OTHERS MIGHT NOT REALIZE.
!
FOUND IT!
HUF
HUF
!

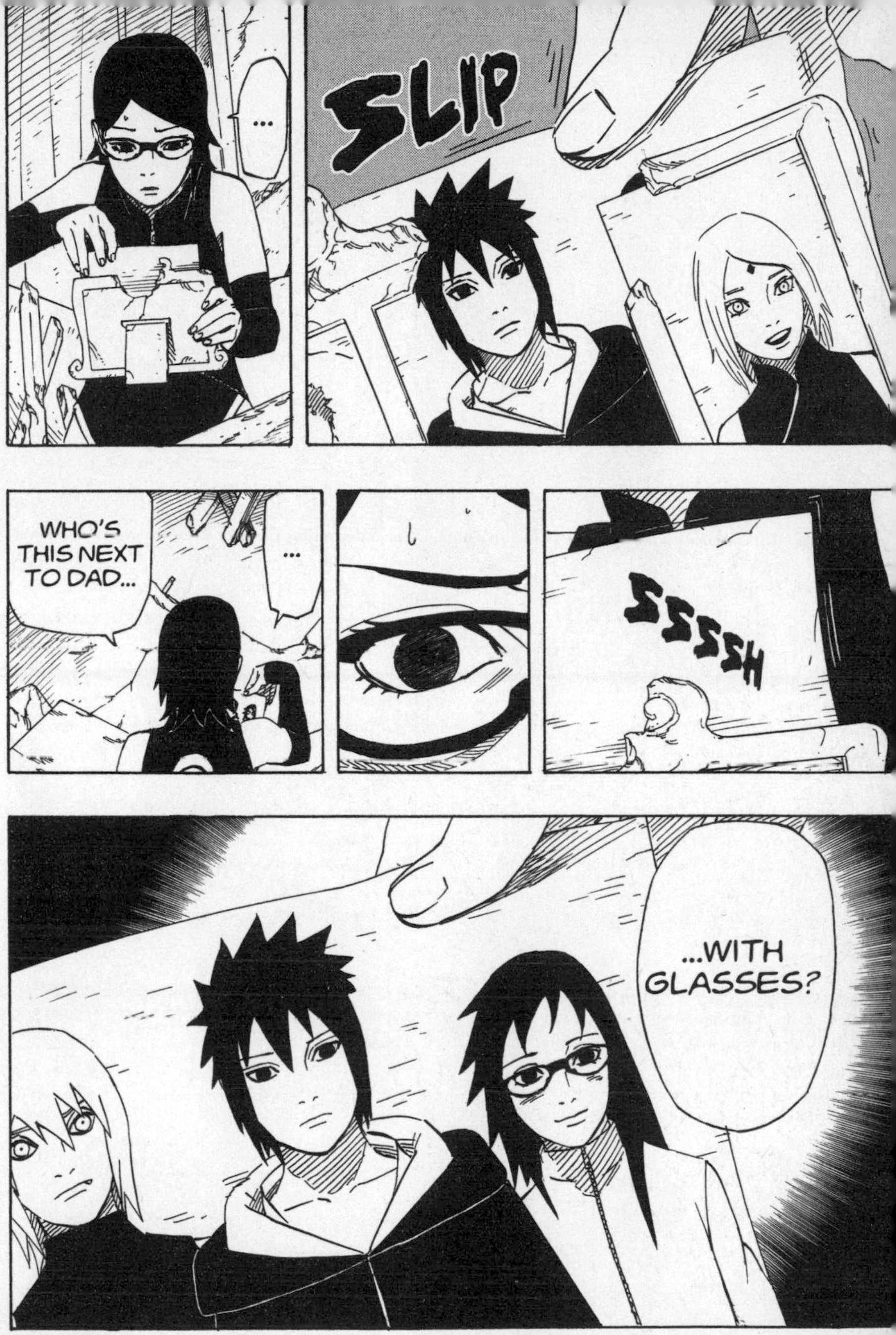
SLIP
...
SSSSH
...
WHO'S THIS NEXT TO DAD...
...WITH GLASSES?

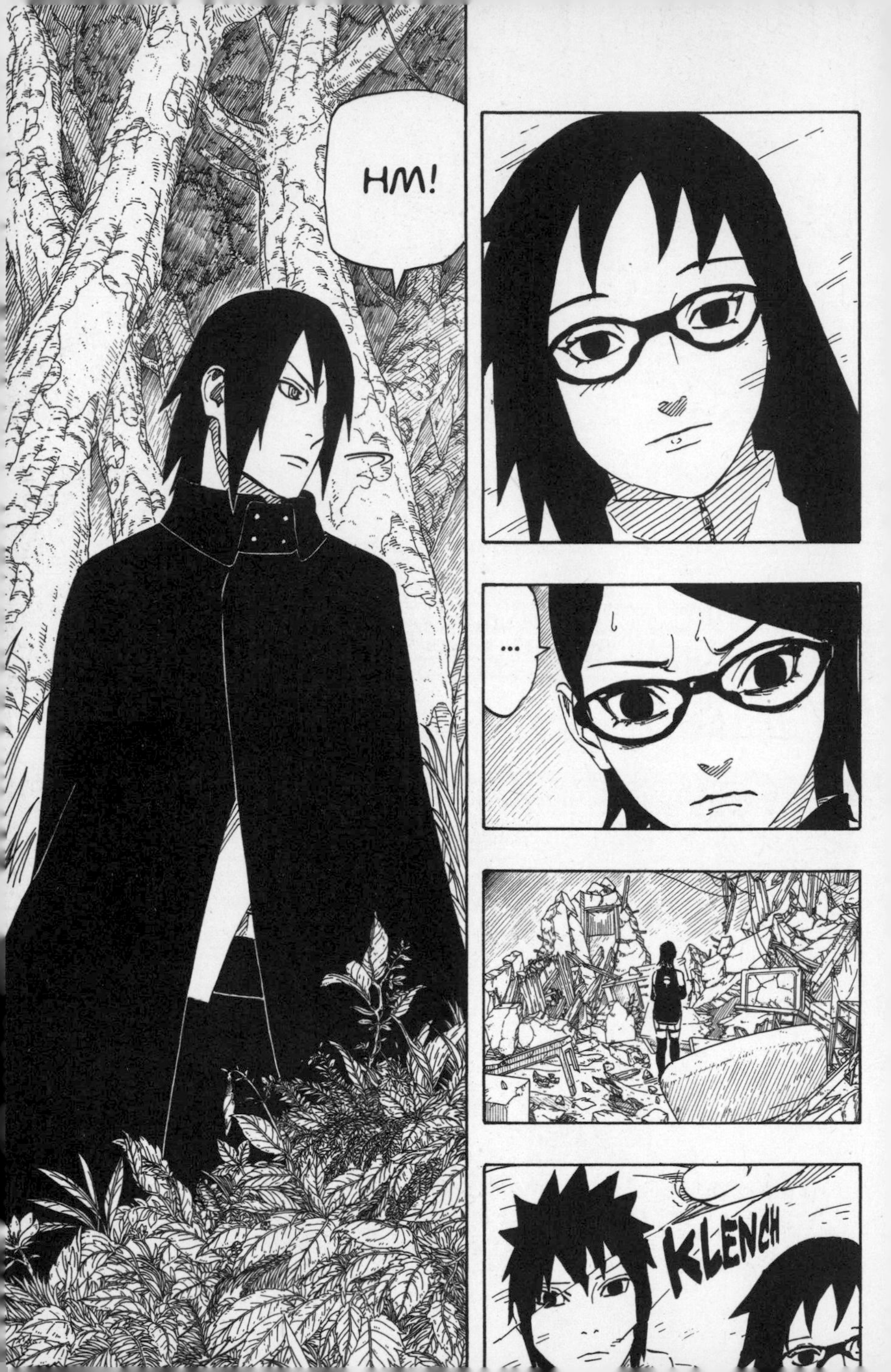
...
KLENCH
HM!

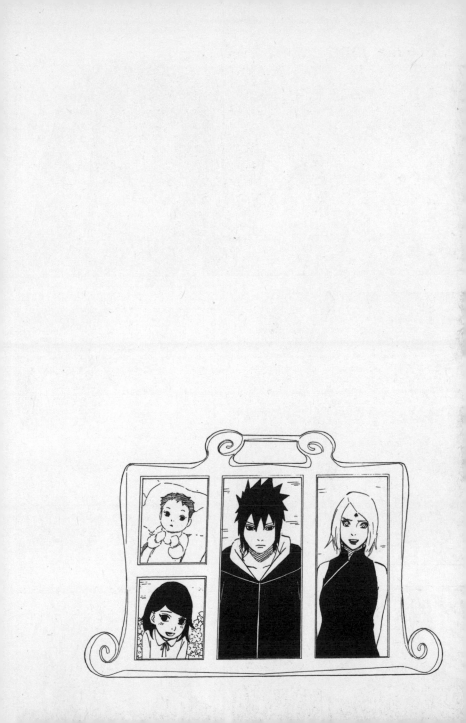

Number 700+2: The Sharingan Boy

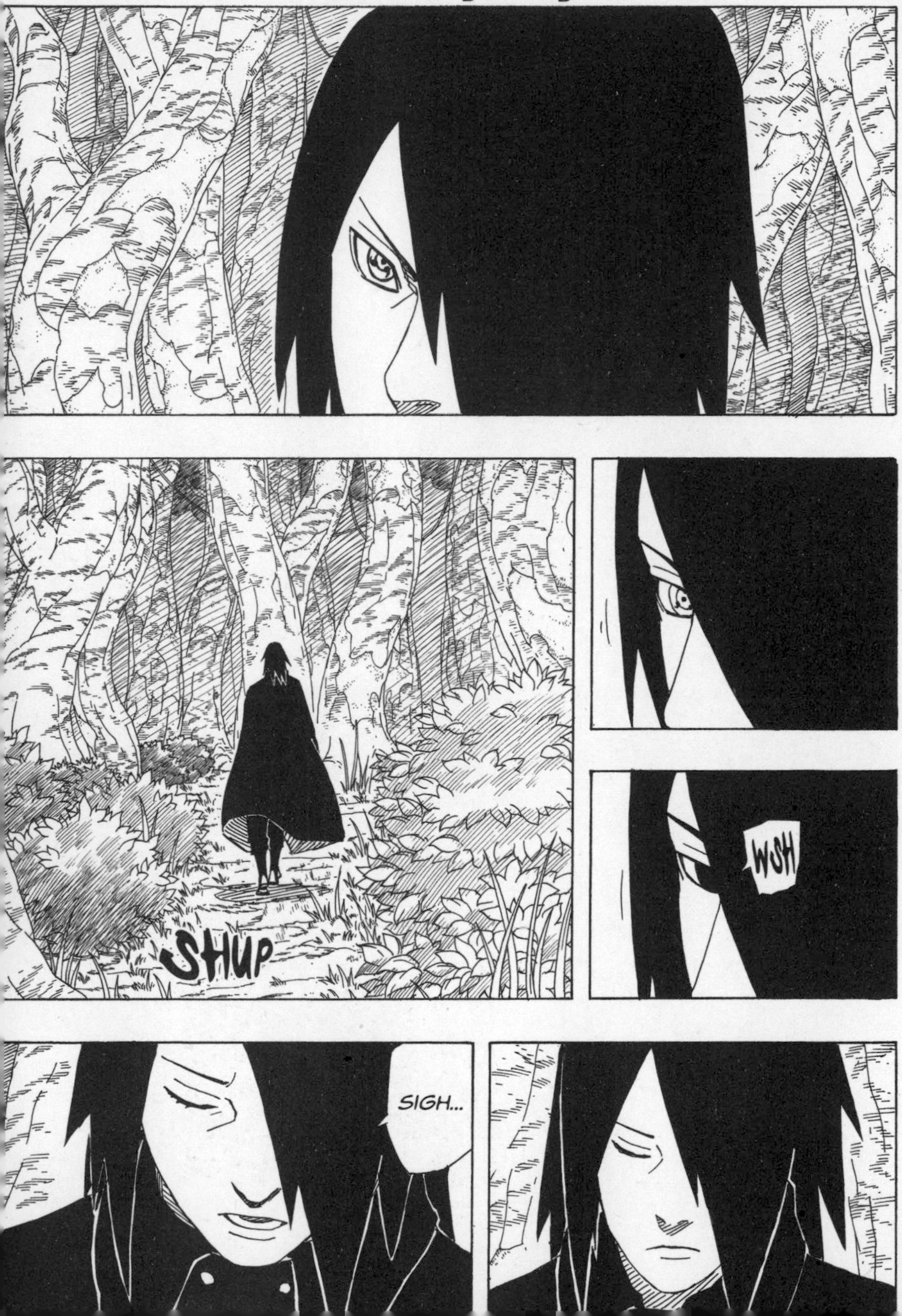
WSH
SHUP
SIGH...

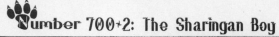

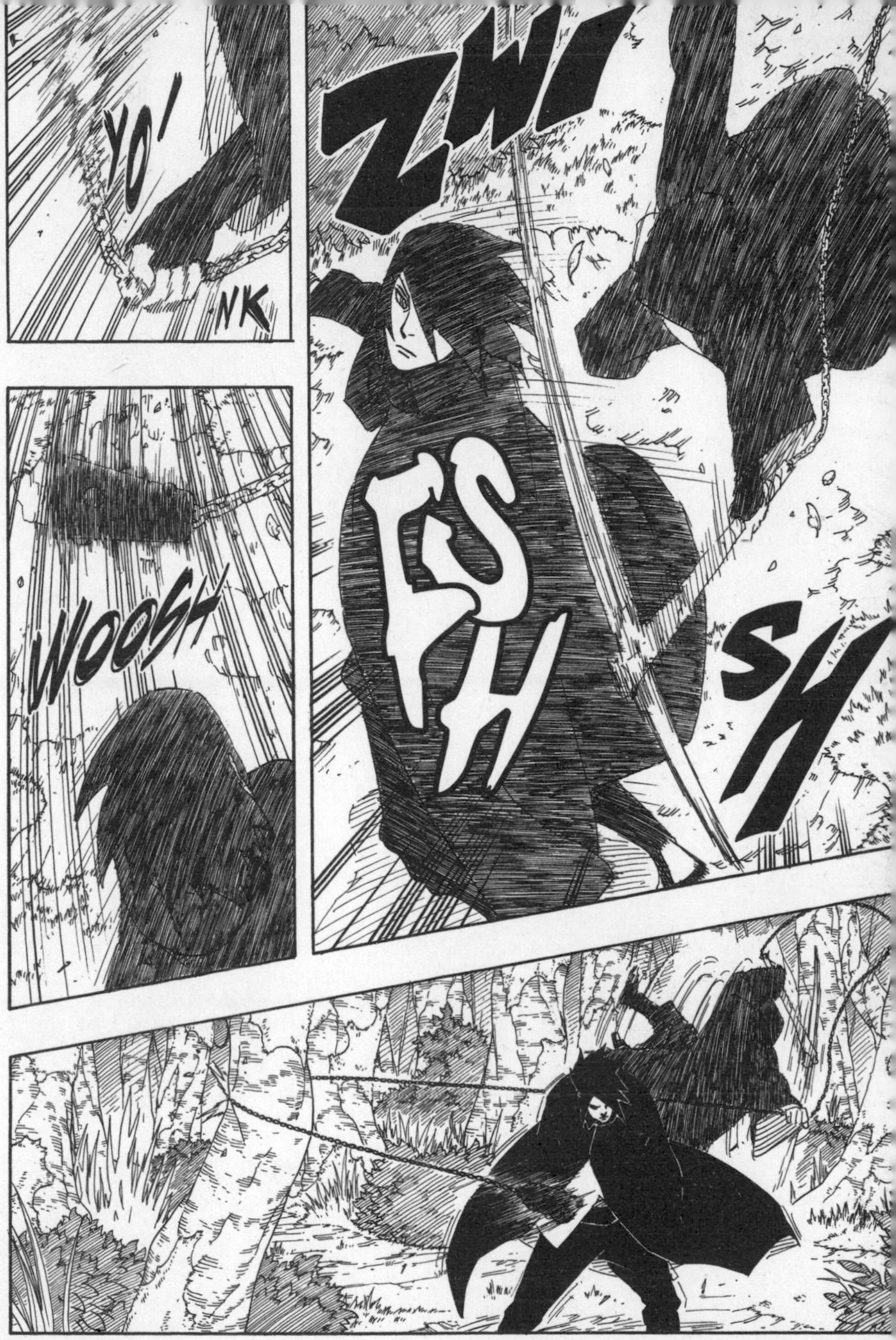
ZWI
FSH
SH
YO'
NK
WOOSH

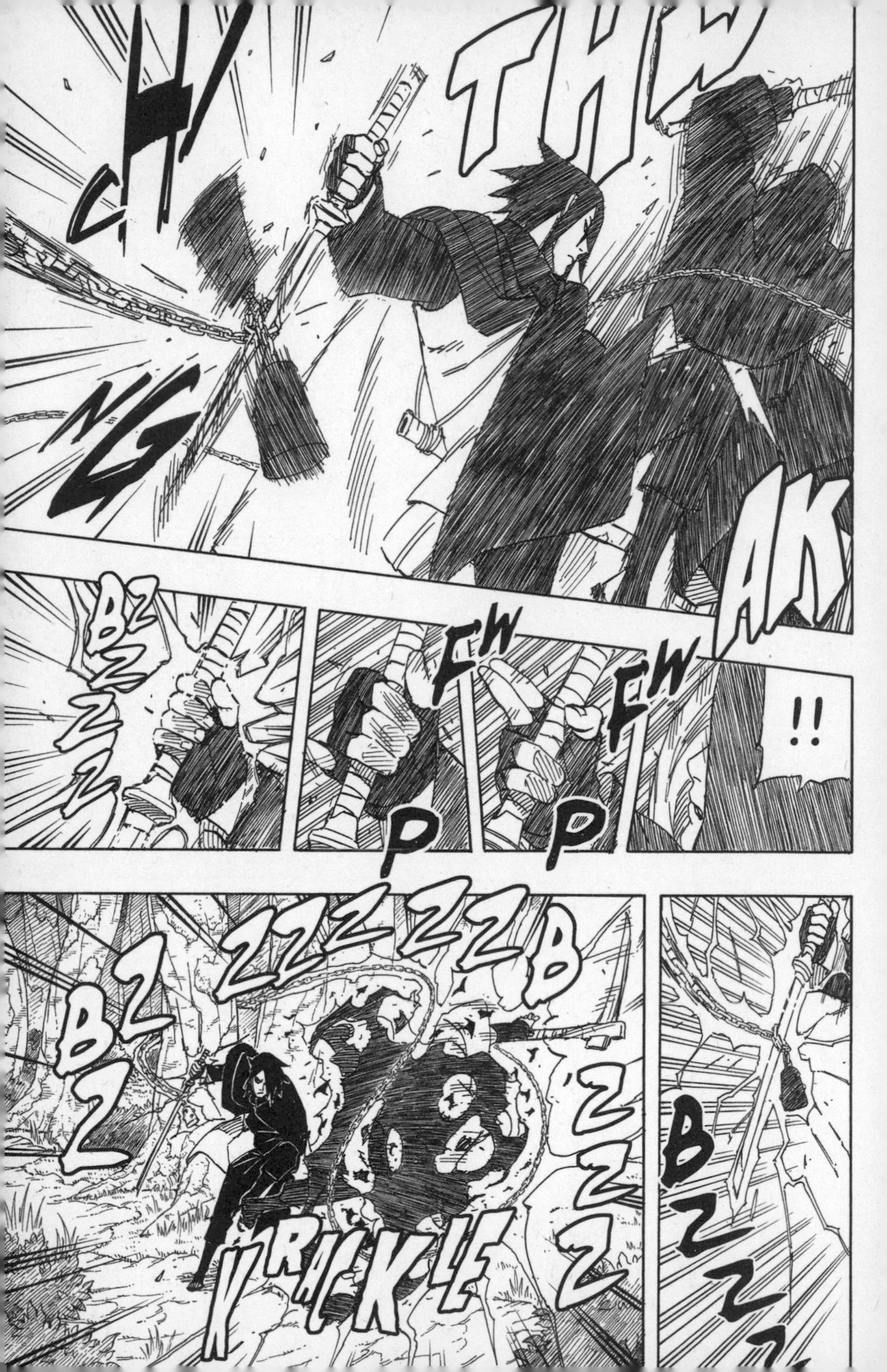
THWAK
CH!
NG
!!
FWP
FWP
BZZZZ
BZZZZ
BZZ
ZZZZZZZB
ZZZZ
KRACKLE

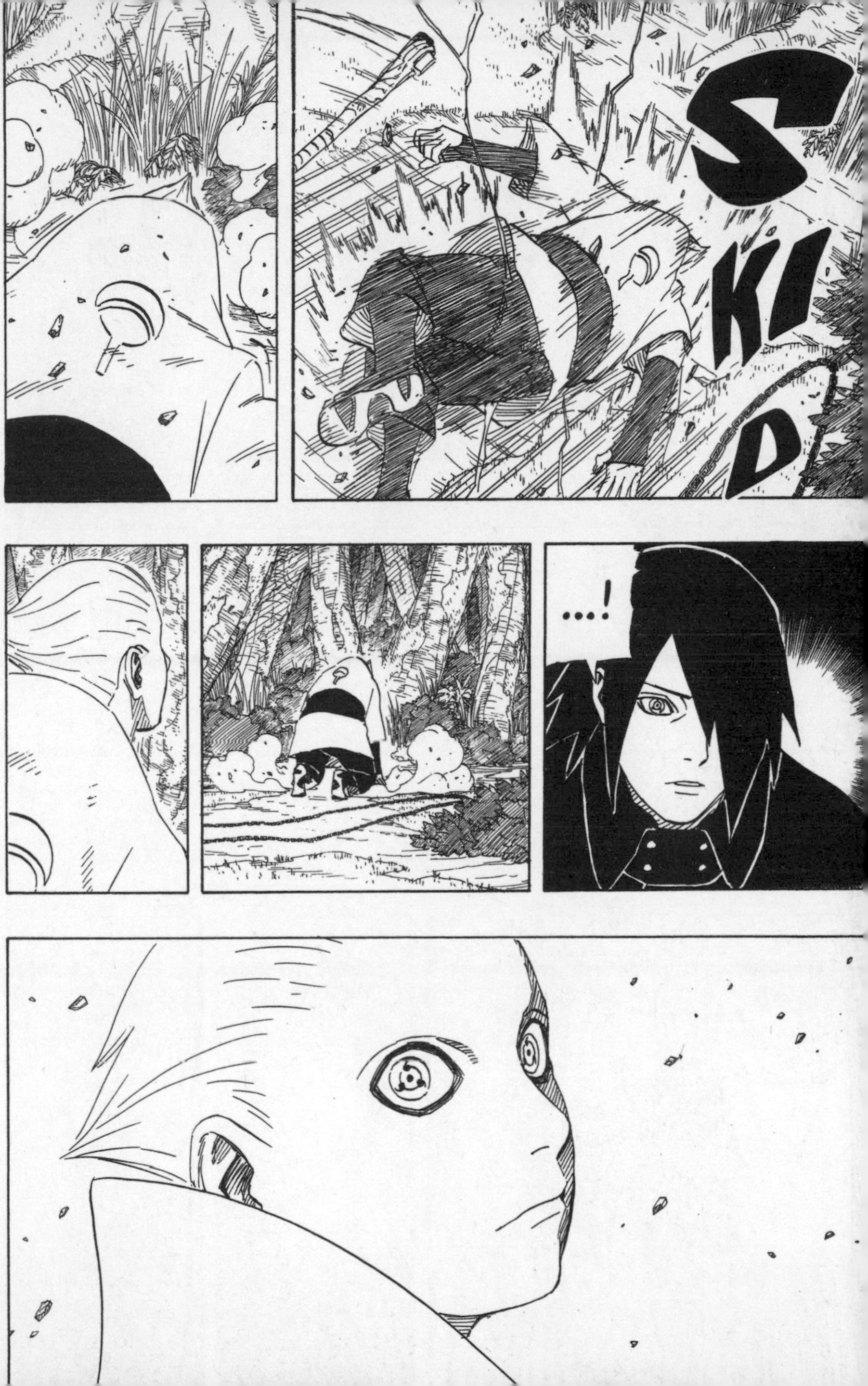
SKID
...!

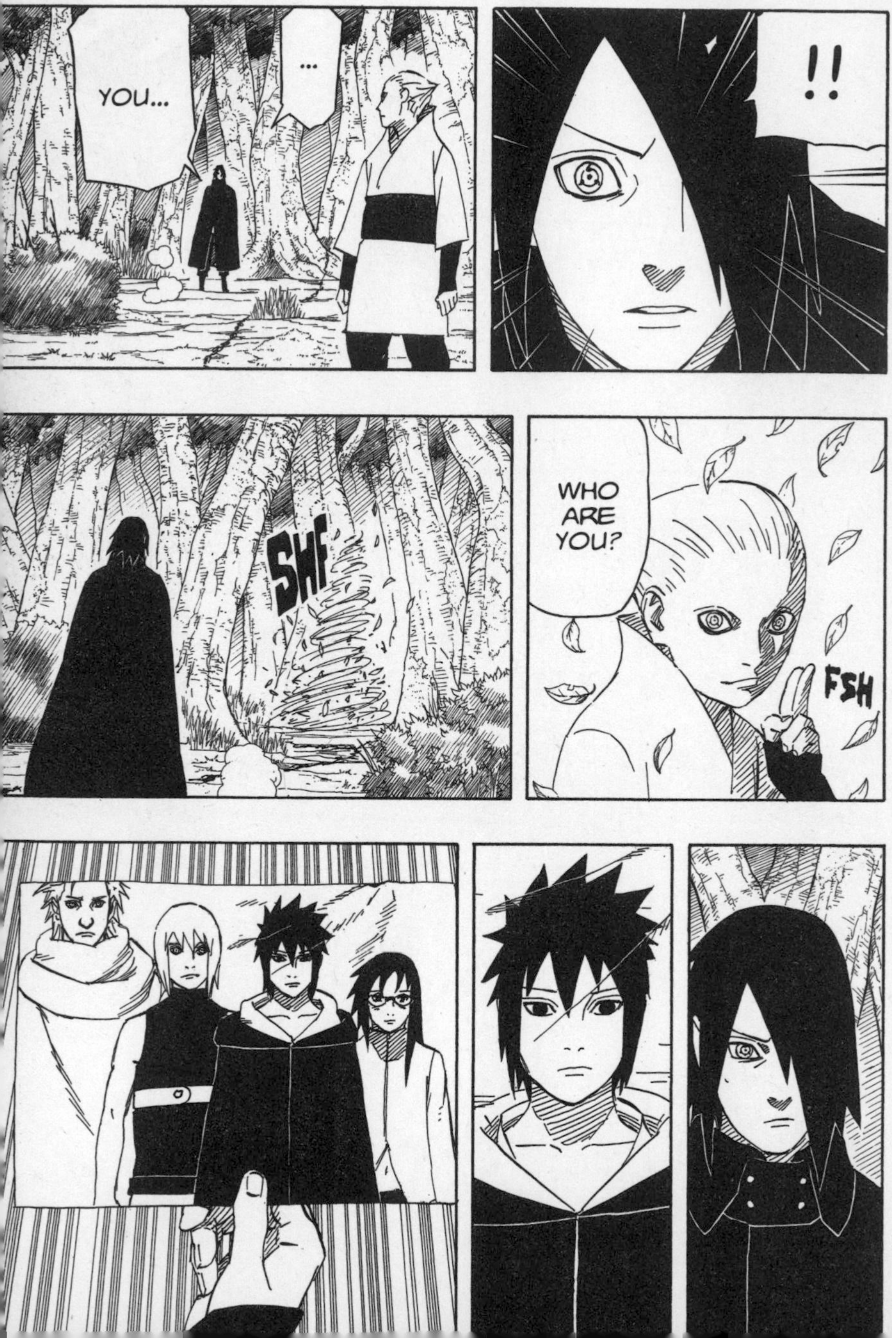
!!
...
YOU...
WHO ARE YOU?
FSH
SHF

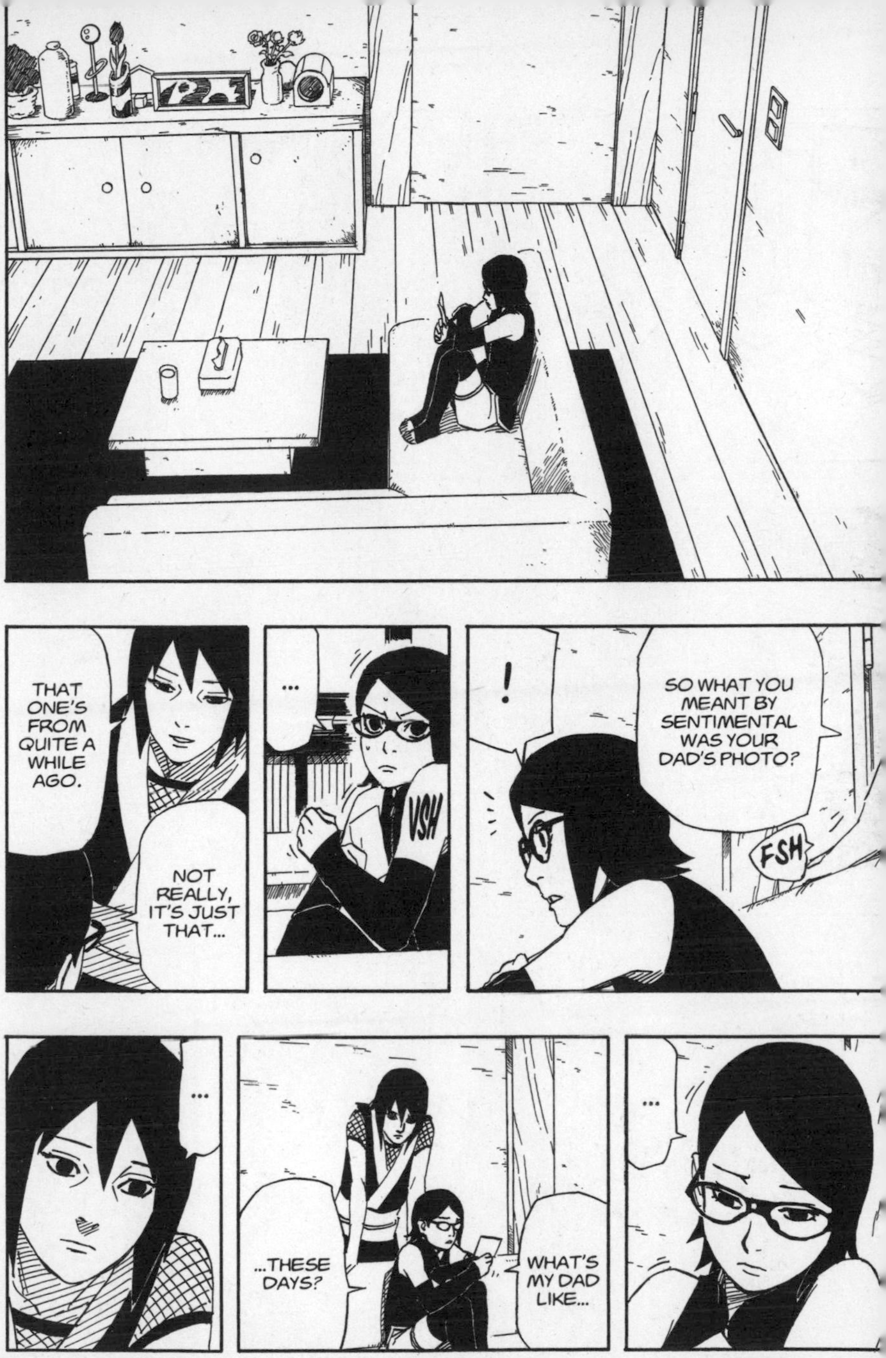
!
SO WHAT YOU MEANT BY SENTIMENTAL WAS YOUR DAD'S PHOTO?
FSH
...
VSH
THAT ONE'S FROM QUITE A WHILE AGO.
NOT REALLY, IT'S JUST THAT...
...
WHAT'S MY DAD LIKE...
...THESE DAYS?
...

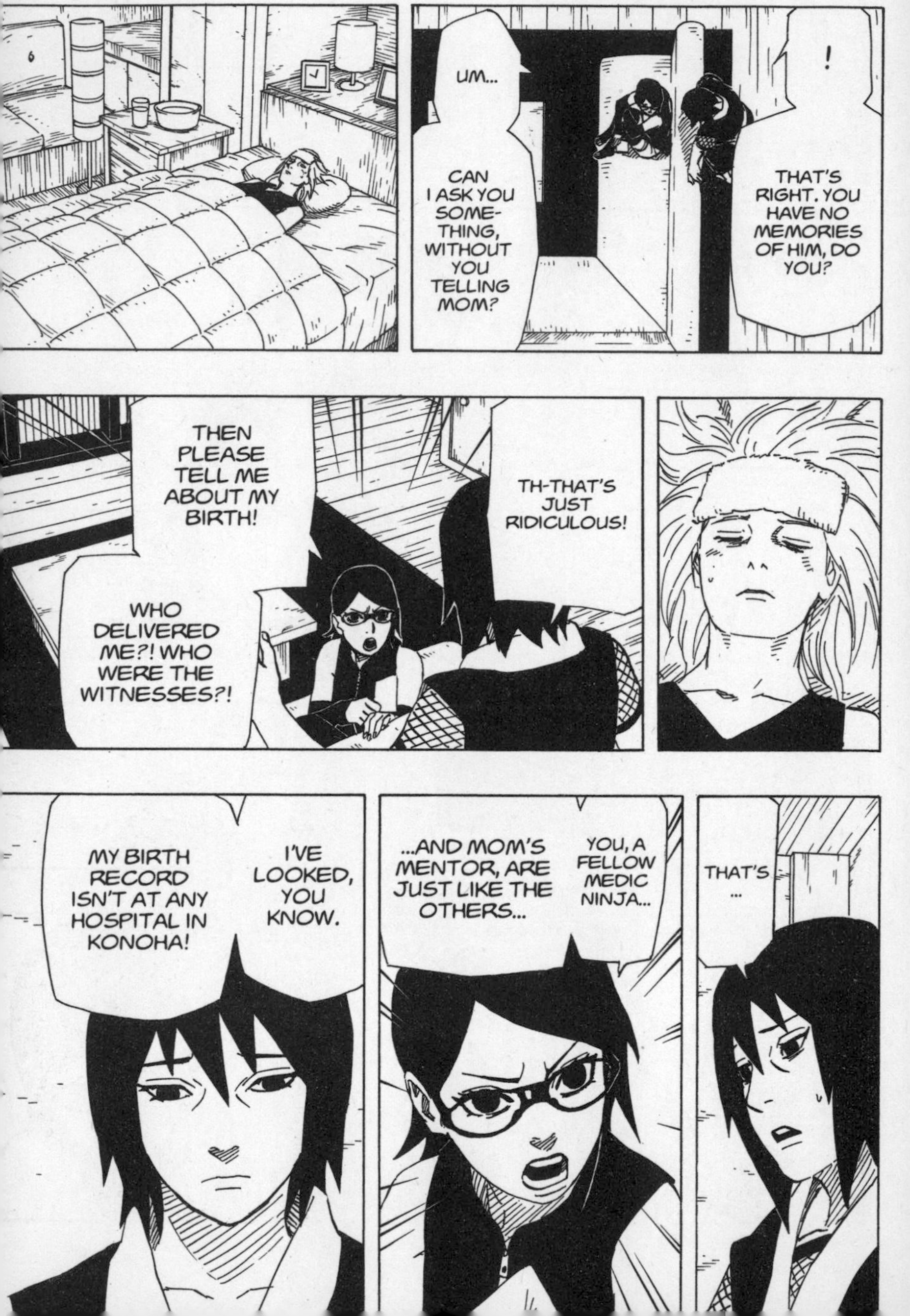
!
THAT'S RIGHT. YOU HAVE NO MEMORIES OF HIM, DO YOU?
UM...
CAN I ASK YOU SOMETHING, WITHOUT YOU TELLING MOM?
TH-THAT'S JUST RIDICULOUS!
THEN PLEASE TELL ME ABOUT MY BIRTH!
WHO DELIVERED ME?! WHO WERE THE WITNESSES?!
THAT'S ...
YOU, A FELLOW MEDIC NINJA...
...AND MOM'S MENTOR, ARE JUST LIKE THE OTHERS...
I'VE LOOKED, YOU KNOW.
MY BIRTH RECORD ISN'T AT ANY HOSPITAL IN KONOHA!

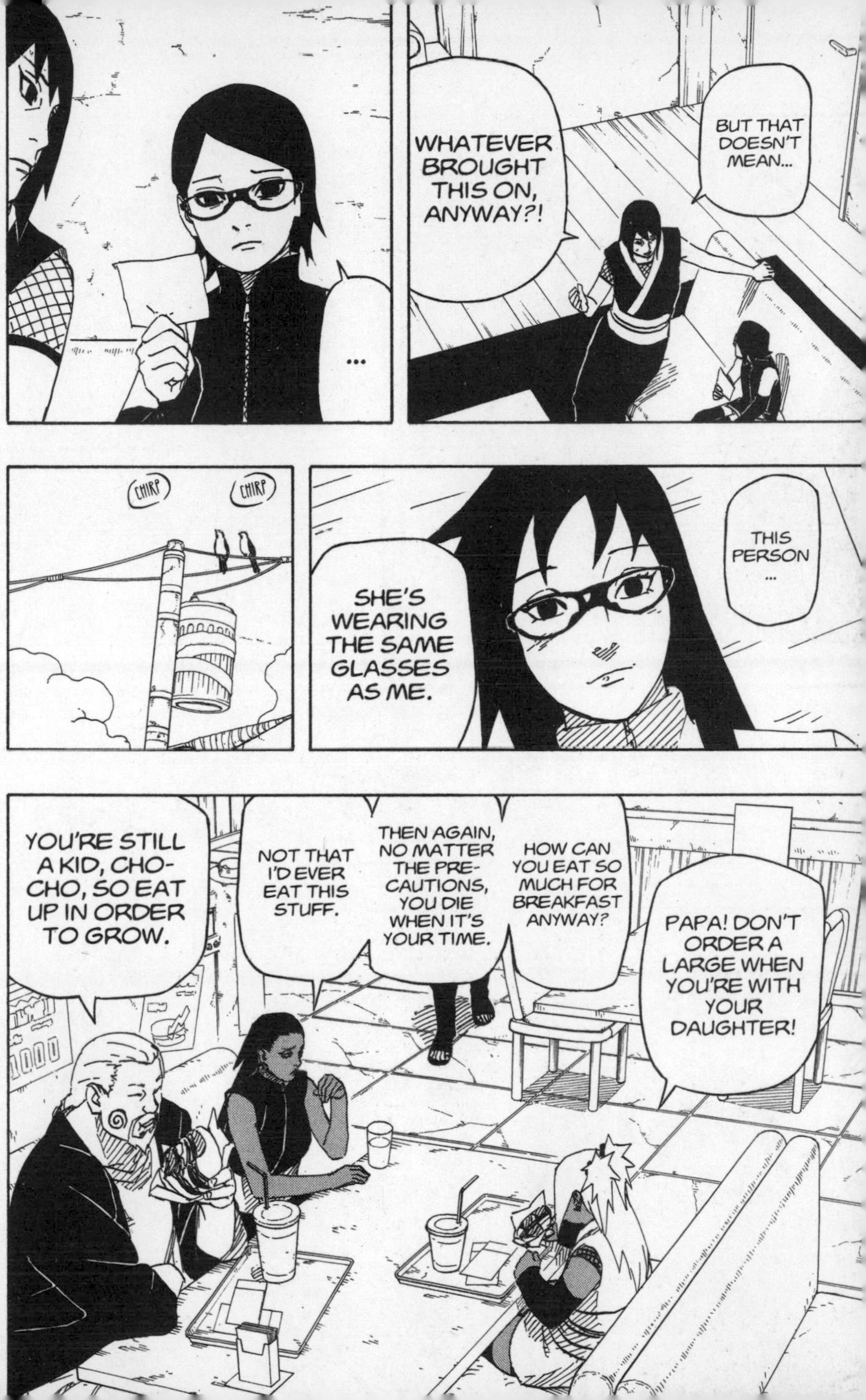
BUT THAT DOESN'T MEAN...
WHATEVER BROUGHT THIS ON, ANYWAY?!
...
THIS PERSON ...
SHE'S WEARING THE SAME GLASSES AS ME.
CHIRP
CHIRP
PAPA! DON'T ORDER A LARGE WHEN YOU'RE WITH YOUR DAUGHTER!
HOW CAN YOU EAT SO MUCH FOR BREAKFAST ANYWAY?
THEN AGAIN, NO MATTER THE PRE-CAUTIONS, YOU DIE WHEN IT'S YOUR TIME.
NOT THAT I'D EVER EAT THIS STUFF.
YOU'RE STILL A KID, CHO-CHO, SO EAT UP IN ORDER TO GROW.

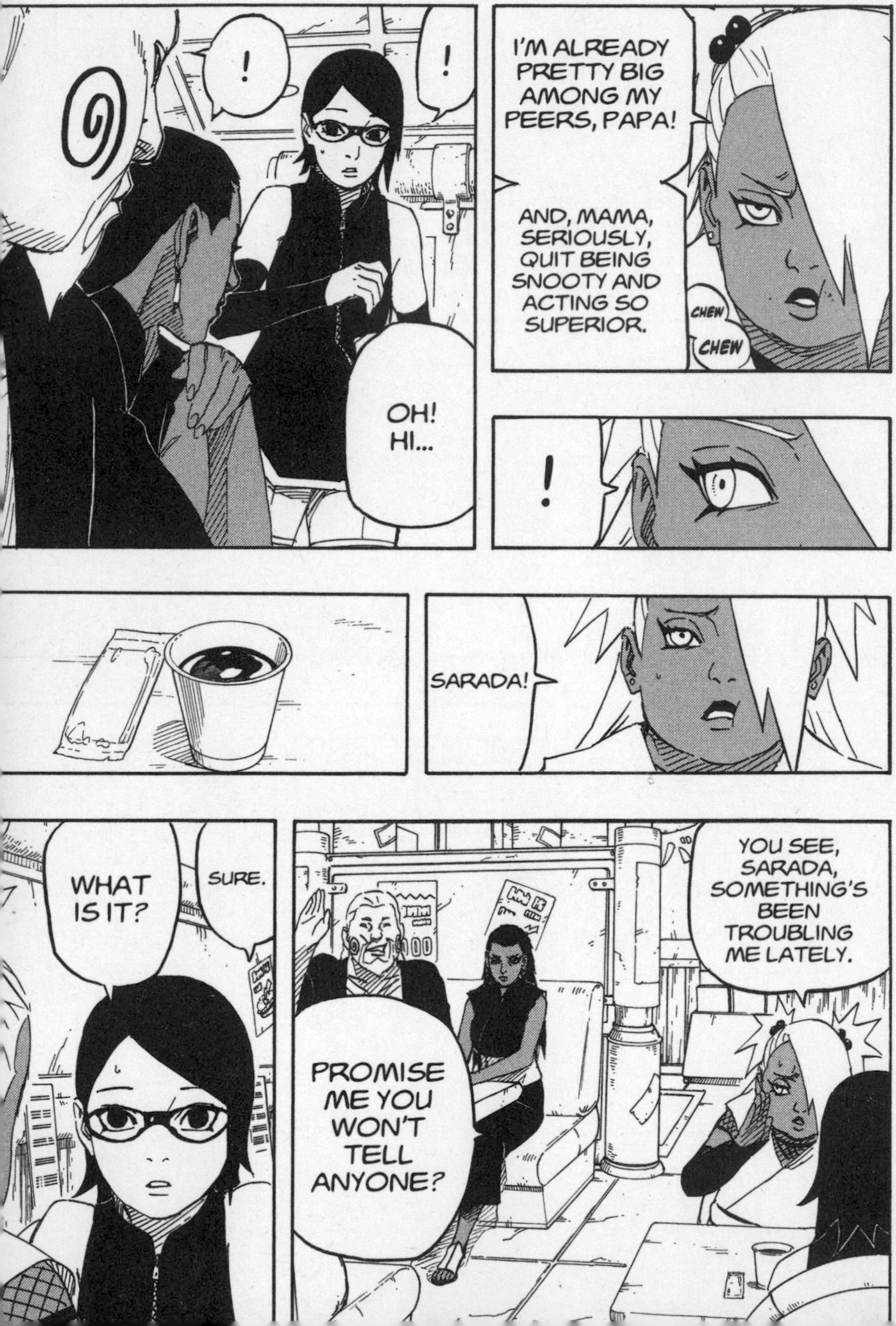
I'M ALREADY PRETTY BIG AMONG MY PEERS, PAPA!
AND, MAMA, SERIOUSLY, QUIT BEING SNOOTY AND ACTING SO SUPERIOR.
CHEW
CHEW
!
!
!
OH! HI...
SARADA!
YOU SEE, SARADA, SOMETHING'S BEEN TROUBLING ME LATELY.
PROMISE ME YOU WON'T TELL ANYONE?
SURE.
WHAT IS IT?

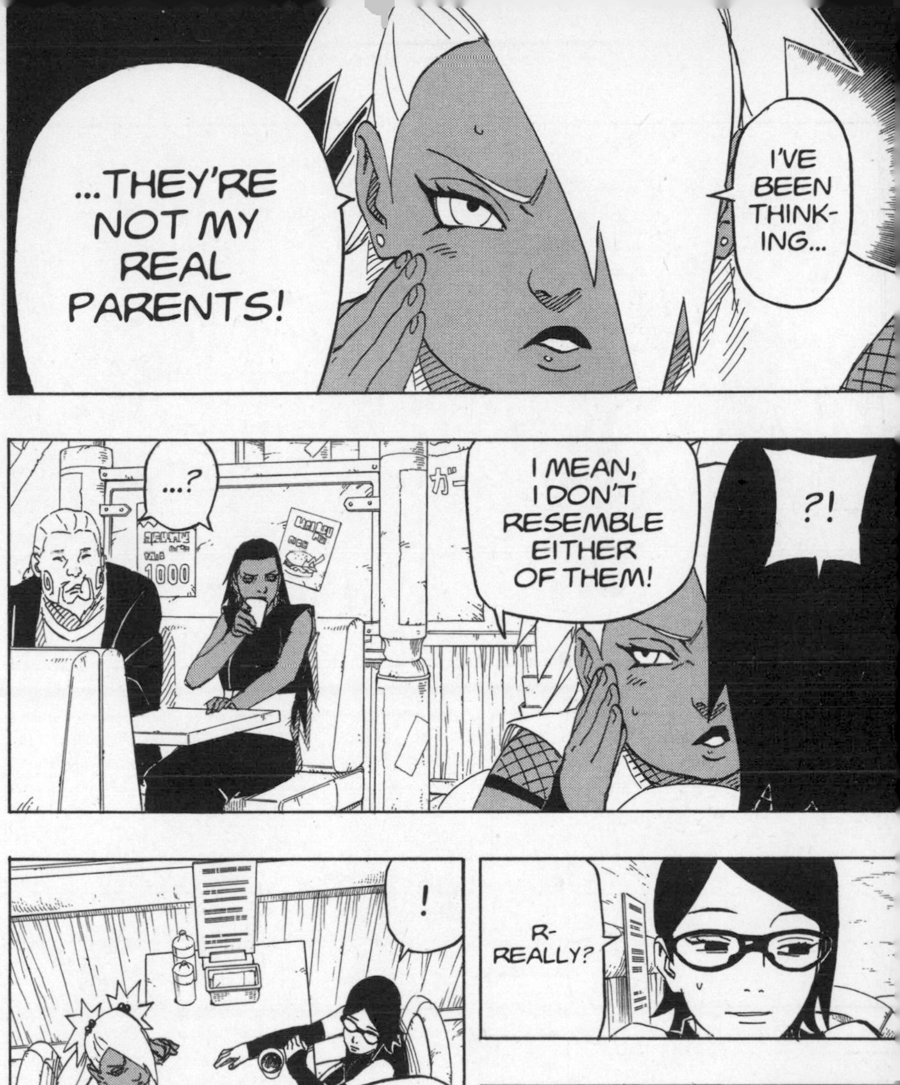
I'VE BEEN THINKING...
...THEY'RE NOT MY REAL PARENTS!
?!
I MEAN, I DON'T RESEMBLE EITHER OF THEM!
...?
1000
R-REALLY?
THAT'S CALLED A TRAGIC-HEROINE SYNDROME.
!
A CONDITION THAT UNCONSCIOUSLY OCCURS IN GIRLS OF A CERTAIN AGE WHEN ATTEMPTING TO DEFINE WHO THEY ARE.
HUH?

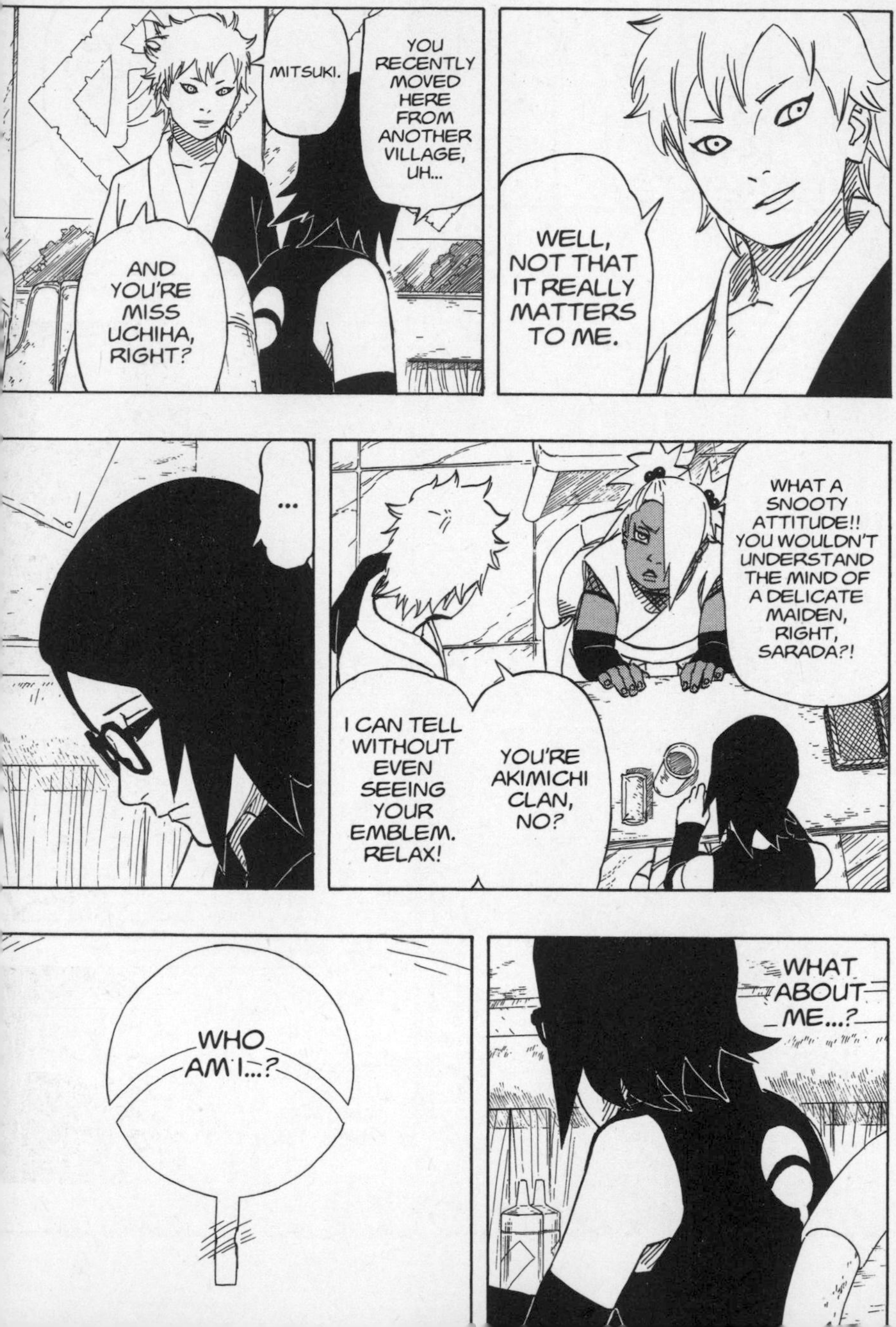
WELL, NOT THAT IT REALLY MATTERS TO ME.
YOU RECENTLY MOVED HERE FROM ANOTHER VILLAGE, UH...
MITSUKI.
AND YOU'RE MISS UCHIHA, RIGHT?
WHAT A SNOOTY ATTITUDE!! YOU WOULDN'T UNDERSTAND THE MIND OF A DELICATE MAIDEN, RIGHT, SARADA?!
YOU'RE AKIMICHI CLAN, NO?
I CAN TELL WITHOUT EVEN SEEING YOUR EMBLEM. RELAX!
...
WHAT ABOUT ME...?
WHO AM I...?

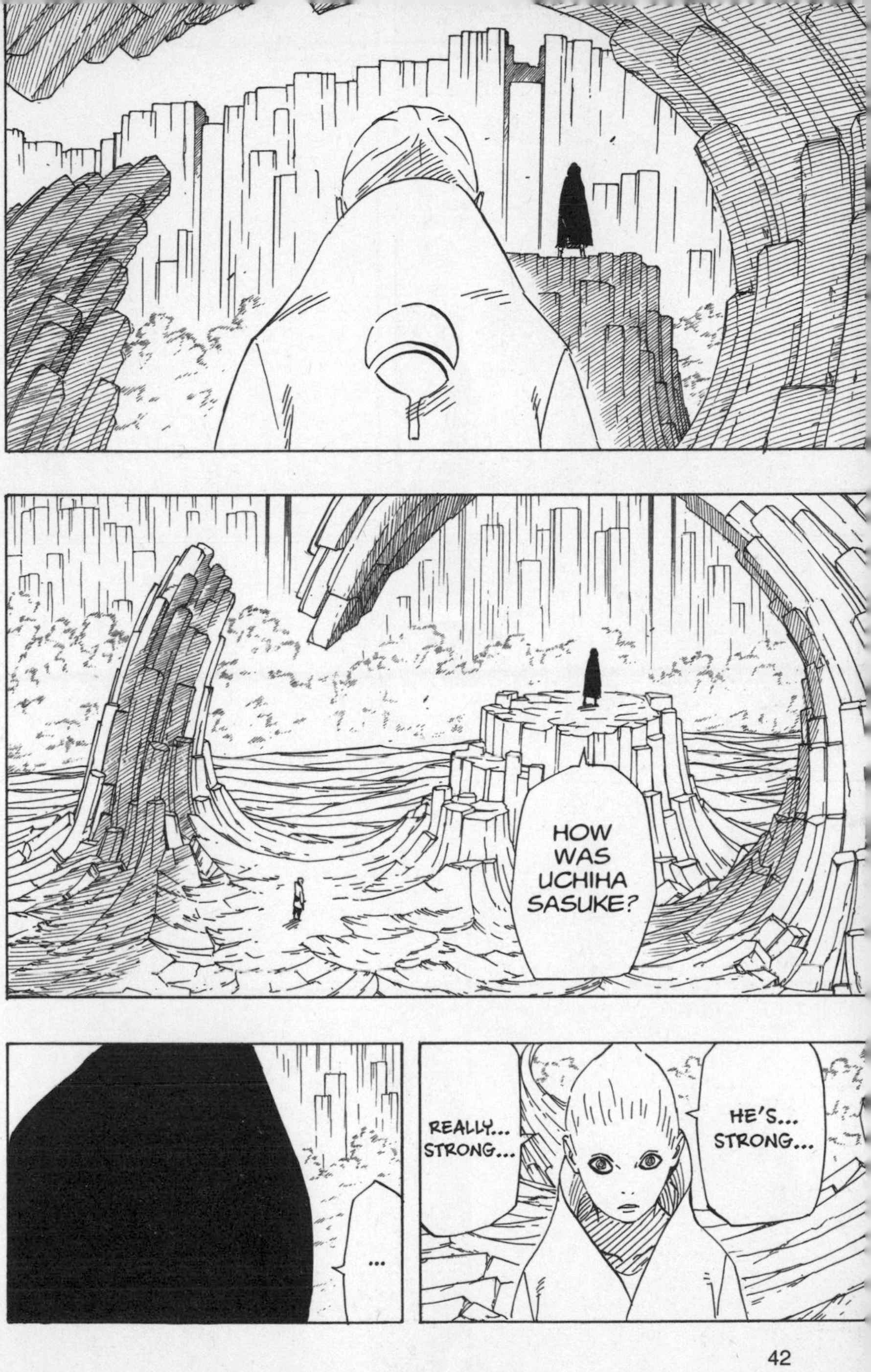
HOW WAS UCHIHA SASUKE?
HE'S... STRONG...
REALLY... STRONG...
...

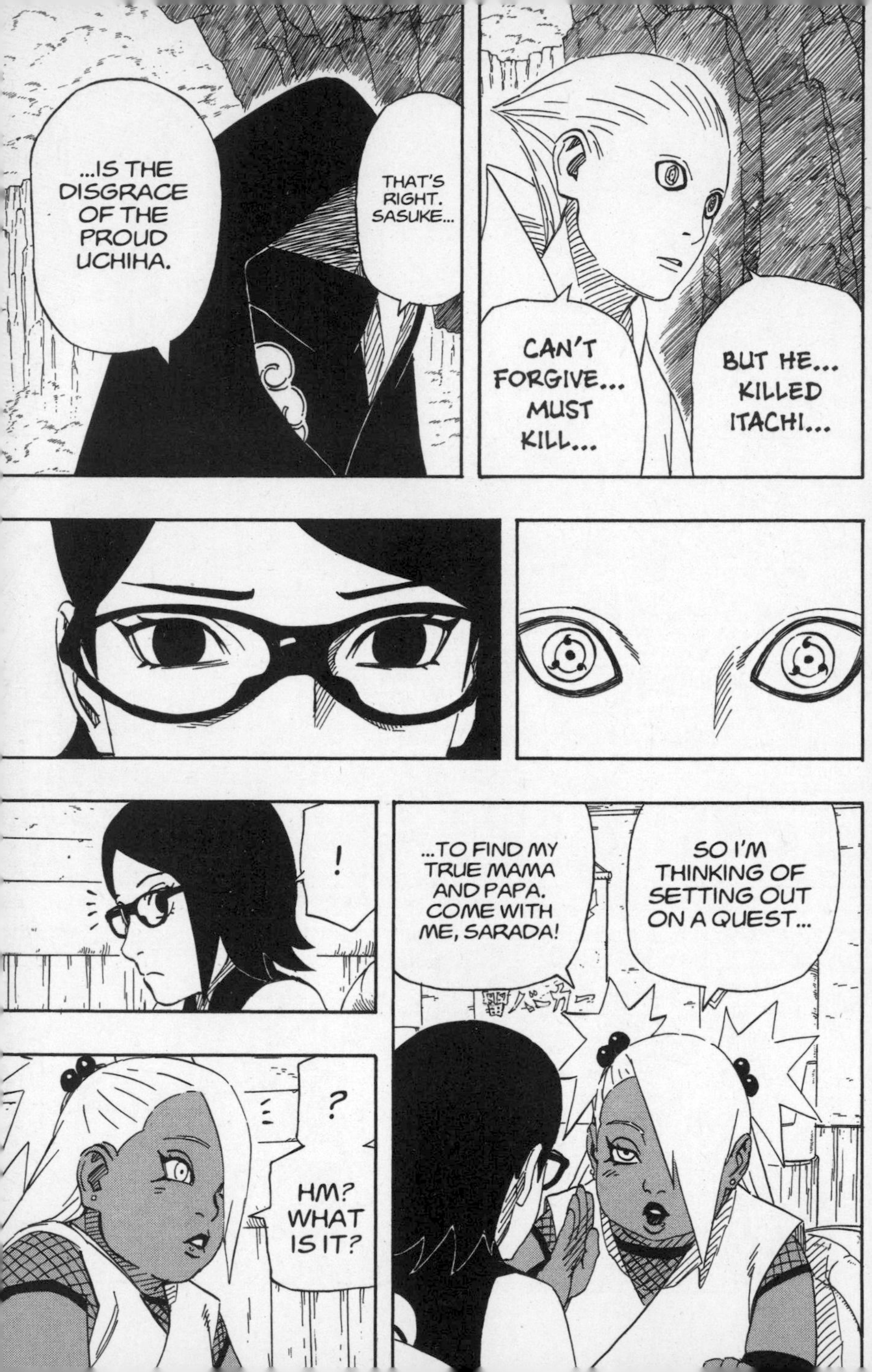
BUT HE... KILLED ITACHI...
CAN'T FORGIVE... MUST KILL...
THAT'S RIGHT. SASUKE...
...IS THE DISGRACE OF THE PROUD UCHIHA.
SO I'M THINKING OF SETTING OUT ON A QUEST...
...TO FIND MY TRUE MAMA AND PAPA. COME WITH ME, SARADA!
!
?
HM? WHAT IS IT?

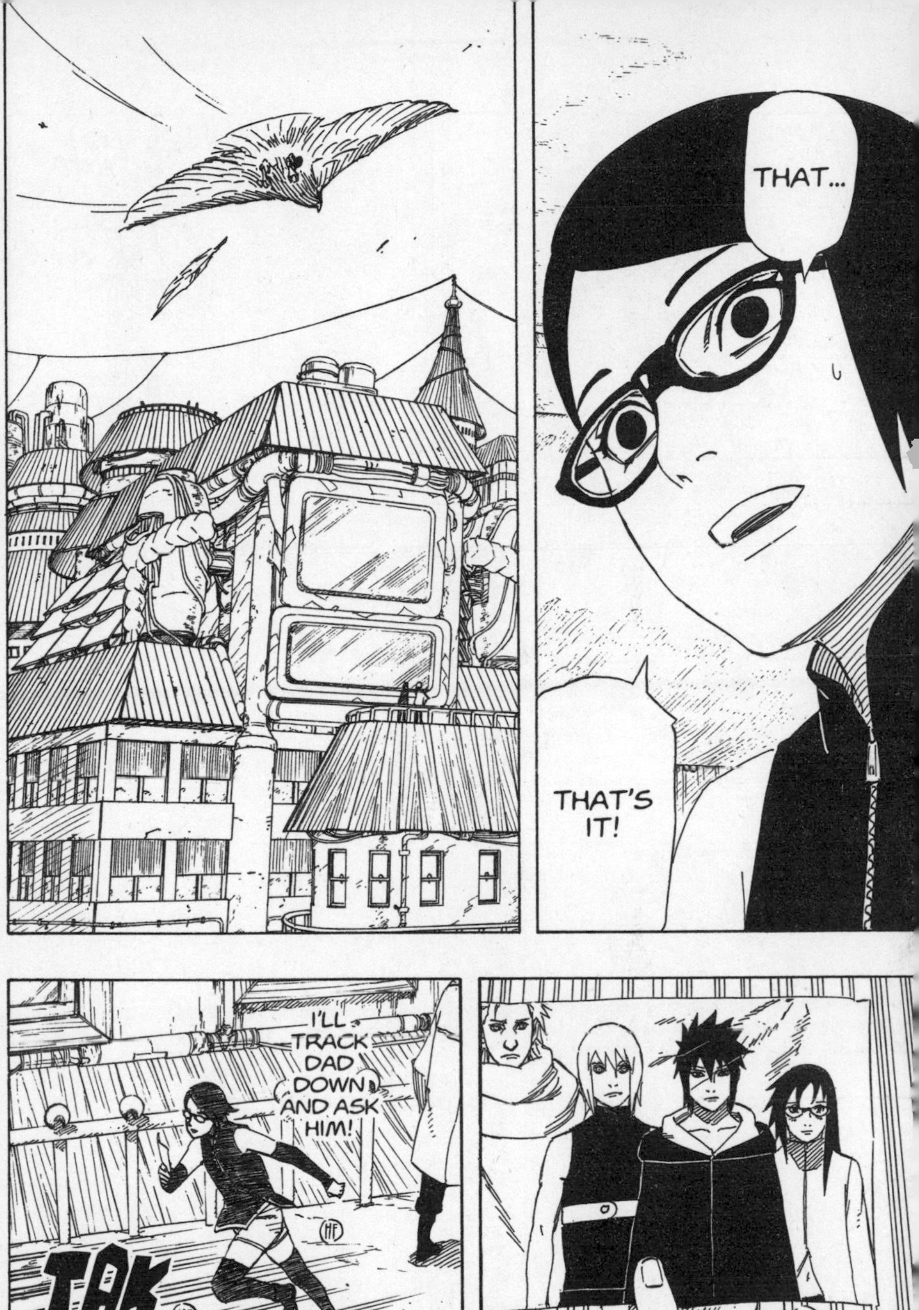
THAT...
THAT'S IT!
HFF
HFF
I'LL TRACK DAD DOWN AND ASK HIM!
HF
TAK
HF

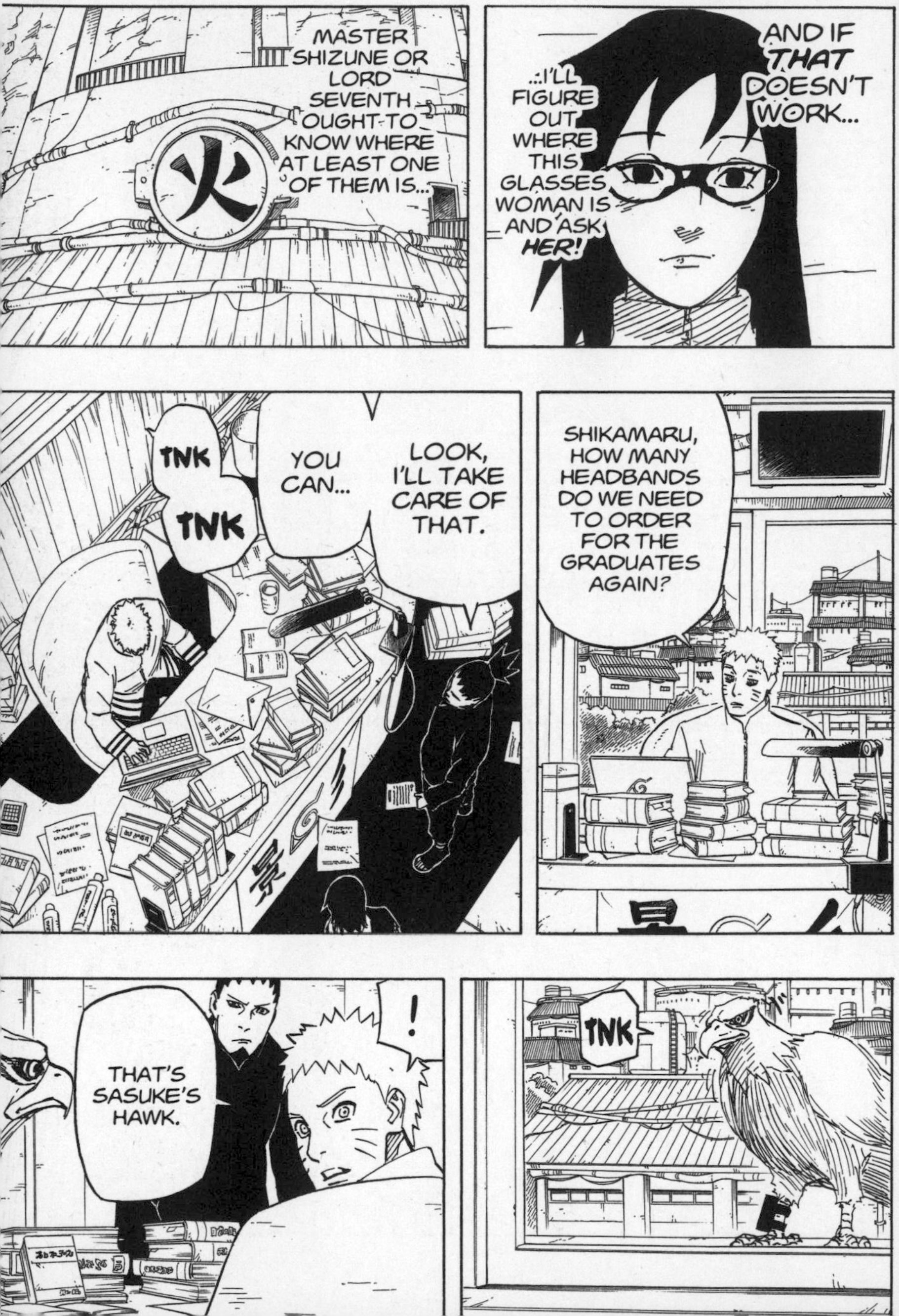
AND IF *THAT* DOESN'T WORK...
...I'LL FIGURE OUT WHERE THIS GLASSES WOMAN IS AND ASK *HER!*
MASTER SHIZUNE OR LORD SEVENTH OUGHT TO KNOW WHERE AT LEAST ONE OF THEM IS...
SHIKAMARU, HOW MANY HEADBANDS DO WE NEED TO ORDER FOR THE GRADUATES AGAIN?
LOOK, I'LL TAKE CARE OF THAT.
YOU CAN...
TNK
TNK
TNK
!
THAT'S SASUKE'S HAWK.

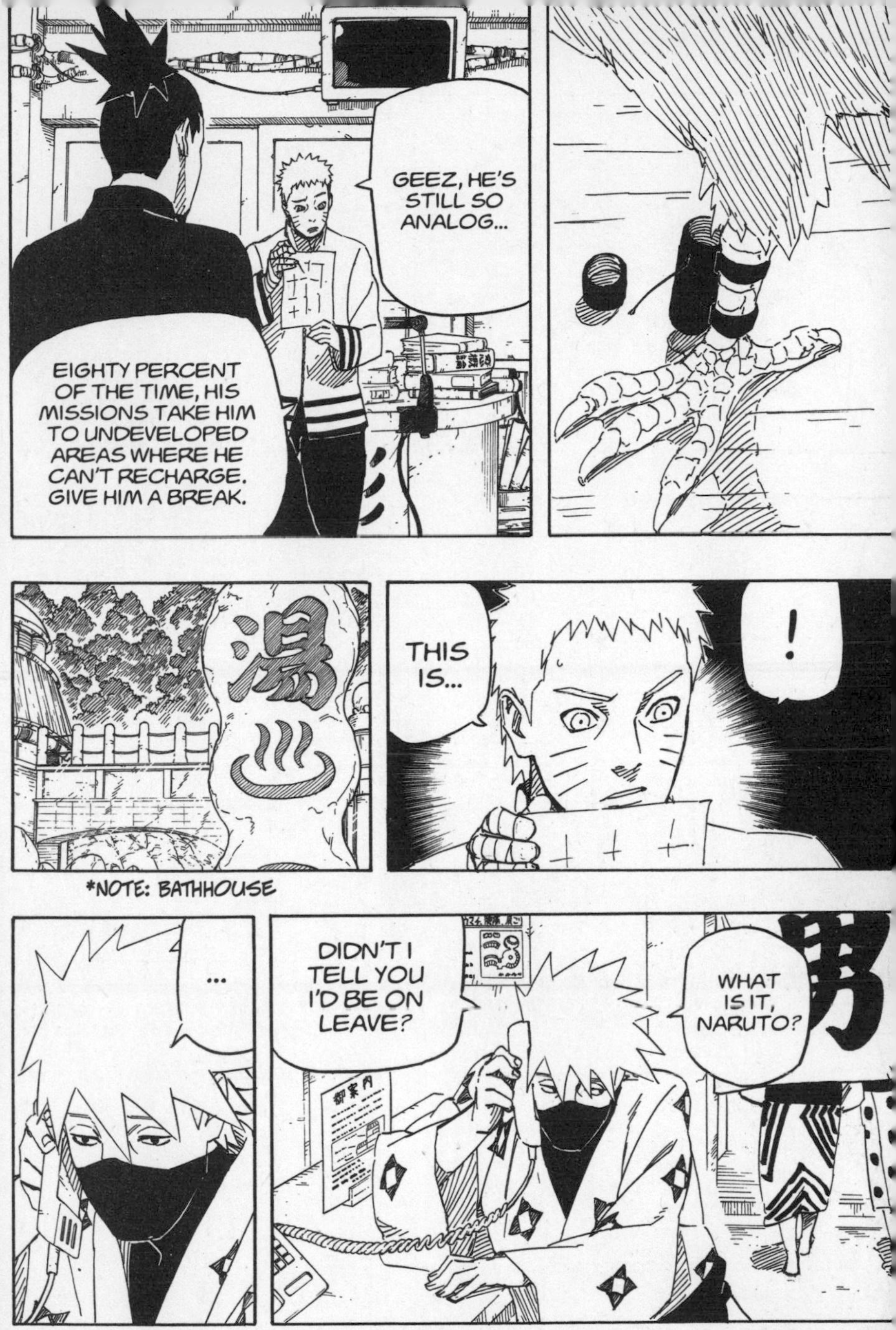
GEEZ, HE'S STILL SO ANALOG...
EIGHTY PERCENT OF THE TIME, HIS MISSIONS TAKE HIM TO UNDEVELOPED AREAS WHERE HE CAN'T RECHARGE. GIVE HIM A BREAK.
!
THIS IS...
湯
*NOTE: BATHHOUSE
男
WHAT IS IT, NARUTO?
DIDN'T I TELL YOU I'D BE ON LEAVE?
...

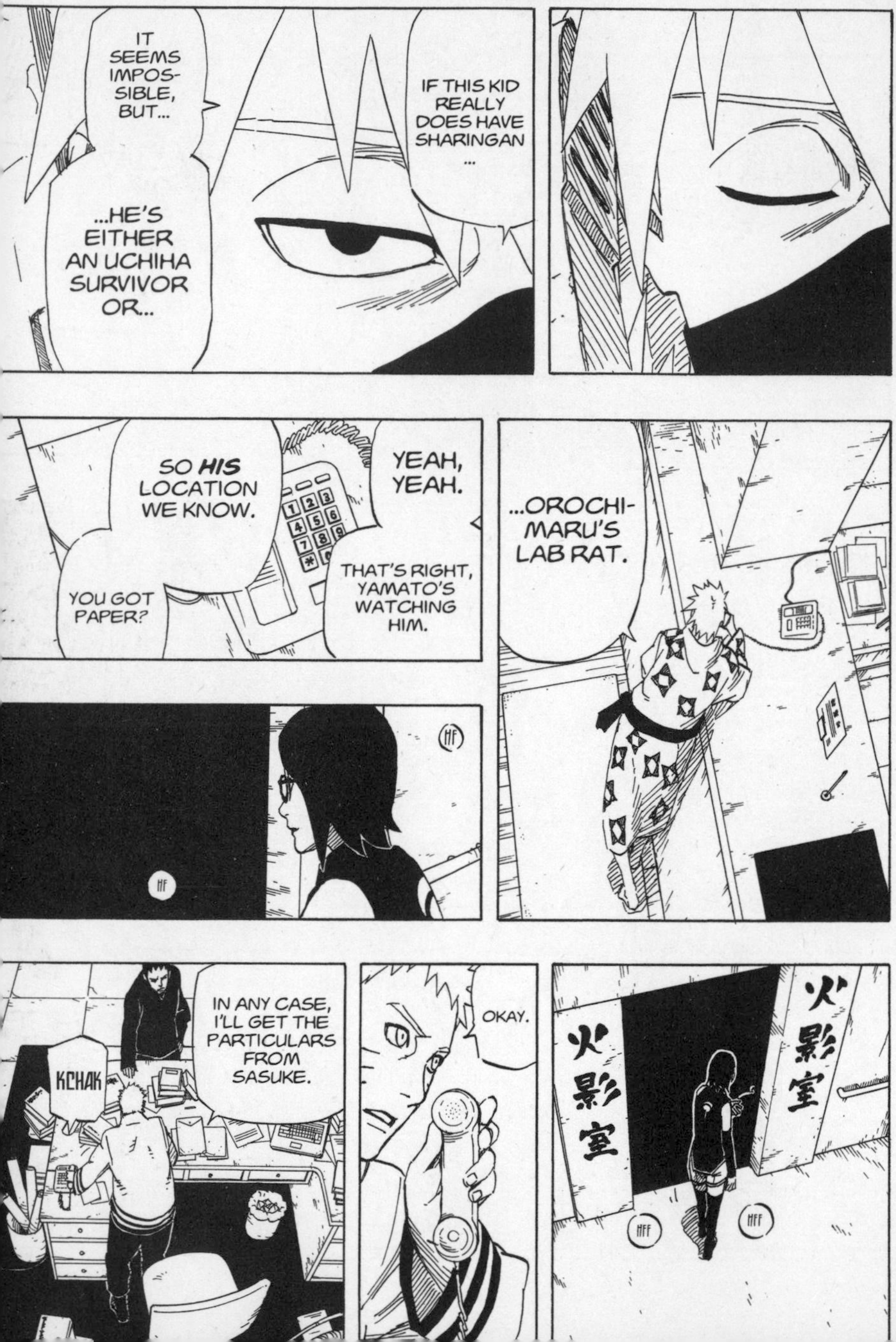
IF THIS KID REALLY DOES HAVE SHARINGAN ...
IT SEEMS IMPOSSIBLE, BUT...
...HE'S EITHER AN UCHIHA SURVIVOR OR...
...OROCHIMARU'S LAB RAT.
YEAH, YEAH.
SO **HIS** LOCATION WE KNOW.
THAT'S RIGHT, YAMATO'S WATCHING HIM.
YOU GOT PAPER?
HF
HF
火影室
火影室
HFF
HFF
OKAY.
IN ANY CASE, I'LL GET THE PARTICULARS FROM SASUKE.
KCHAK

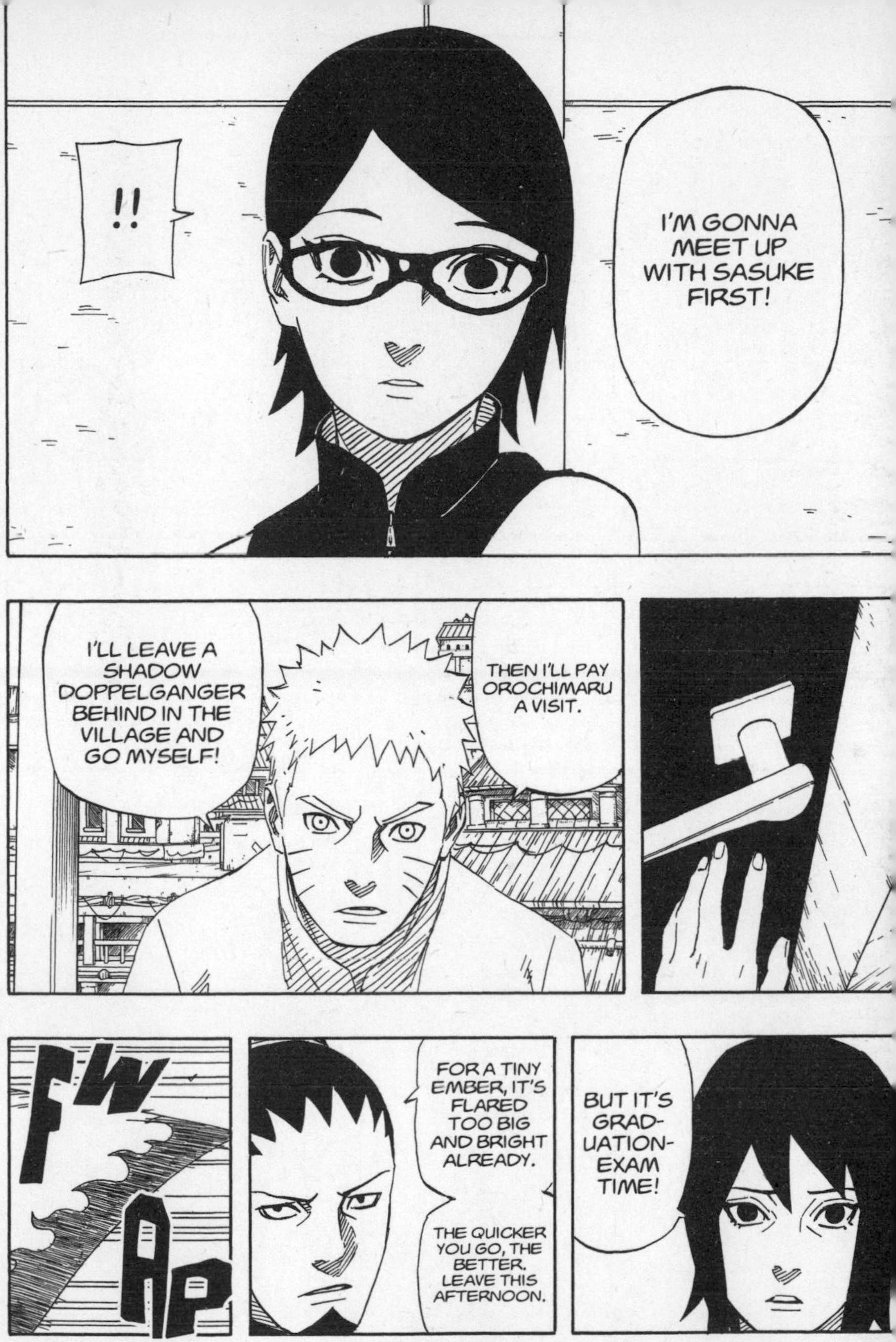
I'M GONNA MEET UP WITH SASUKE FIRST!
!!
I'LL LEAVE A SHADOW DOPPELGANGER BEHIND IN THE VILLAGE AND GO MYSELF!
THEN I'LL PAY OROCHIMARU A VISIT.
BUT IT'S GRAD-UATION-EXAM TIME!
FOR A TINY EMBER, IT'S FLARED TOO BIG AND BRIGHT ALREADY.
THE QUICKER YOU GO, THE BETTER. LEAVE THIS AFTERNOON.
FWAP

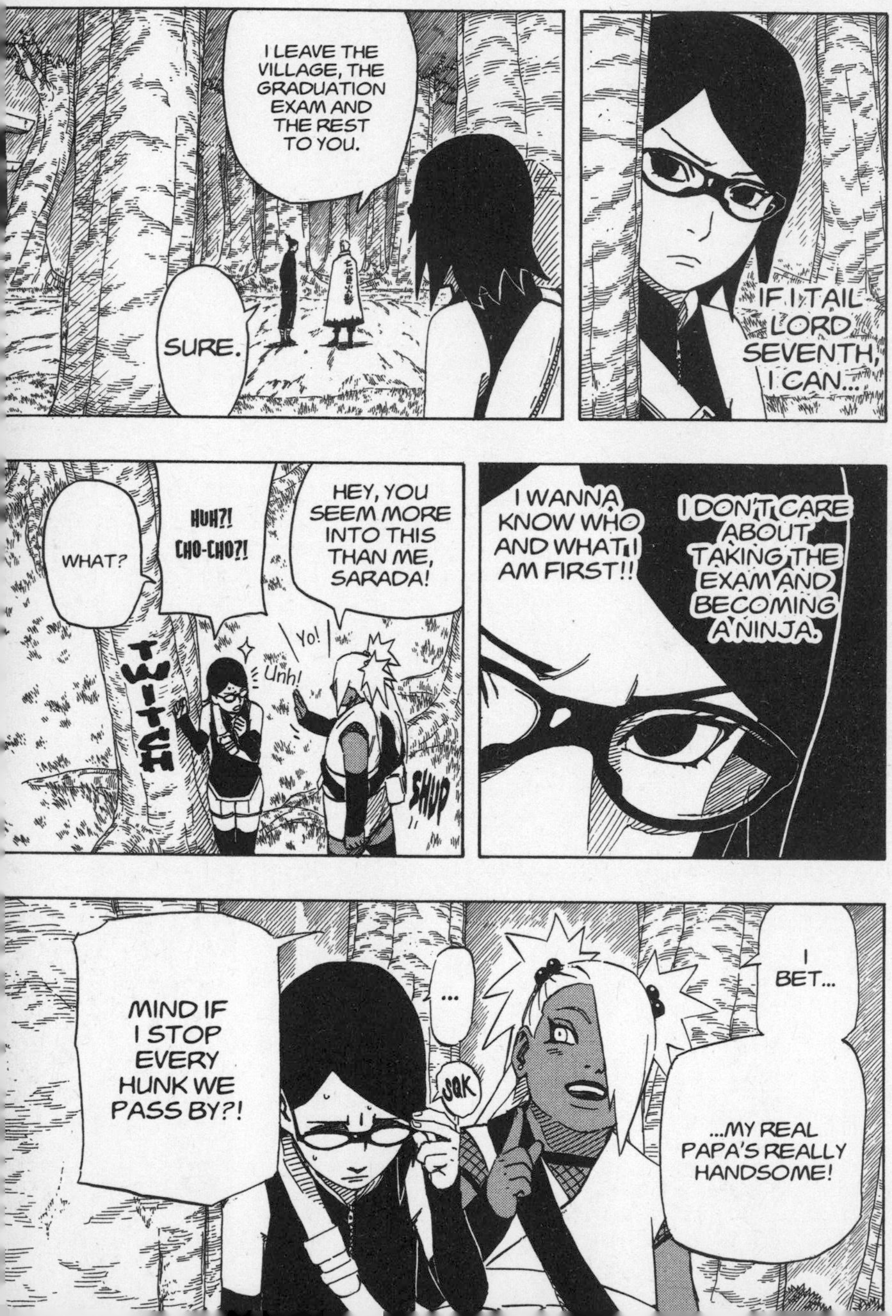
IF I TAIL LORD SEVENTH, I CAN...
I LEAVE THE VILLAGE, THE GRADUATION EXAM AND THE REST TO YOU.
SURE.
I DON'T CARE ABOUT TAKING THE EXAM AND BECOMING A NINJA.
I WANNA KNOW WHO AND WHAT I AM FIRST!!
HEY, YOU SEEM MORE INTO THIS THAN ME, SARADA!
Yo!
Unh!
SHUP
HUH?! CHO-CHO?!
WHAT?
TWITCH
I BET...
...MY REAL PAPA'S REALLY HANDSOME!
SQK
...
MIND IF I STOP EVERY HUNK WE PASS BY?!

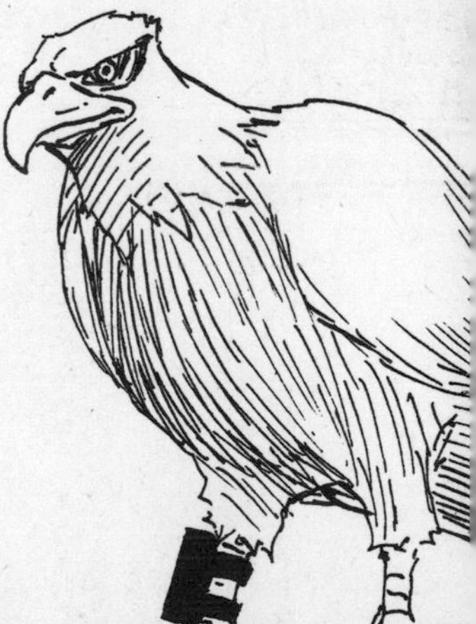

Number 700+3: Chance Meeting: Part 1

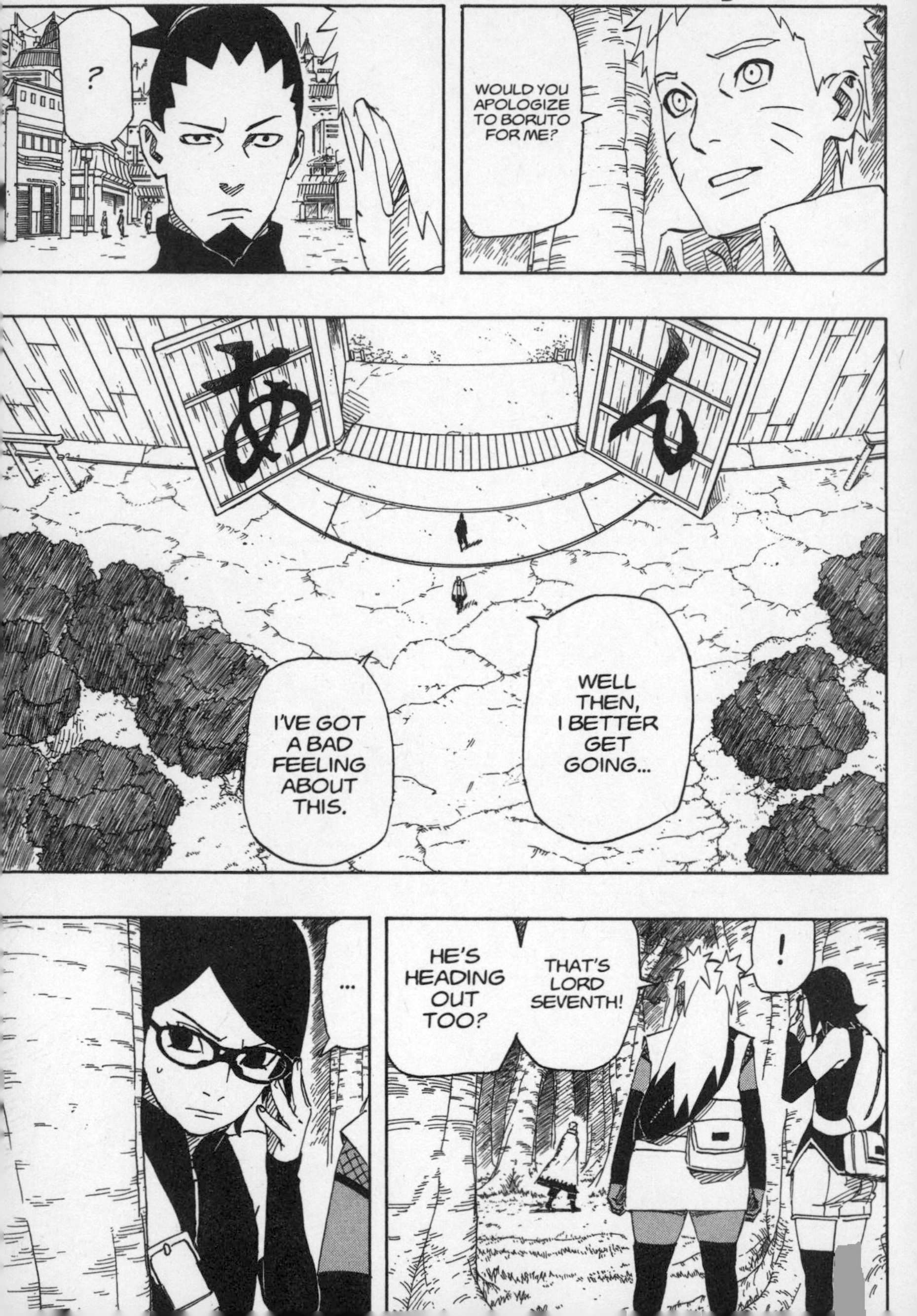
WOULD YOU APOLOGIZE TO BORUTO FOR ME?
?
WELL THEN, I BETTER GET GOING...
I'VE GOT A BAD FEELING ABOUT THIS.
!
THAT'S LORD SEVENTH!
HE'S HEADING OUT TOO?
...

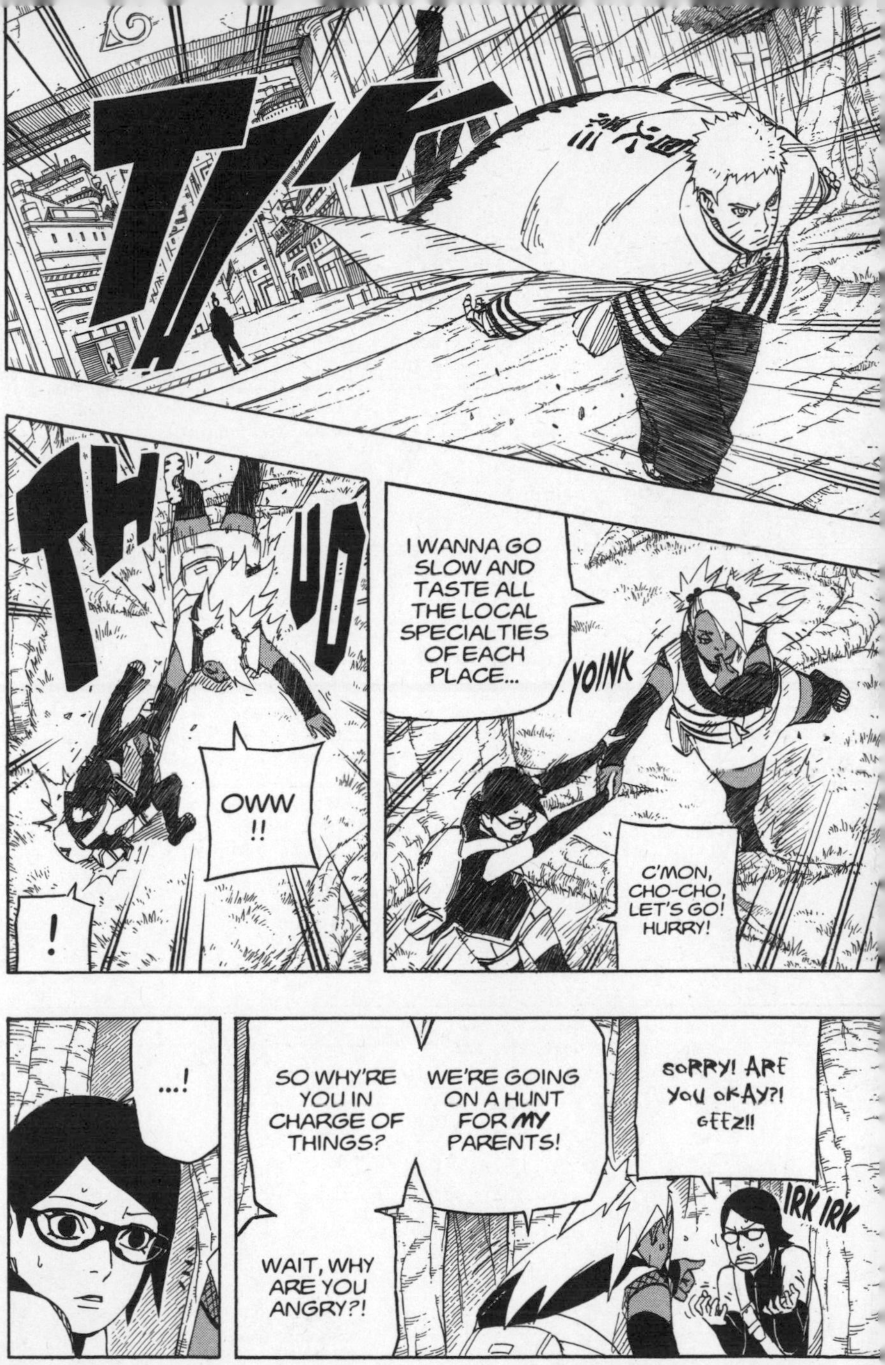
I WANNA GO SLOW AND TASTE ALL THE LOCAL SPECIALTIES OF EACH PLACE...
YOINK
C'MON, CHO-CHO, LET'S GO! HURRY!
THUD
OWW!!
!
SORRY! ARE YOU OKAY?! GEEZ!!
IRK IRK
WE'RE GOING ON A HUNT FOR *MY* PARENTS!
SO WHY'RE YOU IN CHARGE OF THINGS?
WAIT, WHY ARE YOU ANGRY?!
...!

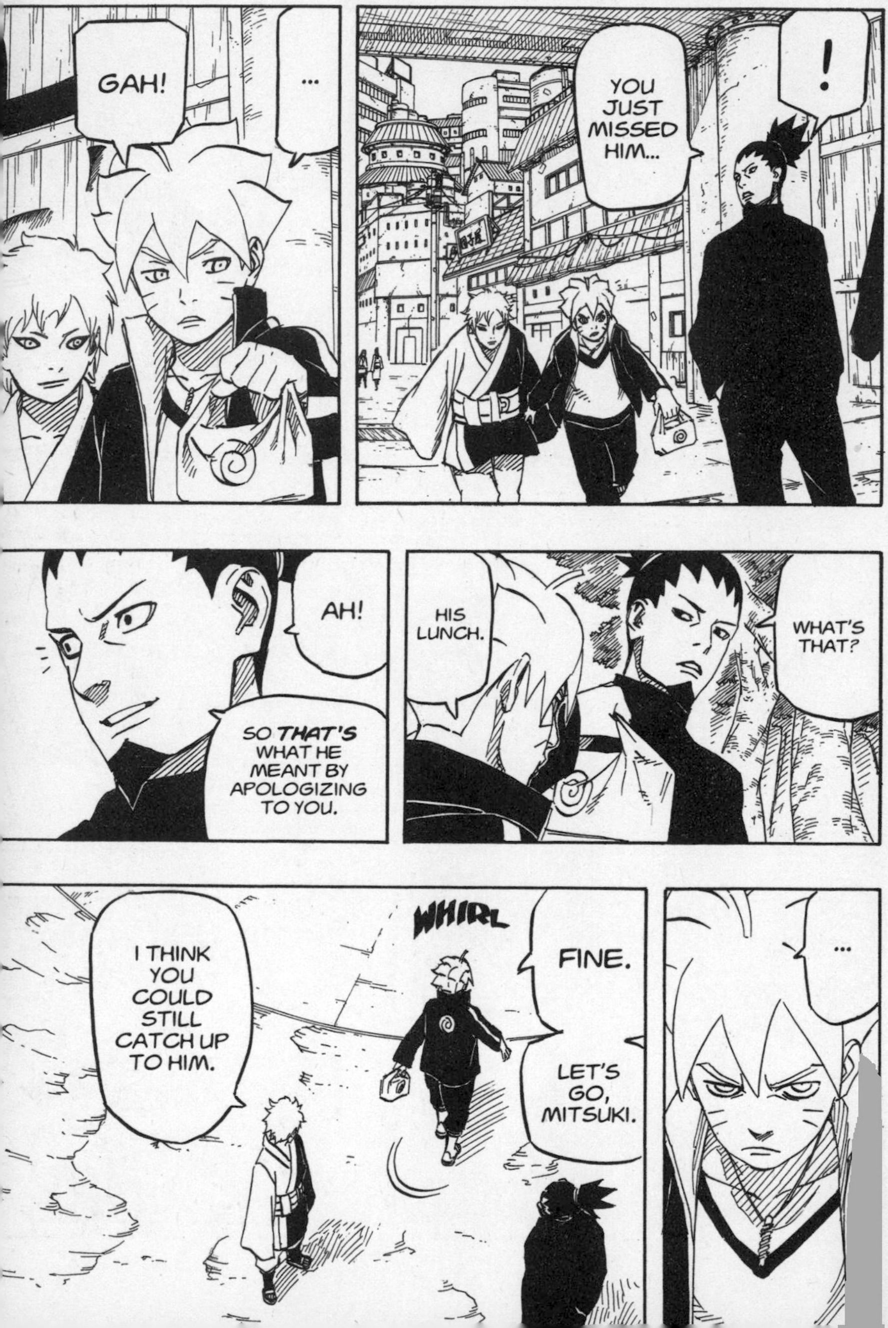
!
YOU JUST MISSED HIM...
...
GAH!
WHAT'S THAT?
HIS LUNCH.
AH!
SO **THAT'S** WHAT HE MEANT BY APOLOGIZING TO YOU.
...
FINE.
LET'S GO, MITSUKI.
WHIRL
I THINK YOU COULD STILL CATCH UP TO HIM.

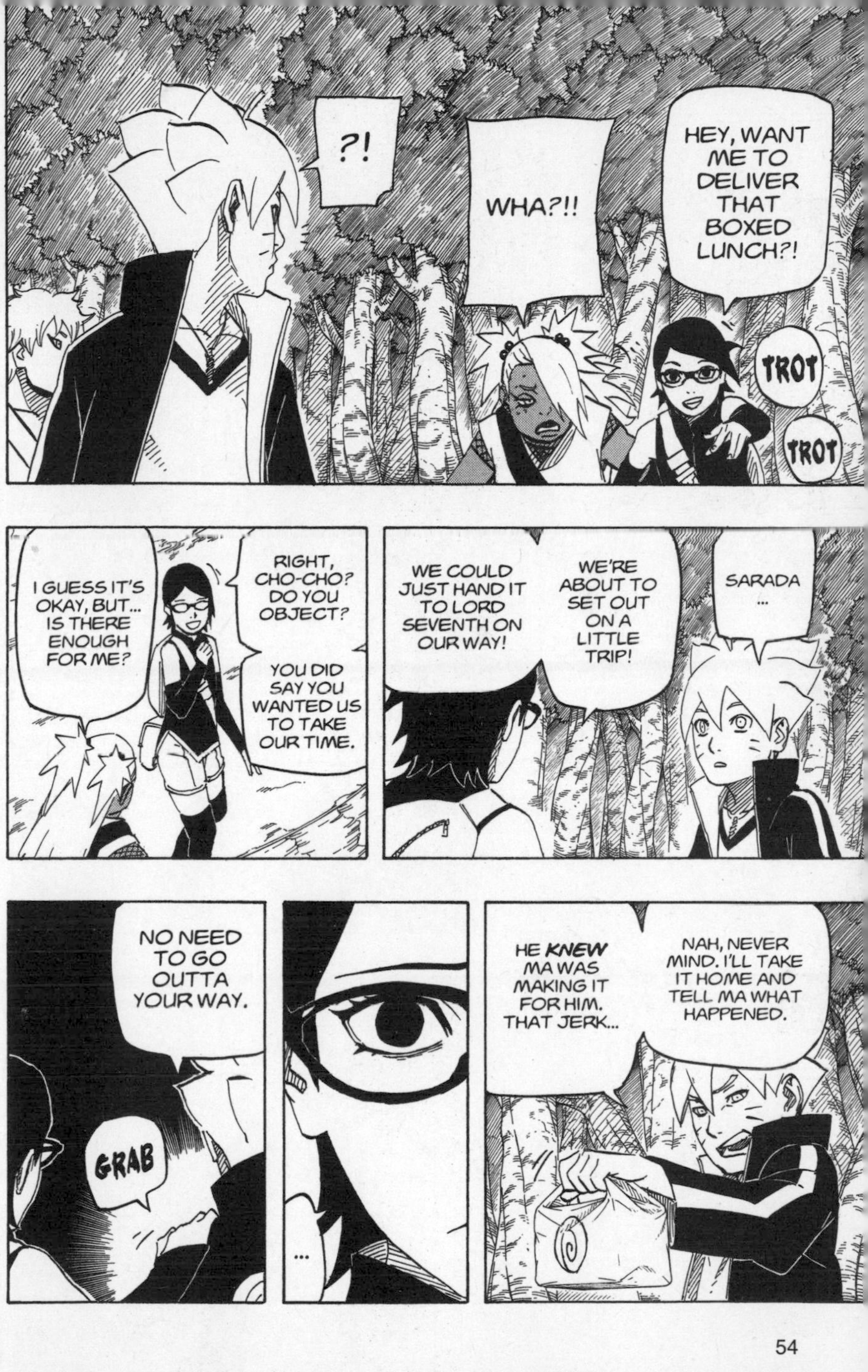
HEY, WANT ME TO DELIVER THAT BOXED LUNCH?!
TROT
TROT
WHA?!!
?!
SARADA ...
WE'RE ABOUT TO SET OUT ON A LITTLE TRIP!
WE COULD JUST HAND IT TO LORD SEVENTH ON OUR WAY!
RIGHT, CHO-CHO? DO YOU OBJECT?
YOU DID SAY YOU WANTED US TO TAKE OUR TIME.
I GUESS IT'S OKAY, BUT... IS THERE ENOUGH FOR ME?
NAH, NEVER MIND. I'LL TAKE IT HOME AND TELL MA WHAT HAPPENED.
HE ***KNEW*** MA WAS MAKING IT FOR HIM. THAT JERK...
...
NO NEED TO GO OUTTA YOUR WAY.
GRAB

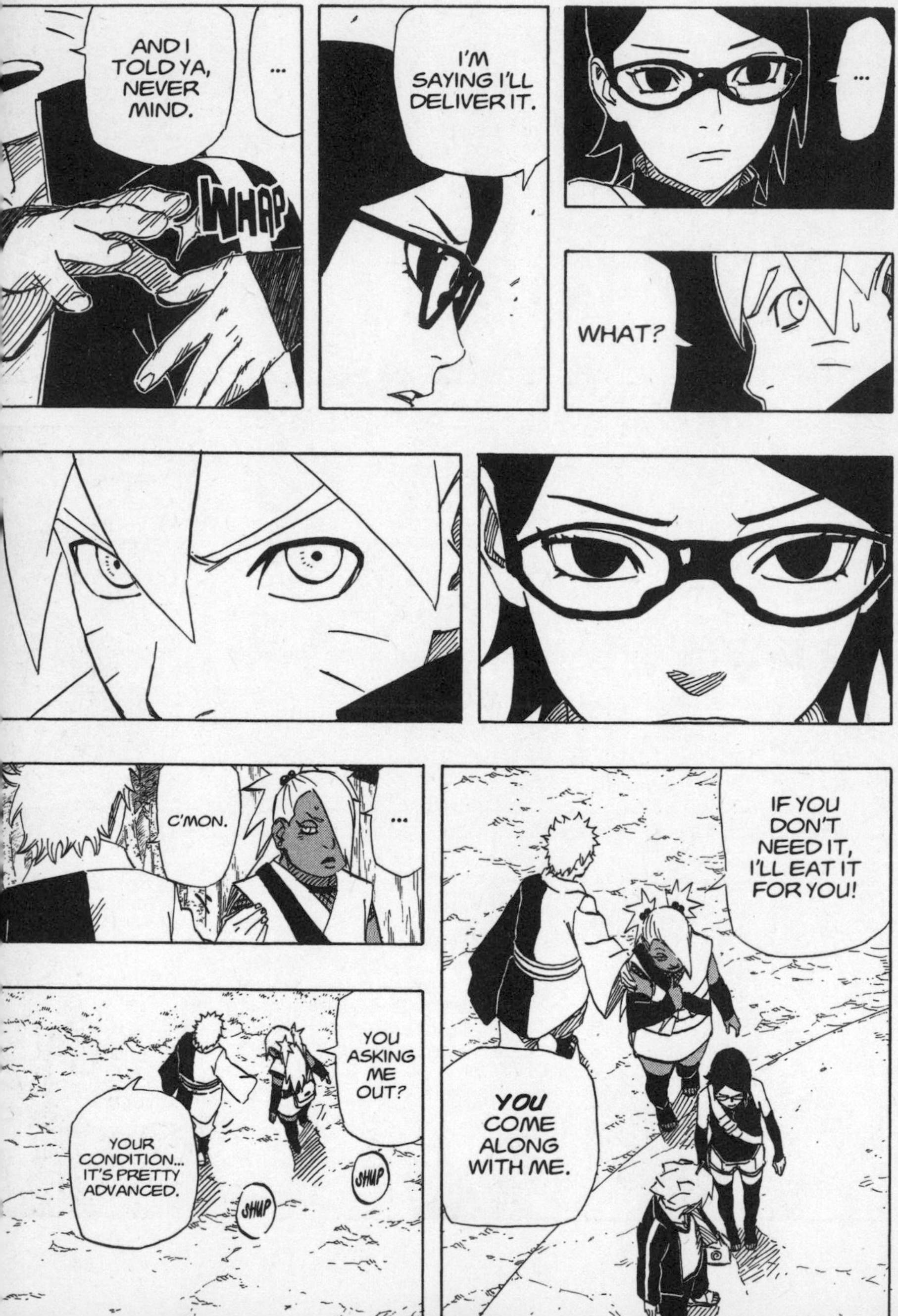
...
WHAT?
I'M SAYING I'LL DELIVER IT.
...
AND I TOLD YA, NEVER MIND.
WHAP
IF YOU DON'T NEED IT, I'LL EAT IT FOR YOU!
YOU COME ALONG WITH ME.
...
C'MON.
YOU ASKING ME OUT?
SHUP
SHUP
YOUR CONDITION... IT'S PRETTY ADVANCED.

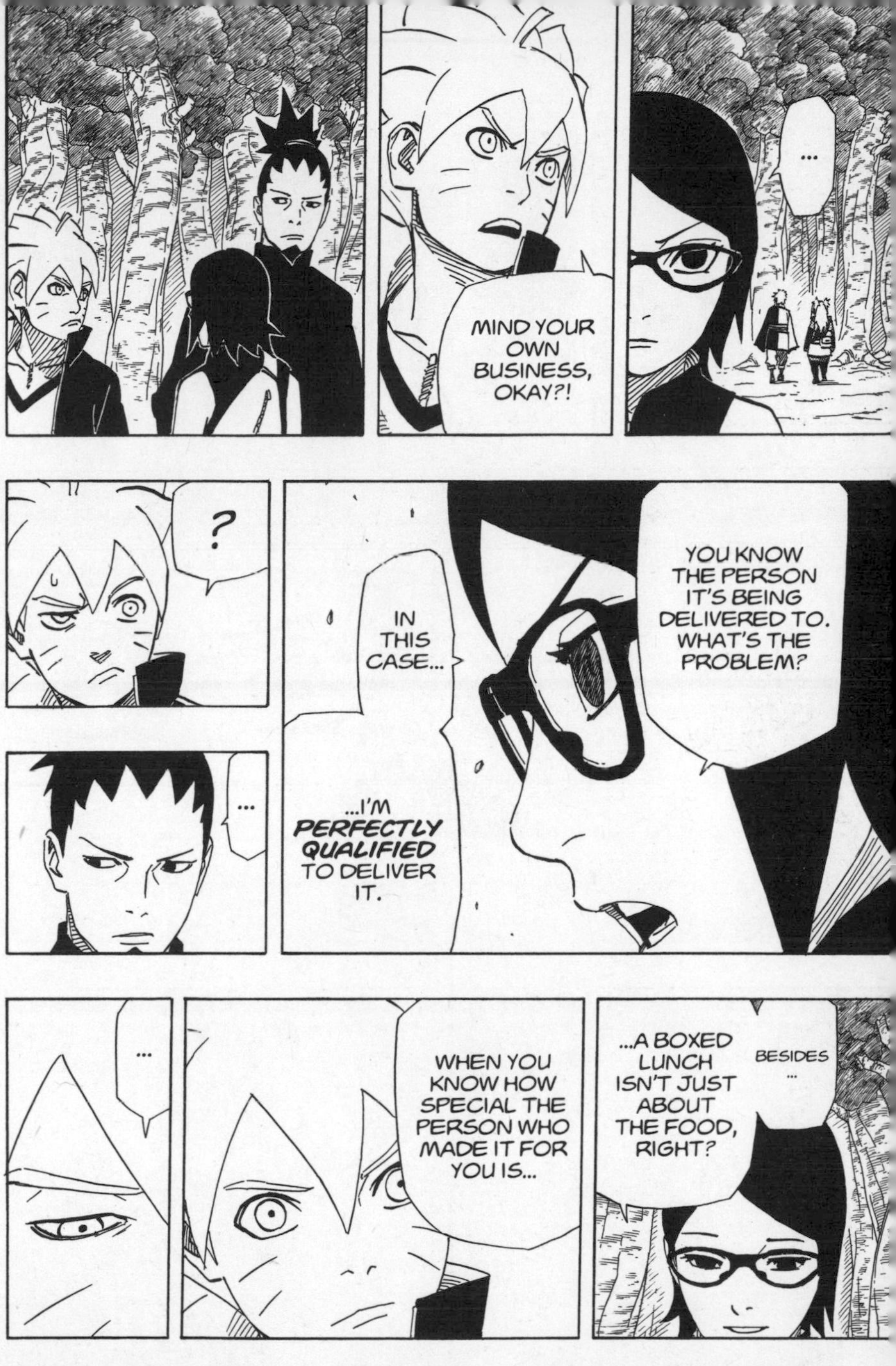
...
MIND YOUR OWN BUSINESS, OKAY?!
YOU KNOW THE PERSON IT'S BEING DELIVERED TO. WHAT'S THE PROBLEM?
IN THIS CASE...
...I'M *PERFECTLY QUALIFIED* TO DELIVER IT.
?
...
BESIDES ...
...A BOXED LUNCH ISN'T JUST ABOUT THE FOOD, RIGHT?
WHEN YOU KNOW HOW SPECIAL THE PERSON WHO MADE IT FOR YOU IS...
...

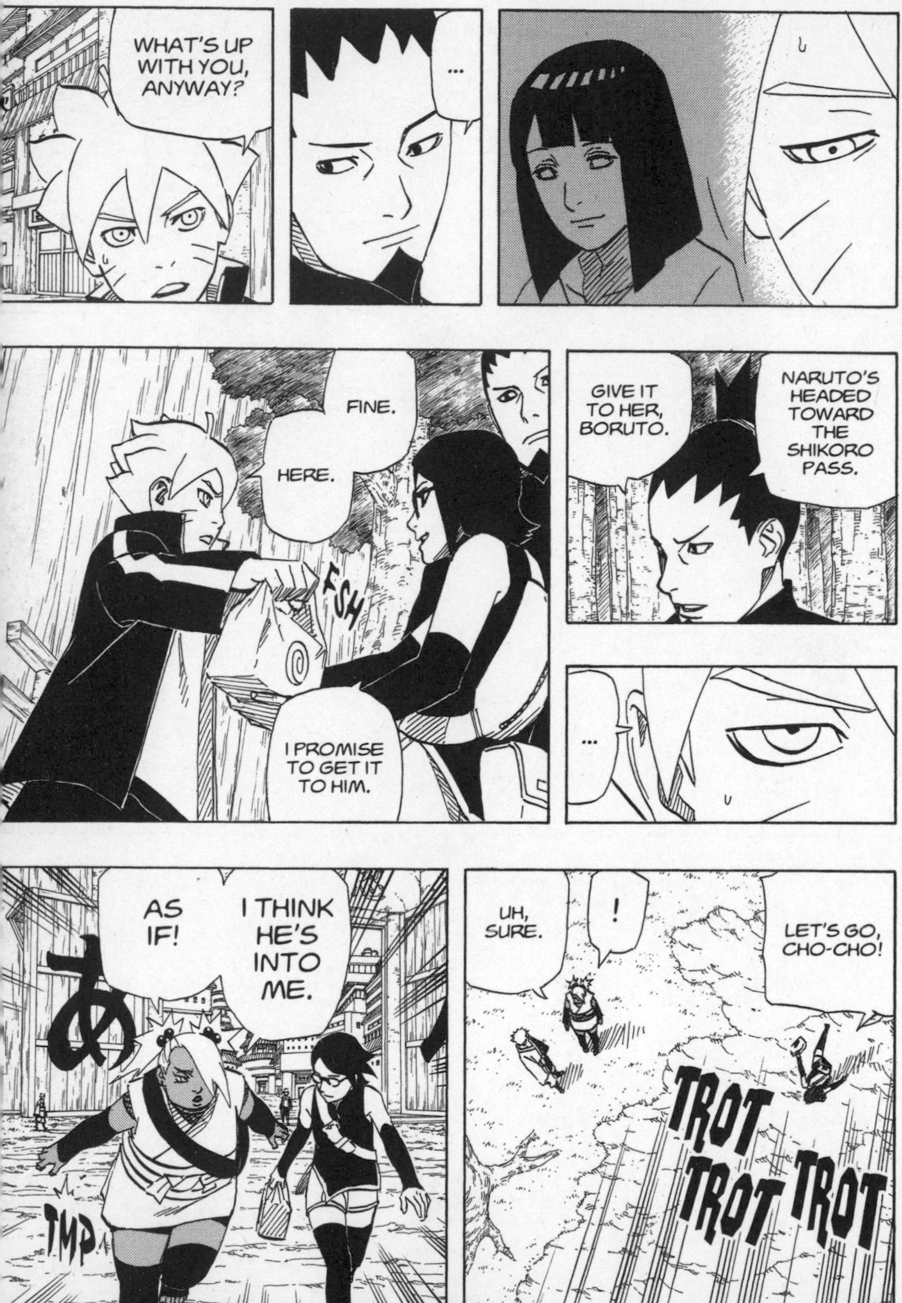
...
WHAT'S UP WITH YOU, ANYWAY?
NARUTO'S HEADED TOWARD THE SHIKORO PASS.
GIVE IT TO HER, BORUTO.
...
FINE.
HERE.
FSH
I PROMISE TO GET IT TO HIM.
LET'S GO, CHO-CHO!
!
UH, SURE.
TROT TROT TROT TROT
I THINK HE'S INTO ME.
AS IF!
あ
TMP

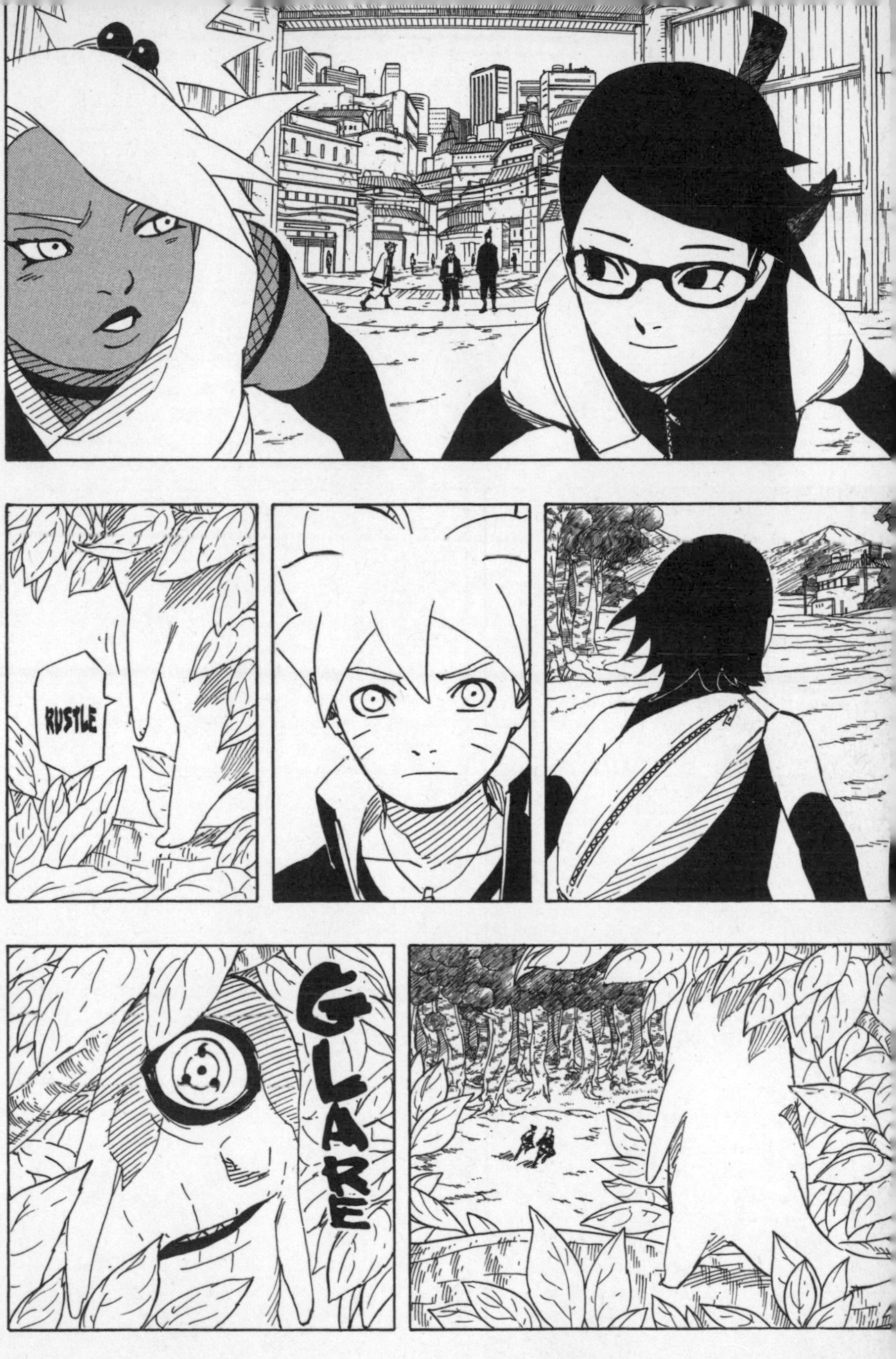
RUSTLE
GLARE

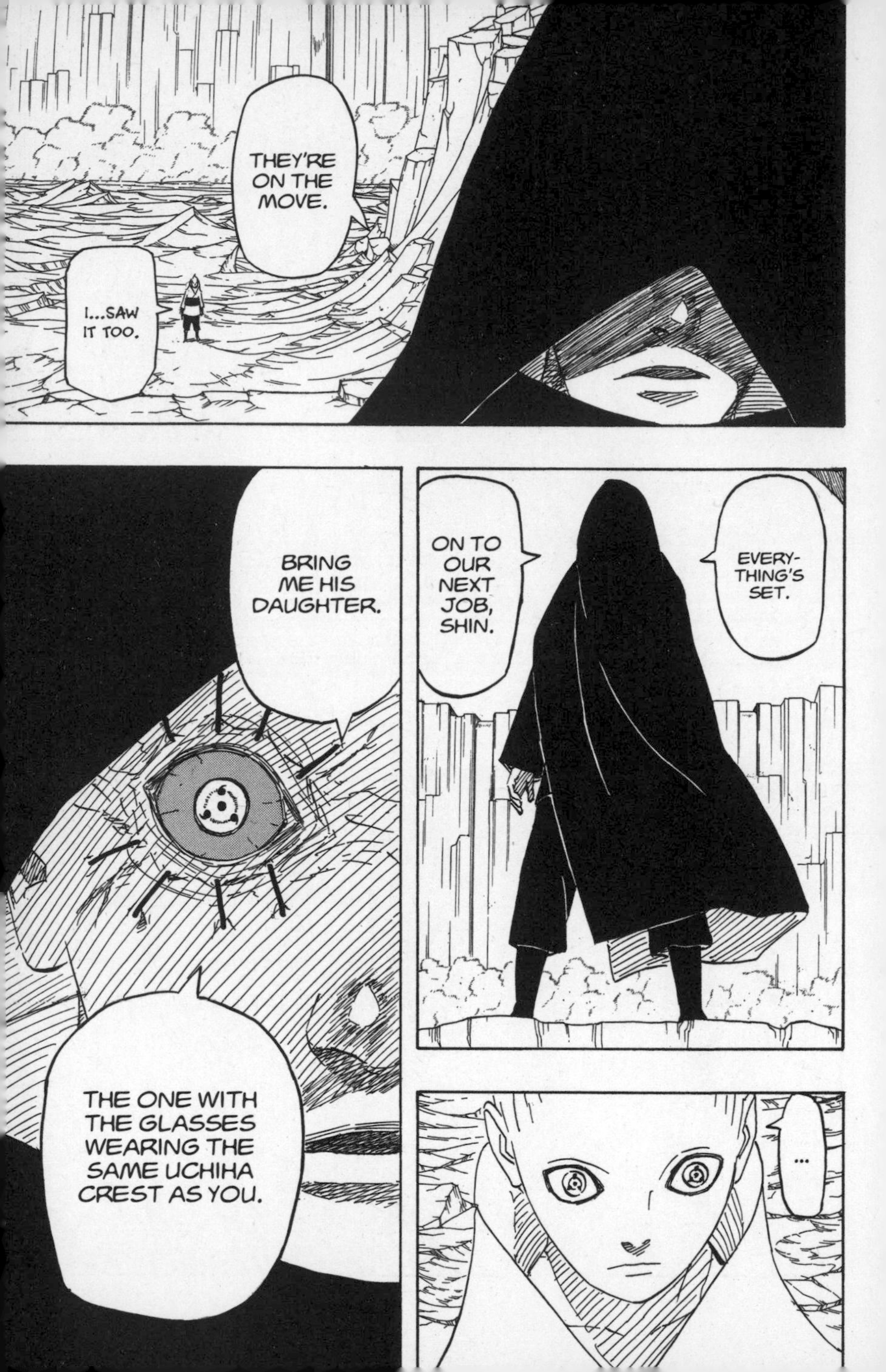
THEY'RE ON THE MOVE.
I...SAW IT TOO.
EVERY-THING'S SET.
ON TO OUR NEXT JOB, SHIN.
...
BRING ME HIS DAUGHTER.
THE ONE WITH THE GLASSES WEARING THE SAME UCHIHA CREST AS YOU.

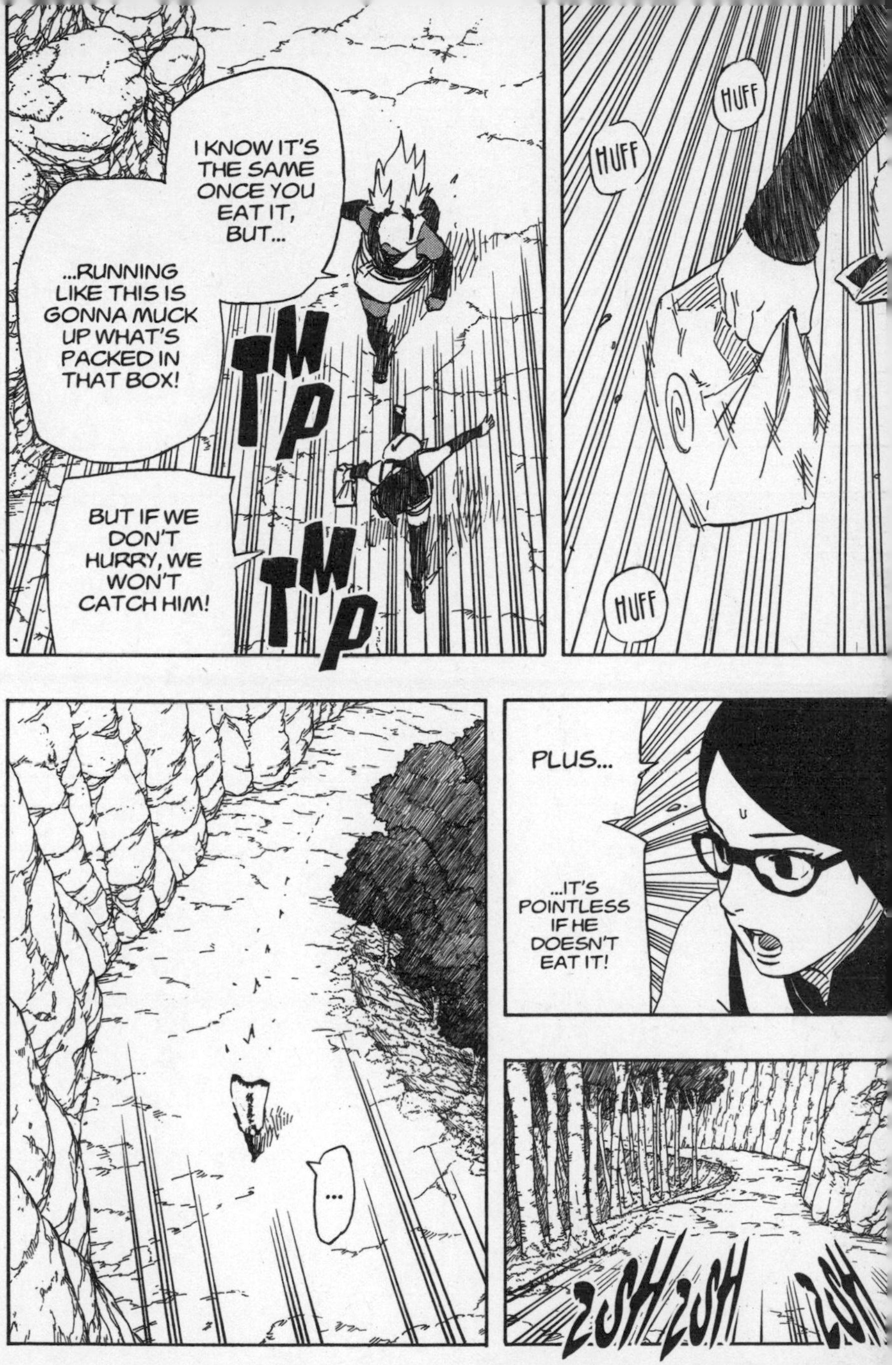
HUFF
HUFF
HUFF
I KNOW IT'S THE SAME ONCE YOU EAT IT, BUT...
...RUNNING LIKE THIS IS GONNA MUCK UP WHAT'S PACKED IN THAT BOX!
TMP TMP
BUT IF WE DON'T HURRY, WE WON'T CATCH HIM!
PLUS...
...IT'S POINTLESS IF HE DOESN'T EAT IT!
ZSH ZSH ZSH
...

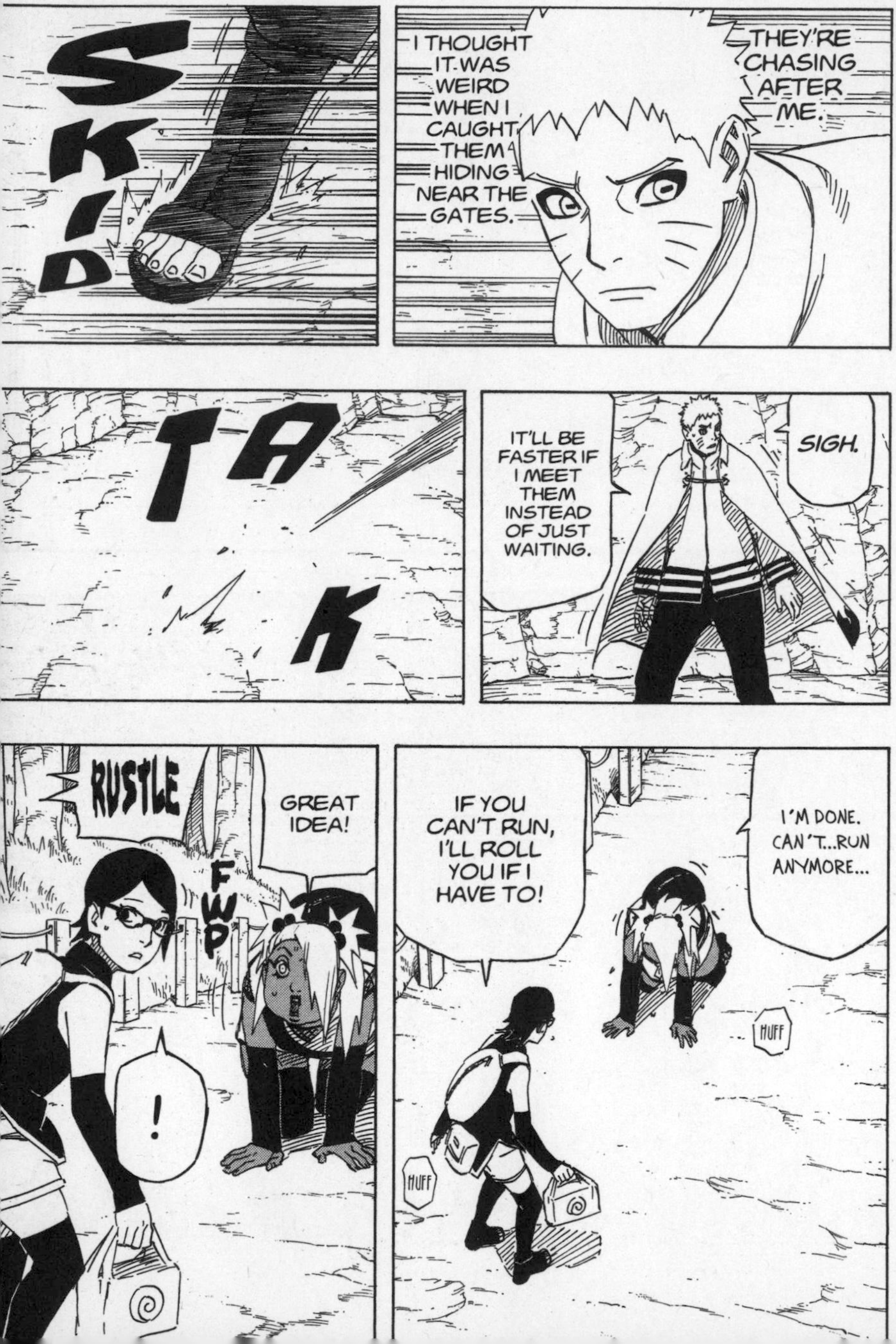
THEY'RE CHASING AFTER ME.
I THOUGHT IT WAS WEIRD WHEN I CAUGHT THEM HIDING NEAR THE GATES.
SKID
SIGH.
IT'LL BE FASTER IF I MEET THEM INSTEAD OF JUST WAITING.
TAK
I'M DONE. CAN'T...RUN ANYMORE...
HUFF
IF YOU CAN'T RUN, I'LL ROLL YOU IF I HAVE TO!
HUFF
RUSTLE
GREAT IDEA!
FWP
!

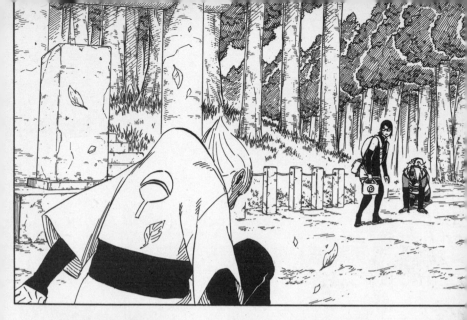

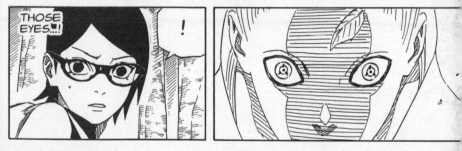

THOSE EYES...!

!

WHO **ARE** YOU?

COME WITH ME. COME.

HUH? HE A FRIEND OF YOURS?

RISE

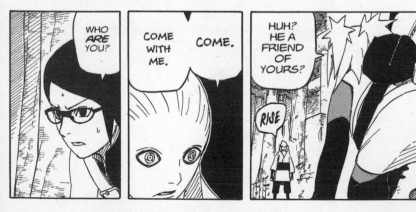

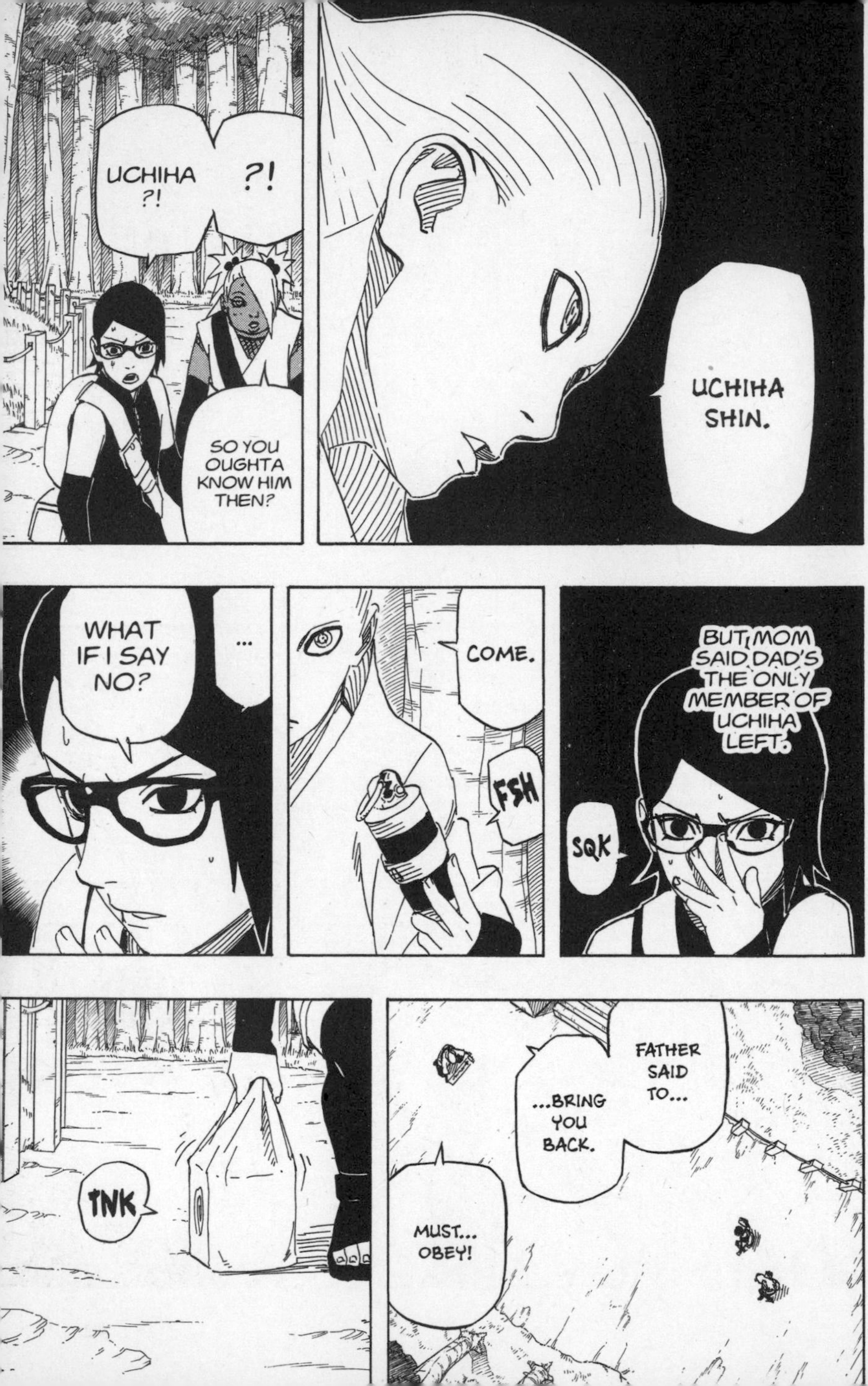
UCHIHA SHIN.
?!
UCHIHA ?!
SO YOU OUGHTA KNOW HIM THEN?
BUT MOM SAID DAD'S THE ONLY MEMBER OF UCHIHA LEFT.
SQK
COME.
FSH
...
WHAT IF I SAY NO?
FATHER SAID TO...
...BRING YOU BACK.
MUST... OBEY!
TNK

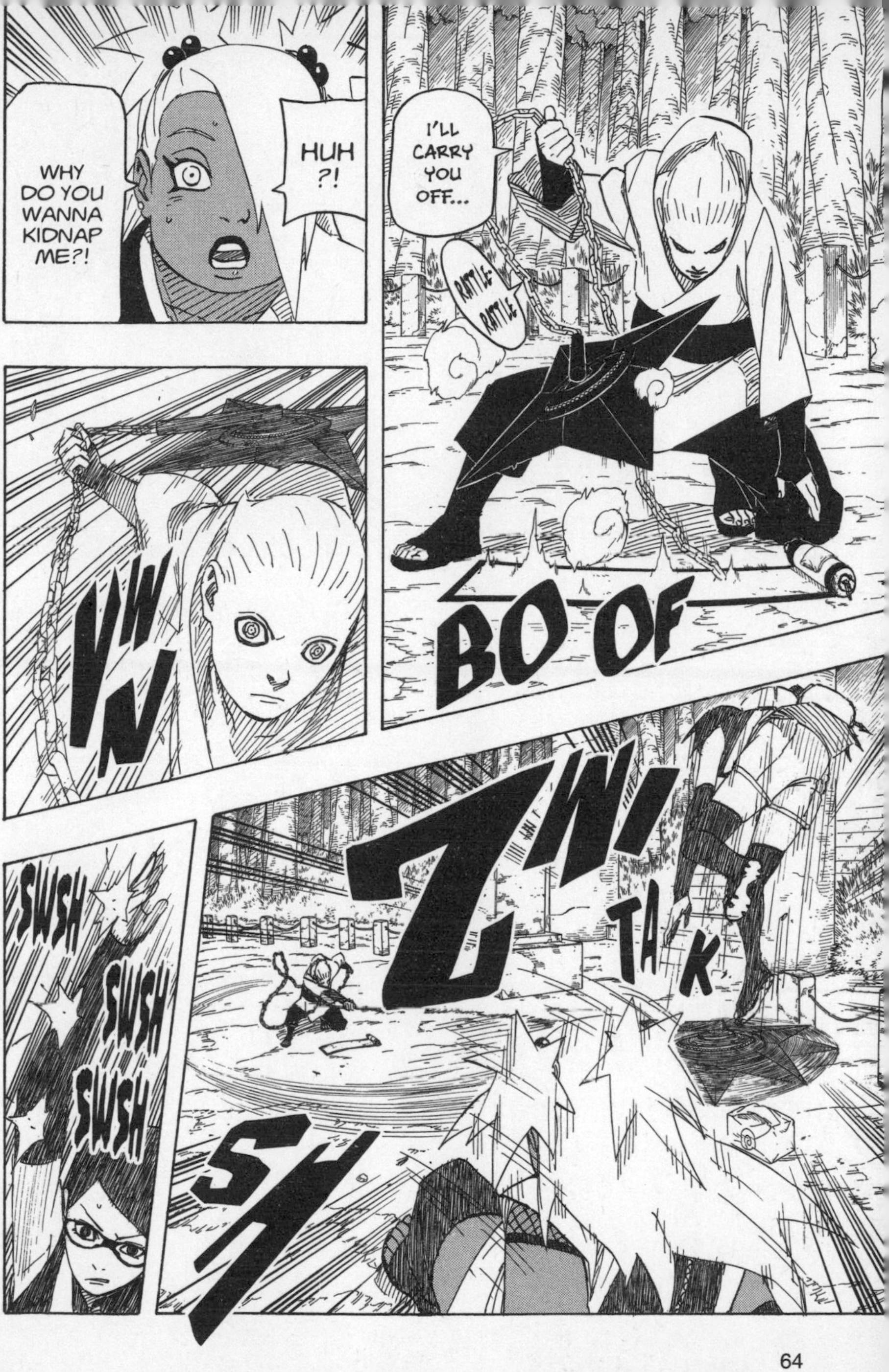

I'LL CARRY YOU OFF...
RATTLE RATTLE
BO OF
HUH ?!
WHY DO YOU WANNA KIDNAP ME?!
VWN
ZWN
TA K
SH
SWSH
SWSH
SWSH

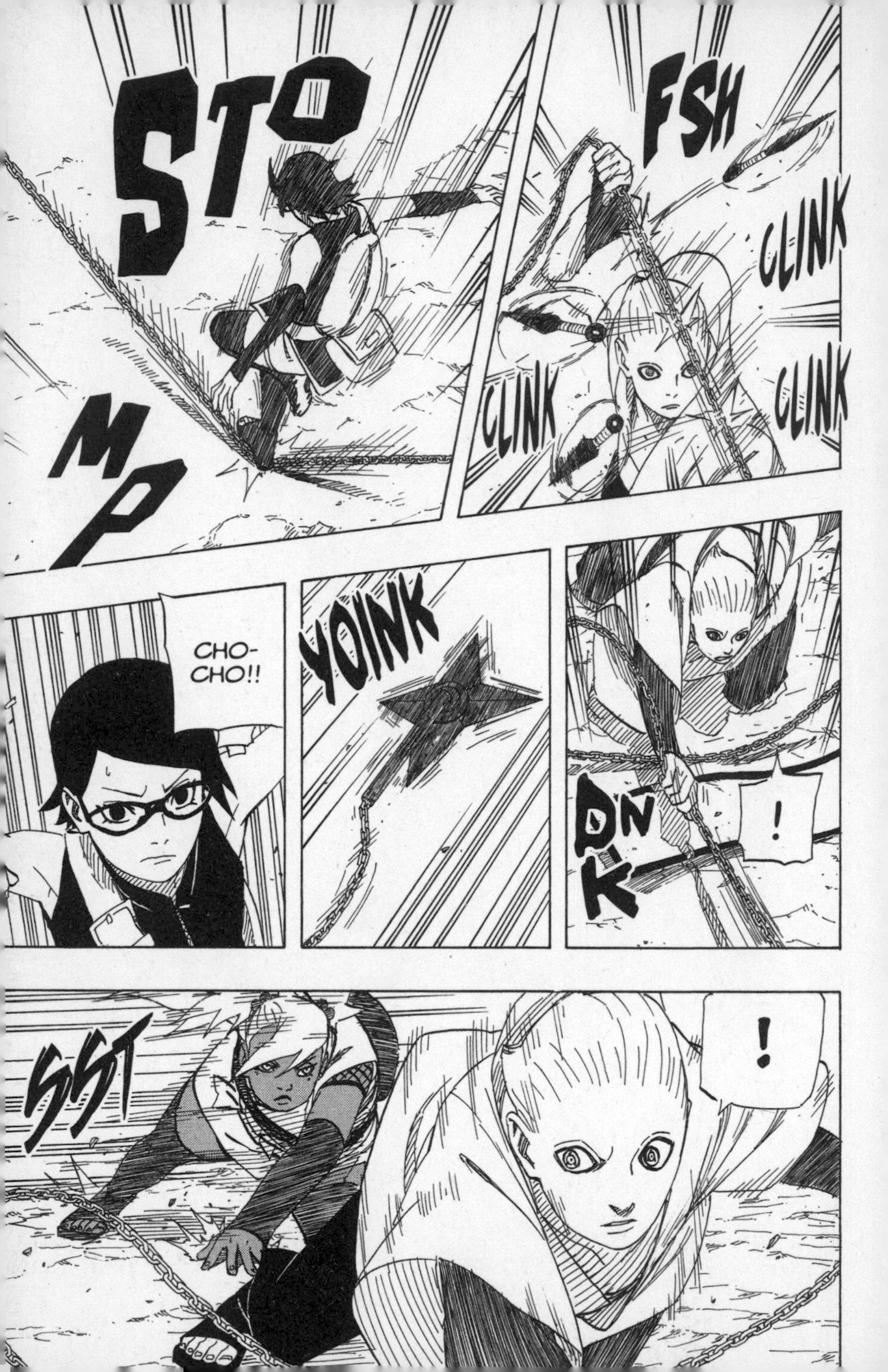
FSH
CLINK
CLINK
CLINK
STOMP
!
DNK
YOINK
CHO-CHO!!
!
SST

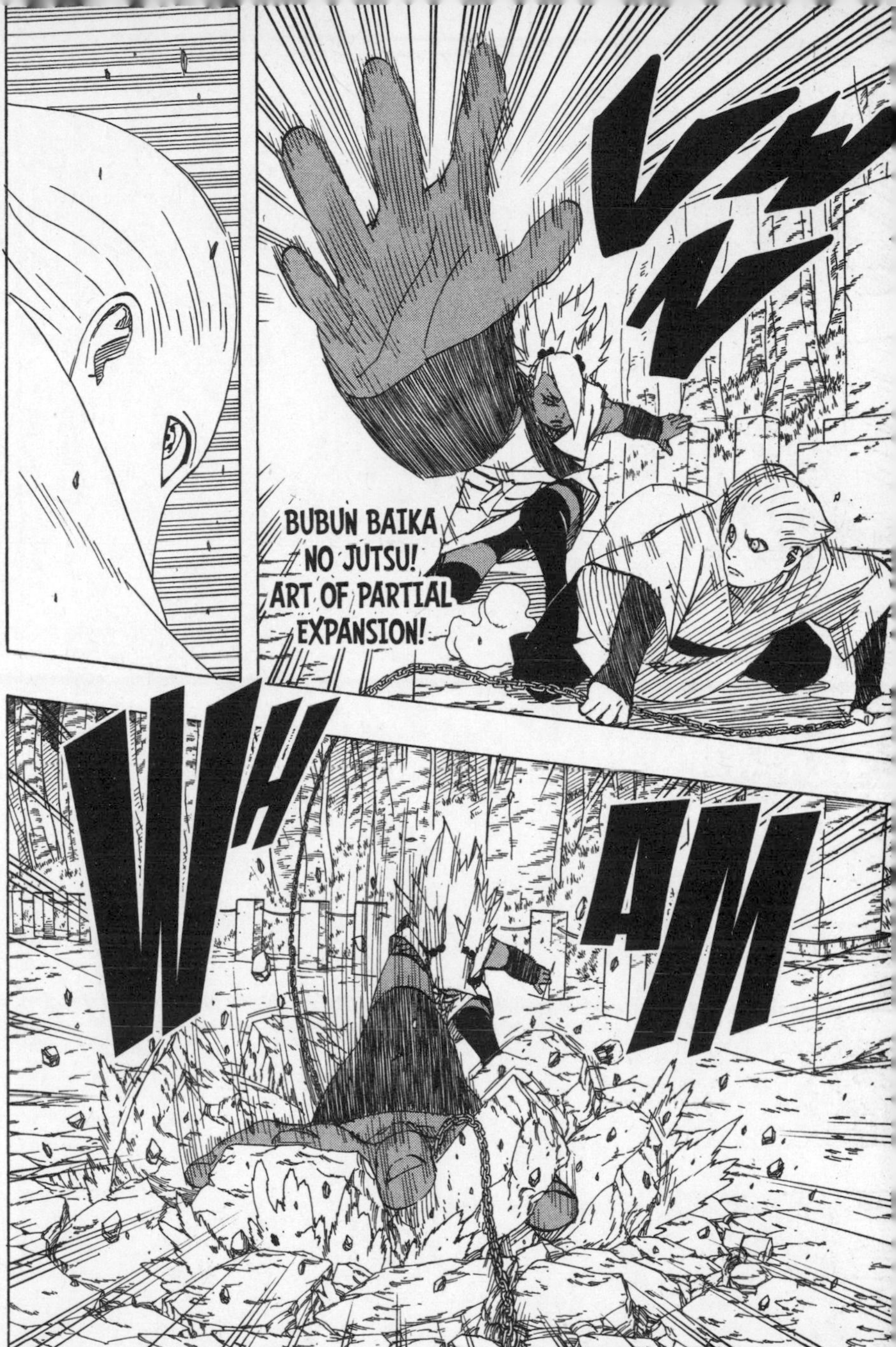
BUBUN BAIKA NO JUTSU! ART OF PARTIAL EXPANSION!
WHAM

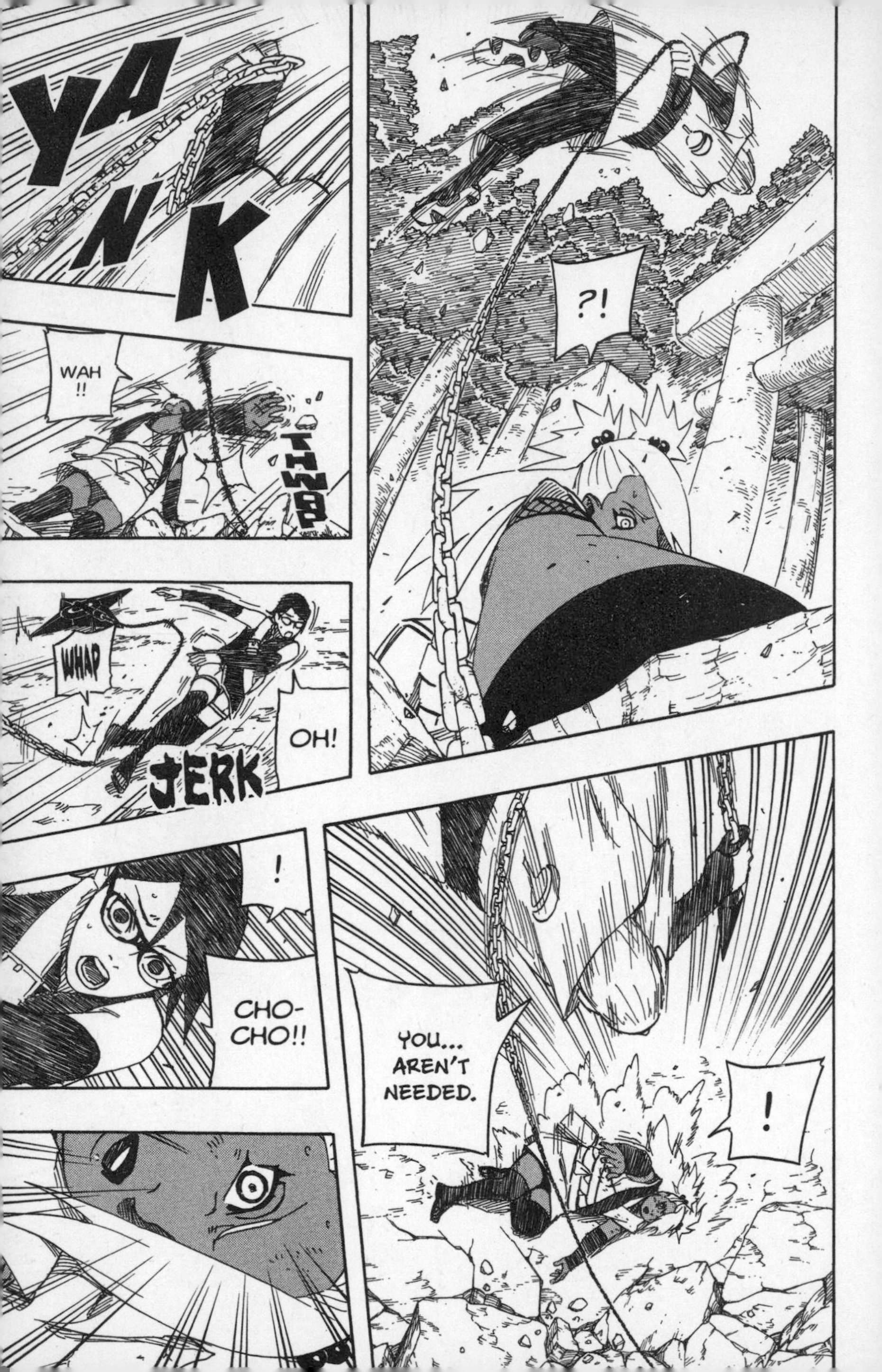

?!
YANK
WAH !!
THWBP
OH!
WHAP
JERK
YOU... AREN'T NEEDED.
!
!
CHO-CHO!!

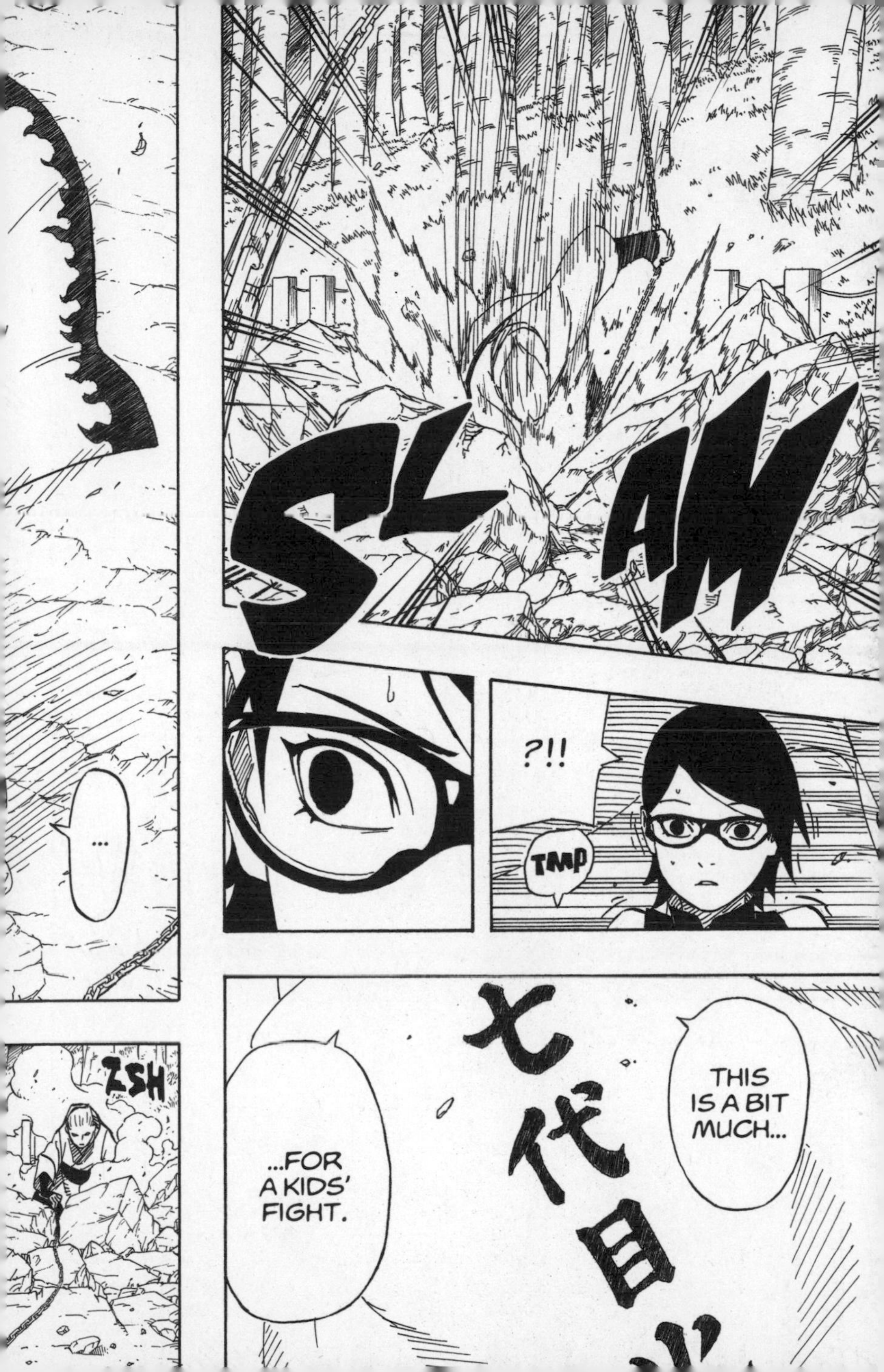

SLAM
?!!
TMP
...
THIS IS A BIT MUCH...
...FOR A KIDS' FIGHT.
七代目
ZSH

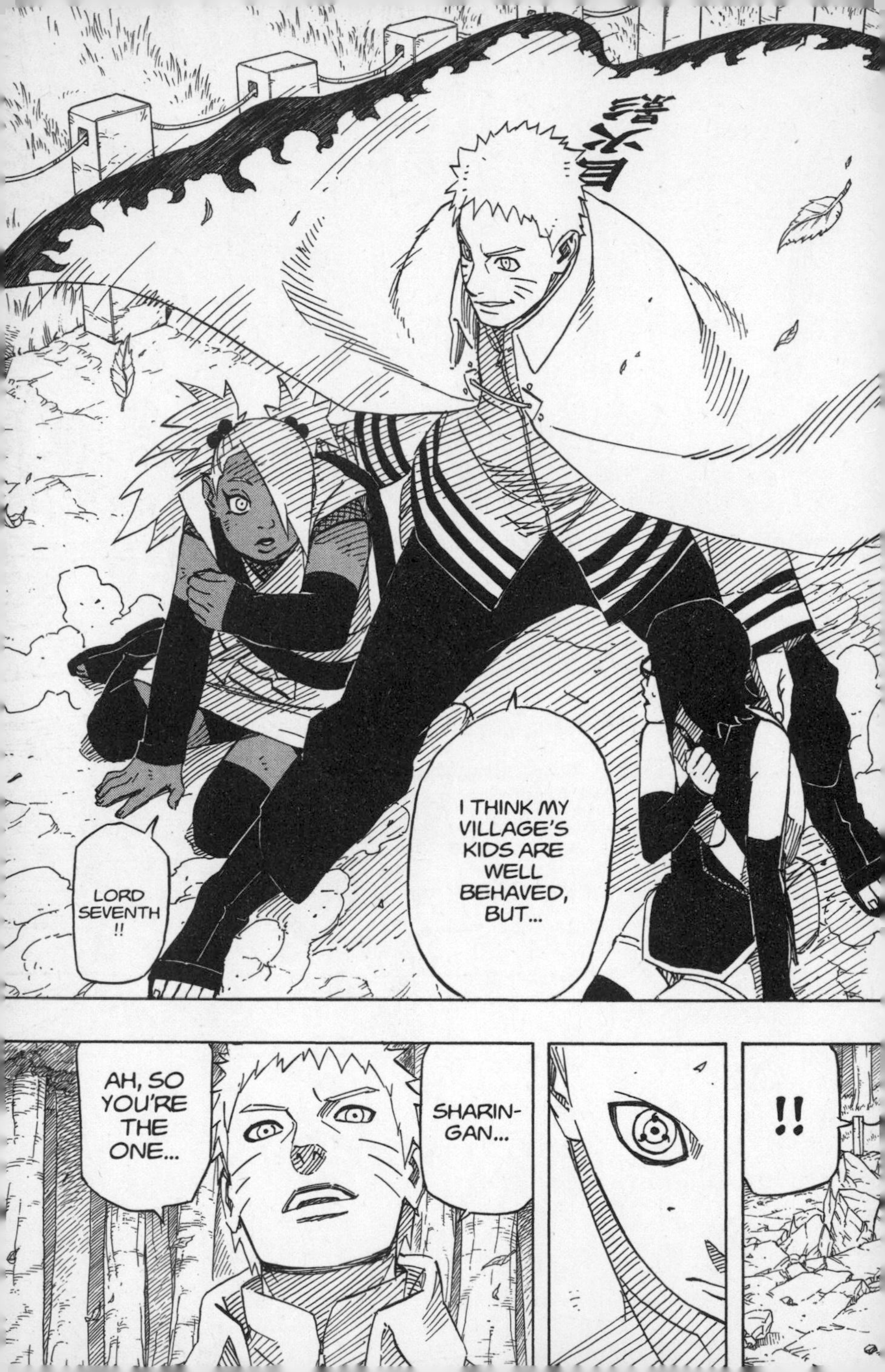
I THINK MY VILLAGE'S KIDS ARE WELL BEHAVED, BUT...
LORD SEVENTH !!
!!
SHARIN-GAN...
AH, SO YOU'RE THE ONE...

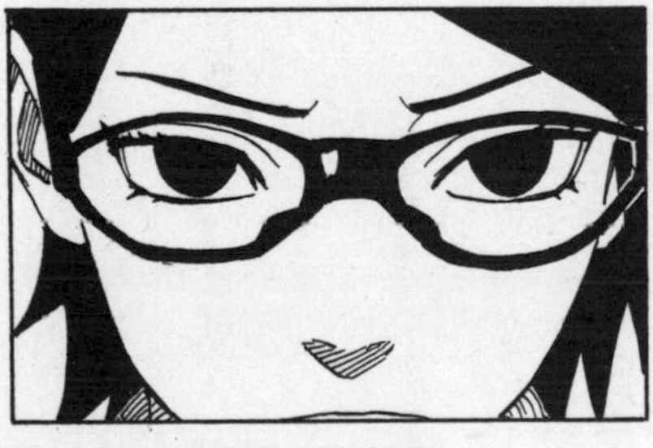
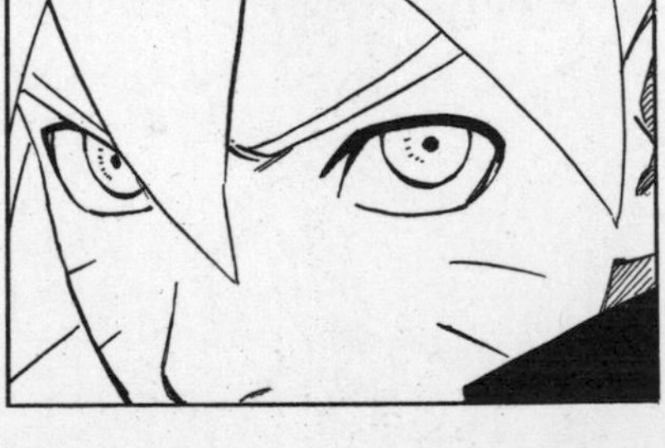

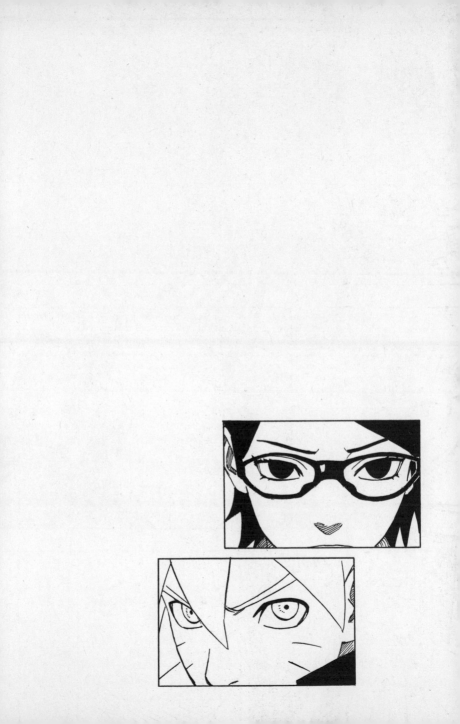

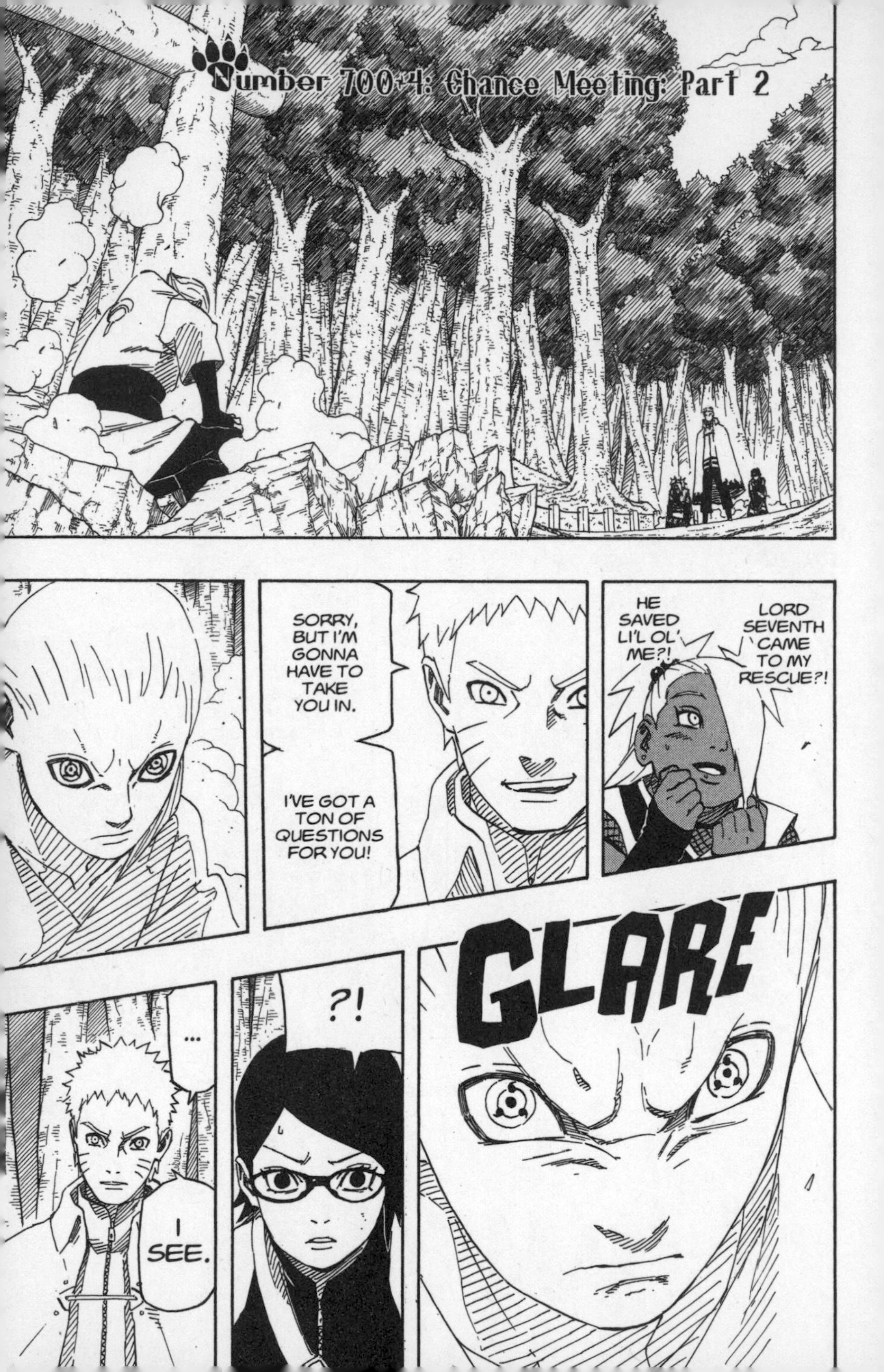
Number 700+4: Chance Meeting: Part 2
LORD SEVENTH CAME TO MY RESCUE?!
HE SAVED LI'L OL' ME?!
SORRY, BUT I'M GONNA HAVE TO TAKE YOU IN.
I'VE GOT A TON OF QUESTIONS FOR YOU!
GLARE
?!
...
I SEE.

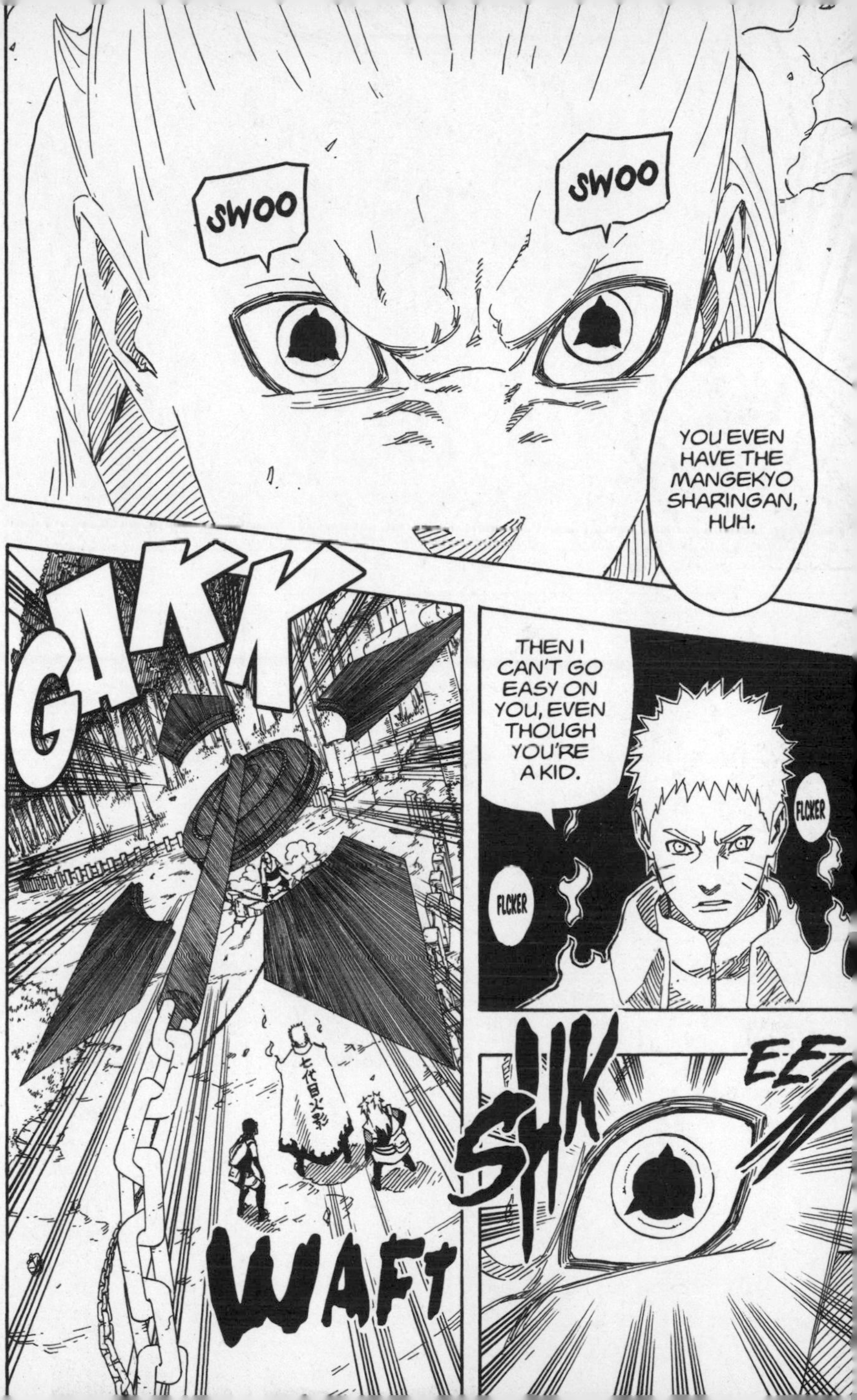
SWOO
SWOO
YOU EVEN HAVE THE MANGEKYO SHARINGAN, HUH.
THEN I CAN'T GO EASY ON YOU, EVEN THOUGH YOU'RE A KID.
FLCKER
FLCKER
EE
SHK
GAKK
WAFT

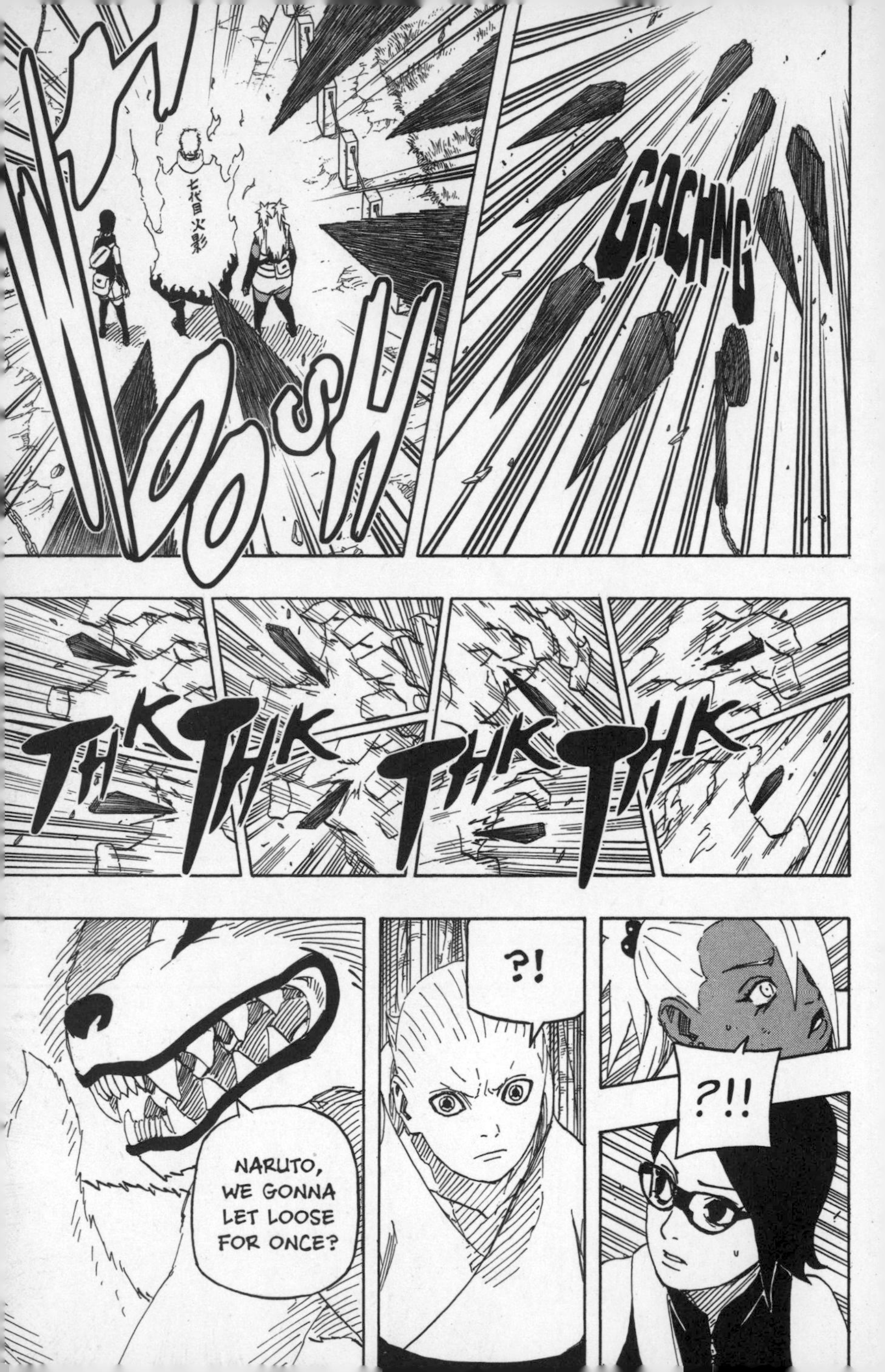
GACHNG
WOOSH
七代目火影
THK THK THK THK
?!!
?!
NARUTO, WE GONNA LET LOOSE FOR ONCE?

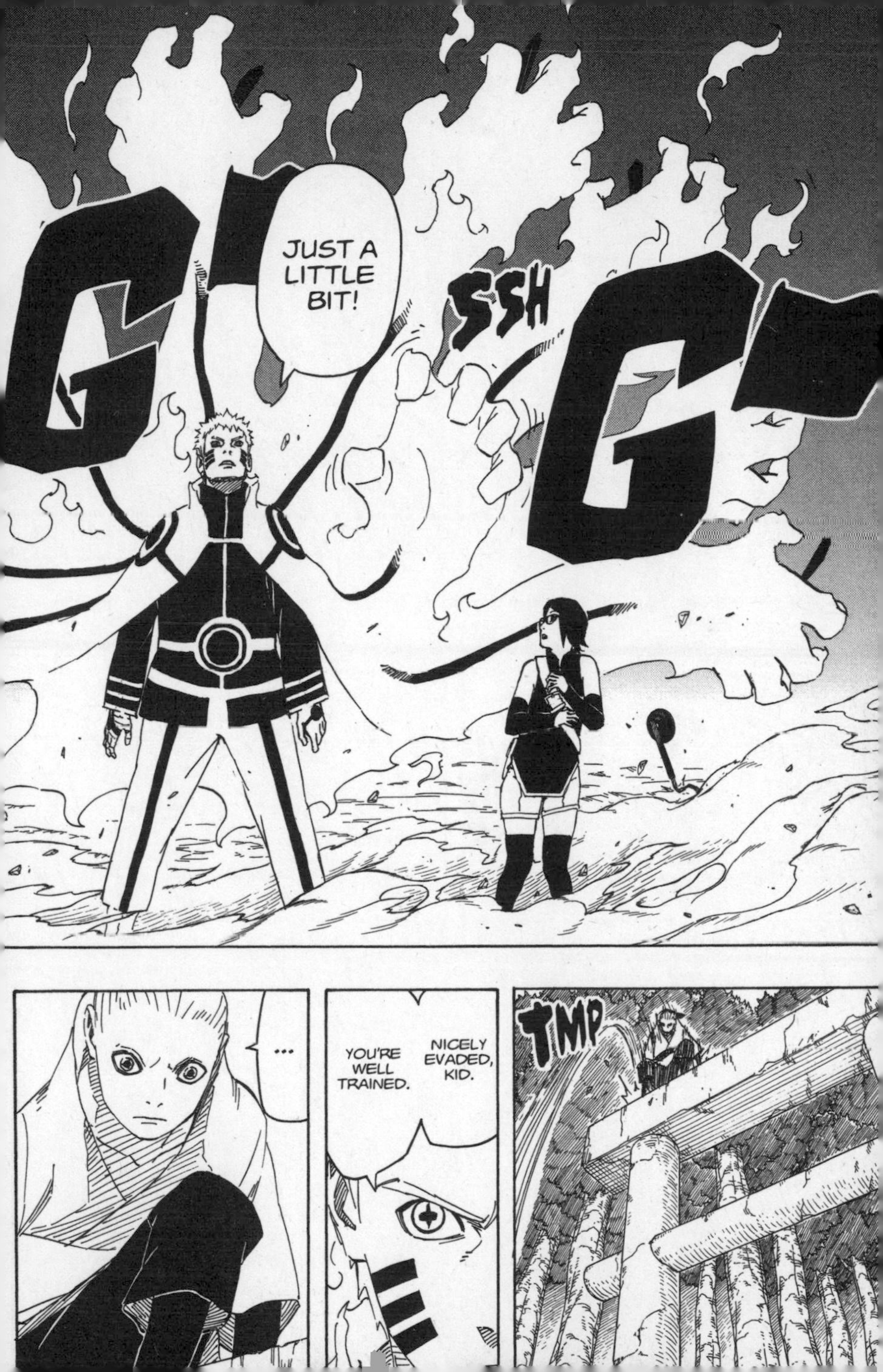
SSH
JUST A LITTLE BIT!
TMP
NICELY EVADED, KID.
YOU'RE WELL TRAINED.
...

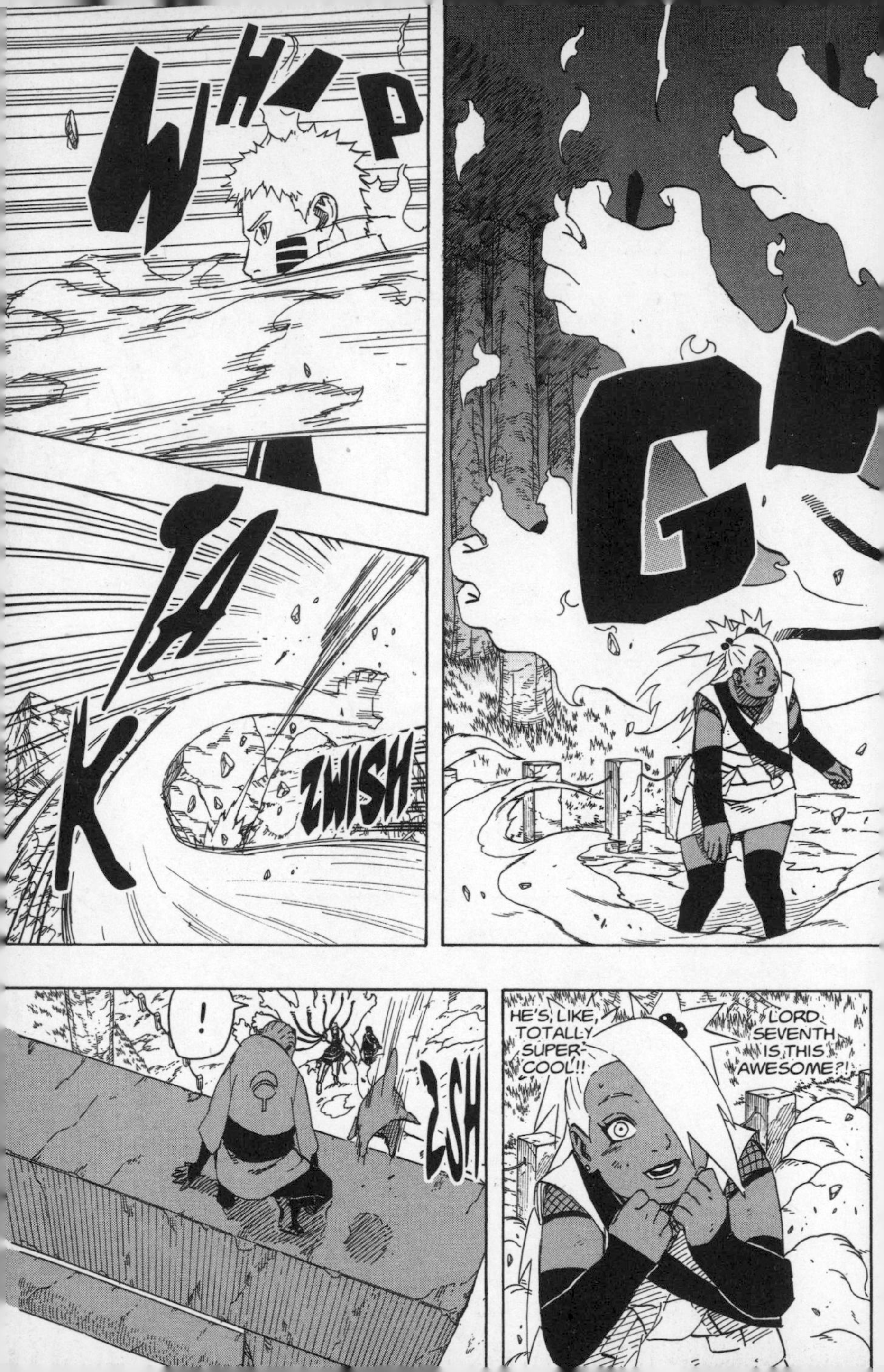
WHIP
ZWISH
LORD SEVENTH IS THIS AWESOME?!
HE'S, LIKE, TOTALLY SUPER-COOL!!
!
ZSH

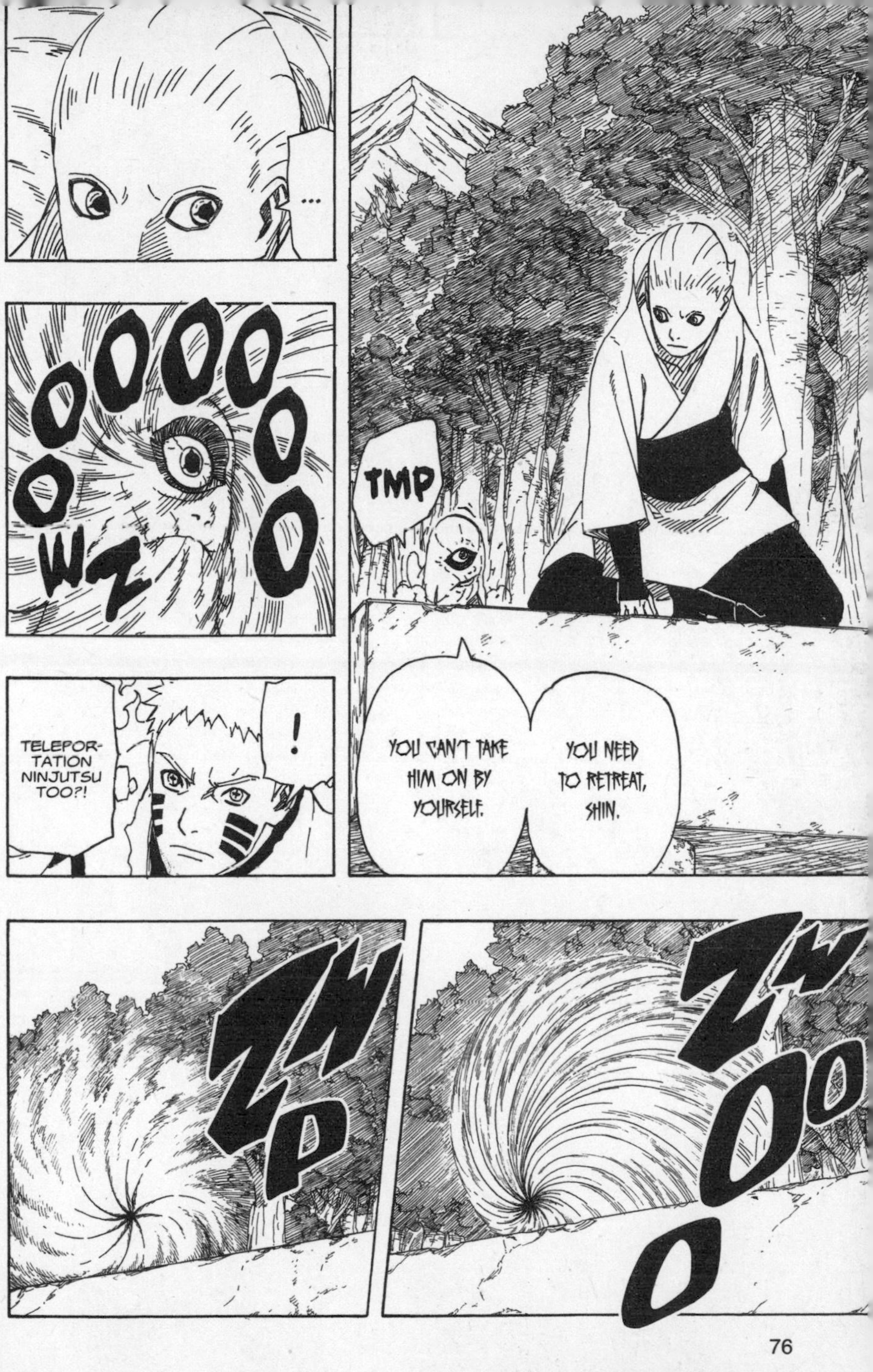
TMP
YOU NEED TO RETREAT, SHIN.
YOU CAN'T TAKE HIM ON BY YOURSELF.
...
WZOOOOOOOOO
!
TELEPORTATION NINJUTSU TOO?!
ZWOOOO
ZWIP

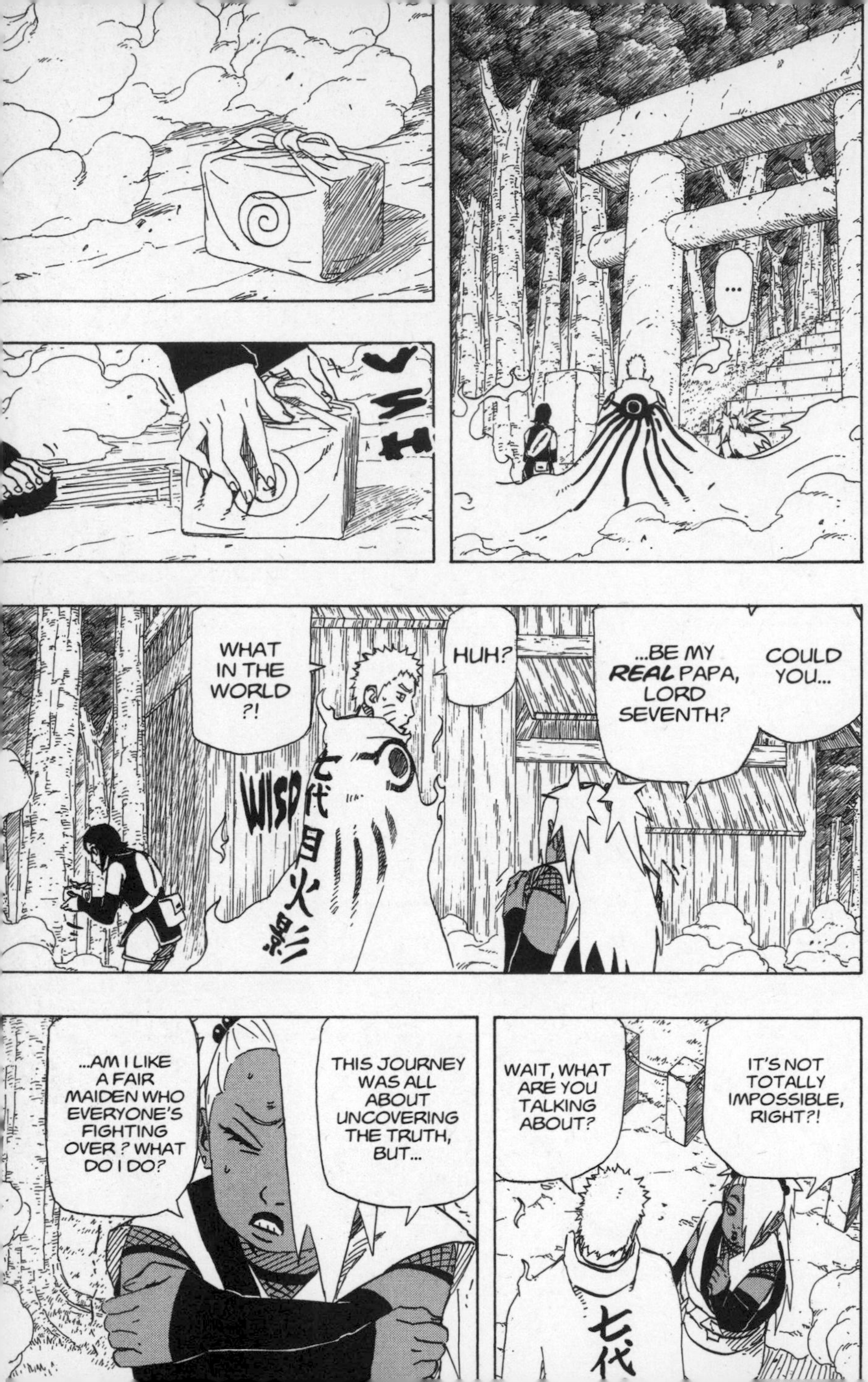
...
COULD YOU...
...BE MY **REAL** PAPA, LORD SEVENTH?
HUH?
WHAT IN THE WORLD ?!
七代目火影
WISP
IT'S NOT TOTALLY IMPOSSIBLE, RIGHT?!
WAIT, WHAT ARE YOU TALKING ABOUT?
七代
THIS JOURNEY WAS ALL ABOUT UNCOVERING THE TRUTH, BUT...
...AM I LIKE A FAIR MAIDEN WHO EVERYONE'S FIGHTING OVER ? WHAT DO I DO?

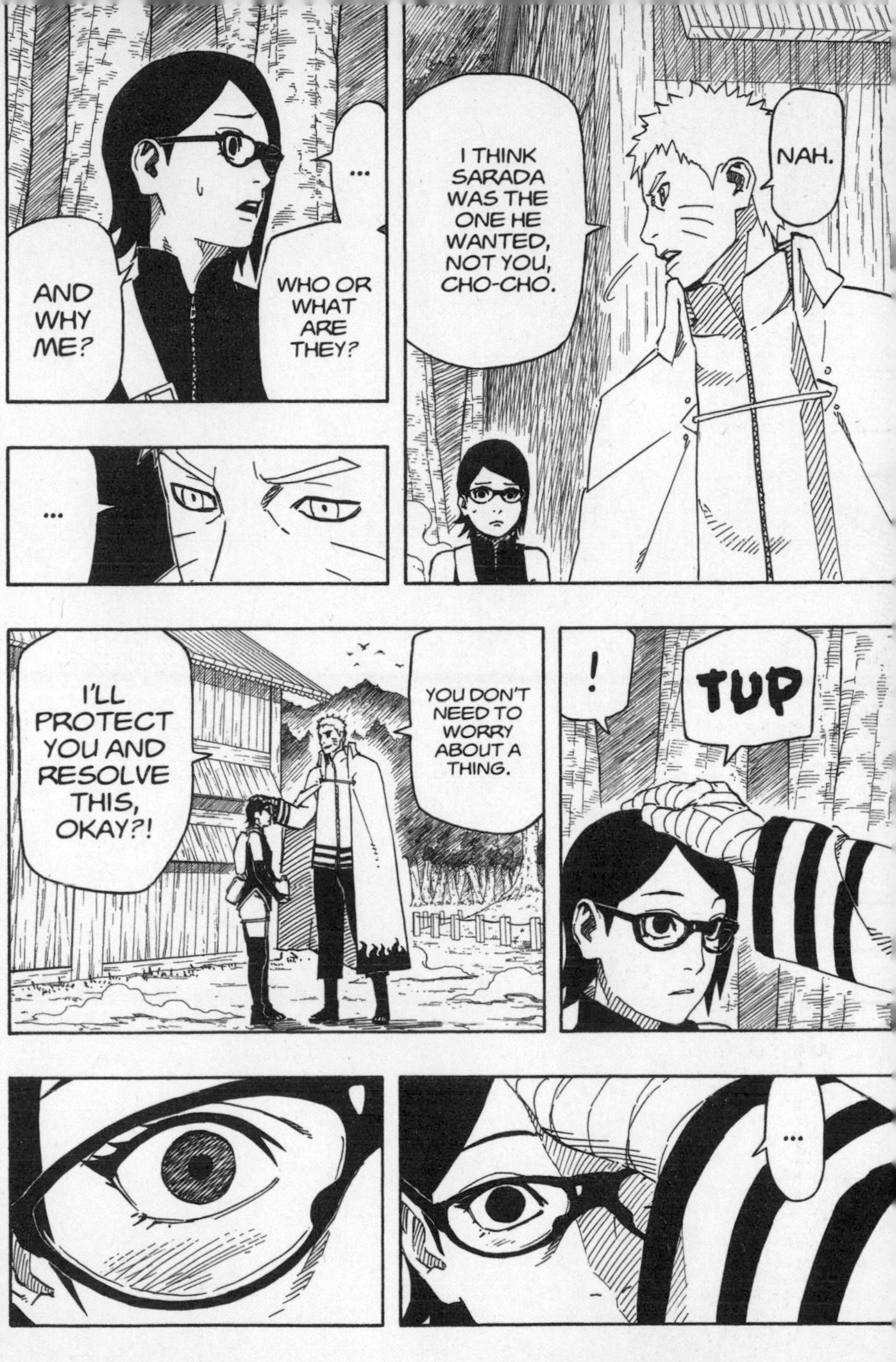
NAH.
I THINK SARADA WAS THE ONE HE WANTED, NOT YOU, CHO-CHO.
...
WHO OR WHAT ARE THEY?
AND WHY ME?
...
TUP
!
YOU DON'T NEED TO WORRY ABOUT A THING.
I'LL PROTECT YOU AND RESOLVE THIS, OKAY?!
...

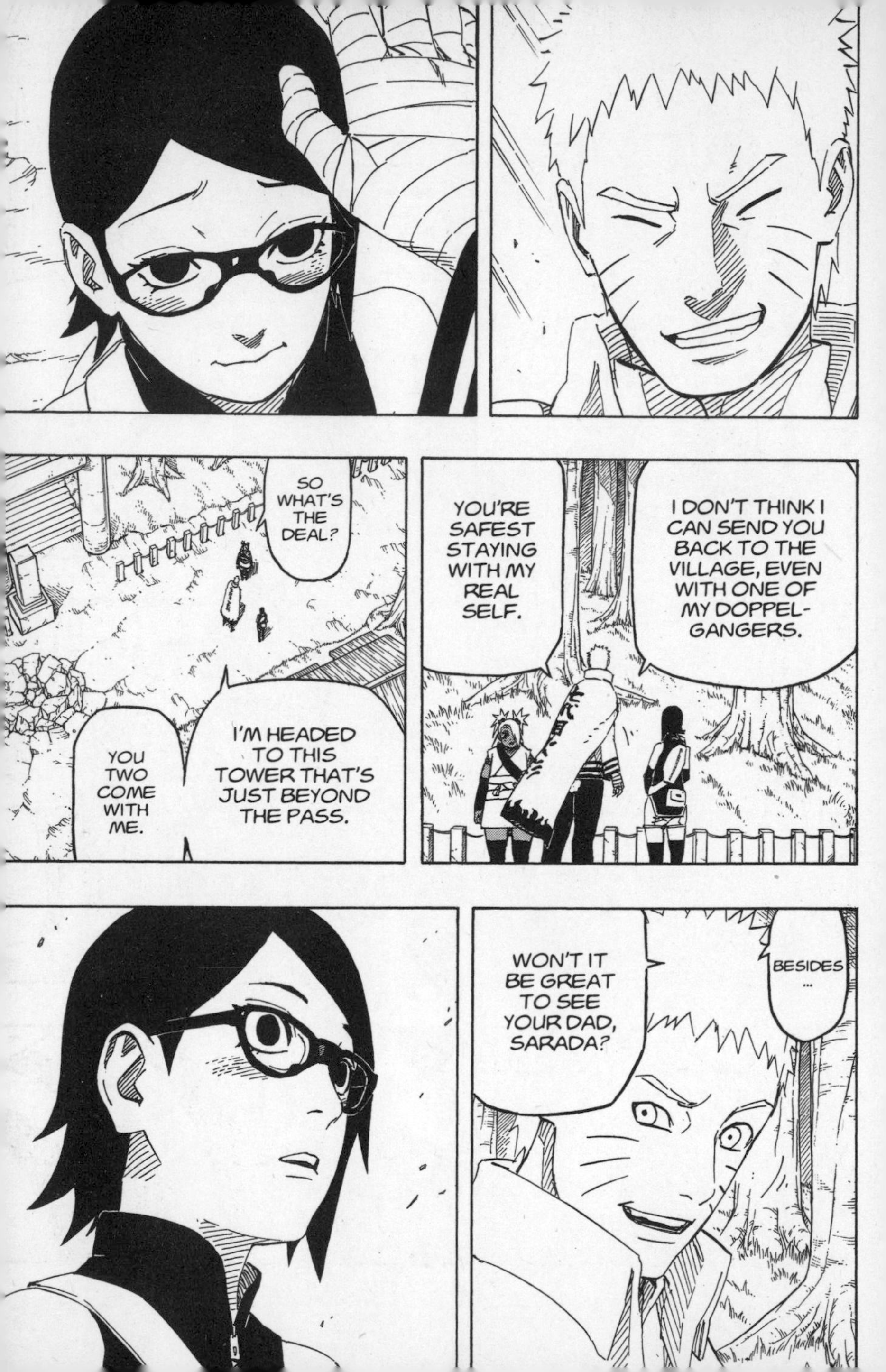
I DON'T THINK I CAN SEND YOU BACK TO THE VILLAGE, EVEN WITH ONE OF MY DOPPEL-GANGERS.
YOU'RE SAFEST STAYING WITH MY REAL SELF.
SO WHAT'S THE DEAL?
I'M HEADED TO THIS TOWER THAT'S JUST BEYOND THE PASS.
YOU TWO COME WITH ME.
BESIDES...
WON'T IT BE GREAT TO SEE YOUR DAD, SARADA?

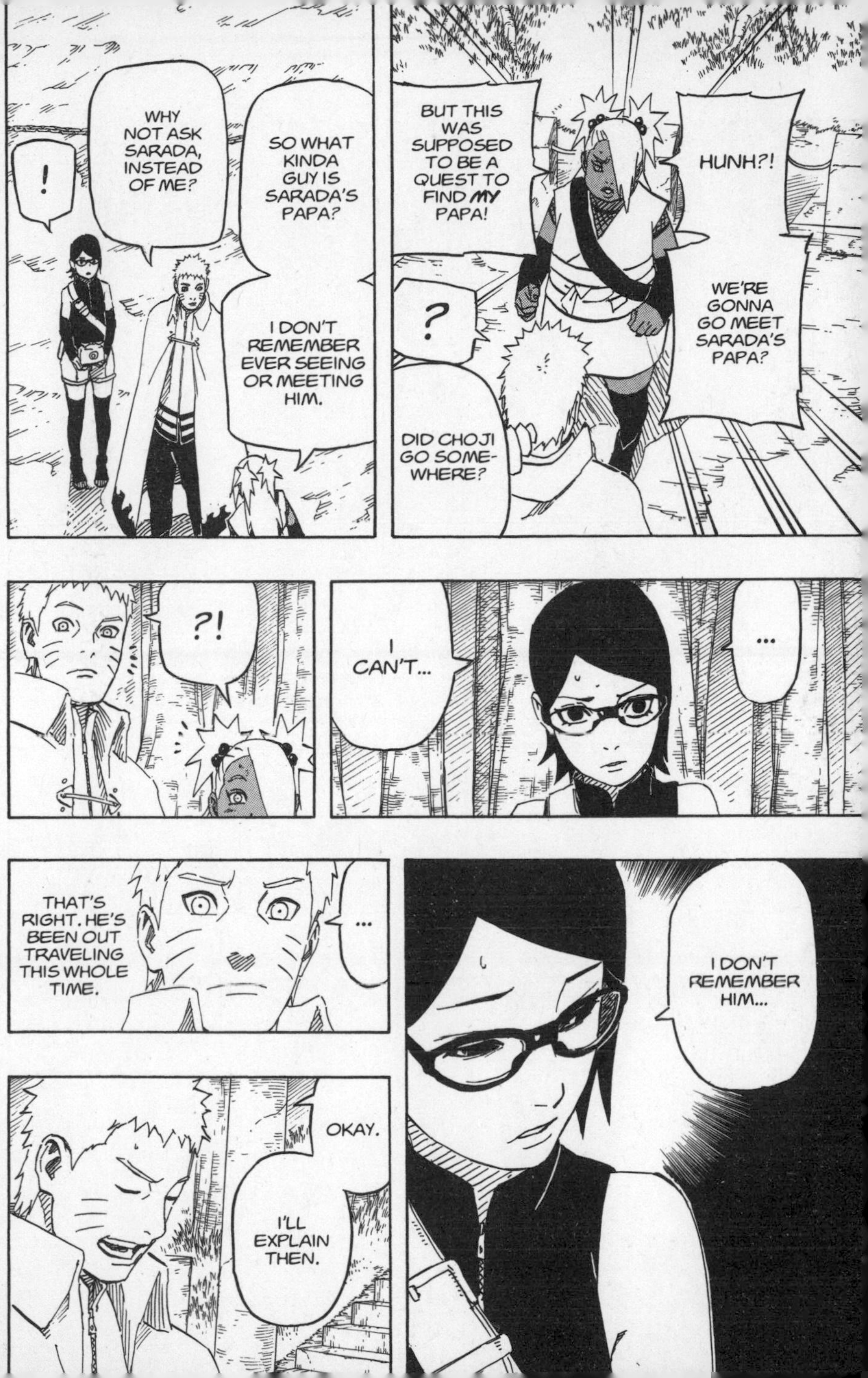
HUNH?!
WE'RE GONNA GO MEET SARADA'S PAPA?
BUT THIS WAS SUPPOSED TO BE A QUEST TO FIND MY PAPA!
?
DID CHOJI GO SOMEWHERE?
SO WHAT KINDA GUY IS SARADA'S PAPA?
I DON'T REMEMBER EVER SEEING OR MEETING HIM.
WHY NOT ASK SARADA, INSTEAD OF ME?
!
...
I CAN'T...
?!
I DON'T REMEMBER HIM...
...
THAT'S RIGHT. HE'S BEEN OUT TRAVELING THIS WHOLE TIME.
OKAY.
I'LL EXPLAIN THEN.

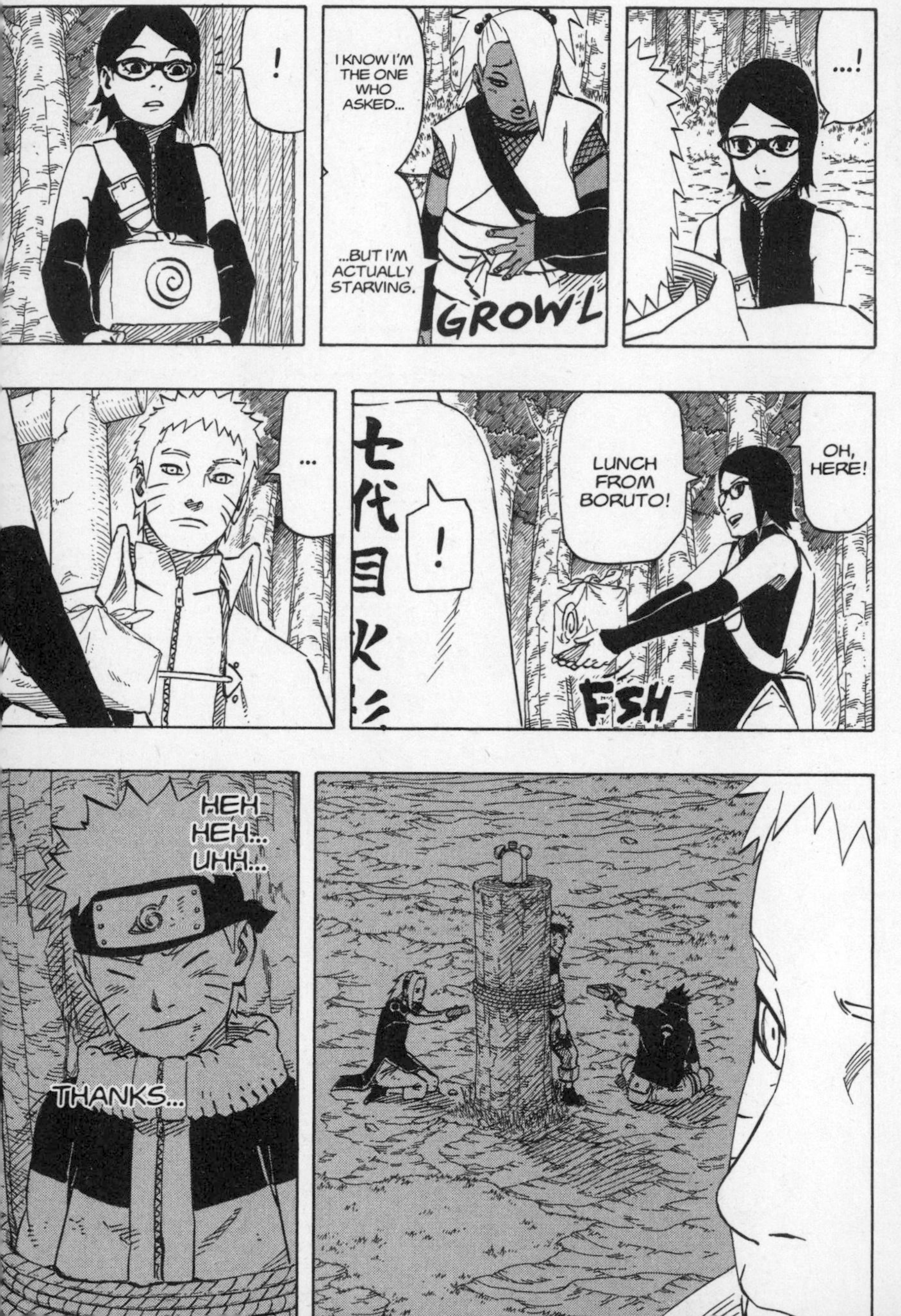
...!
I KNOW I'M THE ONE WHO ASKED...
...BUT I'M ACTUALLY STARVING.
GROWL
!
OH, HERE!
LUNCH FROM BORUTO!
FSH
!
七代目火
...
HEH HEH... UHH...
THANKS...

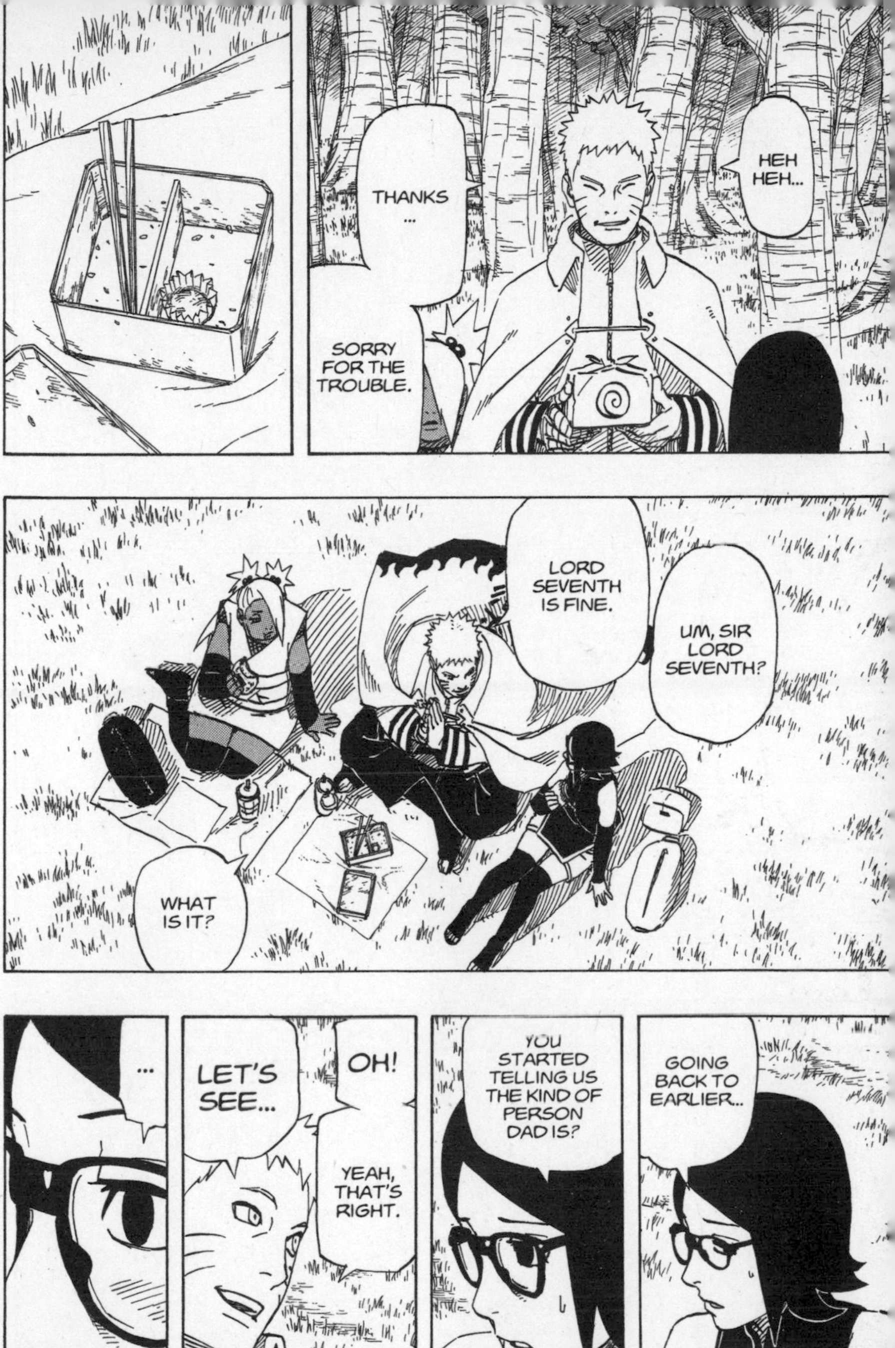
HEH HEH...
THANKS ...
SORRY FOR THE TROUBLE.
UM, SIR LORD SEVENTH?
LORD SEVENTH IS FINE.
WHAT IS IT?
GOING BACK TO EARLIER...
YOU STARTED TELLING US THE KIND OF PERSON DAD IS?
OH!
YEAH, THAT'S RIGHT.
LET'S SEE...
...

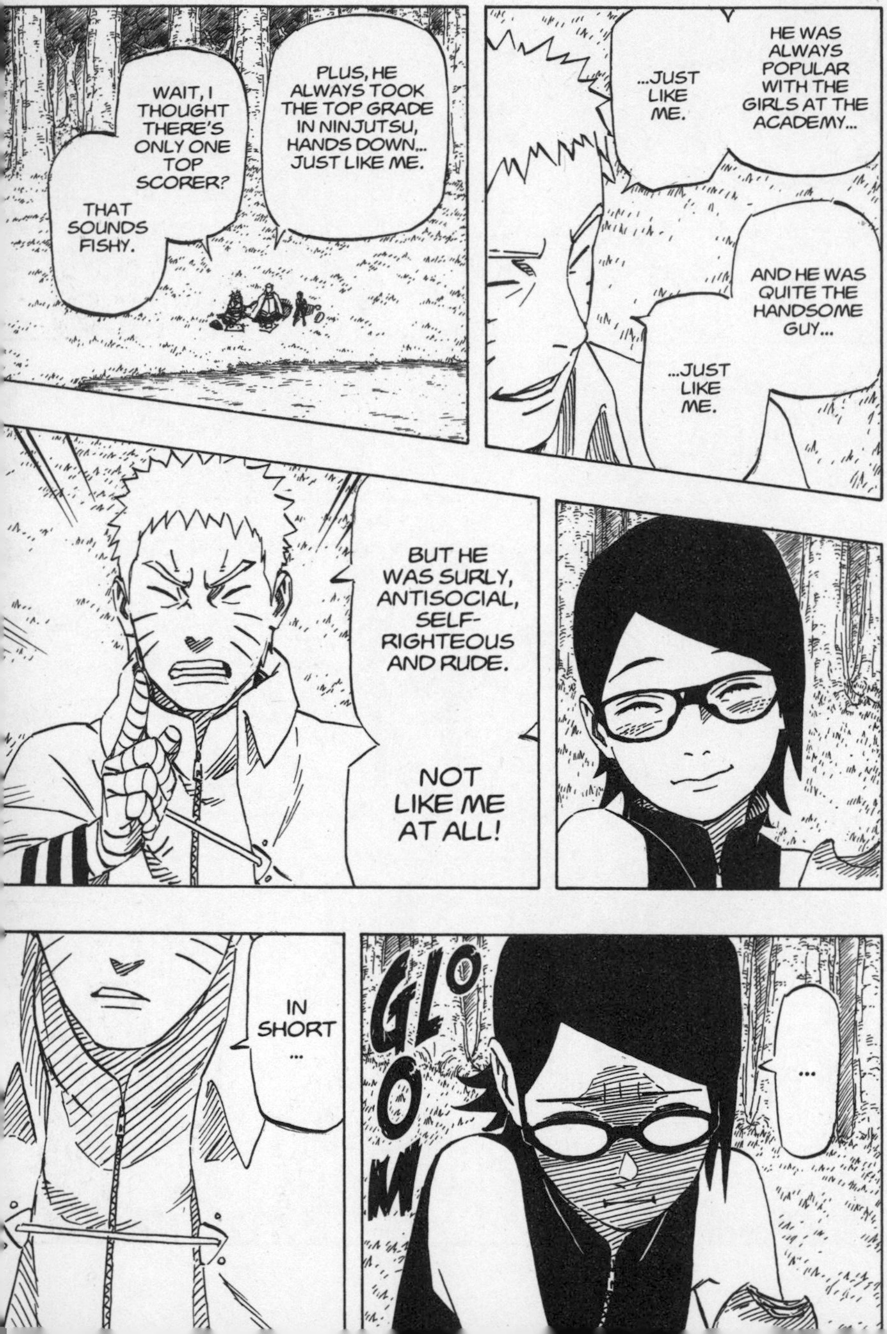
HE WAS ALWAYS POPULAR WITH THE GIRLS AT THE ACADEMY...
...JUST LIKE ME.
AND HE WAS QUITE THE HANDSOME GUY...
...JUST LIKE ME.
PLUS, HE ALWAYS TOOK THE TOP GRADE IN NINJUTSU, HANDS DOWN... JUST LIKE ME.
WAIT, I THOUGHT THERE'S ONLY ONE TOP SCORER?
THAT SOUNDS FISHY.
BUT HE WAS SURLY, ANTISOCIAL, SELF-RIGHTEOUS AND RUDE.
NOT LIKE ME AT ALL!
GLOOM
...
IN SHORT ...

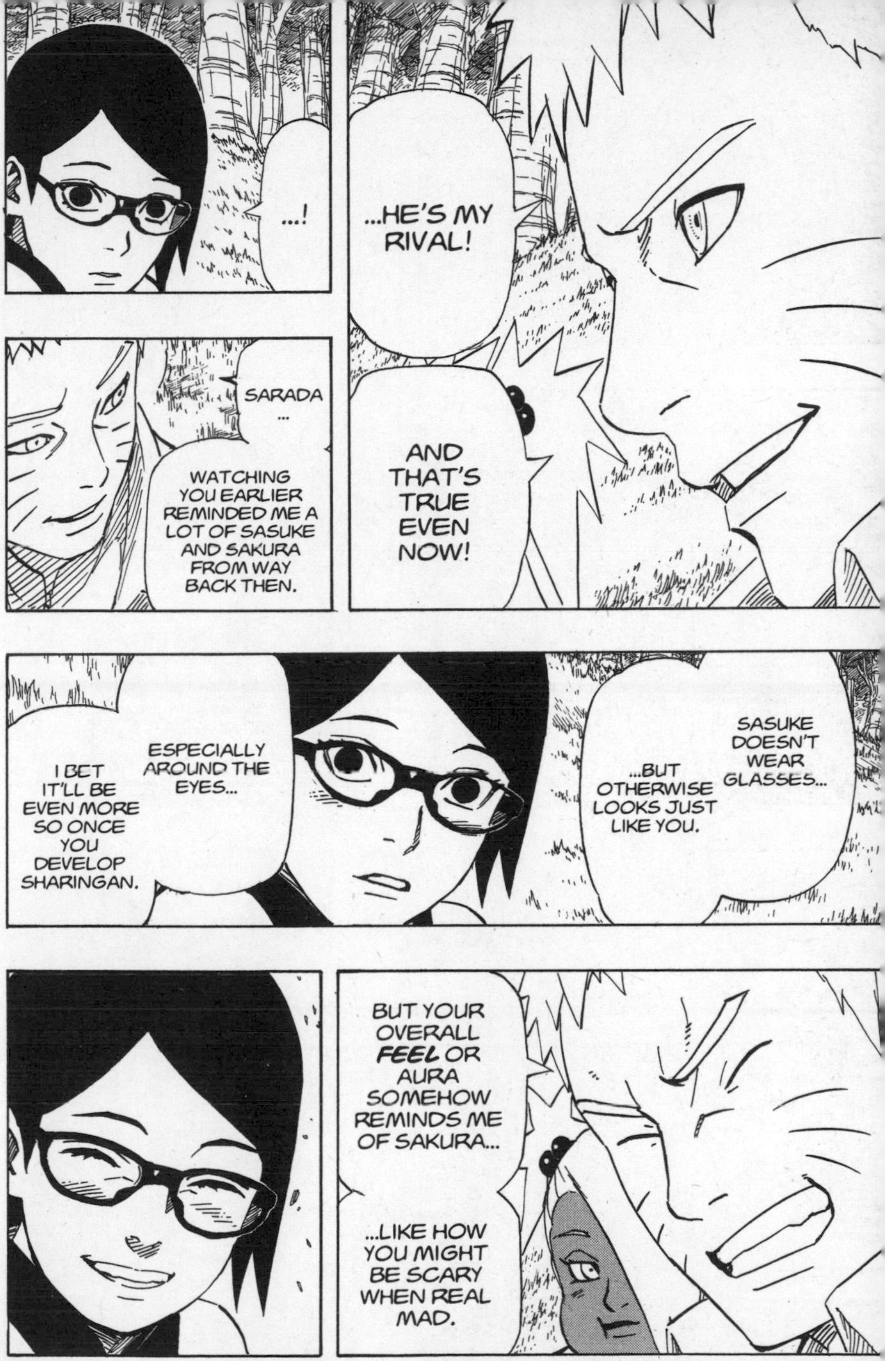
...HE'S MY RIVAL!
AND THAT'S TRUE EVEN NOW!
...!
SARADA...
WATCHING YOU EARLIER REMINDED ME A LOT OF SASUKE AND SAKURA FROM WAY BACK THEN.
SASUKE DOESN'T WEAR GLASSES...
...BUT OTHERWISE LOOKS JUST LIKE YOU.
ESPECIALLY AROUND THE EYES...
I BET IT'LL BE EVEN MORE SO ONCE YOU DEVELOP SHARINGAN.
BUT YOUR OVERALL ***FEEL*** OR AURA SOMEHOW REMINDS ME OF SAKURA...
...LIKE HOW YOU MIGHT BE SCARY WHEN REAL MAD.

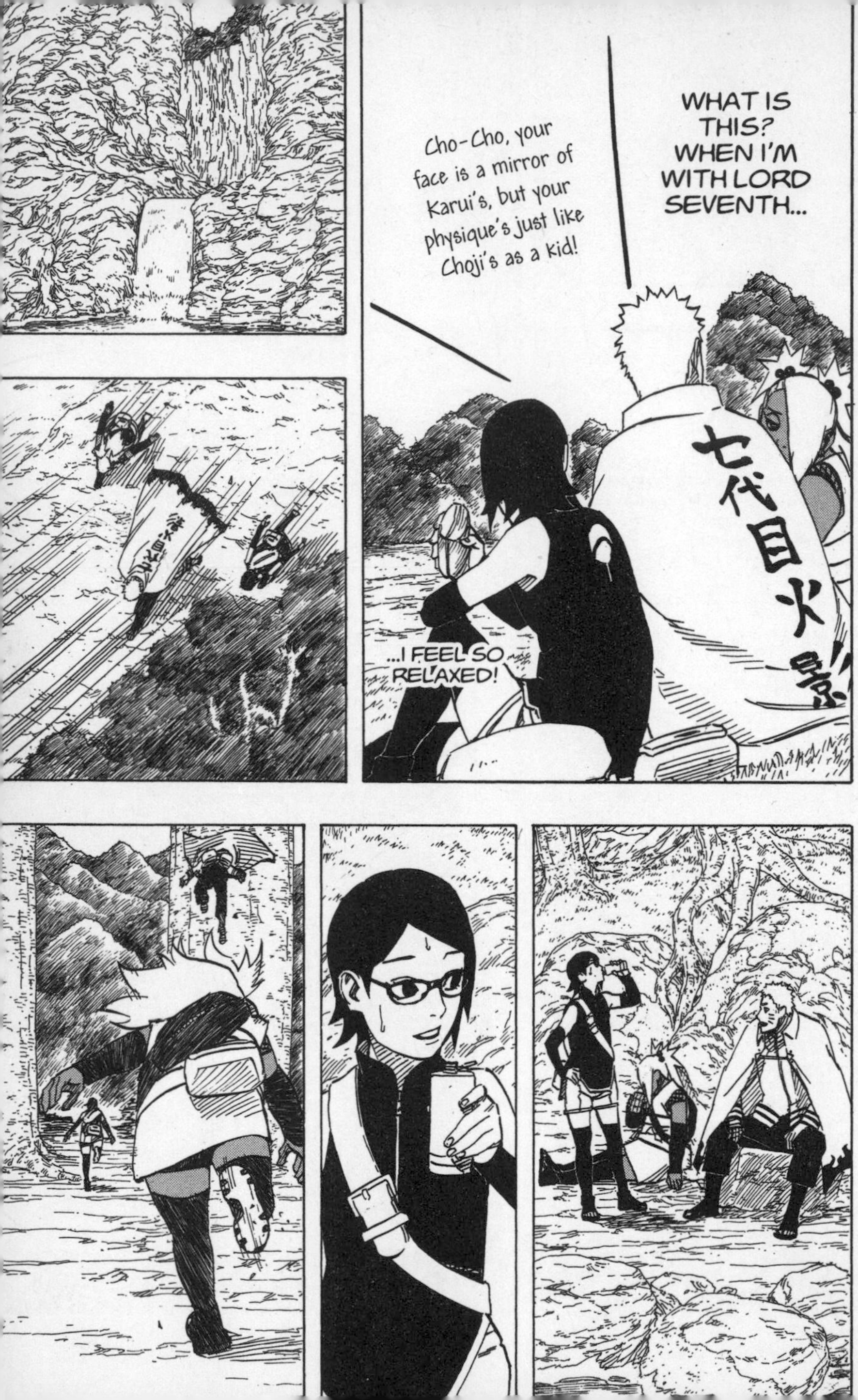
WHAT IS THIS? WHEN I'M WITH LORD SEVENTH...
Cho-Cho, your face is a mirror of Karui's, but your physique's just like Choji's as a kid!
七代目火影
...I FEEL SO RELAXED!

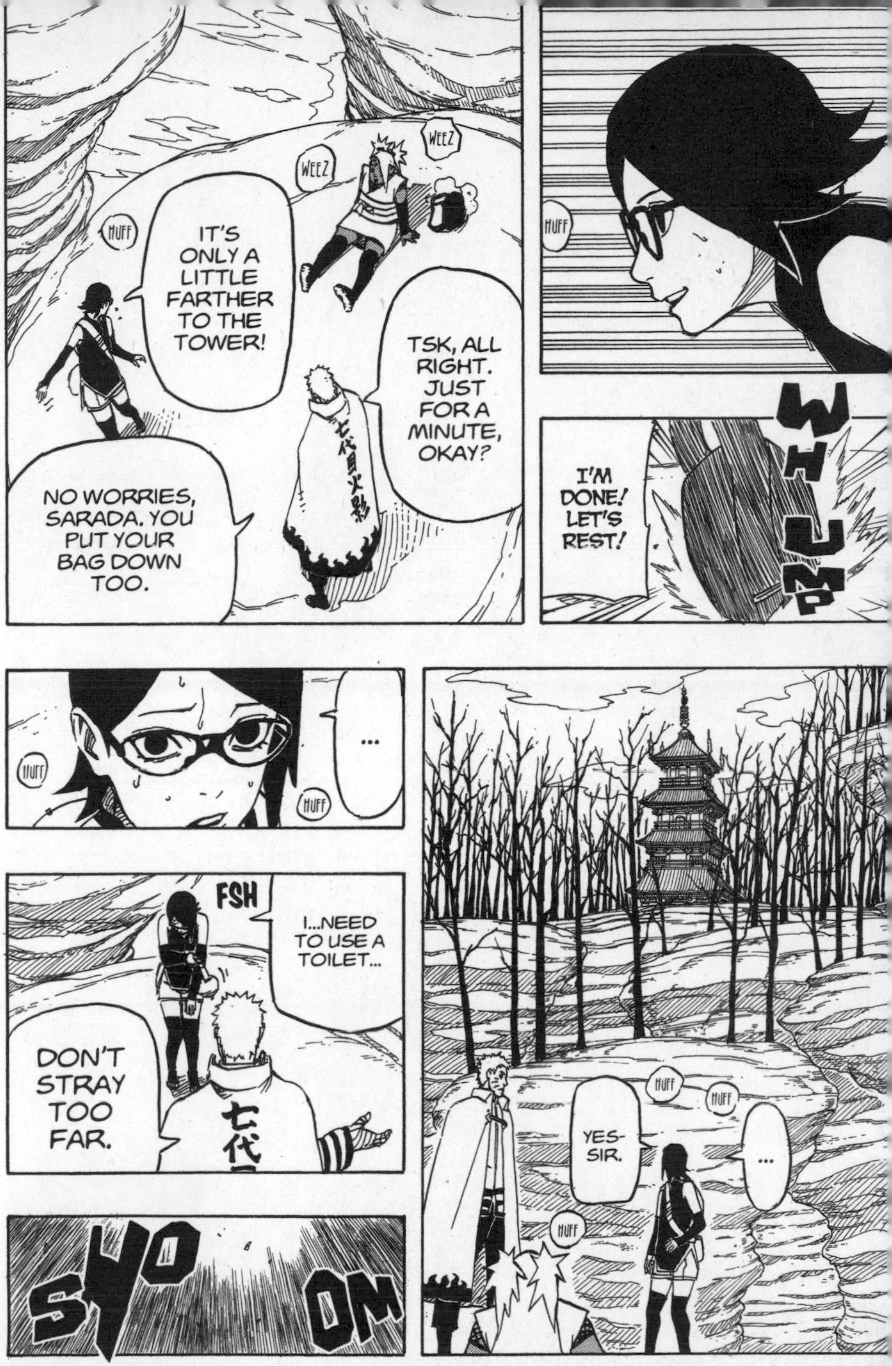
HUFF
WHUMP
I'M DONE! LET'S REST!
WEEZ
WEEZ
HUFF
IT'S ONLY A LITTLE FARTHER TO THE TOWER!
TSK, ALL RIGHT. JUST FOR A MINUTE, OKAY?
NO WORRIES, SARADA. YOU PUT YOUR BAG DOWN TOO.
HUFF
HUFF
...
YES-SIR.
HUFF
...
HUFF
HUFF
FSH
I...NEED TO USE A TOILET...
DON'T STRAY TOO FAR.
SHOOM

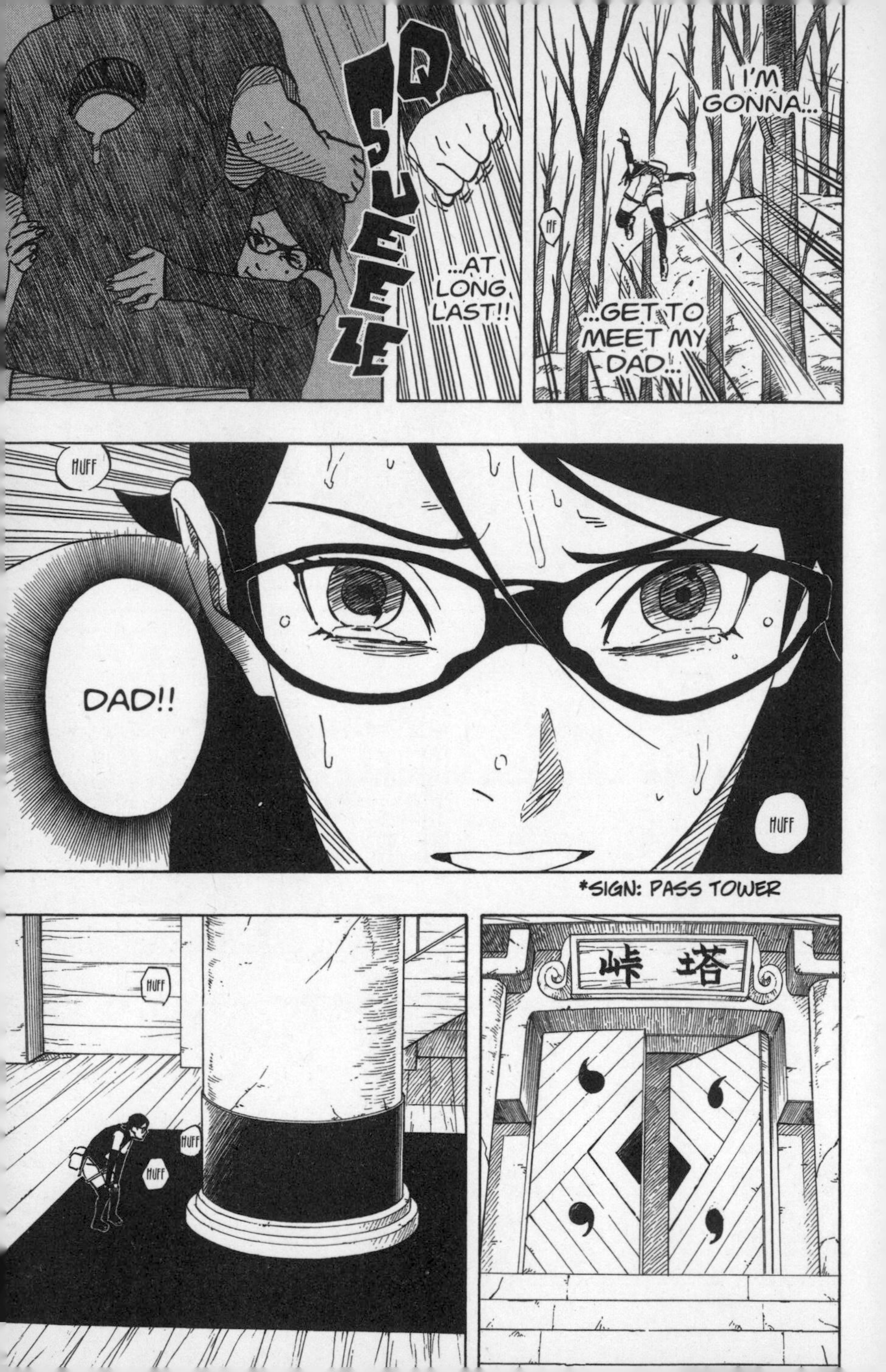
I'M GONNA...
HF
...GET TO MEET MY DAD...
...AT LONG LAST!!
SQUEEZE
HUFF
DAD!!
HUFF
*SIGN: PASS TOWER
峠塔
HUFF
HUFF
HUFF

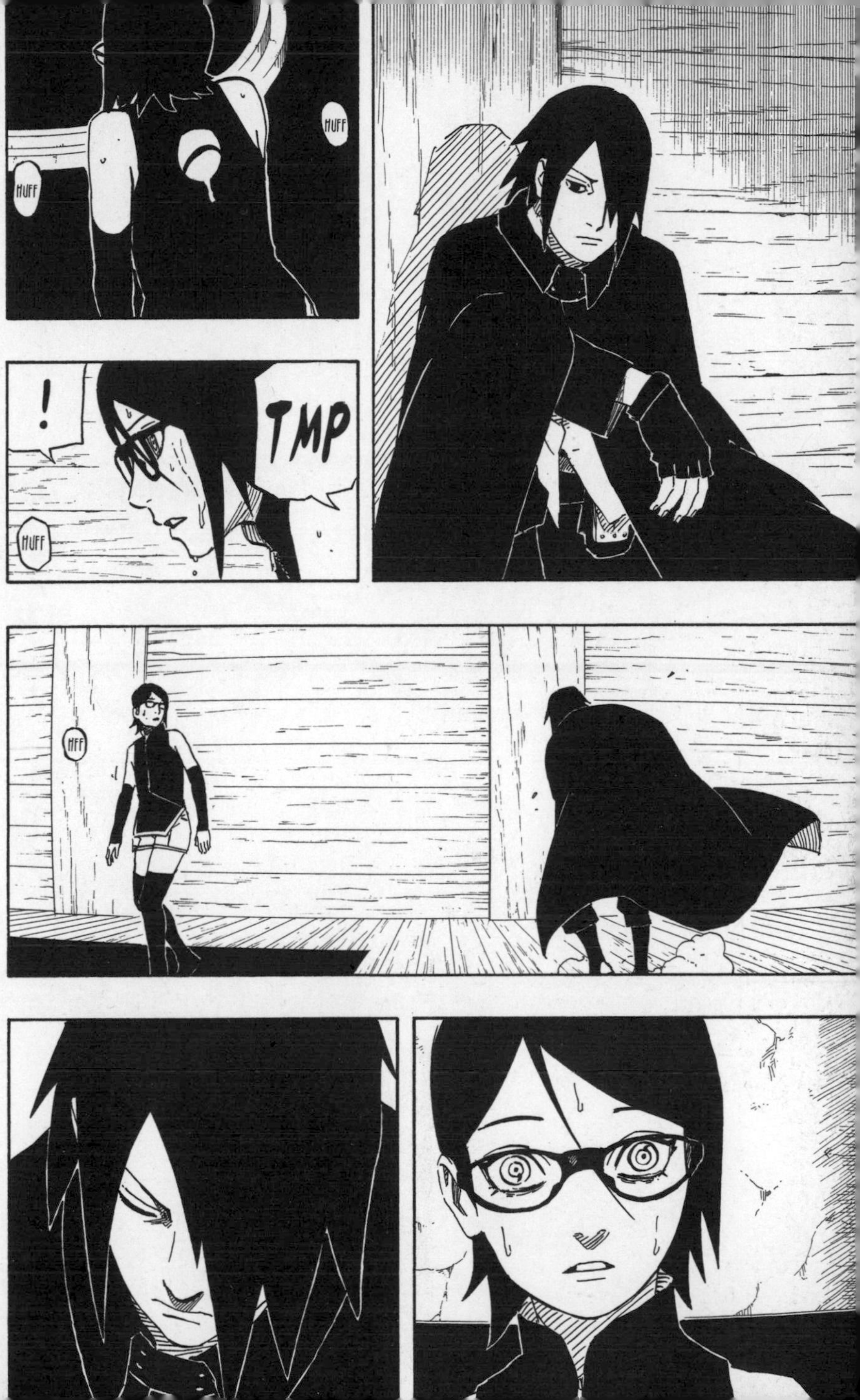
HUFF
HUFF
TMP
!
HUFF
HFF

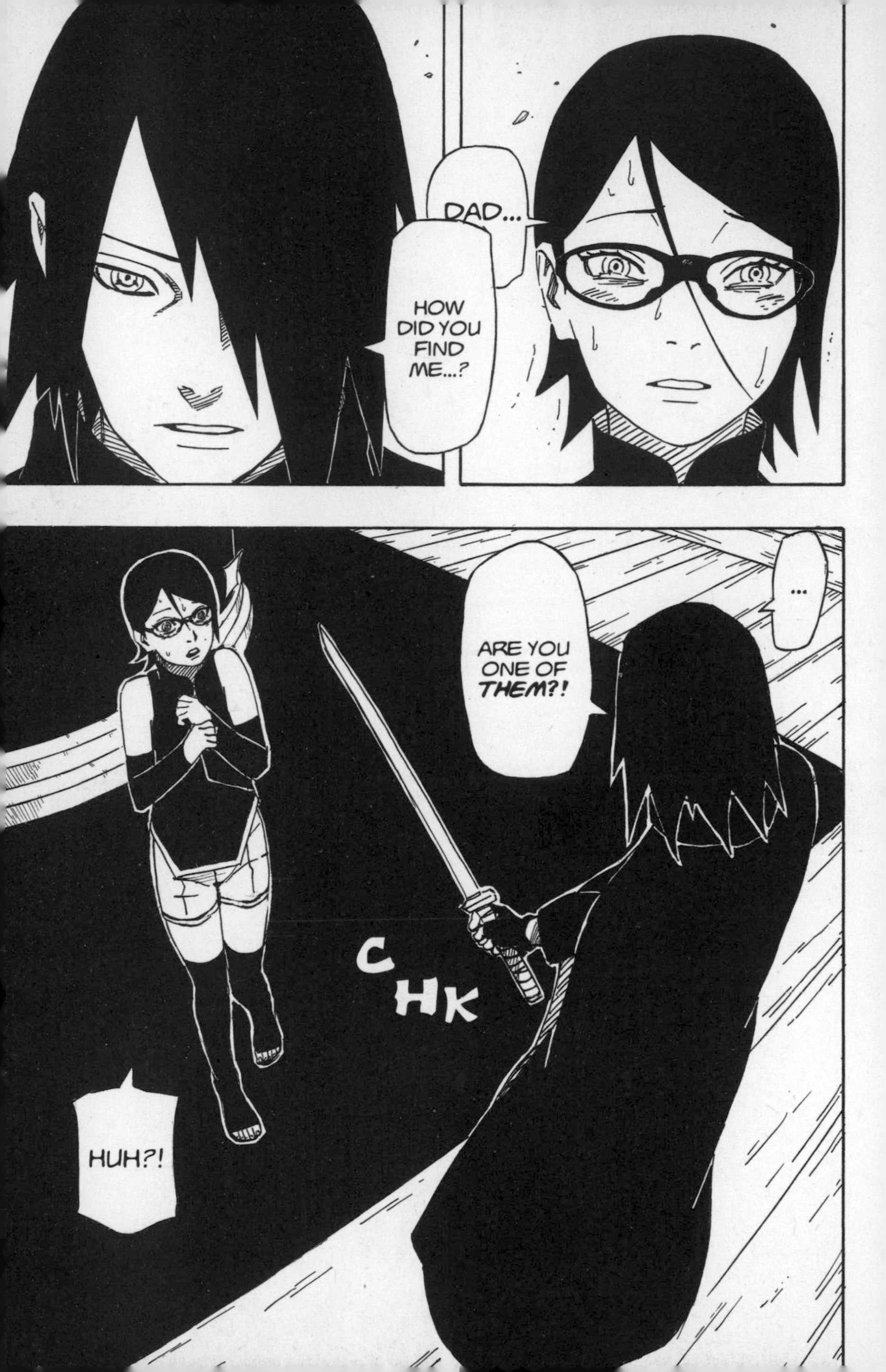
DAD...
HOW DID YOU FIND ME...?
...
ARE YOU ONE OF *THEM?!*
CHK
HUH?!

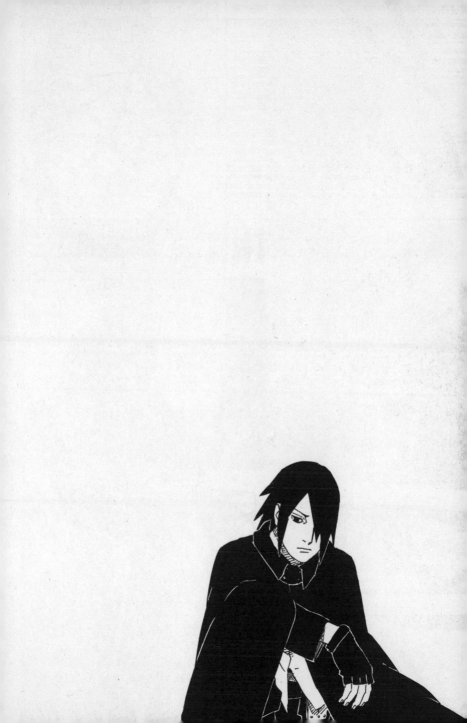

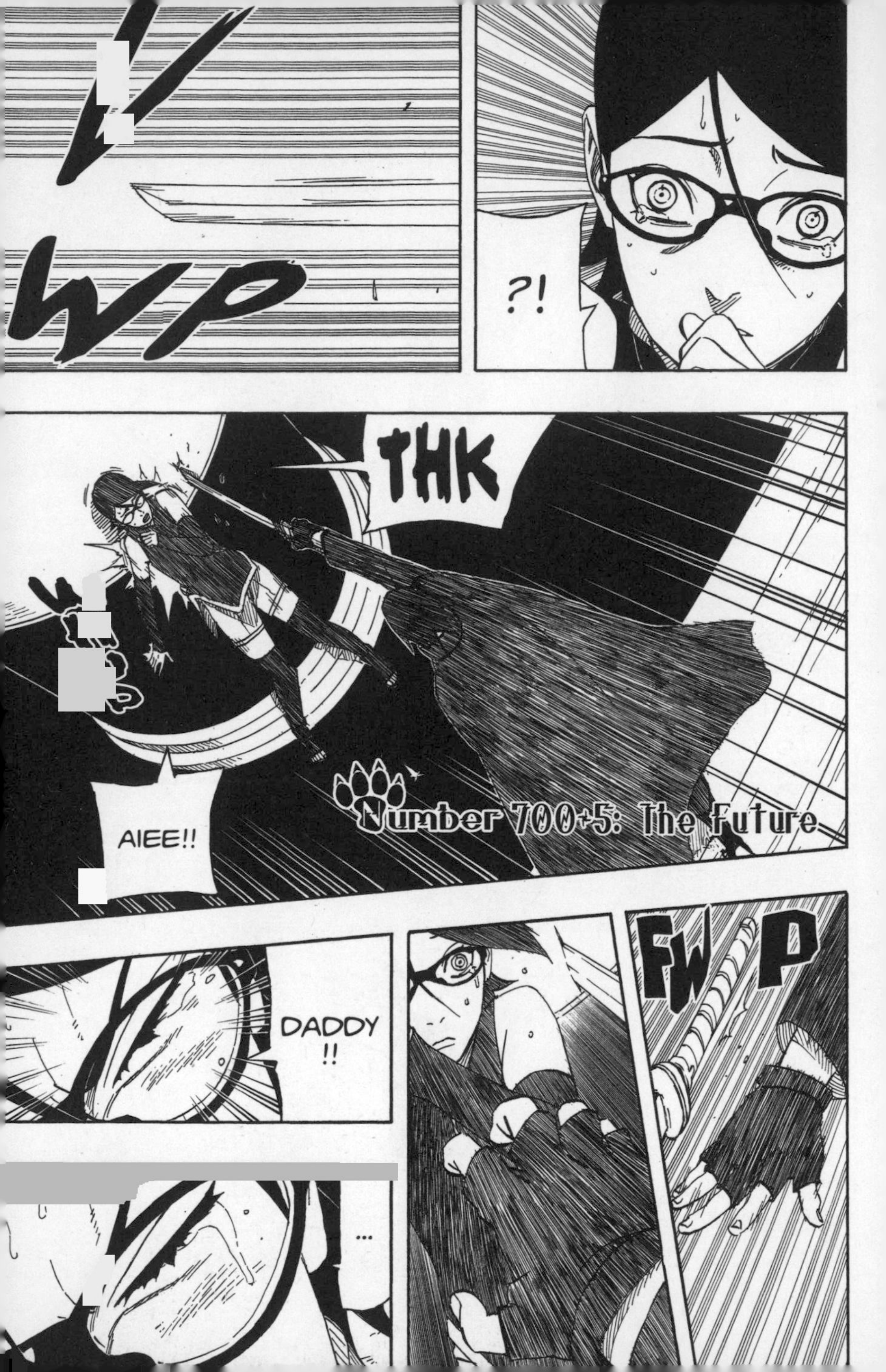
?!
WP
THK
Number 700+5: The Future
AIEE!!
FWP
DADDY !!
...

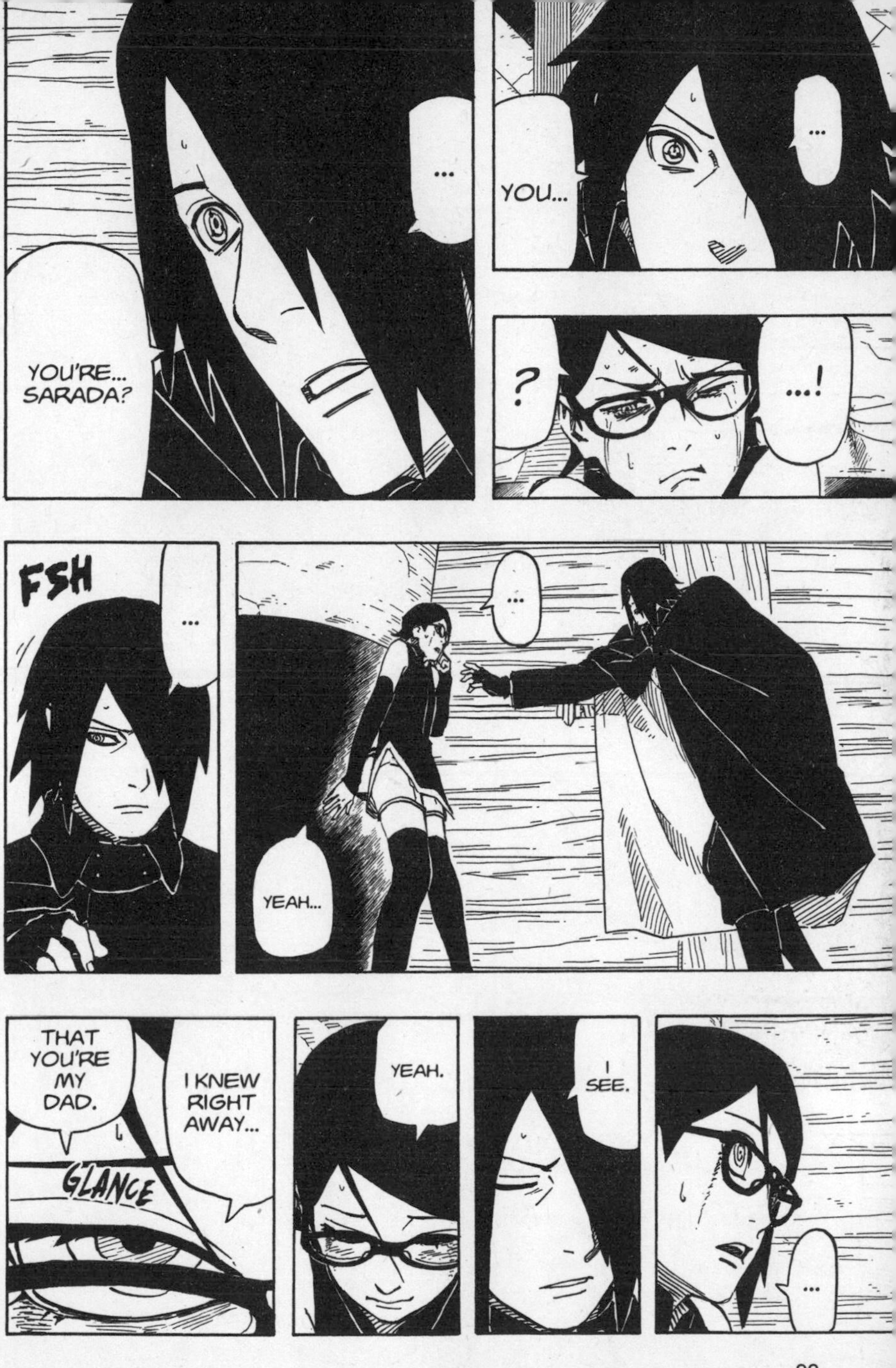
...
YOU...
...!
?
...
YOU'RE... SARADA?
...
YEAH...
FSH
...
...
I SEE.
YEAH.
I KNEW RIGHT AWAY...
THAT YOU'RE MY DAD.
GLANCE

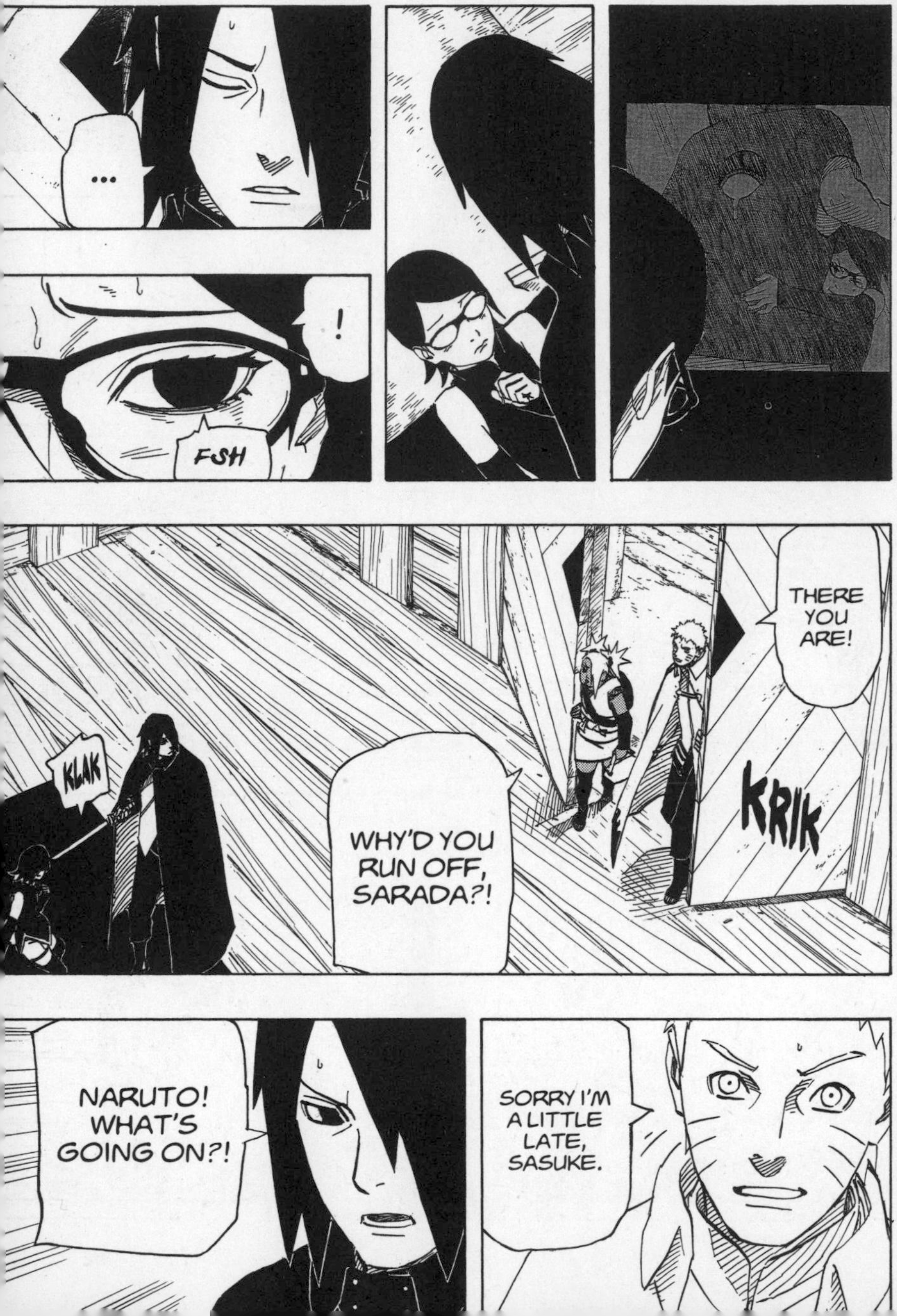
...
!
FSH
THERE YOU ARE!
KRIK
WHY'D YOU RUN OFF, SARADA?!
KLAK
SORRY I'M A LITTLE LATE, SASUKE.
NARUTO! WHAT'S GOING ON?!

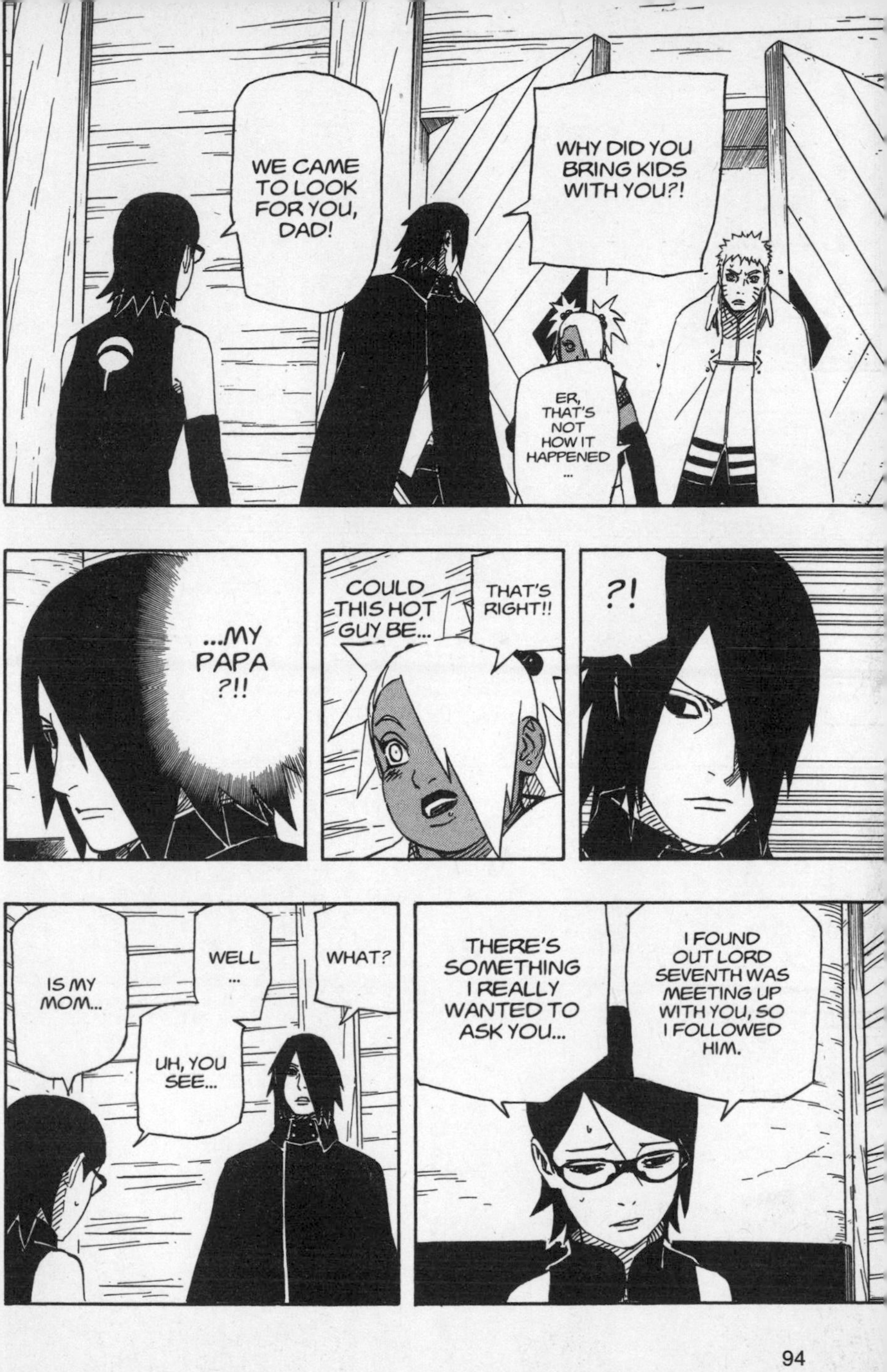
WHY DID YOU BRING KIDS WITH YOU?!
WE CAME TO LOOK FOR YOU, DAD!
ER, THAT'S NOT HOW IT HAPPENED ...
?!
THAT'S RIGHT!!
COULD THIS HOT GUY BE...
...MY PAPA ?!!
I FOUND OUT LORD SEVENTH WAS MEETING UP WITH YOU, SO I FOLLOWED HIM.
THERE'S SOMETHING I REALLY WANTED TO ASK YOU...
WHAT?
WELL ...
UH, YOU SEE...
IS MY MOM...

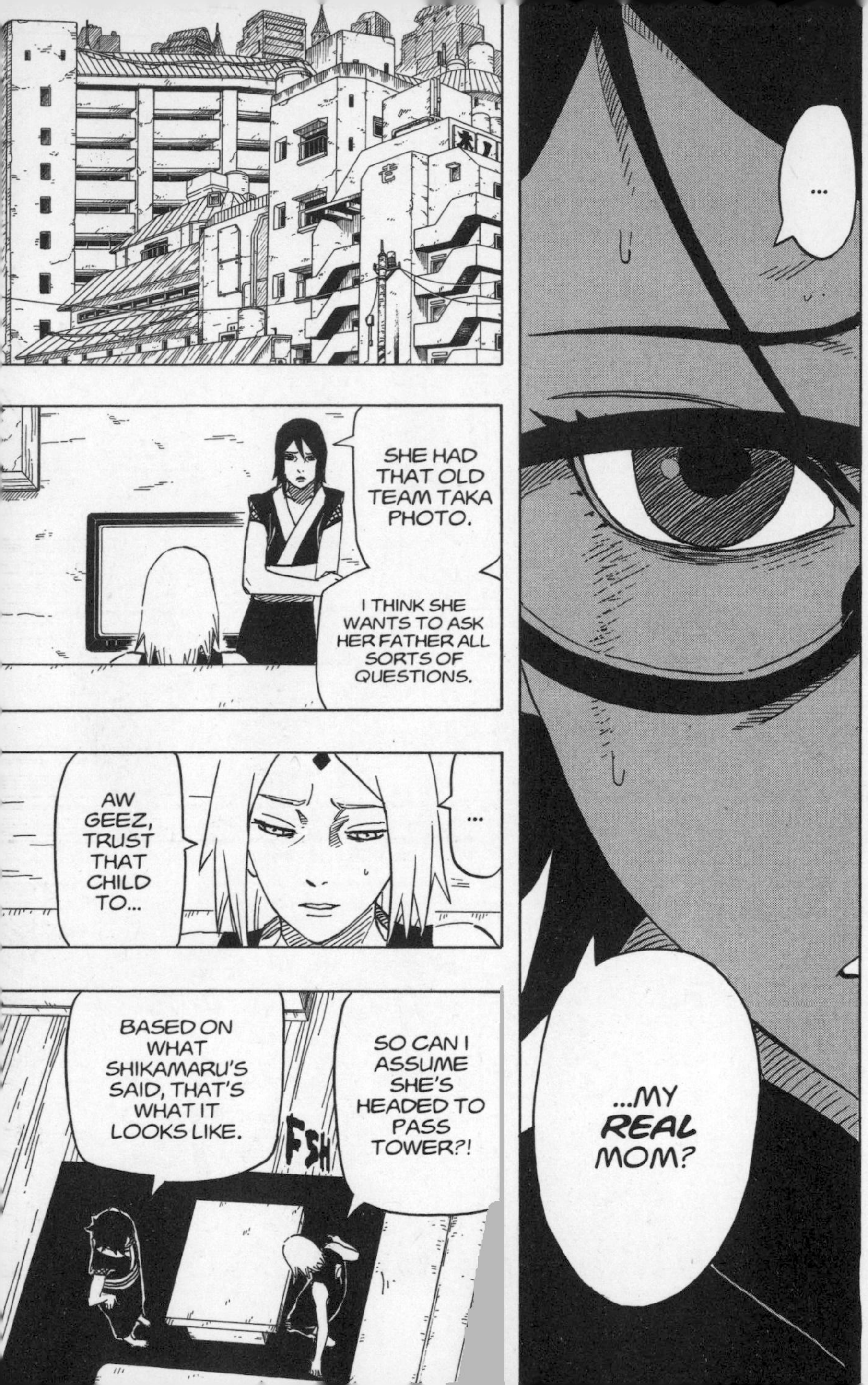
...
...MY *REAL* MOM?
SHE HAD THAT OLD TEAM TAKA PHOTO.
I THINK SHE WANTS TO ASK HER FATHER ALL SORTS OF QUESTIONS.
...
AW GEEZ, TRUST THAT CHILD TO...
SO CAN I ASSUME SHE'S HEADED TO PASS TOWER?!
FSH
BASED ON WHAT SHIKAMARU'S SAID, THAT'S WHAT IT LOOKS LIKE.

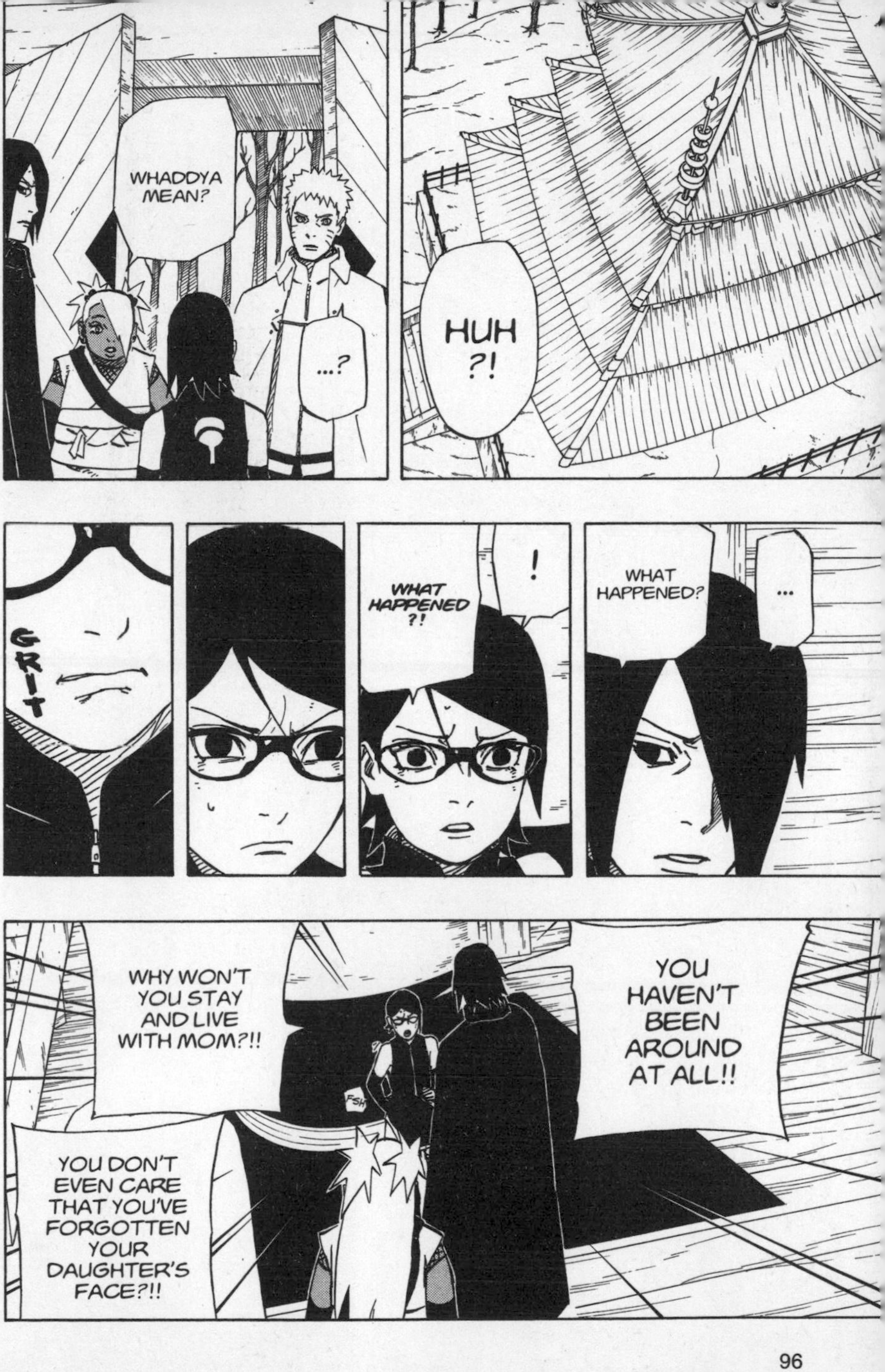
HUH ?!
WHADDYA MEAN?
...?
...
WHAT HAPPENED?
!
WHAT HAPPENED ?!
GRIT
YOU HAVEN'T BEEN AROUND AT ALL!!
WHY WON'T YOU STAY AND LIVE WITH MOM?!!
FSH
YOU DON'T EVEN CARE THAT YOU'VE FORGOTTEN YOUR DAUGHTER'S FACE?!!

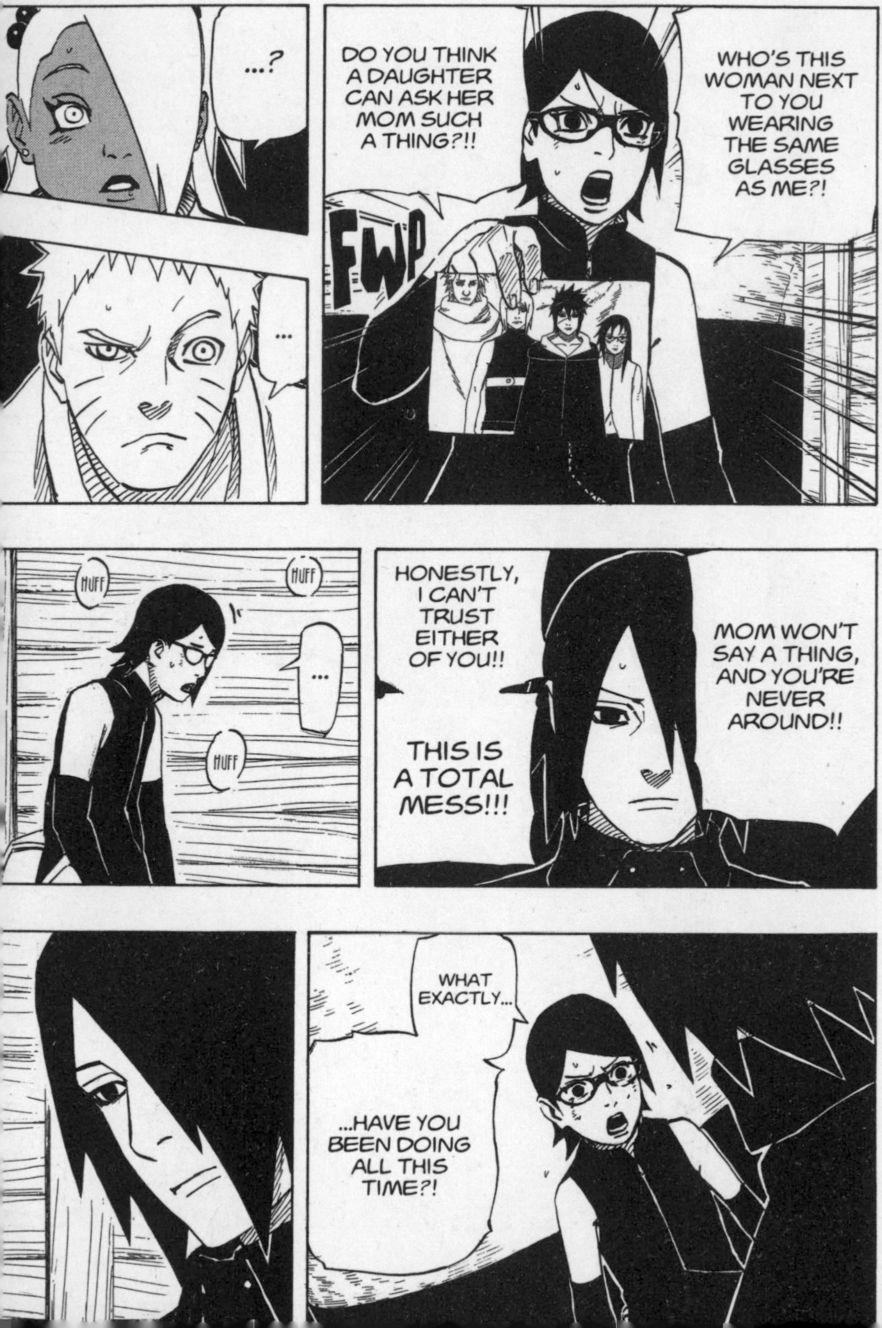
WHO'S THIS WOMAN NEXT TO YOU WEARING THE SAME GLASSES AS ME?!
DO YOU THINK A DAUGHTER CAN ASK HER MOM SUCH A THING?!!
FWP
...?
...
MOM WON'T SAY A THING, AND YOU'RE NEVER AROUND!!
HONESTLY, I CAN'T TRUST EITHER OF YOU!!
THIS IS A TOTAL MESS!!!
HUFF
HUFF
...
HUFF
WHAT EXACTLY...
...HAVE YOU BEEN DOING ALL THIS TIME?!

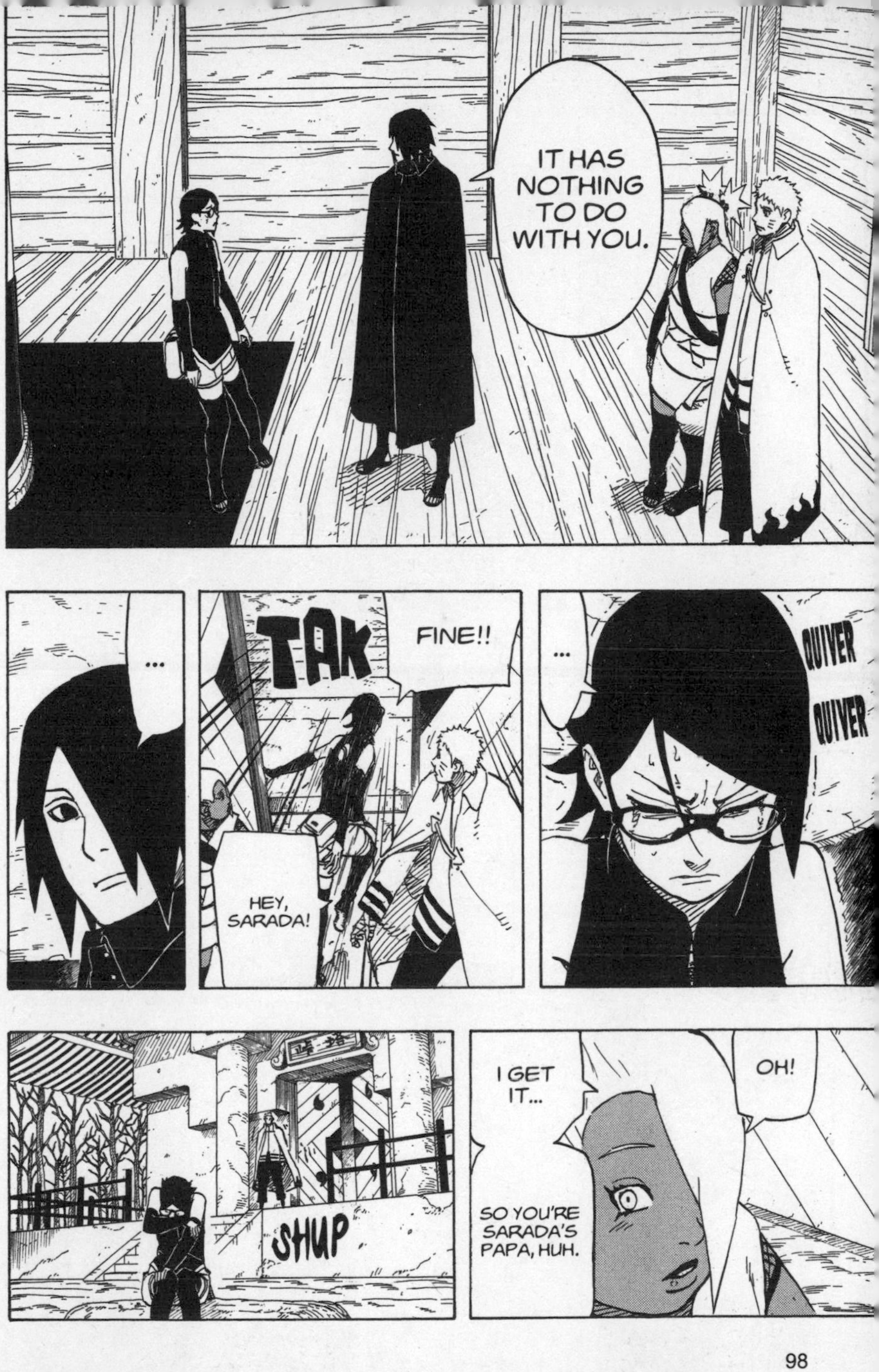
IT HAS NOTHING TO DO WITH YOU.
QUIVER
QUIVER
...
FINE!!
TAK
HEY, SARADA!
...
OH!
I GET IT...
SO YOU'RE SARADA'S PAPA, HUH.
SHUP

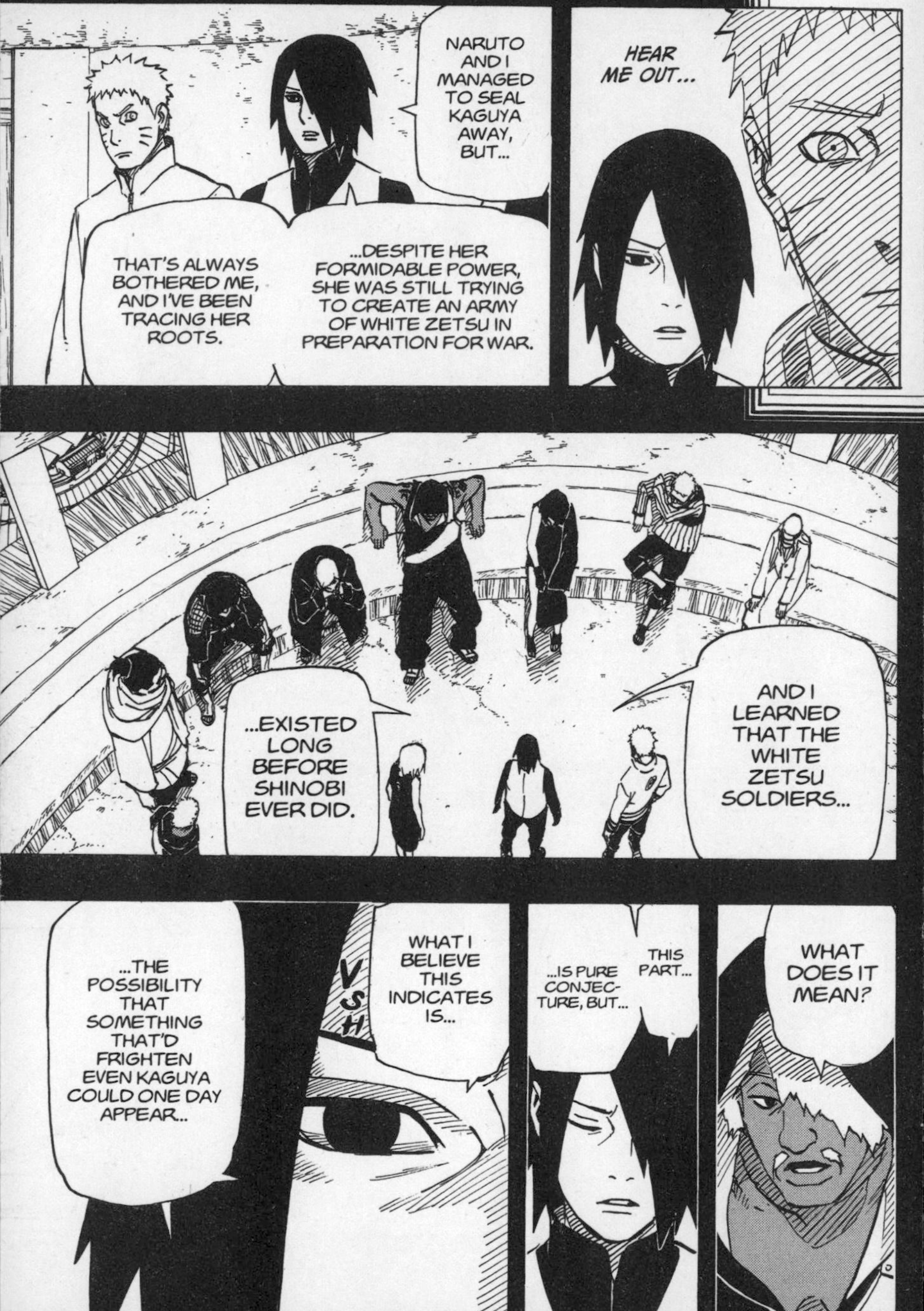
HEAR ME OUT...
NARUTO AND I MANAGED TO SEAL KAGUYA AWAY, BUT...
...DESPITE HER FORMIDABLE POWER, SHE WAS STILL TRYING TO CREATE AN ARMY OF WHITE ZETSU IN PREPARATION FOR WAR.
THAT'S ALWAYS BOTHERED ME, AND I'VE BEEN TRACING HER ROOTS.
AND I LEARNED THAT THE WHITE ZETSU SOLDIERS...
...EXISTED LONG BEFORE SHINOBI EVER DID.
WHAT DOES IT MEAN?
THIS PART...
...IS PURE CONJECTURE, BUT...
WHAT I BELIEVE THIS INDICATES IS...
VSH
...THE POSSIBILITY THAT SOMETHING THAT'D FRIGHTEN EVEN KAGUYA COULD ONE DAY APPEAR...

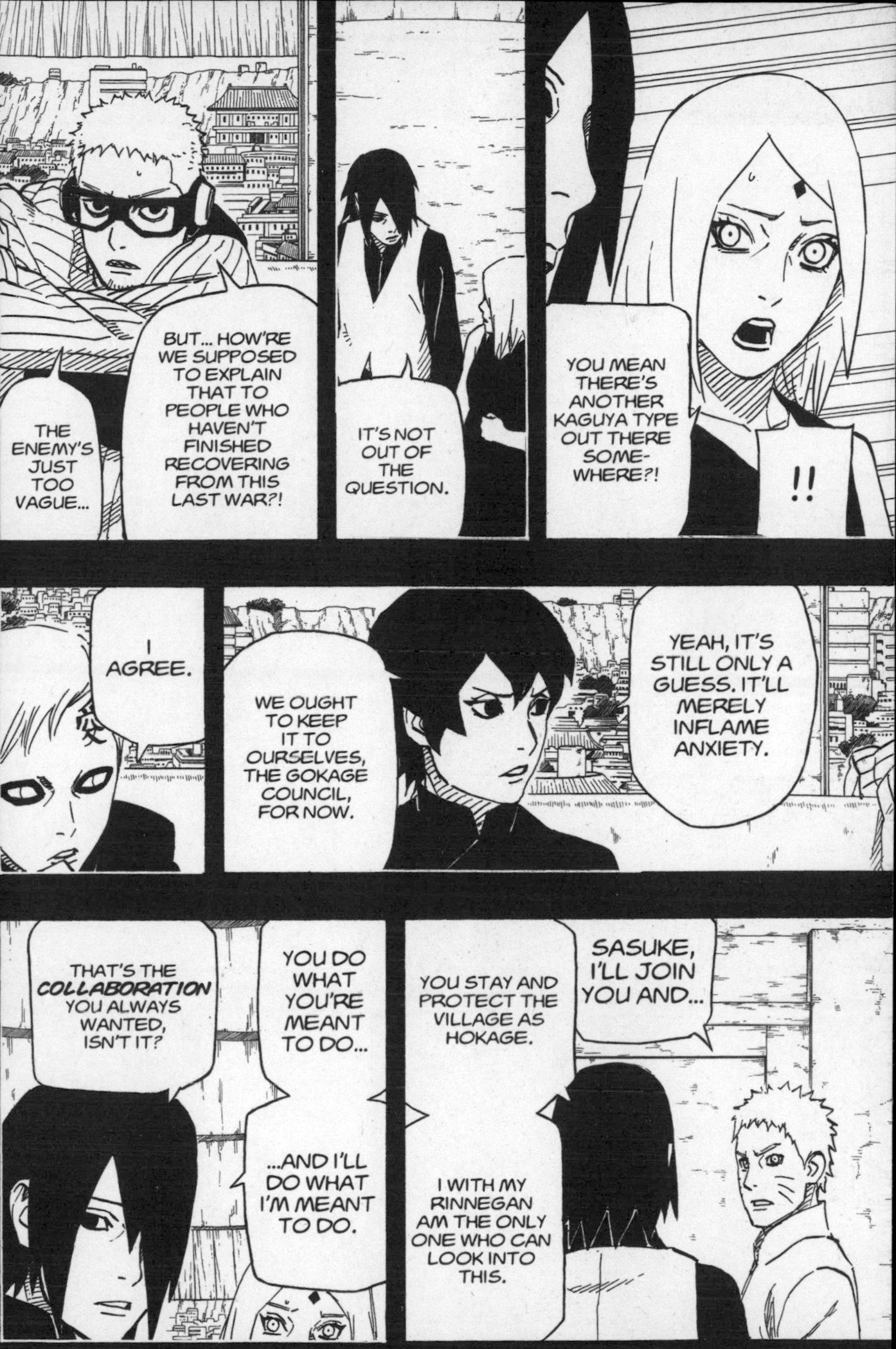
YOU MEAN THERE'S ANOTHER KAGUYA TYPE OUT THERE SOME-WHERE?!
!!
IT'S NOT OUT OF THE QUESTION.
BUT... HOW'RE WE SUPPOSED TO EXPLAIN THAT TO PEOPLE WHO HAVEN'T FINISHED RECOVERING FROM THIS LAST WAR?!
THE ENEMY'S JUST TOO VAGUE...
YEAH, IT'S STILL ONLY A GUESS. IT'LL MERELY INFLAME ANXIETY.
WE OUGHT TO KEEP IT TO OURSELVES, THE GOKAGE COUNCIL, FOR NOW.
I AGREE.
SASUKE, I'LL JOIN YOU AND...
YOU STAY AND PROTECT THE VILLAGE AS HOKAGE.
I WITH MY RINNEGAN AM THE ONLY ONE WHO CAN LOOK INTO THIS.
YOU DO WHAT YOU'RE MEANT TO DO...
...AND I'LL DO WHAT I'M MEANT TO DO.
THAT'S THE *COLLABORATION* YOU ALWAYS WANTED, ISN'T IT?

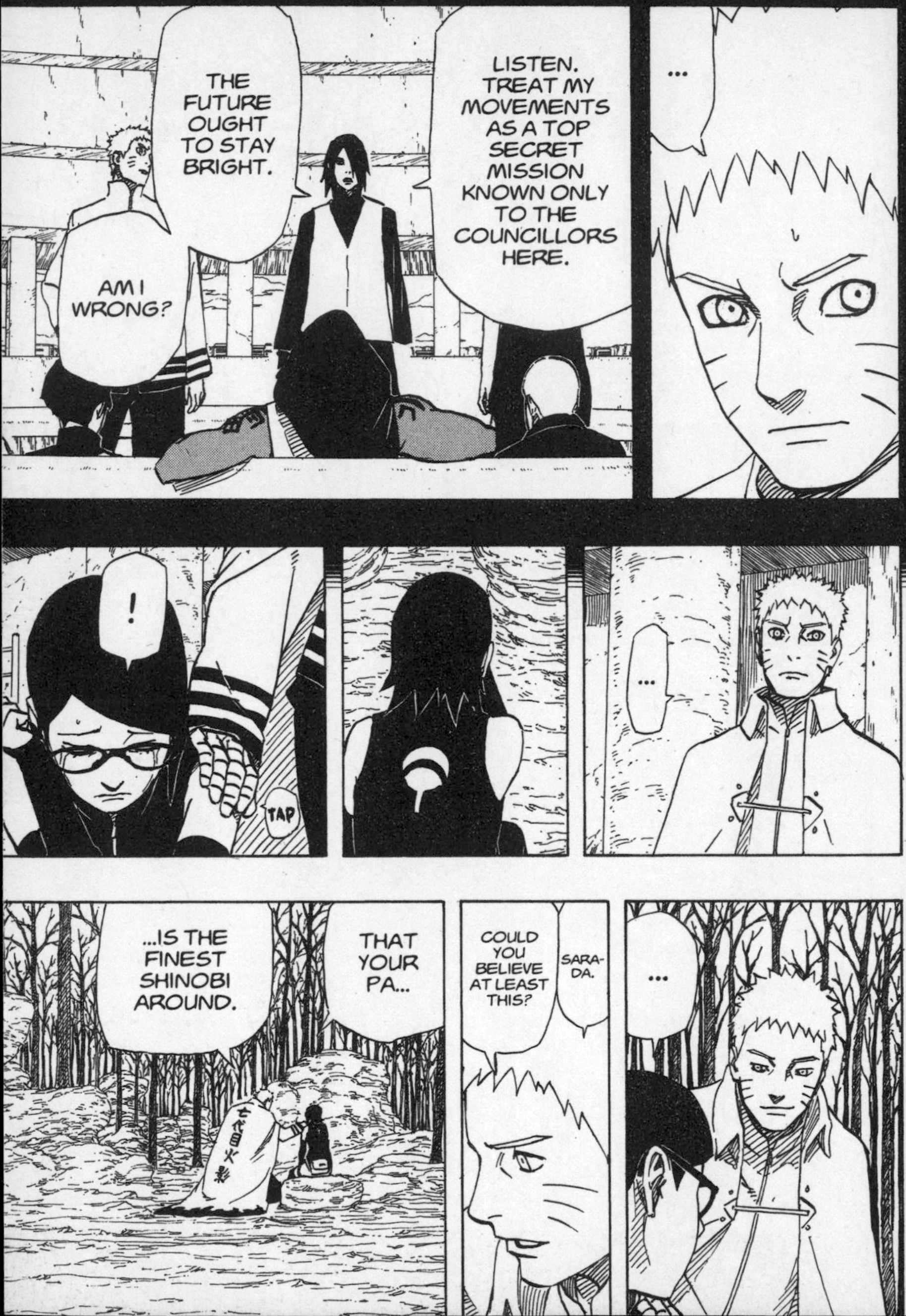
...
LISTEN. TREAT MY MOVEMENTS AS A TOP SECRET MISSION KNOWN ONLY TO THE COUNCILLORS HERE.
THE FUTURE OUGHT TO STAY BRIGHT.
AM I WRONG?
...
!
TAP
...
SARA-DA.
COULD YOU BELIEVE AT LEAST THIS?
THAT YOUR PA...
...IS THE FINEST SHINOBI AROUND.

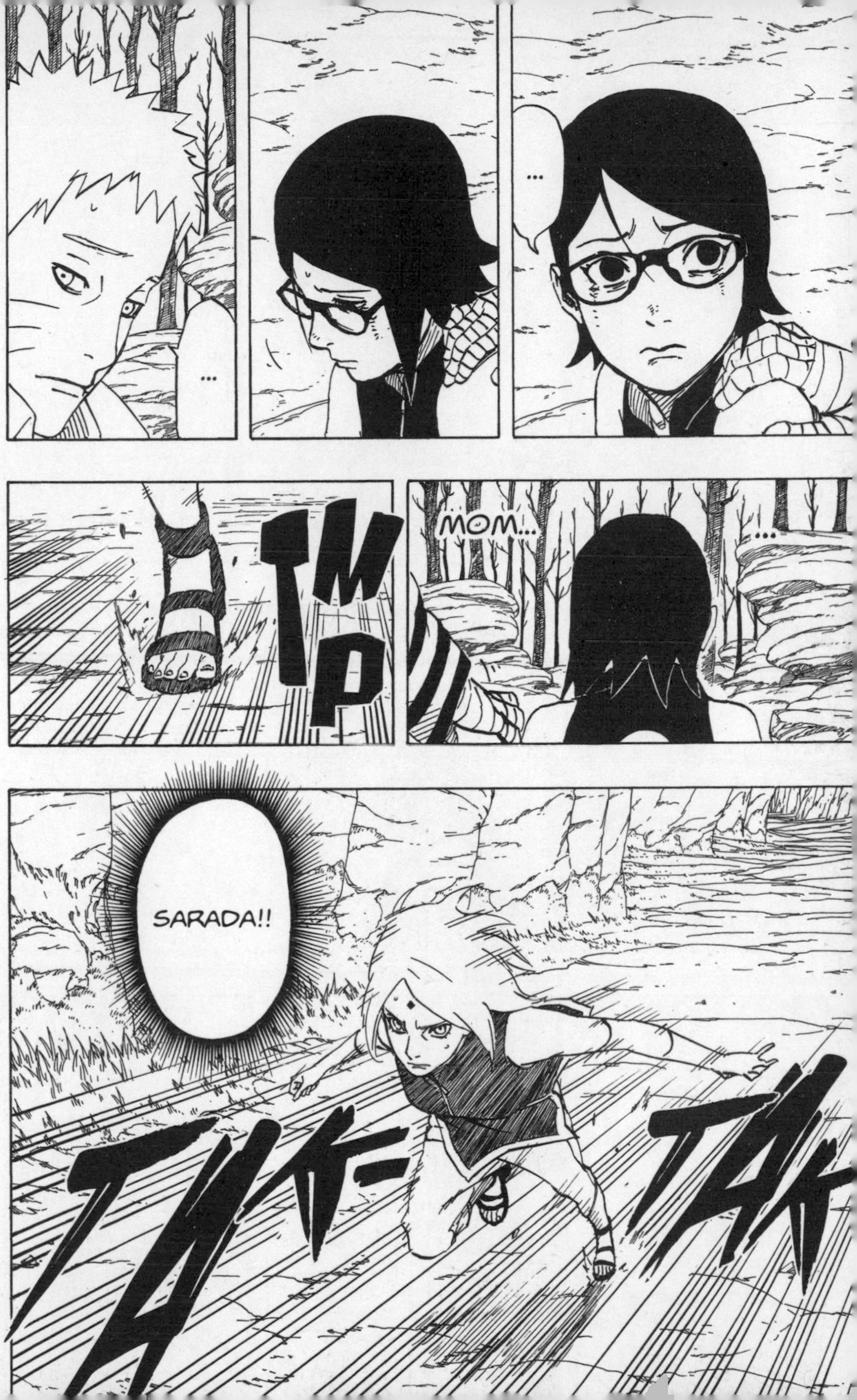
...
...
...
MOM...
TMP
SARADA!!

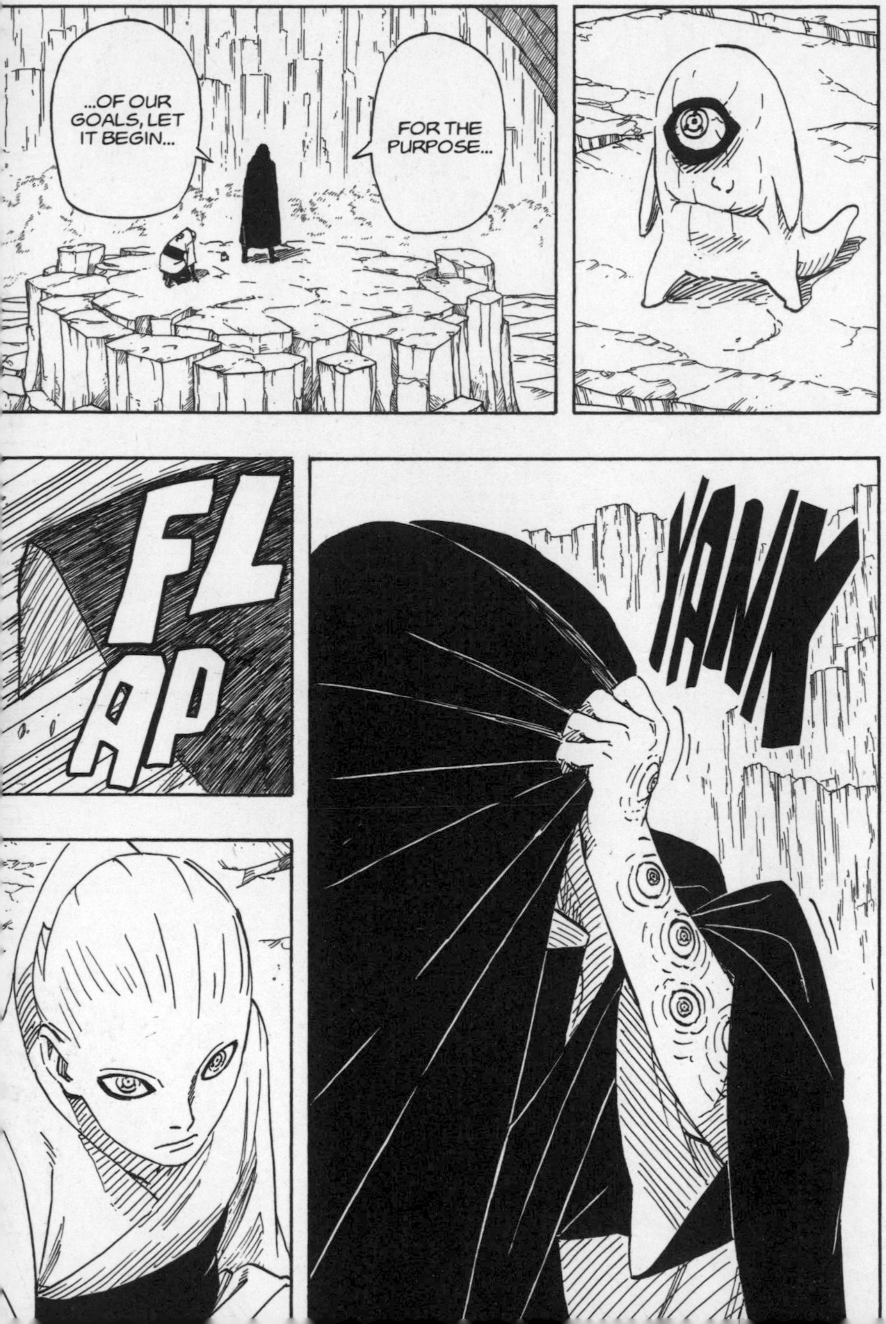
FOR THE PURPOSE...
...OF OUR GOALS, LET IT BEGIN...
YANK
FLAP

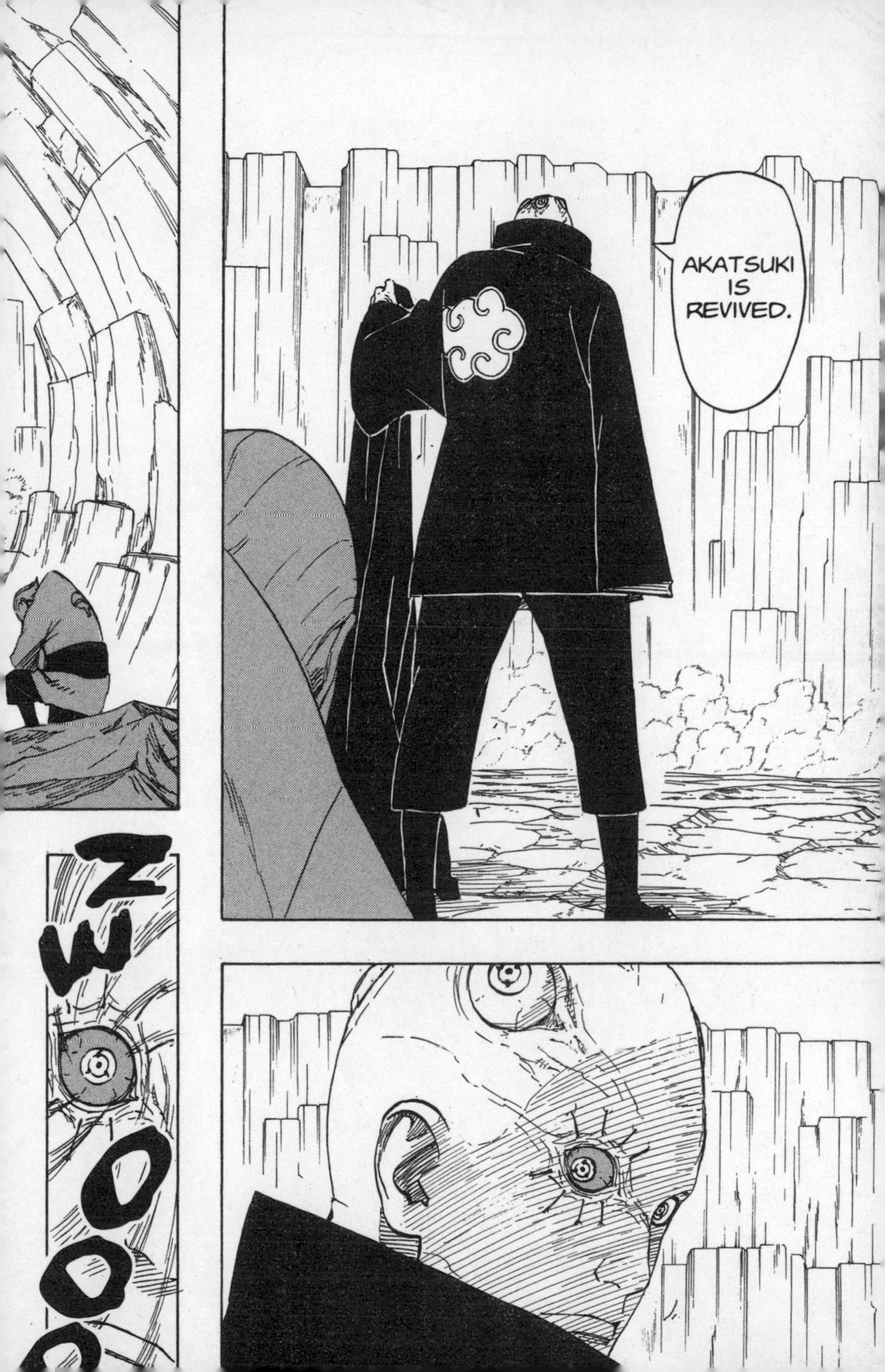
AKATSUKI IS REVIVED.

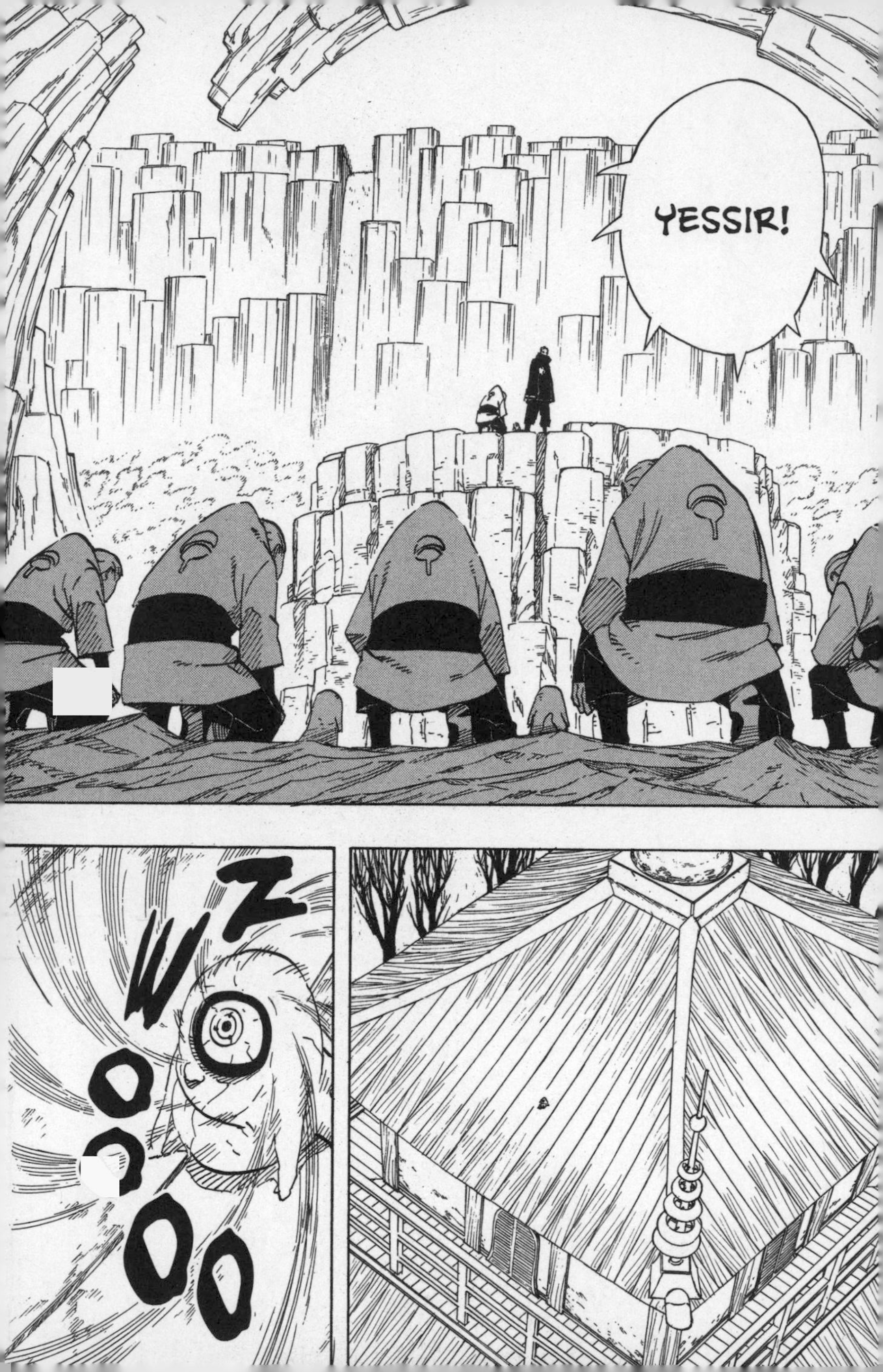
YESSIR!
WZOOOO

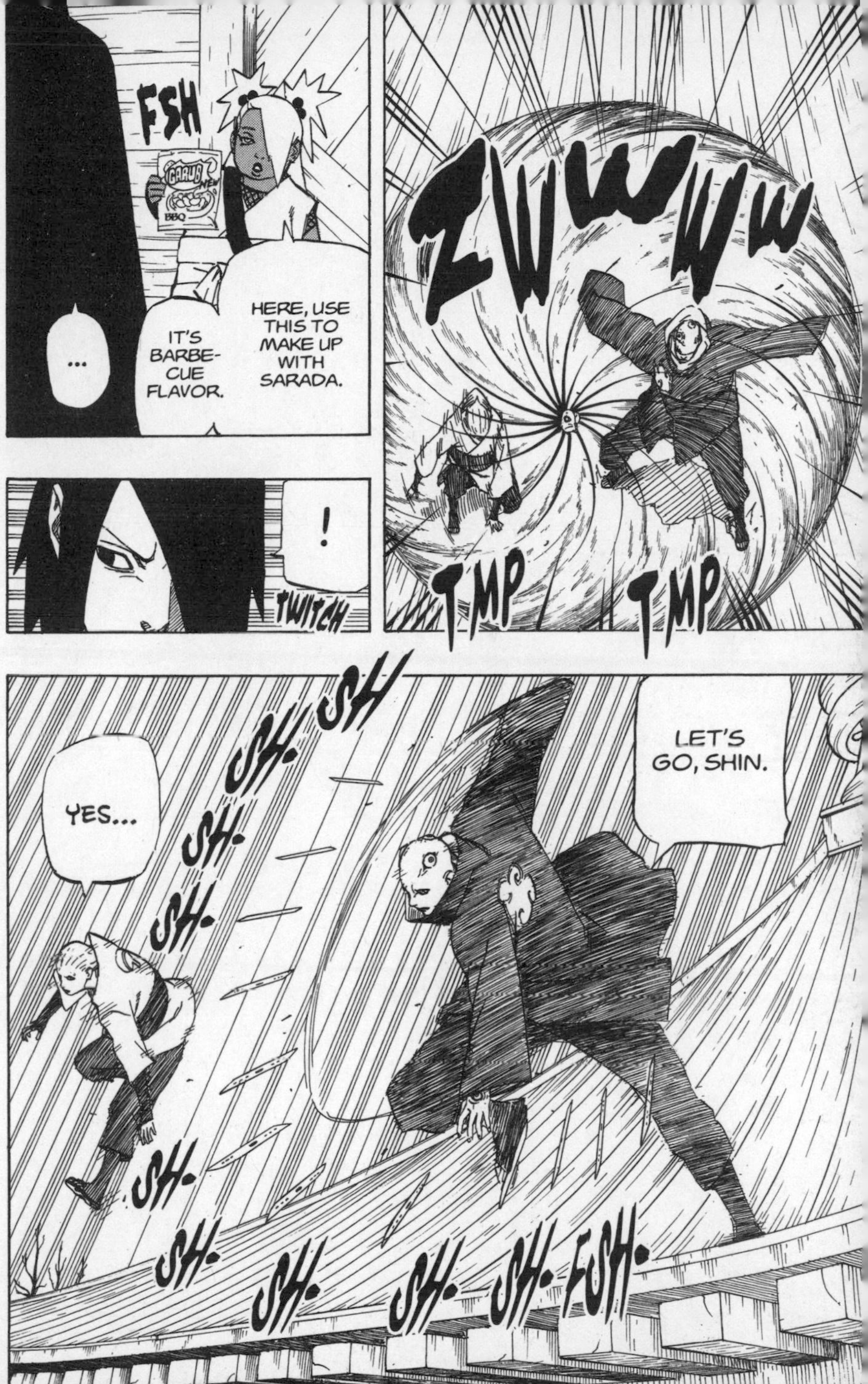
ZWWWWW
TMP TMP
FSH
HERE, USE THIS TO MAKE UP WITH SARADA.
IT'S BARBE-CUE FLAVOR.
...
!
TWITCH
LET'S GO, SHIN.
YES...
SH SH SH SH SH SH
SH SH SH SH SH FSH

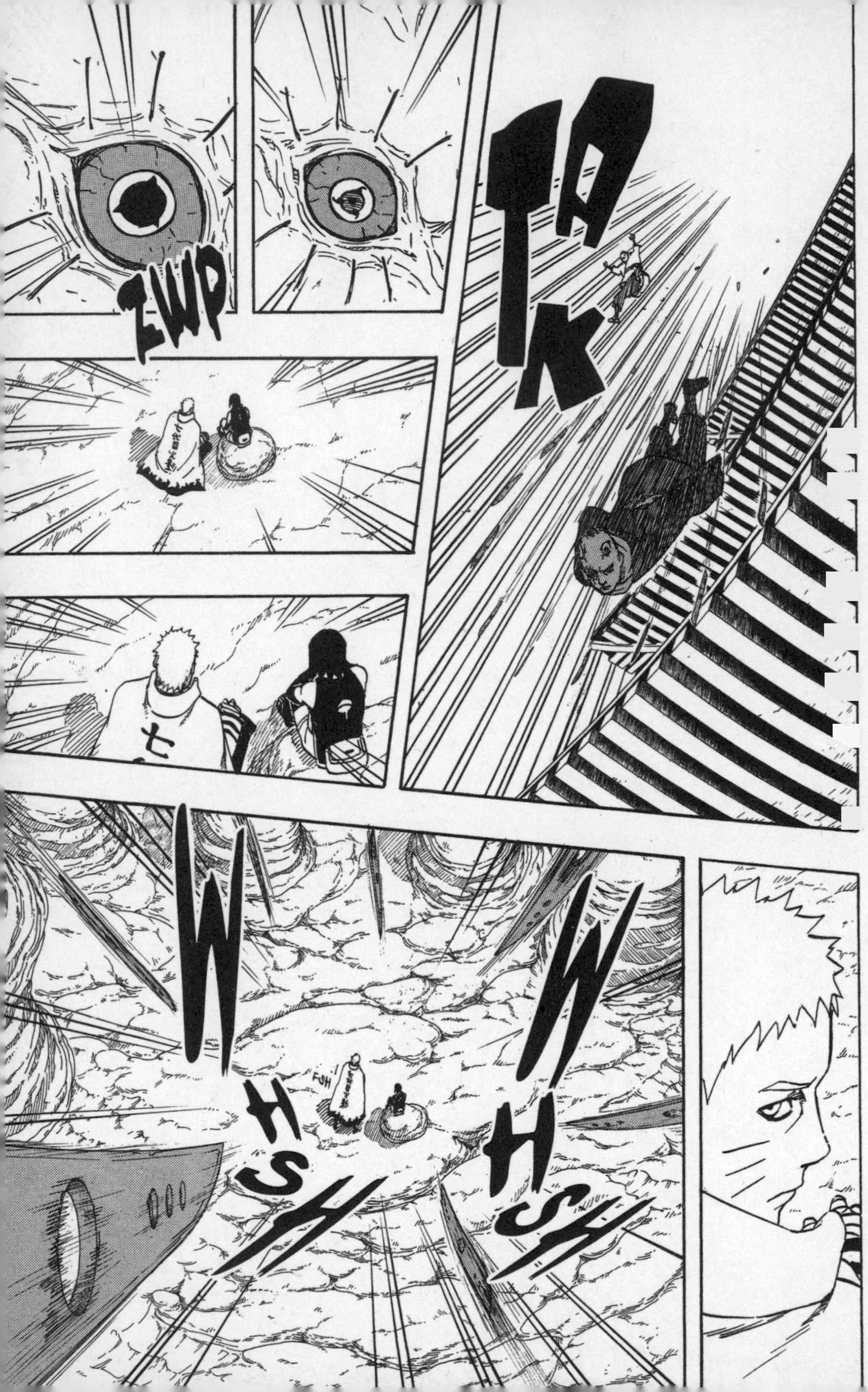
TAK
ZWP
WHSH
FSH
WHSH

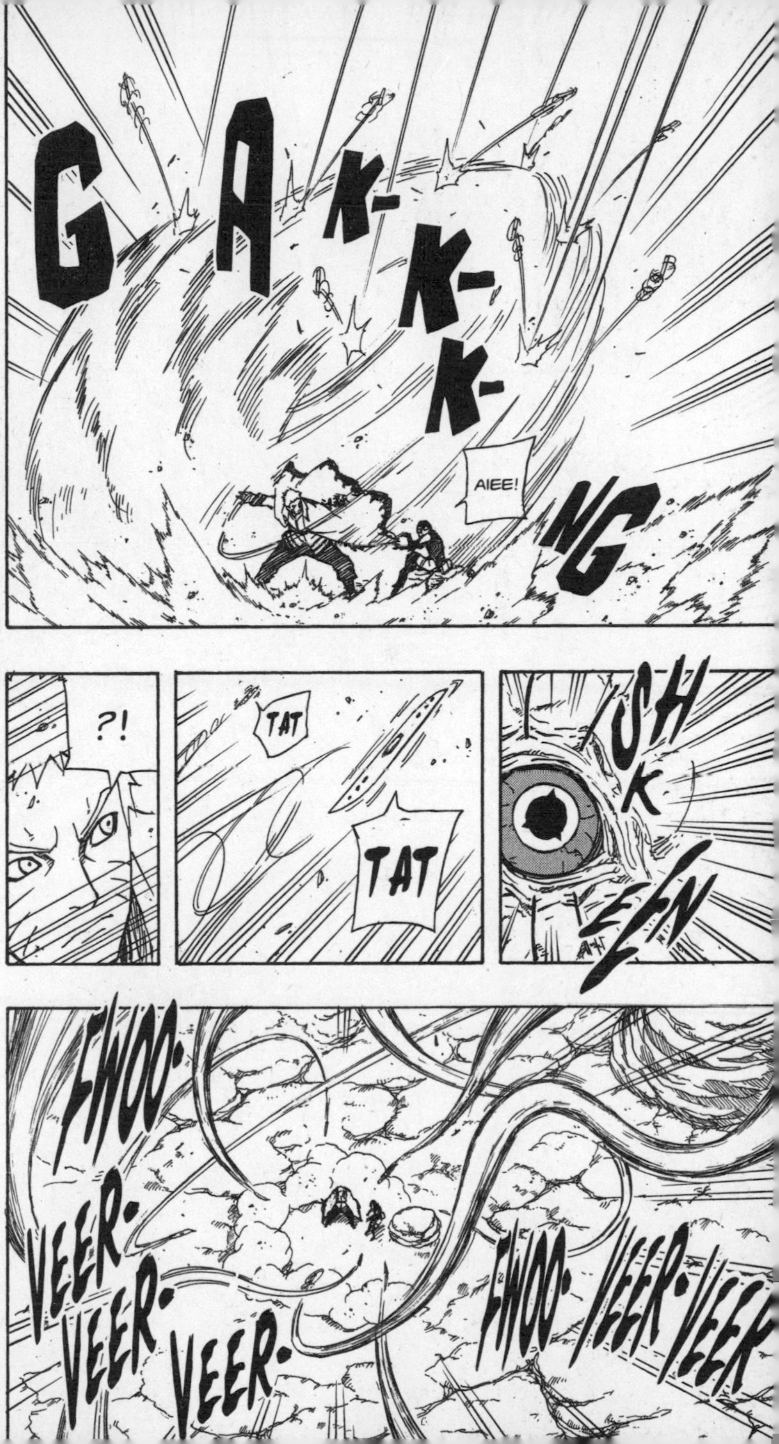
GAK-K-K-NG
AIEE!
SHKEEN
TAT
TAT
?!
FWOO-VEER-VEER-VEER-
FWOO-VEER-VEER

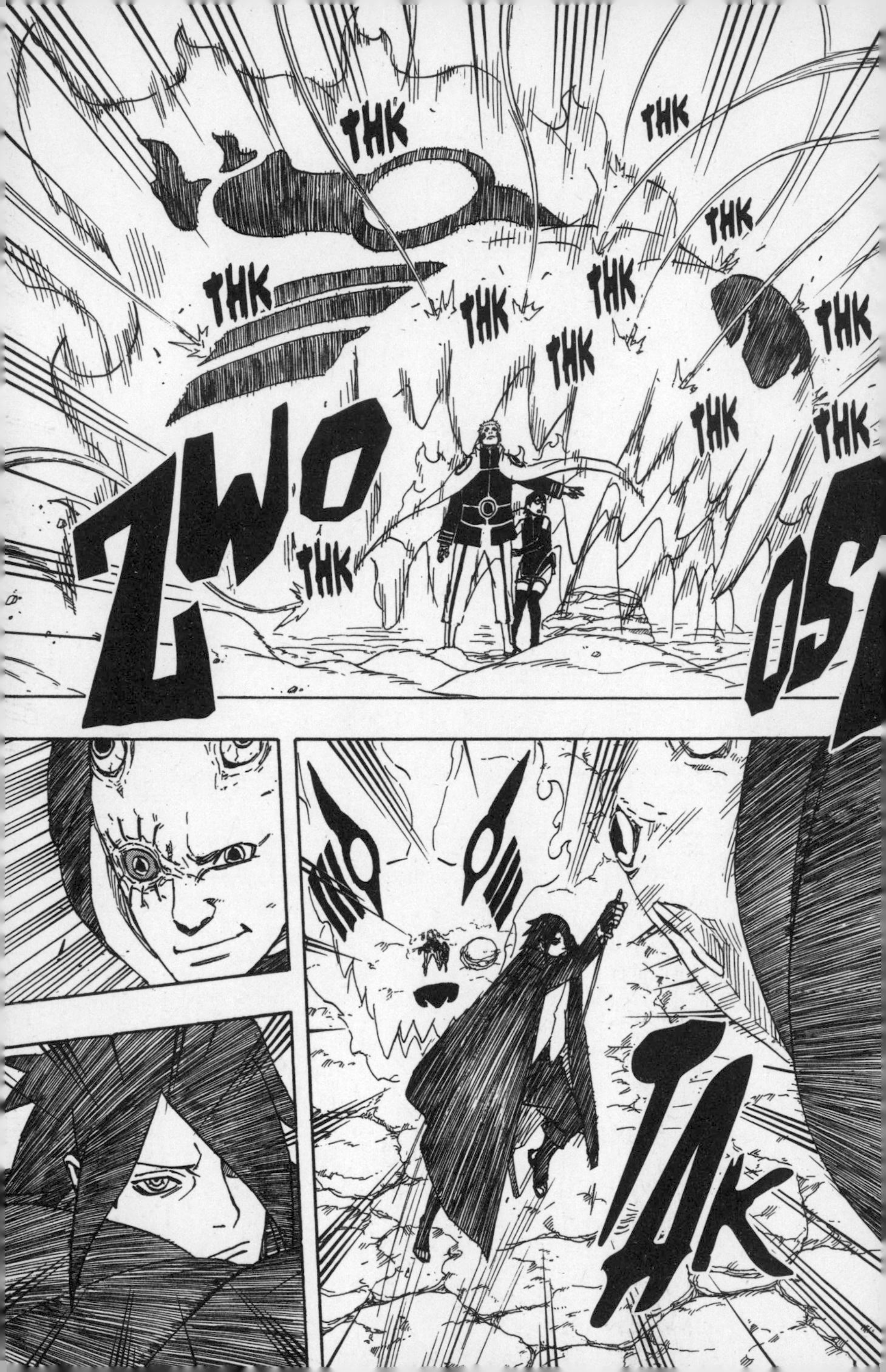
THK
THK
THK
THK
THK
THK
THK
THK
THK
THK
OS
ZWO
THK
TAK

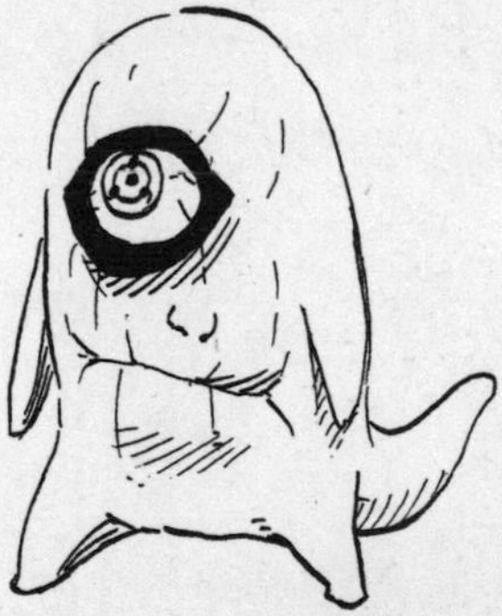

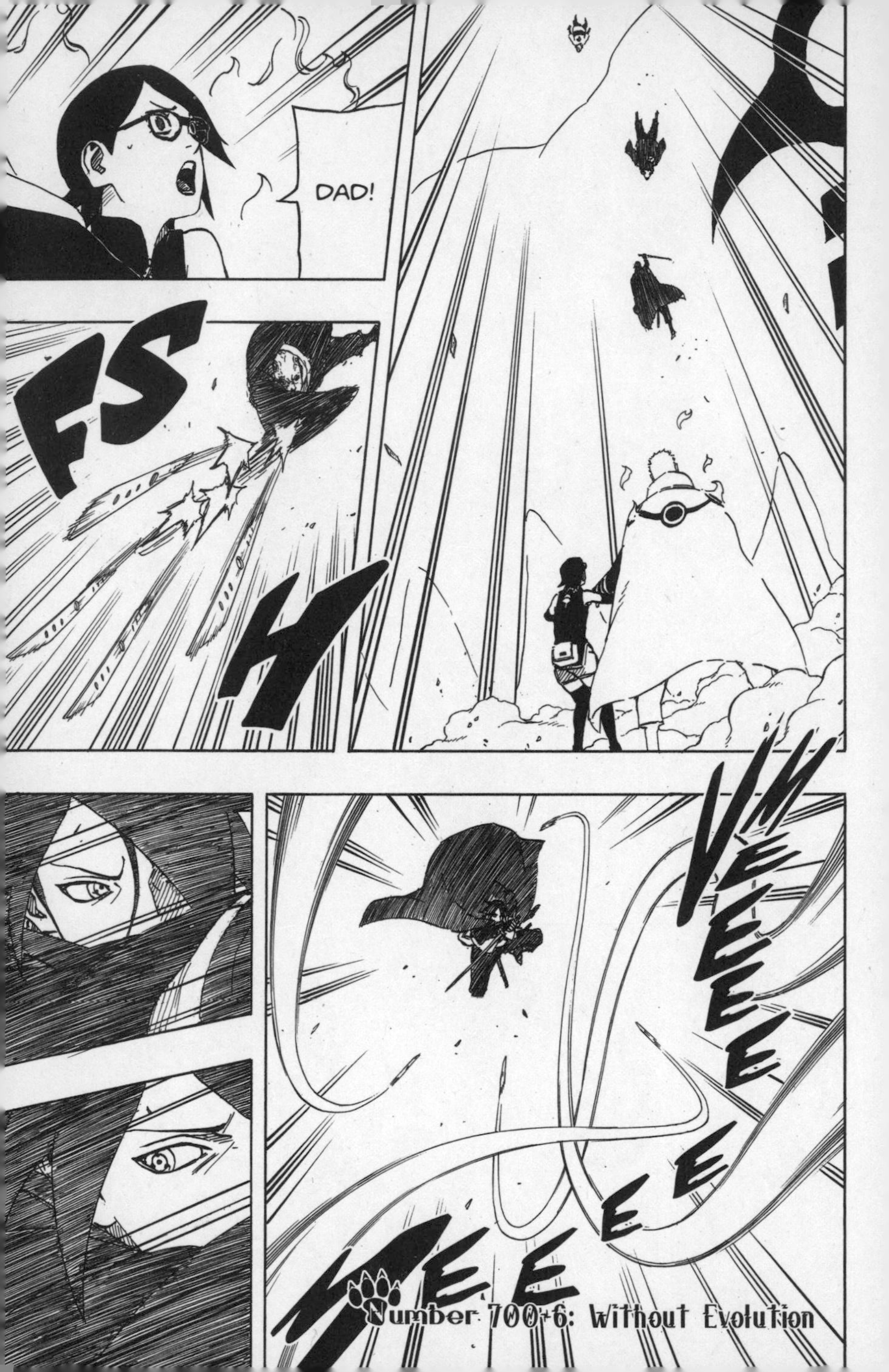
DAD!
FSH
VMEEEEEEEEEE

Number 700+6: Without Evolution

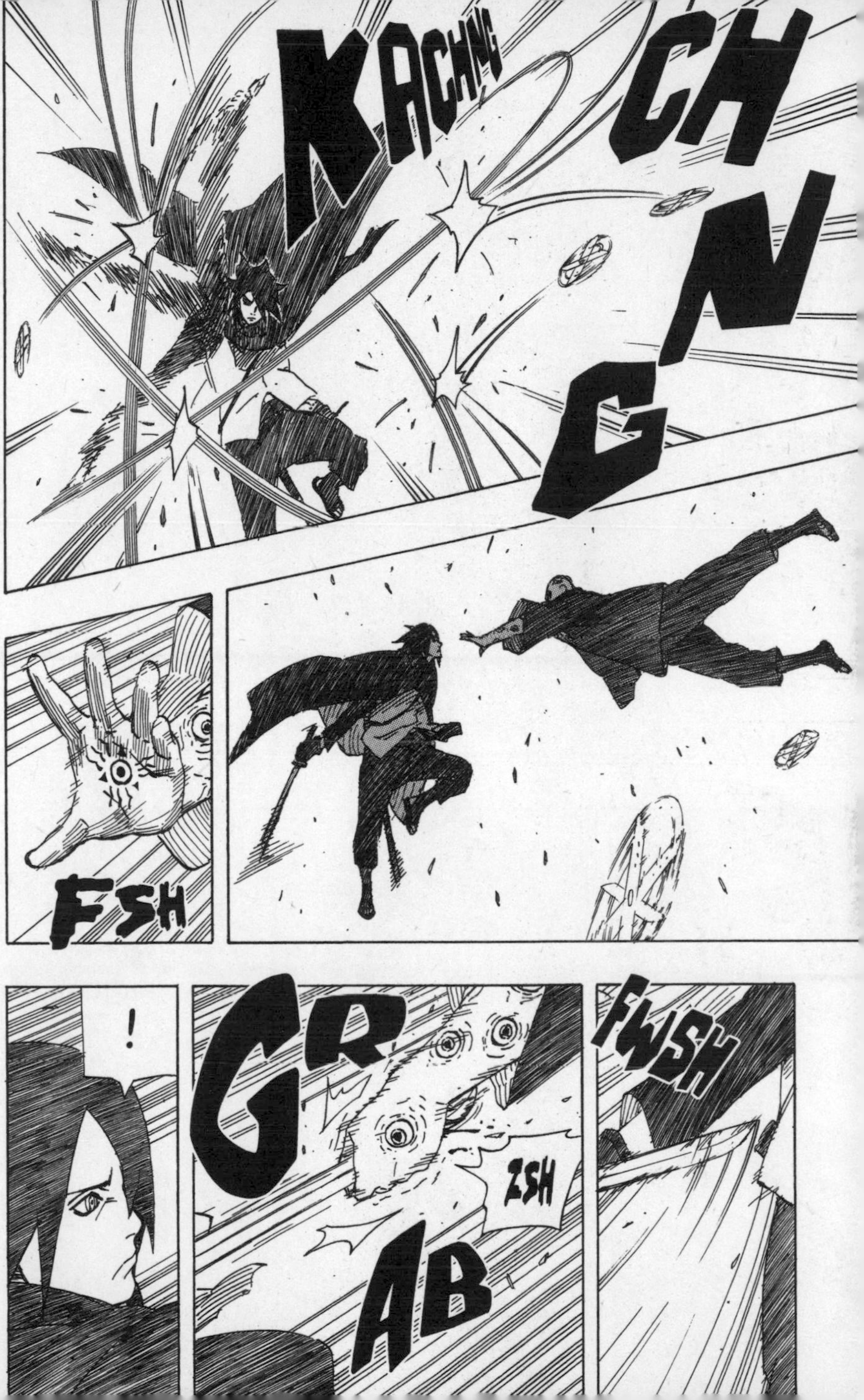

KACHNG
CHNG
FSH
FWSH
GRAB
ZSH
!

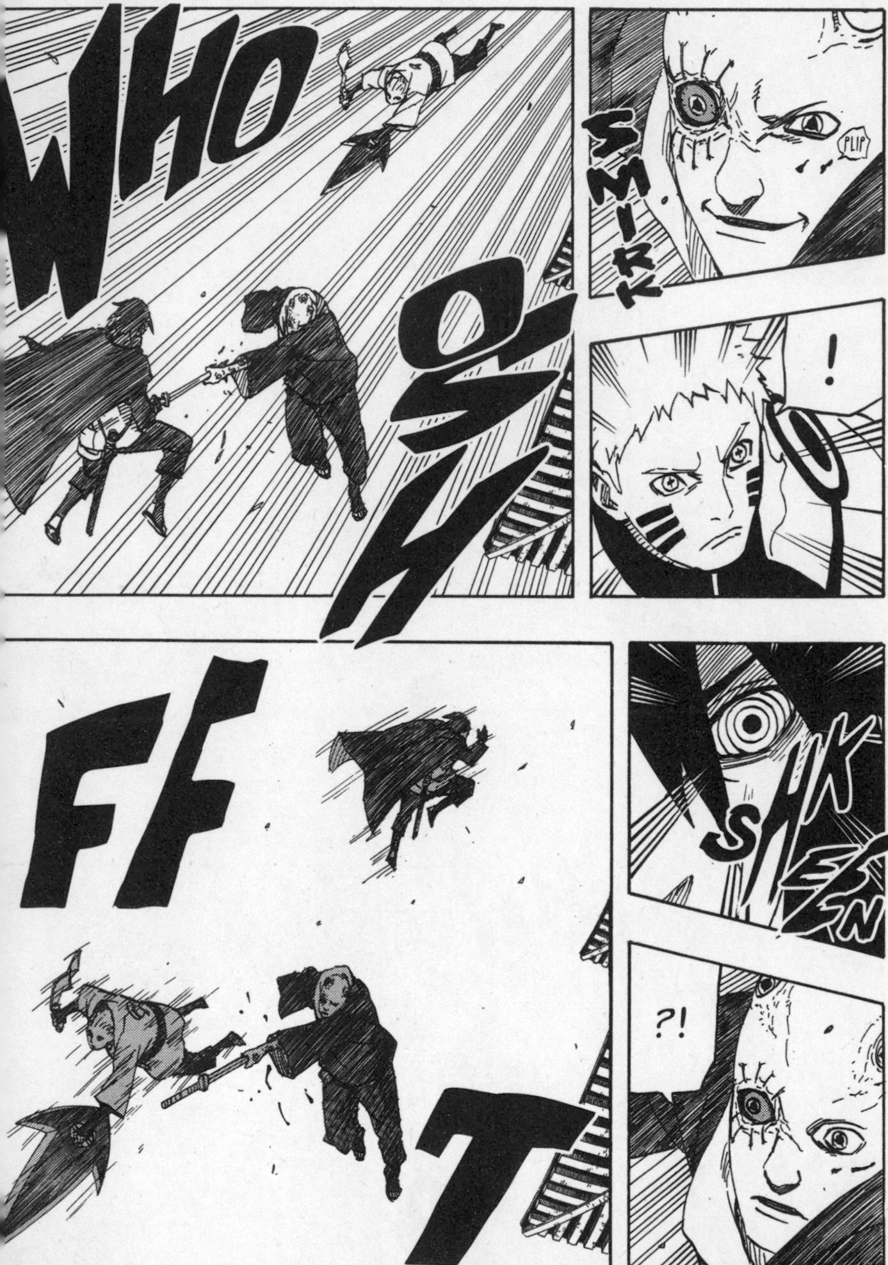
SMIRK
PLIP
!
WHOOSH
SHK
SHEEN
?!
FFT

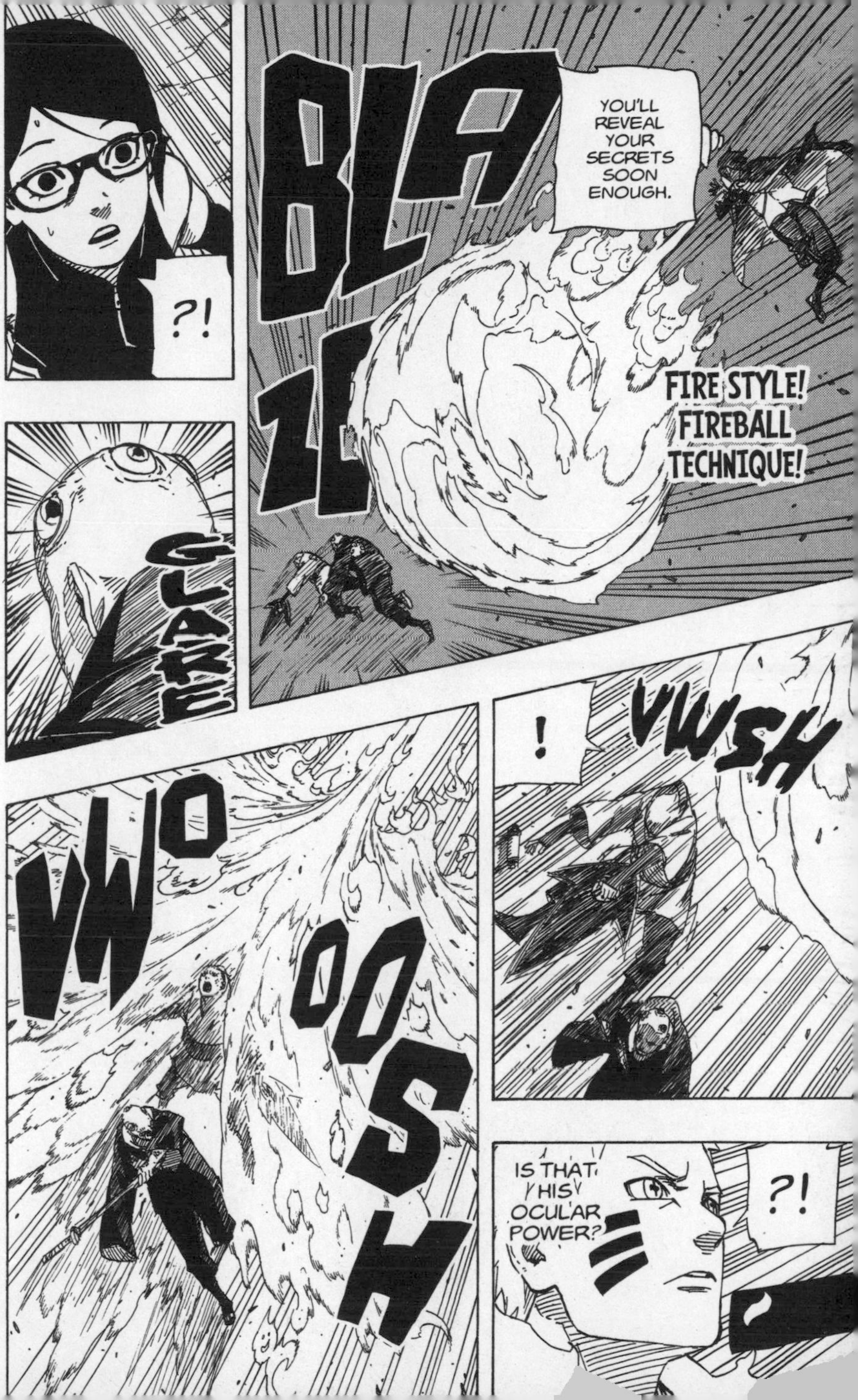
YOU'LL REVEAL YOUR SECRETS SOON ENOUGH.
FIRE STYLE! FIREBALL TECHNIQUE!
BLAZE
?!
GLARE
!
VWSH
?!
IS THAT HIS OCULAR POWER?
WHOOOSH

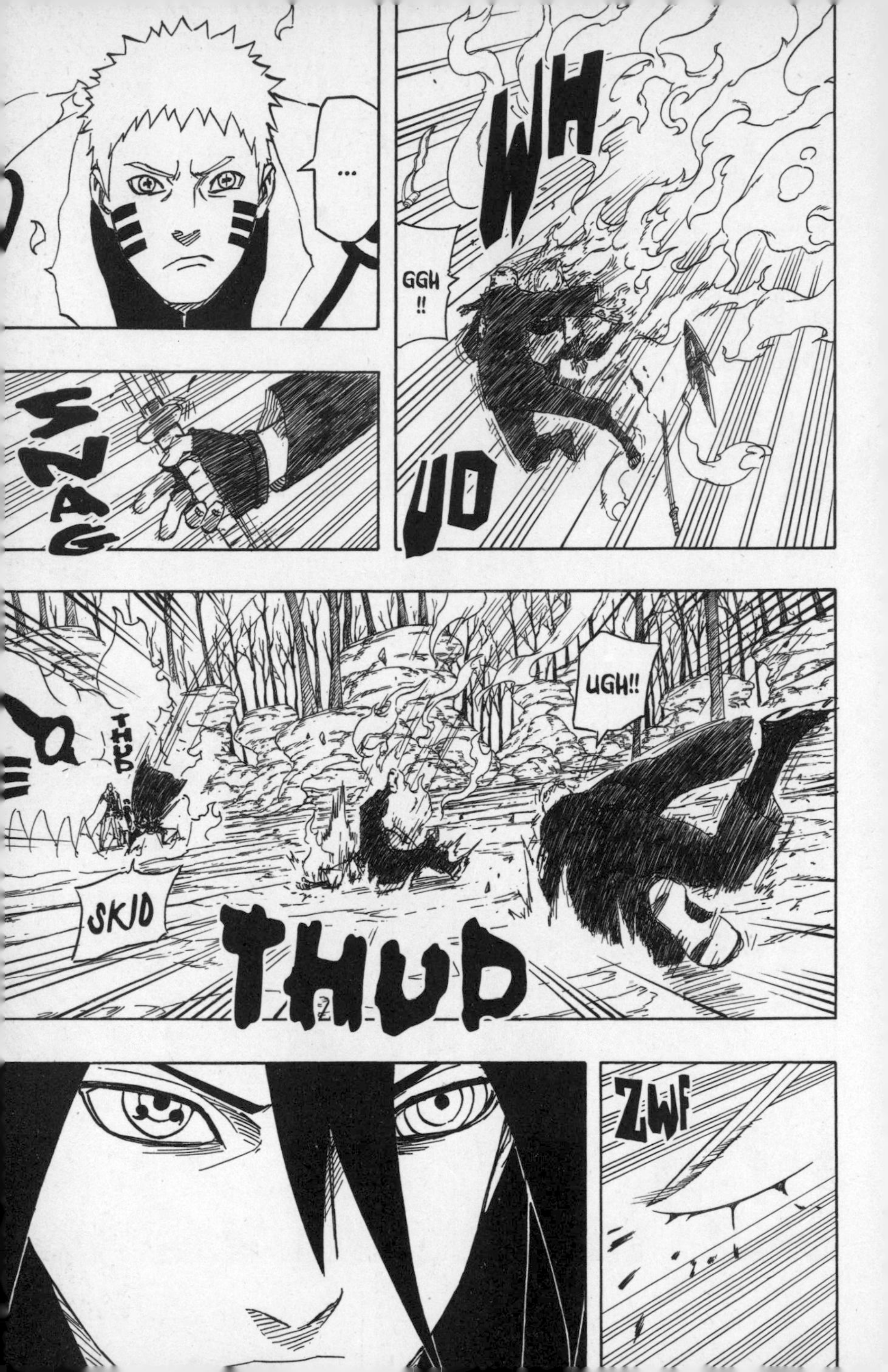
WHUD
GGH!!
...
SNAG
UGH!!
THUD
SKID
THUD
ZWF

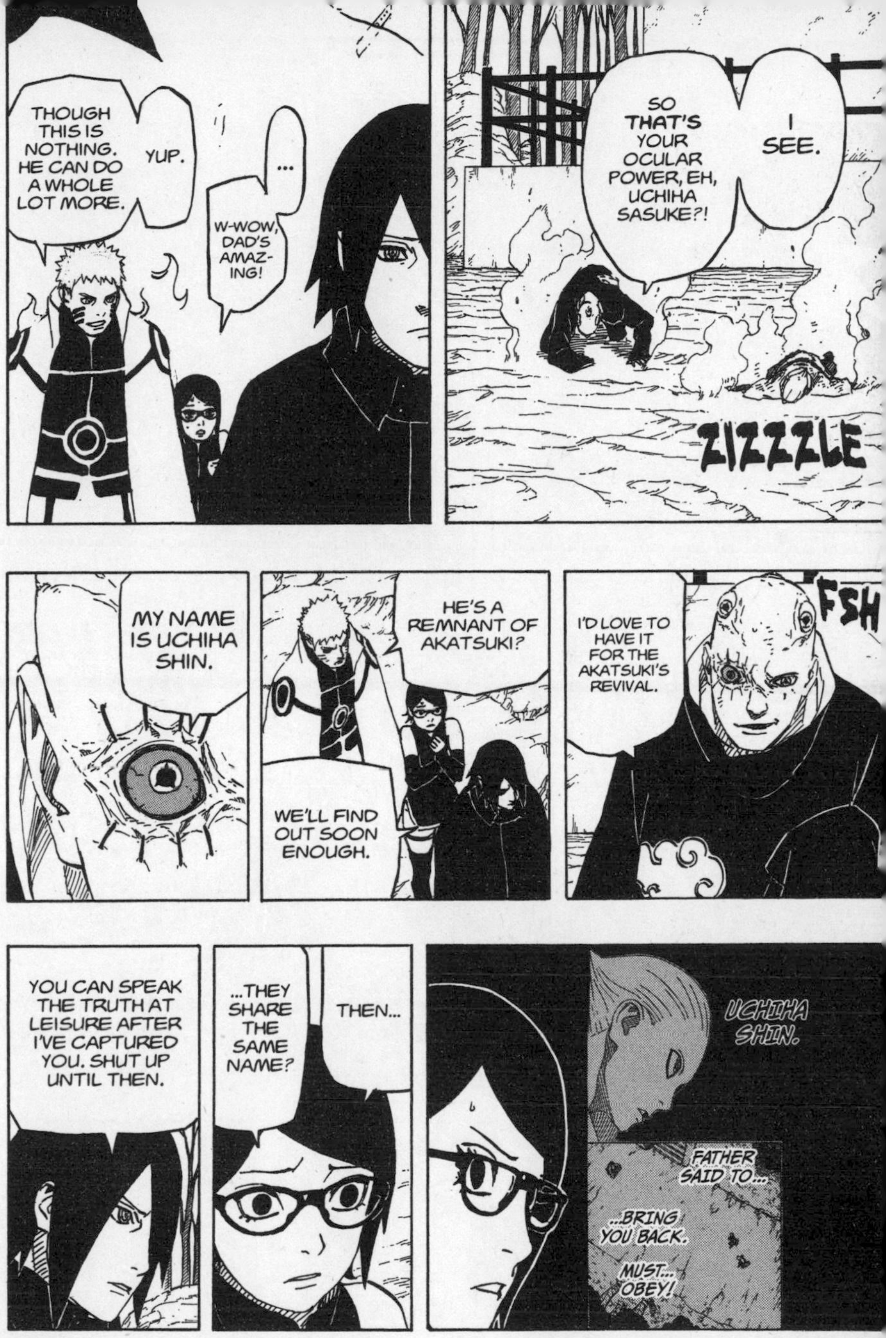
I SEE.
SO THAT'S YOUR OCULAR POWER, EH, UCHIHA SASUKE?!
ZIZZZLE
...
W-WOW, DAD'S AMAZ-ING!
YUP.
THOUGH THIS IS NOTHING. HE CAN DO A WHOLE LOT MORE.
FSH
I'D LOVE TO HAVE IT FOR THE AKATSUKI'S REVIVAL.
HE'S A REMNANT OF AKATSUKI?
WE'LL FIND OUT SOON ENOUGH.
MY NAME IS UCHIHA SHIN.
UCHIHA SHIN.
FATHER SAID TO...
...BRING YOU BACK.
MUST... OBEY!
THEN...
...THEY SHARE THE SAME NAME?
YOU CAN SPEAK THE TRUTH AT LEISURE AFTER I'VE CAPTURED YOU. SHUT UP UNTIL THEN.

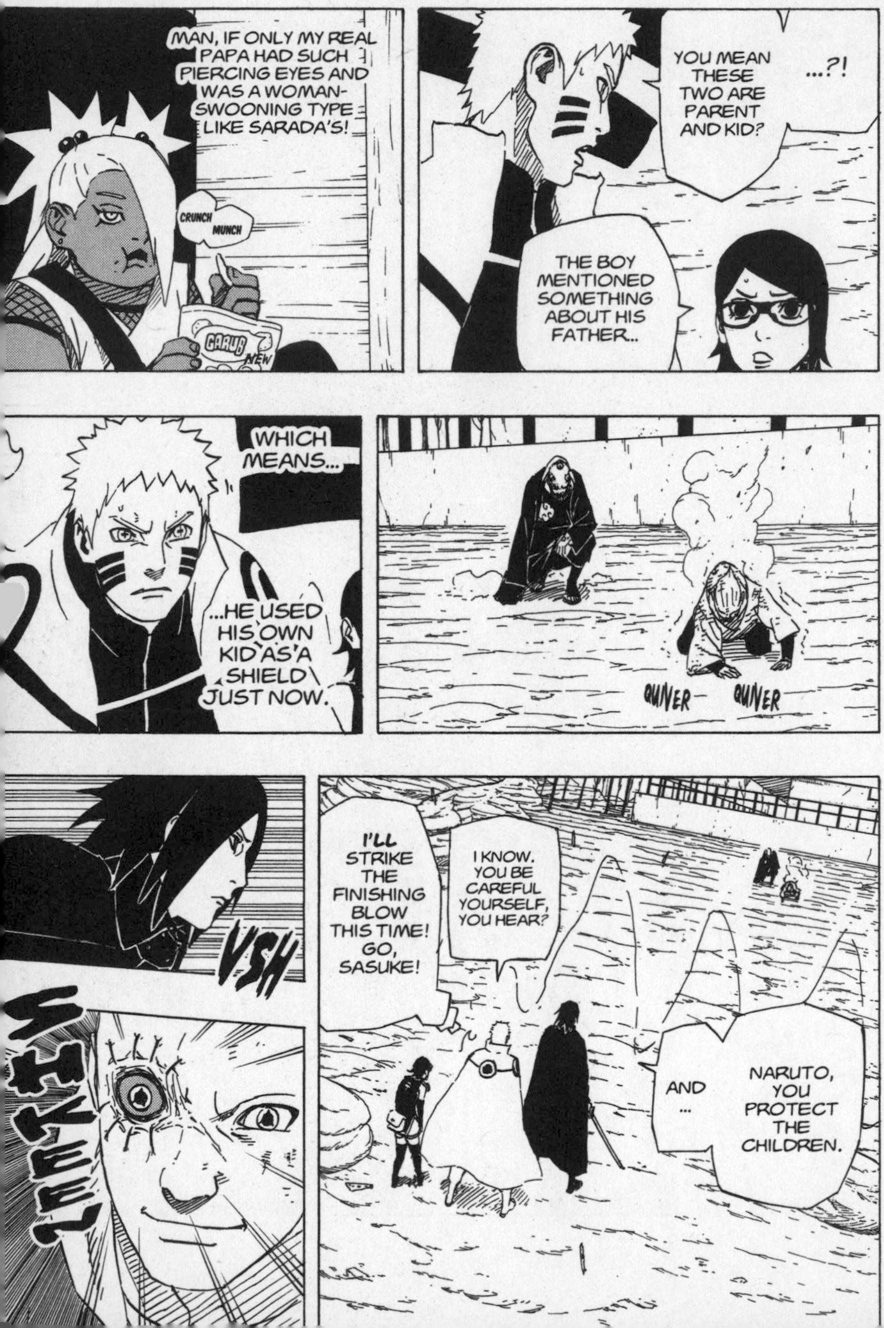
YOU MEAN THESE TWO ARE PARENT AND KID?
...?!
THE BOY MENTIONED SOMETHING ABOUT HIS FATHER...
MAN, IF ONLY MY REAL PAPA HAD SUCH PIERCING EYES AND WAS A WOMAN-SWOONING TYPE LIKE SARADA'S!
CRUNCH
MUNCH
GARUB
NEW
QUIVER
QUIVER
WHICH MEANS...
...HE USED HIS OWN KID AS A SHIELD JUST NOW.
NARUTO, YOU PROTECT THE CHILDREN.
AND ...
I KNOW. YOU BE CAREFUL YOURSELF, YOU HEAR?
I'LL STRIKE THE FINISHING BLOW THIS TIME! GO, SASUKE!
VSH

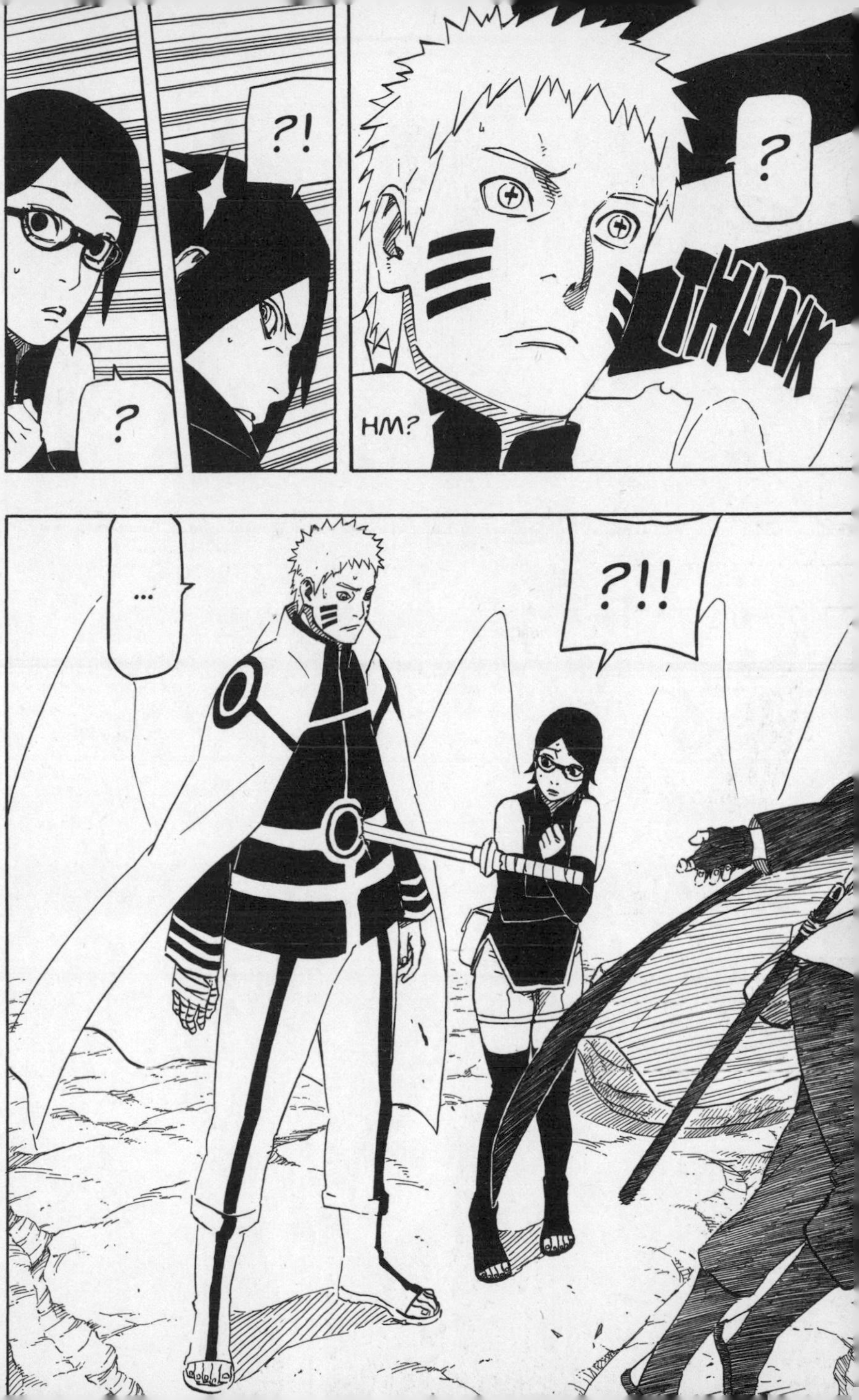
?
THUNK
HM?
?!
?
?!!
...

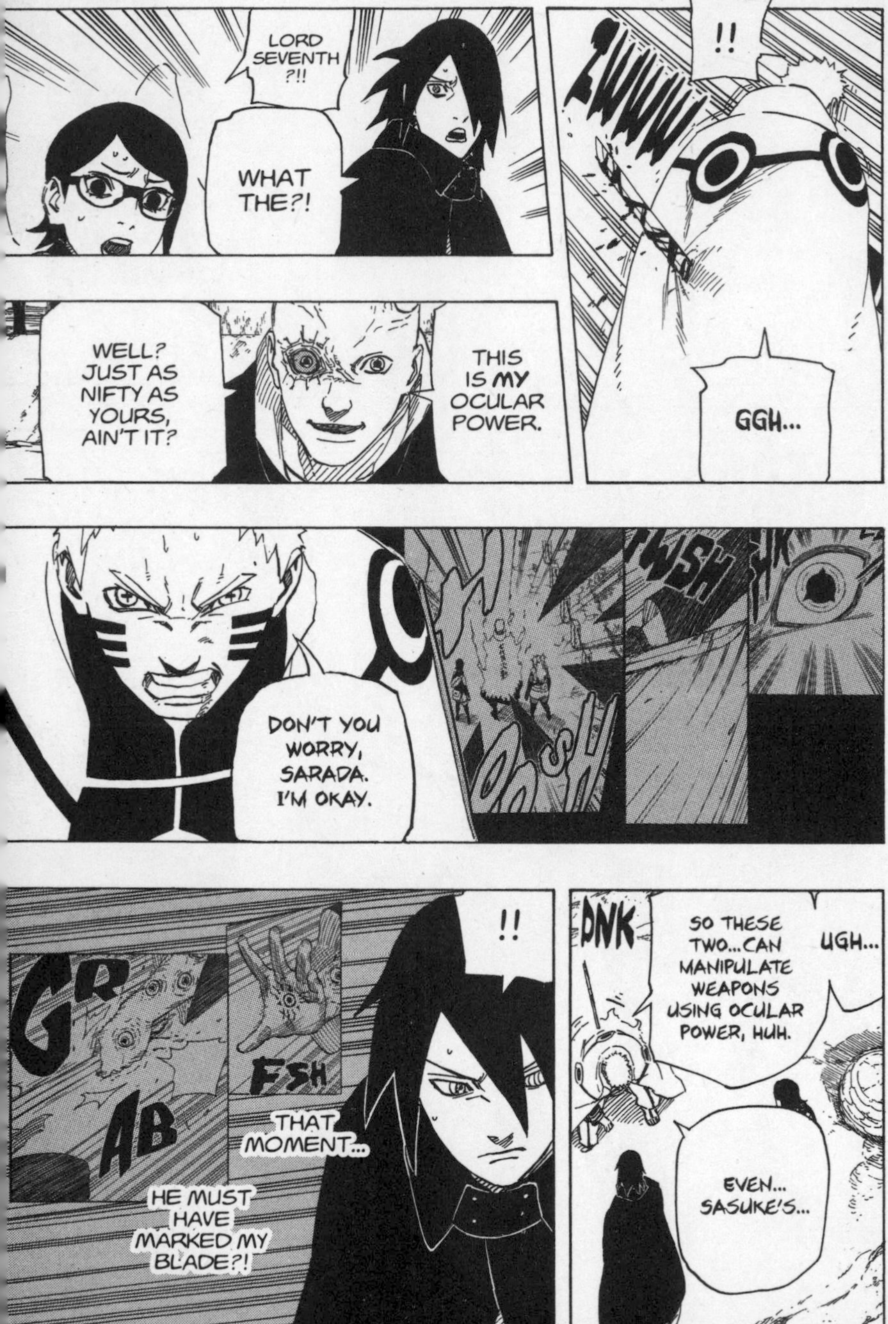
!!
GGH...
LORD SEVENTH ?!!
WHAT THE?!
THIS IS MY OCULAR POWER.
WELL? JUST AS NIFTY AS YOURS, AIN'T IT?
FWSH
DON'T YOU WORRY, SARADA. I'M OKAY.
UGH...
DNK
SO THESE TWO...CAN MANIPULATE WEAPONS USING OCULAR POWER, HUH.
EVEN... SASUKE'S...
!!
THAT MOMENT...
FSH
GRAB
HE MUST HAVE MARKED MY BLADE?!

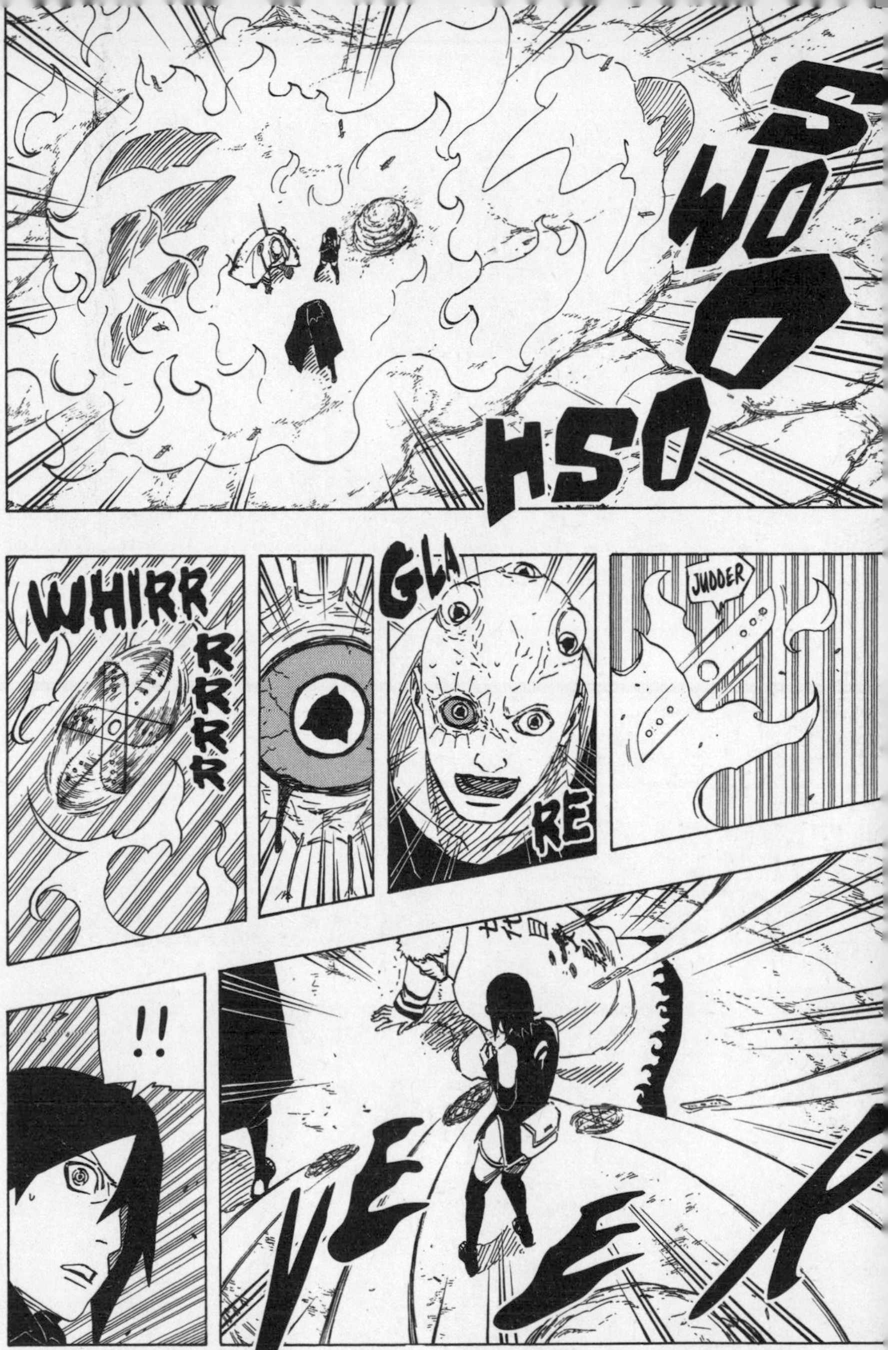
SWOOSH
JUDDER
GLARE
WHIRR RRRRR
!!

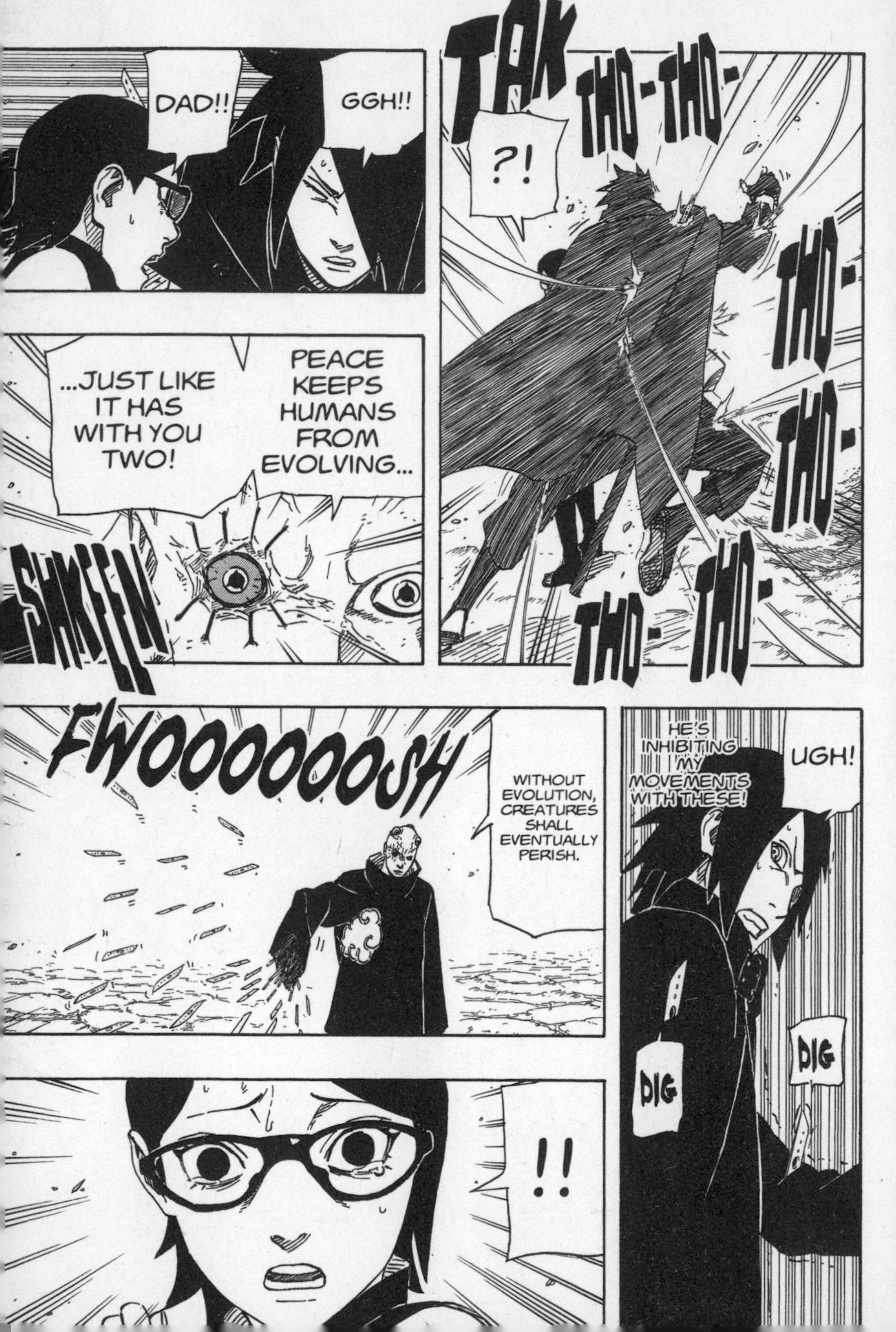
TAK
THO-THO-
?!
THO-
THO-
THO-
THO-
GGH!!
DAD!!
PEACE KEEPS HUMANS FROM EVOLVING...
...JUST LIKE IT HAS WITH YOU TWO!
SHKEEN
UGH!
HE'S INHIBITING MY MOVEMENTS WITH THESE!
DIG
DIG
FWOOOOOOSH
WITHOUT EVOLUTION, CREATURES SHALL EVENTUALLY PERISH.
!!

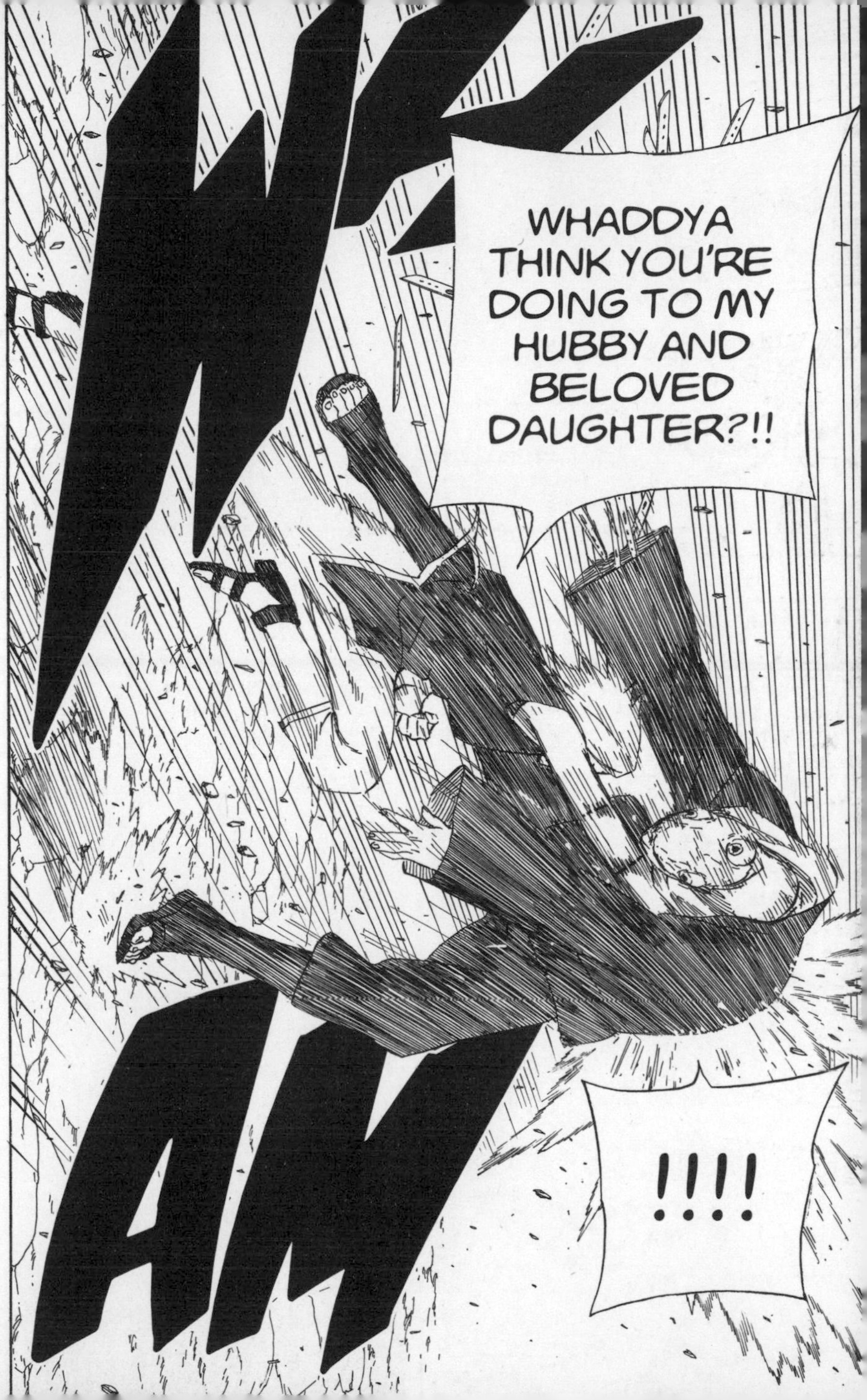
WHADDYA THINK YOU'RE DOING TO MY HUBBY AND BELOVED DAUGHTER?!!
!!!!

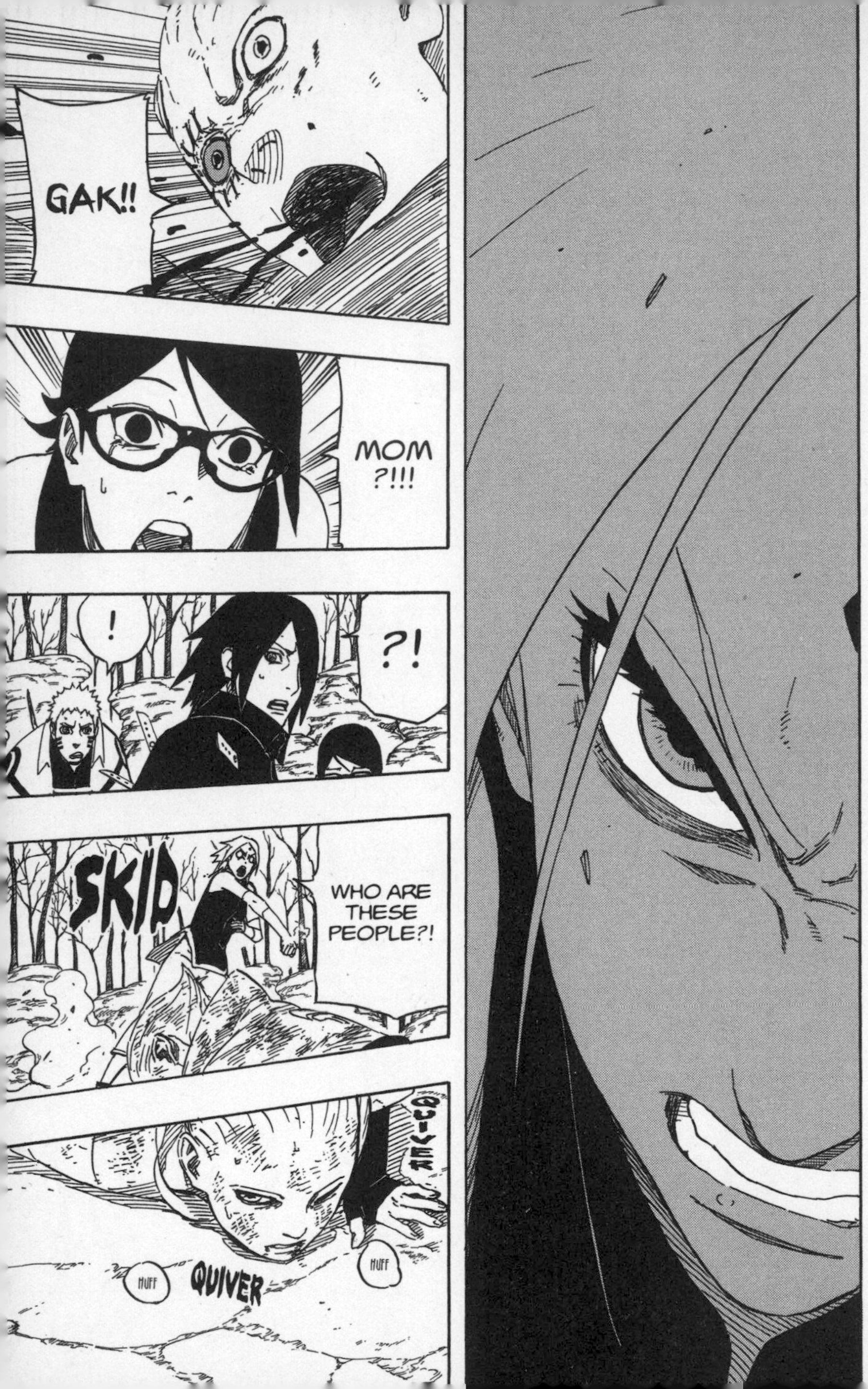
GAK!!
MOM ?!!!
?!
!
WHO ARE THESE PEOPLE?!
SKID
QUIVER
HUFF
QUIVER
HUFF

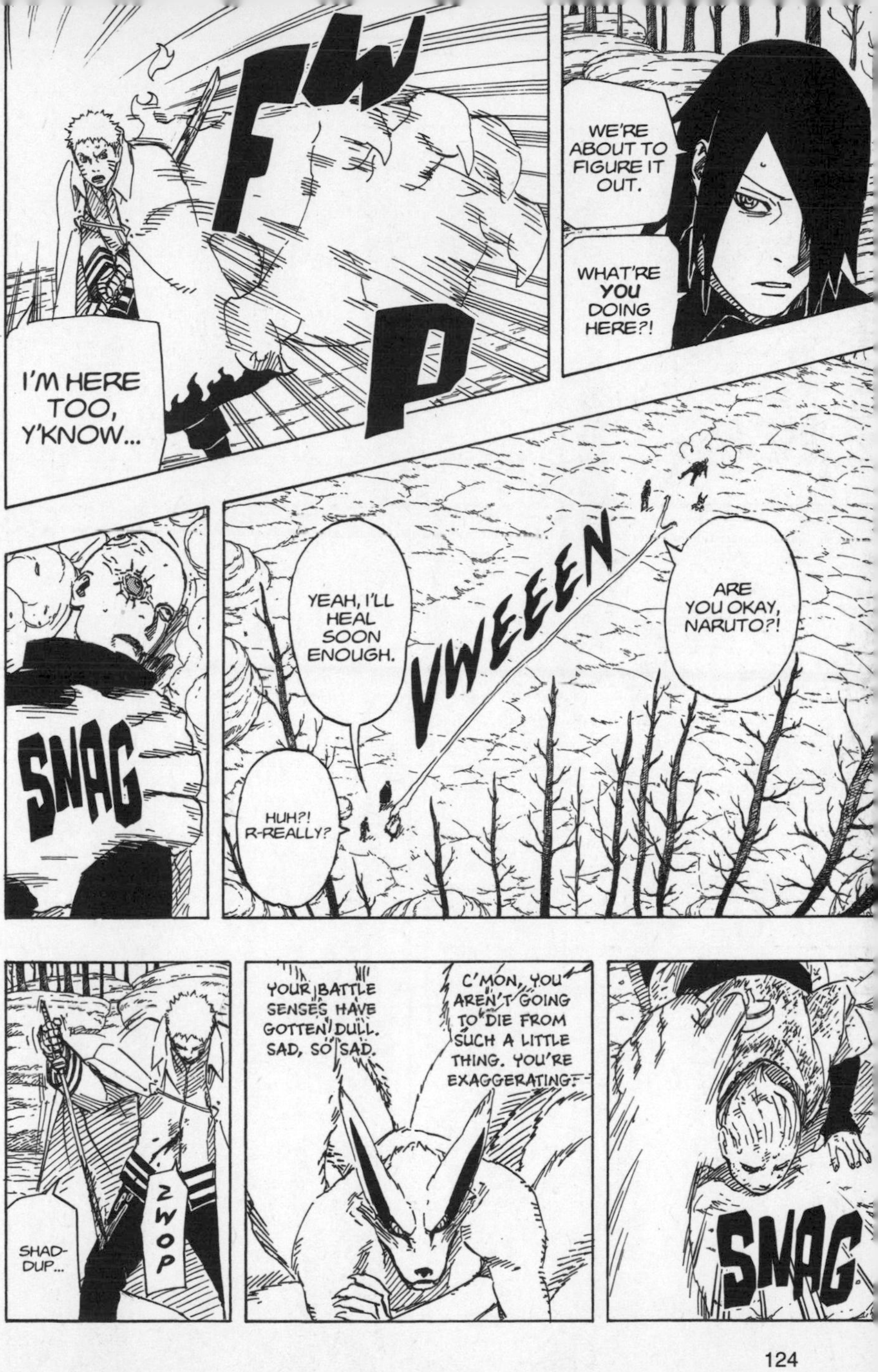

WE'RE ABOUT TO FIGURE IT OUT.
WHAT'RE YOU DOING HERE?!
FWP
I'M HERE TOO, Y'KNOW...
ARE YOU OKAY, NARUTO?!
YEAH, I'LL HEAL SOON ENOUGH.
VWEEEN
HUH?! R-REALLY?
SNAG
SNAG
C'MON, YOU AREN'T GOING TO DIE FROM SUCH A LITTLE THING. YOU'RE EXAGGERATING.
YOUR BATTLE SENSES HAVE GOTTEN DULL. SAD, SO SAD.
ZWOP
SHAD-DUP...

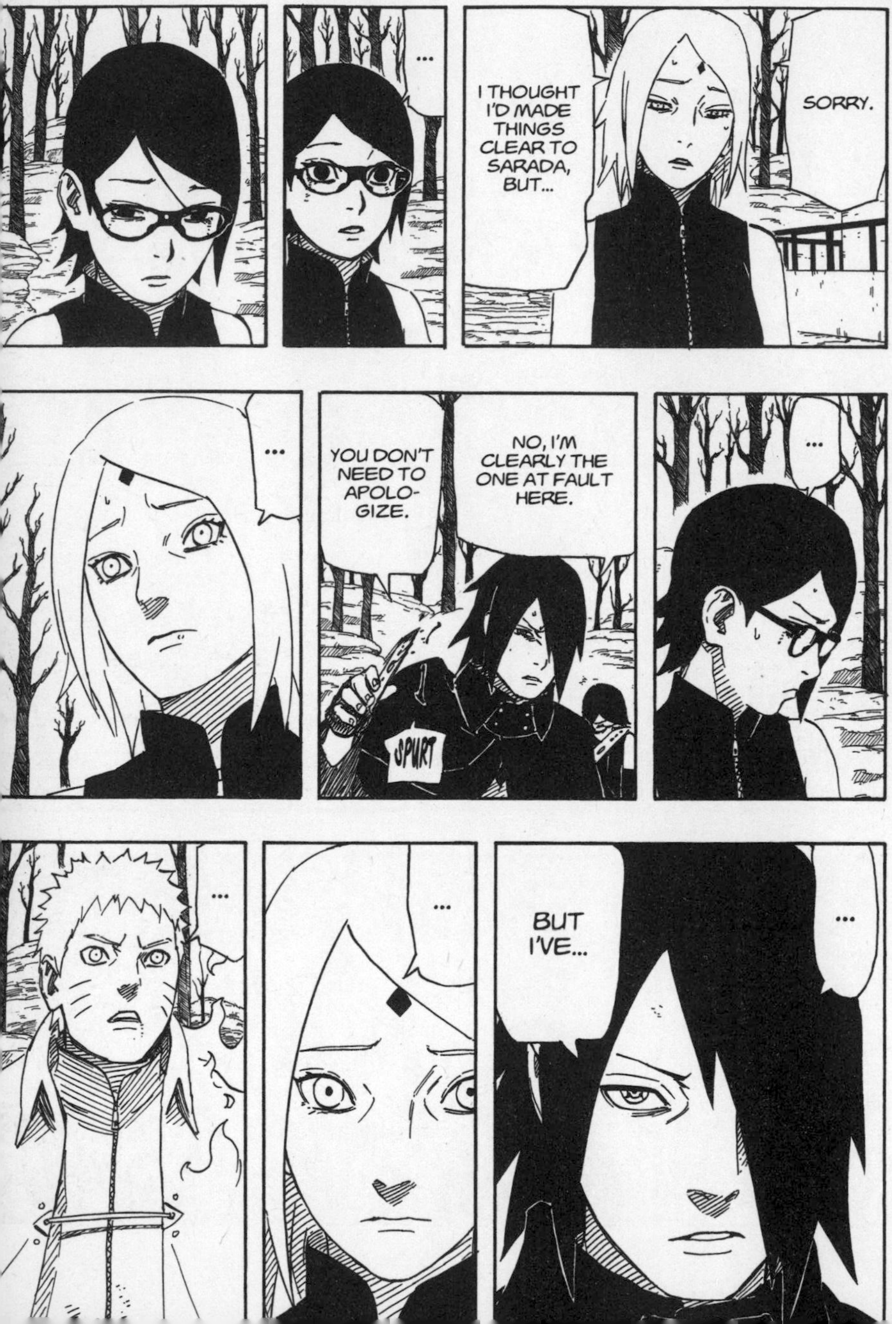
SORRY.
I THOUGHT I'D MADE THINGS CLEAR TO SARADA, BUT...
...
...
NO, I'M CLEARLY THE ONE AT FAULT HERE.
YOU DON'T NEED TO APOLO-GIZE.
SPURT
...
...
BUT I'VE...
...
...

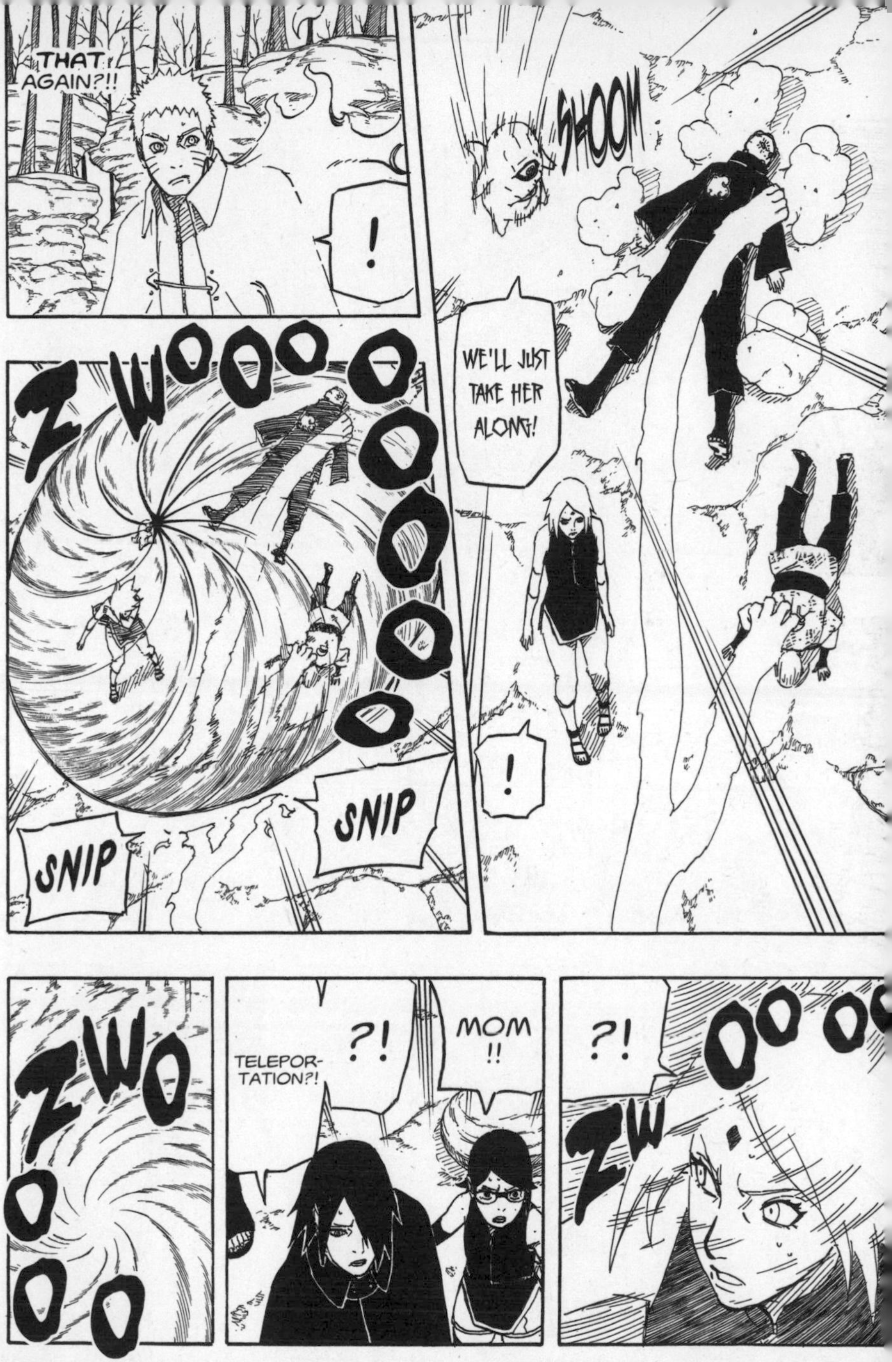
SHOOM
WE'LL JUST TAKE HER ALONG!
!
THAT AGAIN?!!
!
ZWOOOOOOOOOO
SNIP
SNIP
?!
OO OO
ZW
MOM !!
?!
TELEPORTATION?!
ZWO
OOO
OO

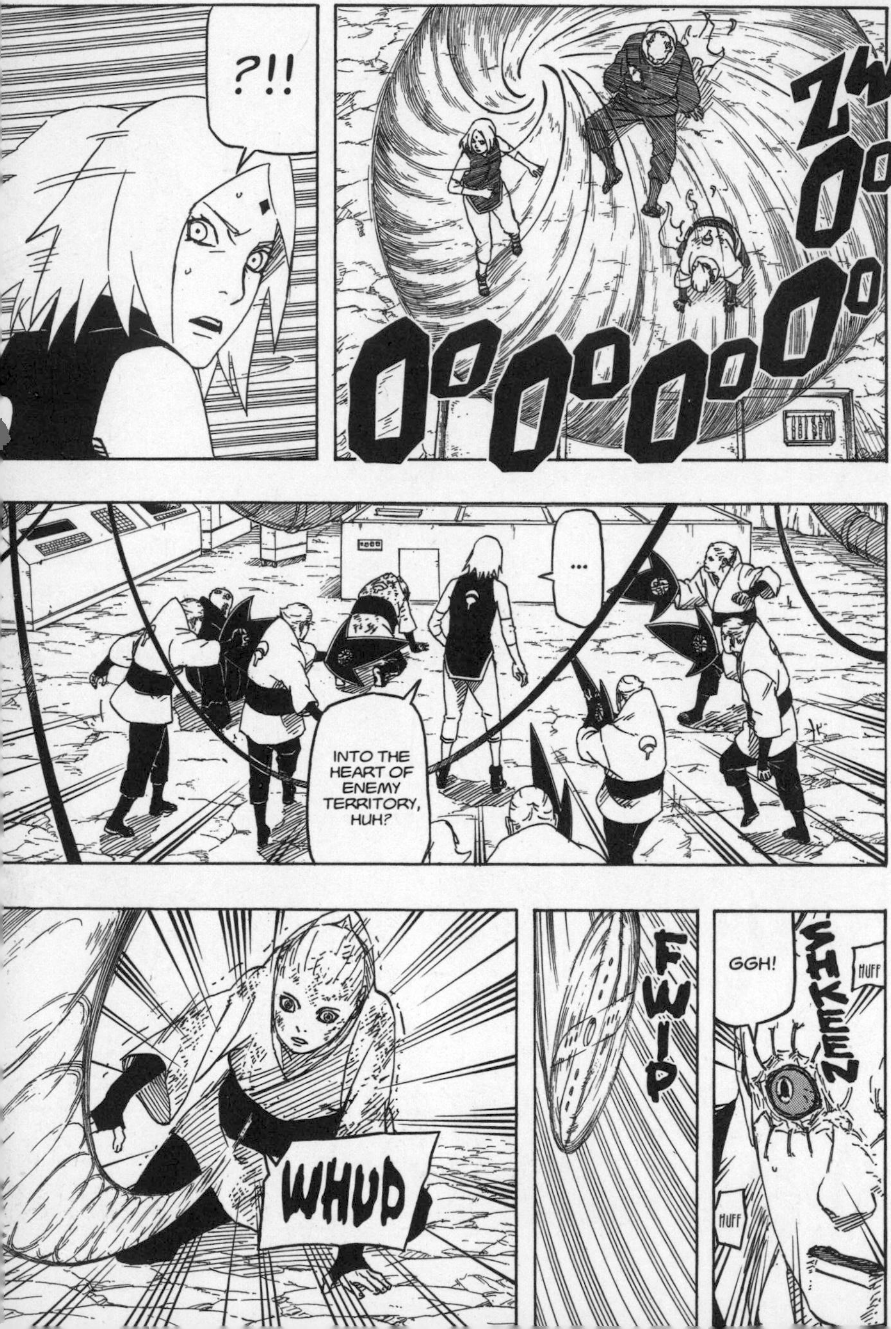
ZWOOOOOOOOOO
?!!
...
INTO THE HEART OF ENEMY TERRITORY, HUH?
SHKEEN
HUFF
GGH!
HUFF
FWIP
WHUD

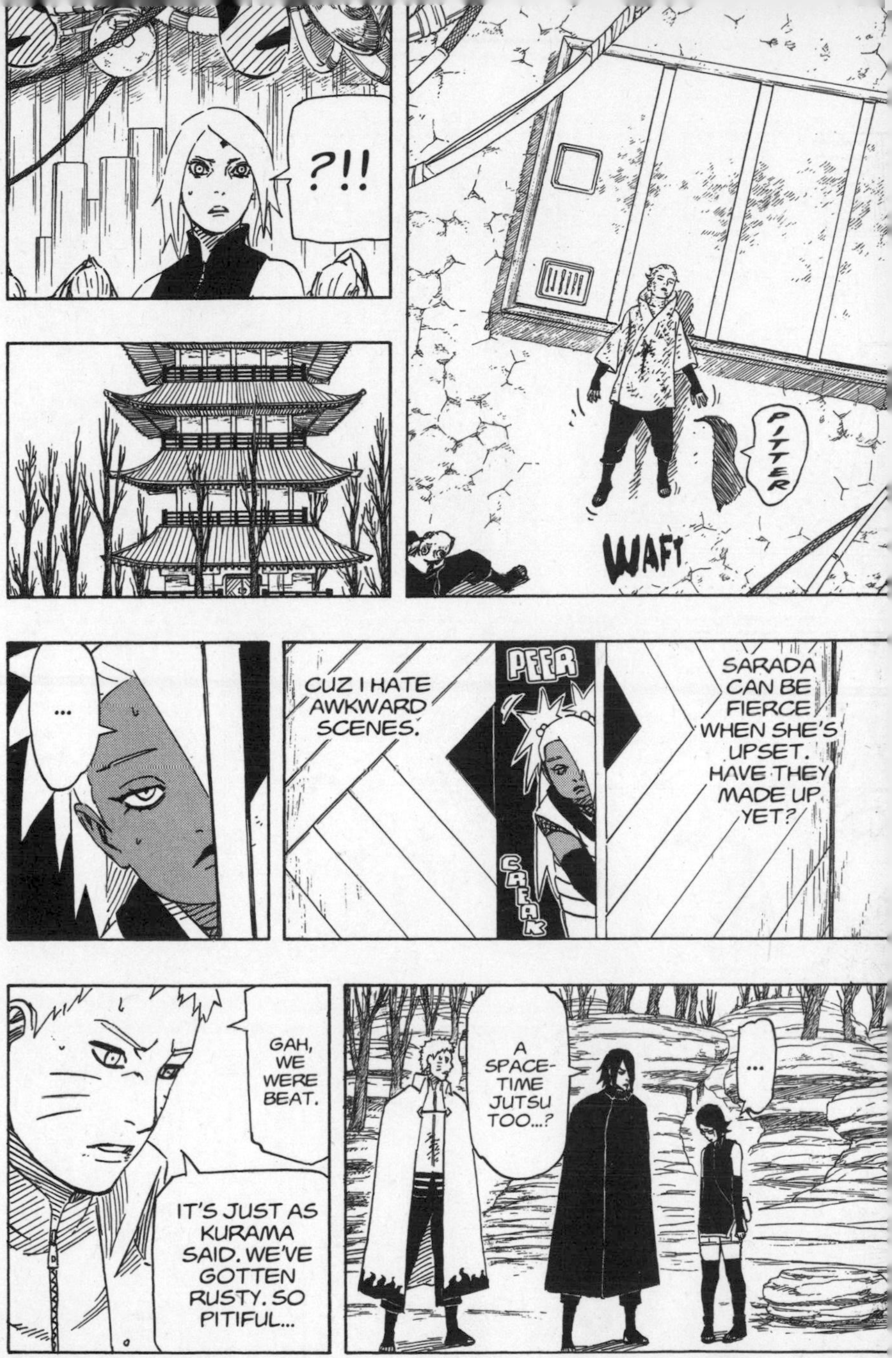
PITTER
WAFT
?!!
SARADA CAN BE FIERCE WHEN SHE'S UPSET. HAVE THEY MADE UP YET?
PEER
CREAK
CUZ I HATE AWKWARD SCENES.
...
...
A SPACE-TIME JUTSU TOO...?
GAH, WE WERE BEAT.
IT'S JUST AS KURAMA SAID. WE'VE GOTTEN RUSTY. SO PITIFUL...

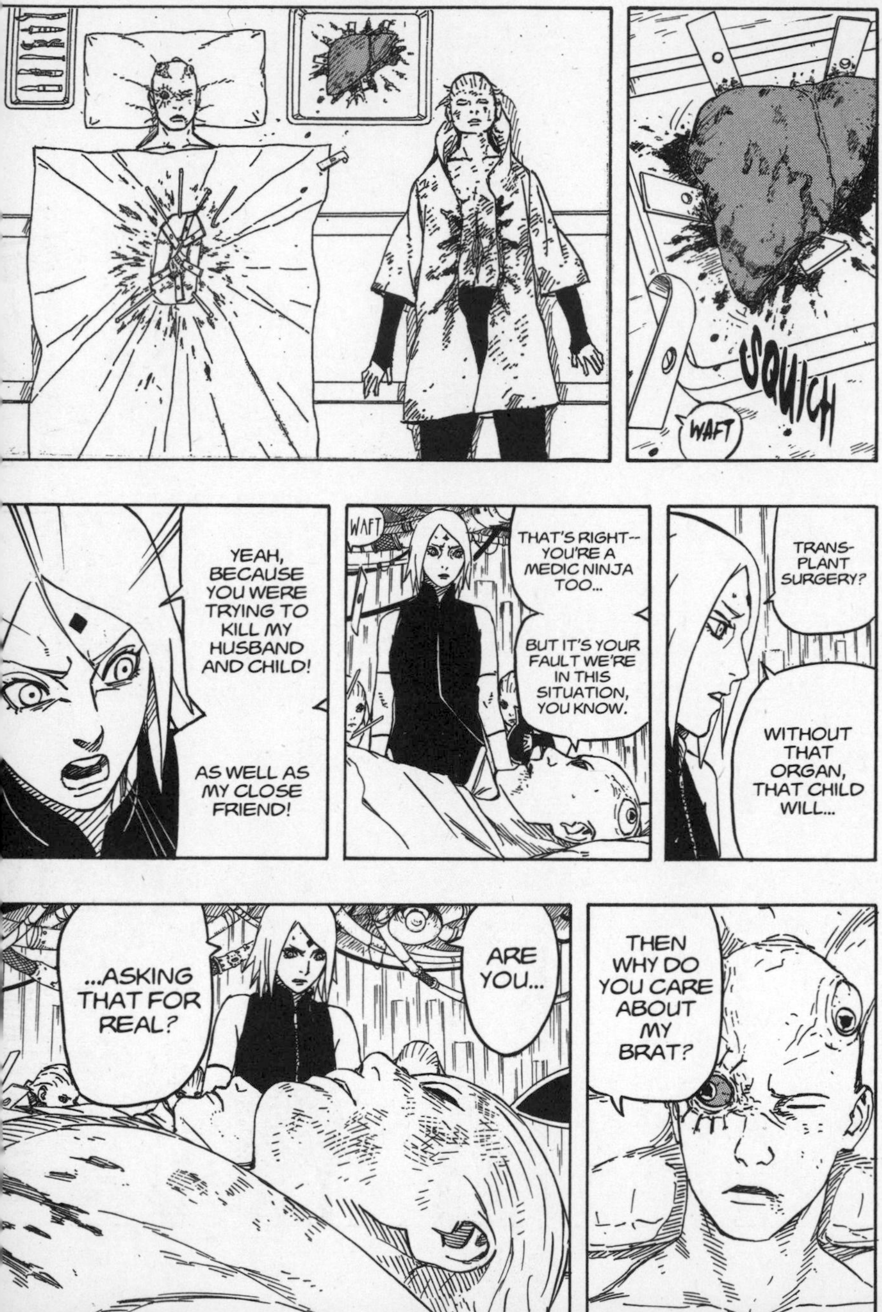
SQUICH
WAFT
TRANS-PLANT SURGERY?
WITHOUT THAT ORGAN, THAT CHILD WILL...
WAFT
THAT'S RIGHT-- YOU'RE A MEDIC NINJA TOO...
BUT IT'S YOUR FAULT WE'RE IN THIS SITUATION, YOU KNOW.
YEAH, BECAUSE YOU WERE TRYING TO KILL MY HUSBAND AND CHILD!
AS WELL AS MY CLOSE FRIEND!
THEN WHY DO YOU CARE ABOUT MY BRAT?
ARE YOU...
...ASKING THAT FOR REAL?

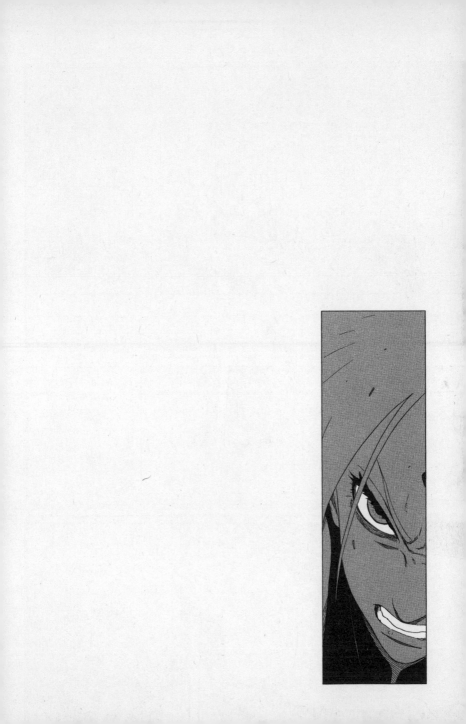

Number 700+7: Genetic Slaves

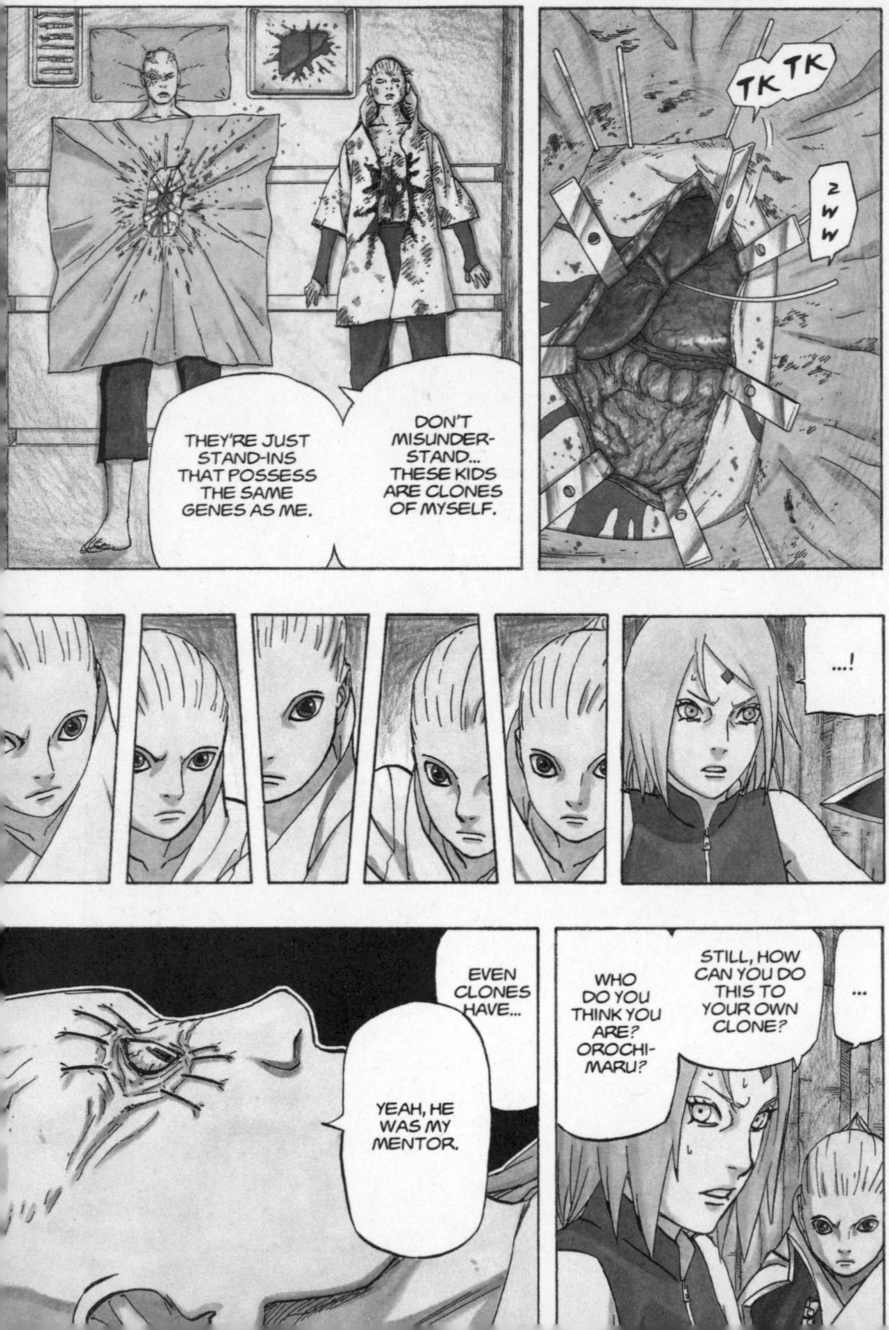
TK TK
ZWW
DON'T MISUNDERSTAND... THESE KIDS ARE CLONES OF MYSELF.
THEY'RE JUST STAND-INS THAT POSSESS THE SAME GENES AS ME.
...!
...
STILL, HOW CAN YOU DO THIS TO YOUR OWN CLONE?
WHO DO YOU THINK YOU ARE? OROCHIMARU?
EVEN CLONES HAVE...
YEAH, HE WAS MY MENTOR.

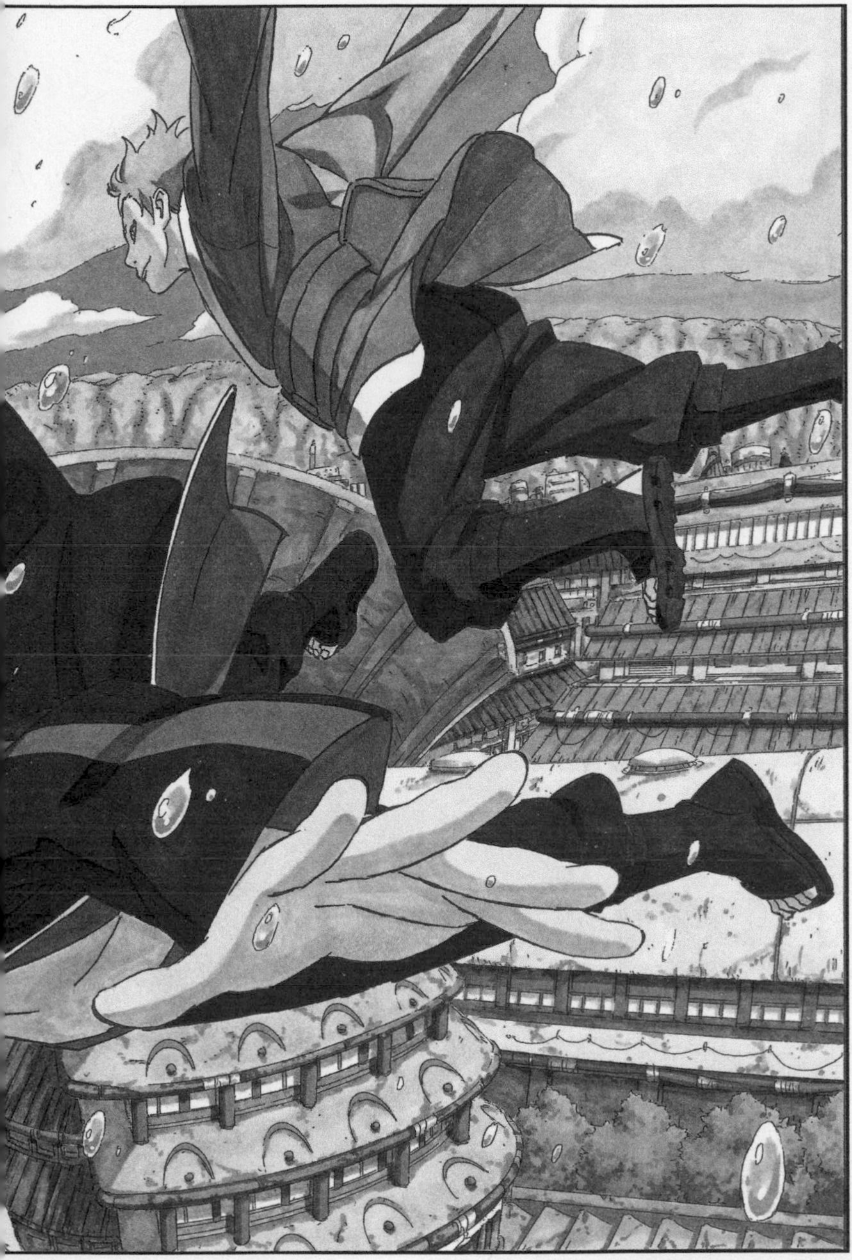

Number 700+7: Genetic Slaves

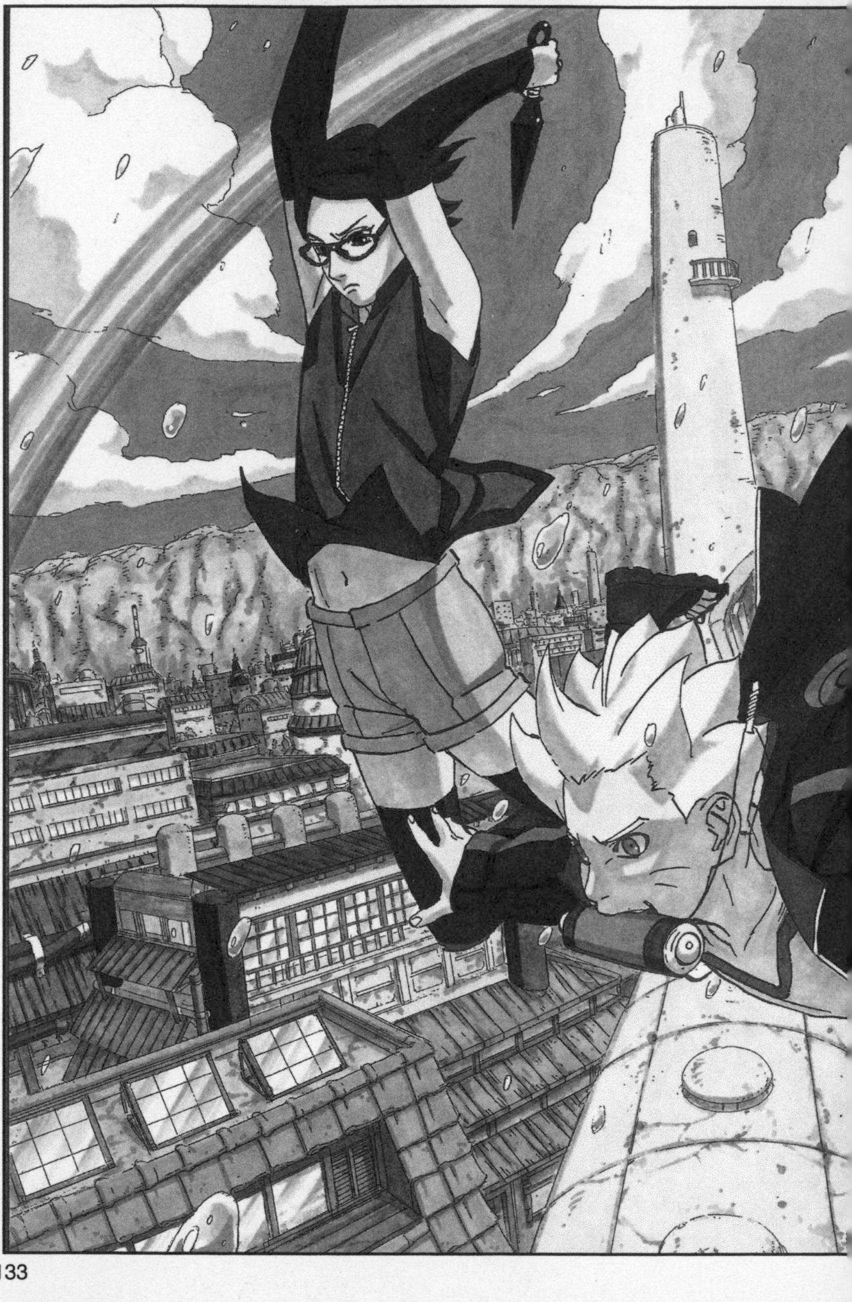

NARUTO
The Seventh Hokage and the Scarlet Spring

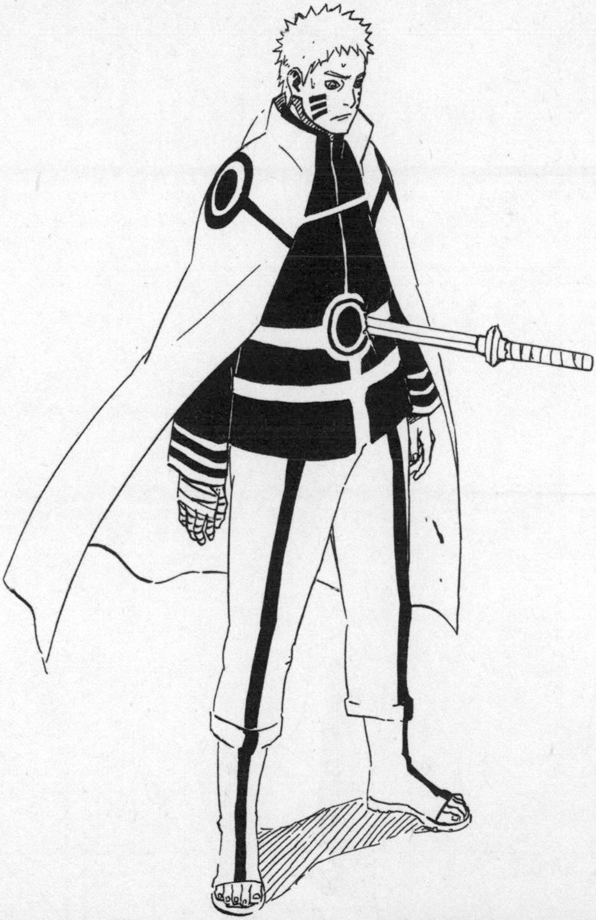

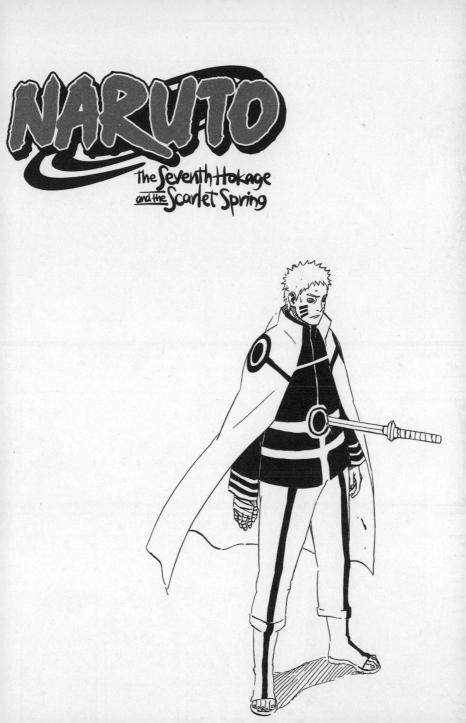

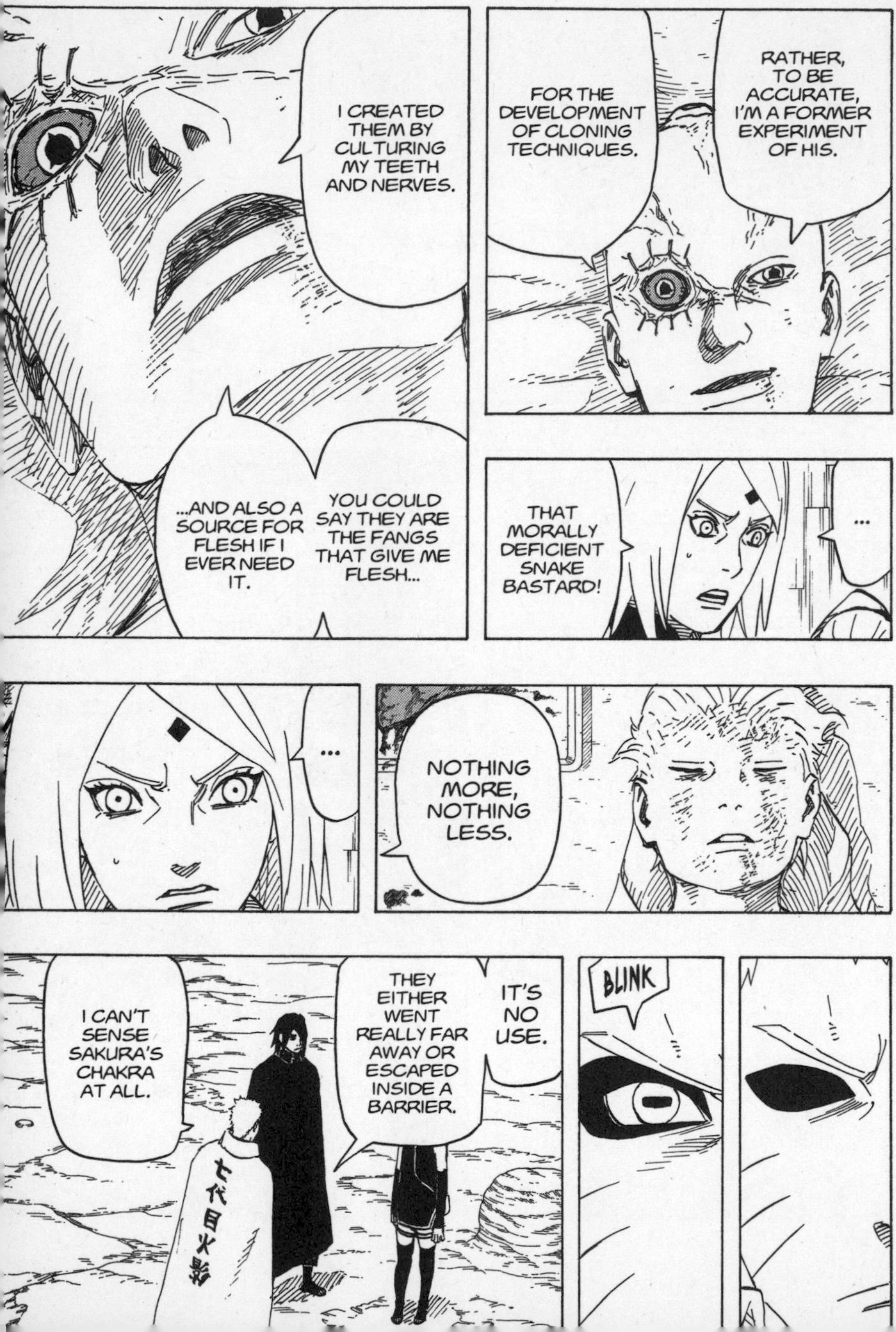
RATHER, TO BE ACCURATE, I'M A FORMER EXPERIMENT OF HIS.
FOR THE DEVELOPMENT OF CLONING TECHNIQUES.
...
THAT MORALLY DEFICIENT SNAKE BASTARD!
I CREATED THEM BY CULTURING MY TEETH AND NERVES.
YOU COULD SAY THEY ARE THE FANGS THAT GIVE ME FLESH...
...AND ALSO A SOURCE FOR FLESH IF I EVER NEED IT.
NOTHING MORE, NOTHING LESS.
...
BLINK
IT'S NO USE.
THEY EITHER WENT REALLY FAR AWAY OR ESCAPED INSIDE A BARRIER.
I CAN'T SENSE SAKURA'S CHAKRA AT ALL.
七代目火影

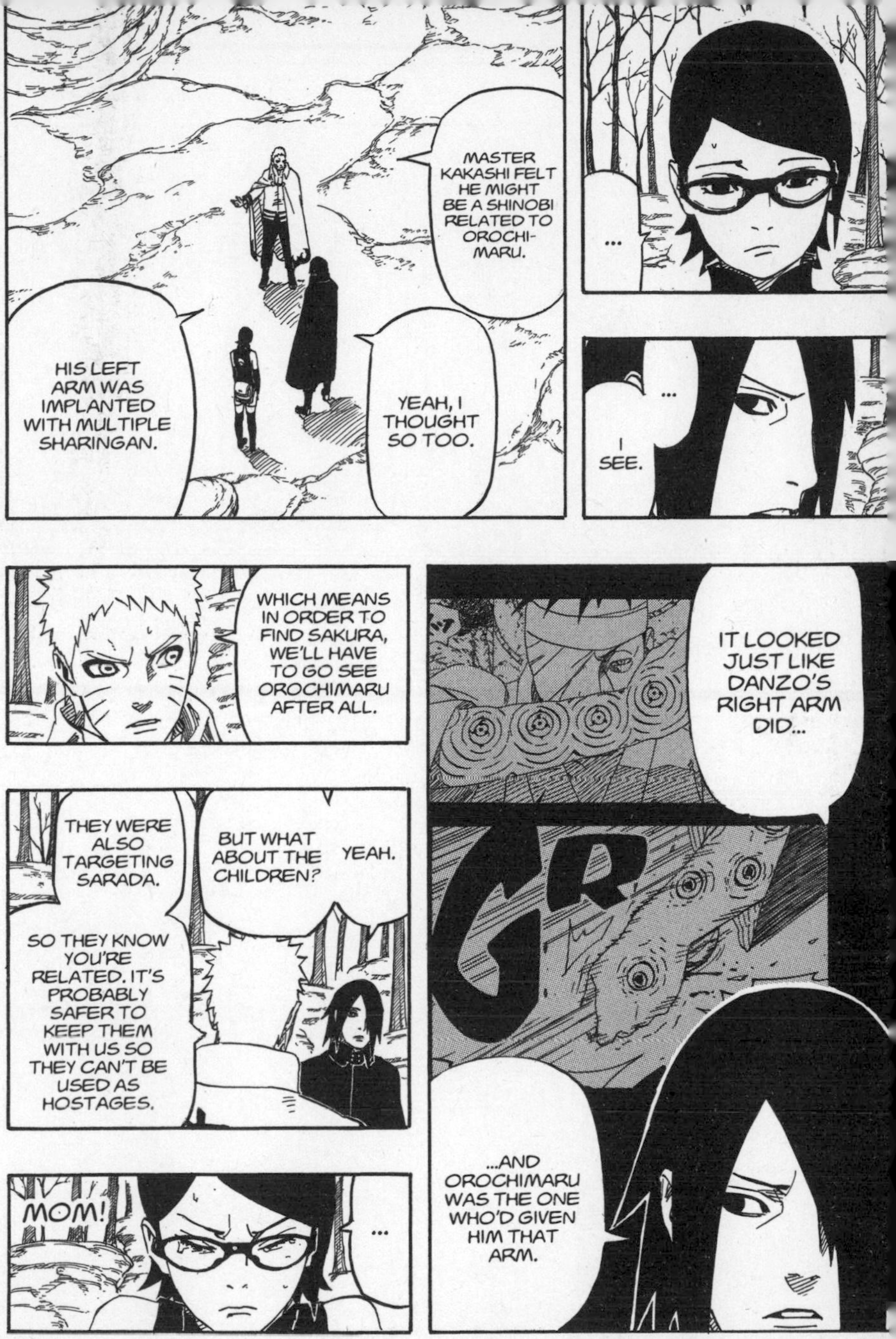
...
...
I SEE.
MASTER KAKASHI FELT HE MIGHT BE A SHINOBI RELATED TO OROCHI-MARU.
YEAH, I THOUGHT SO TOO.
HIS LEFT ARM WAS IMPLANTED WITH MULTIPLE SHARINGAN.
IT LOOKED JUST LIKE DANZO'S RIGHT ARM DID...
GR
...AND OROCHIMARU WAS THE ONE WHO'D GIVEN HIM THAT ARM.
WHICH MEANS IN ORDER TO FIND SAKURA, WE'LL HAVE TO GO SEE OROCHIMARU AFTER ALL.
YEAH.
BUT WHAT ABOUT THE CHILDREN?
THEY WERE ALSO TARGETING SARADA.
SO THEY KNOW YOU'RE RELATED. IT'S PROBABLY SAFER TO KEEP THEM WITH US SO THEY CAN'T BE USED AS HOSTAGES.
...
MOM!

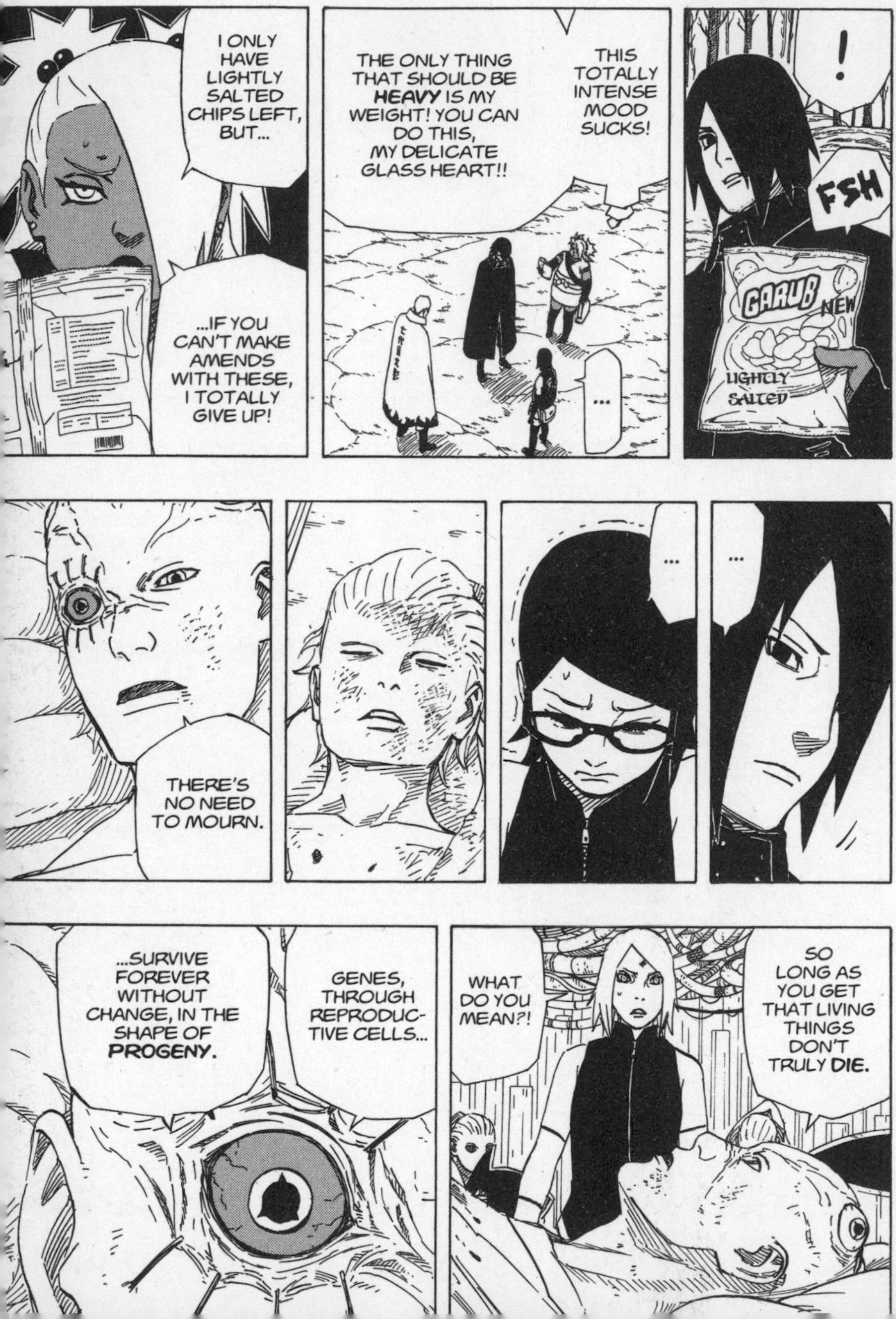
!
FSH
GARUB
NEW
LIGHTLY SALTED
THIS TOTALLY INTENSE MOOD SUCKS!
THE ONLY THING THAT SHOULD BE **HEAVY** IS MY WEIGHT! YOU CAN DO THIS, MY DELICATE GLASS HEART!!
...
I ONLY HAVE LIGHTLY SALTED CHIPS LEFT, BUT...
...IF YOU CAN'T MAKE AMENDS WITH THESE, I TOTALLY GIVE UP!
...
...
THERE'S NO NEED TO MOURN.
SO LONG AS YOU GET THAT LIVING THINGS DON'T TRULY **DIE.**
WHAT DO YOU MEAN?!
GENES, THROUGH REPRODUCTIVE CELLS...
...SURVIVE FOREVER WITHOUT CHANGE, IN THE SHAPE OF **PROGENY.**

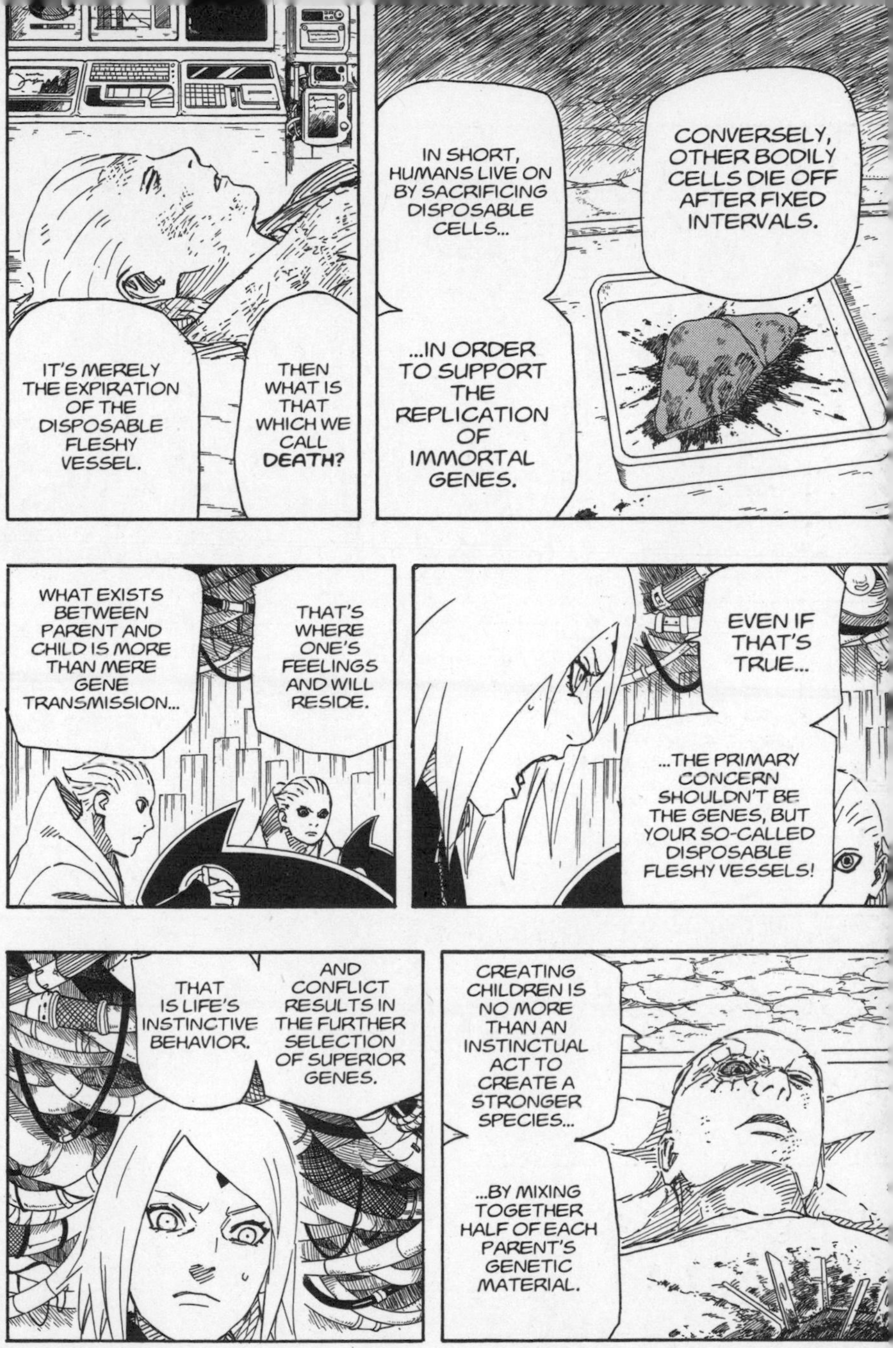
CONVERSELY, OTHER BODILY CELLS DIE OFF AFTER FIXED INTERVALS.
IN SHORT, HUMANS LIVE ON BY SACRIFICING DISPOSABLE CELLS...
...IN ORDER TO SUPPORT THE REPLICATION OF IMMORTAL GENES.
THEN WHAT IS THAT WHICH WE CALL DEATH?
IT'S MERELY THE EXPIRATION OF THE DISPOSABLE FLESHY VESSEL.
EVEN IF THAT'S TRUE...
...THE PRIMARY CONCERN SHOULDN'T BE THE GENES, BUT YOUR SO-CALLED DISPOSABLE FLESHY VESSELS!
THAT'S WHERE ONE'S FEELINGS AND WILL RESIDE.
WHAT EXISTS BETWEEN PARENT AND CHILD IS MORE THAN MERE GENE TRANSMISSION...
CREATING CHILDREN IS NO MORE THAN AN INSTINCTUAL ACT TO CREATE A STRONGER SPECIES...
...BY MIXING TOGETHER HALF OF EACH PARENT'S GENETIC MATERIAL.
AND CONFLICT RESULTS IN THE FURTHER SELECTION OF SUPERIOR GENES.
THAT IS LIFE'S INSTINCTIVE BEHAVIOR.

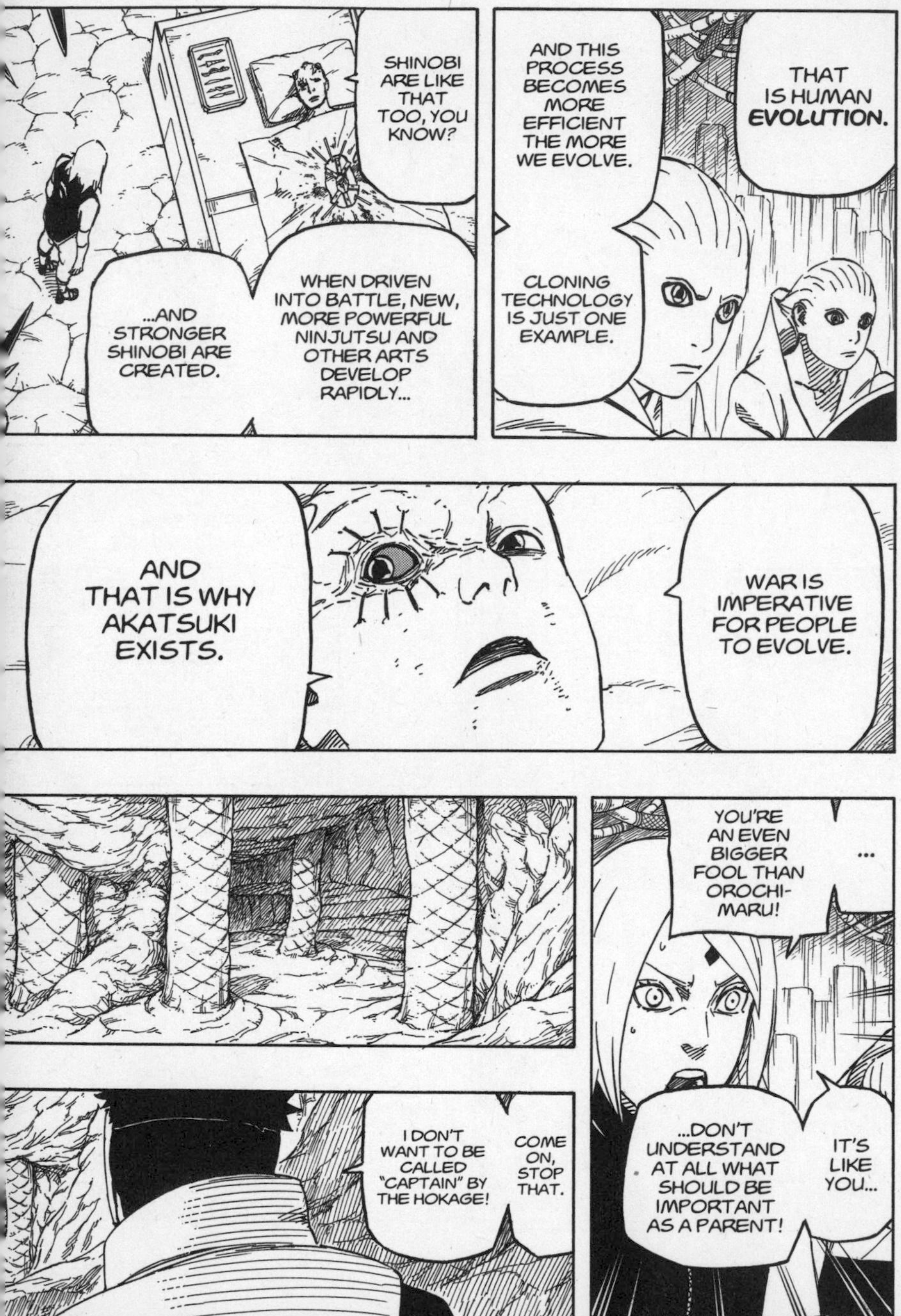
THAT IS HUMAN **EVOLUTION.**
AND THIS PROCESS BECOMES MORE EFFICIENT THE MORE WE EVOLVE.
CLONING TECHNOLOGY IS JUST ONE EXAMPLE.
SHINOBI ARE LIKE THAT TOO, YOU KNOW?
WHEN DRIVEN INTO BATTLE, NEW, MORE POWERFUL NINJUTSU AND OTHER ARTS DEVELOP RAPIDLY...
...AND STRONGER SHINOBI ARE CREATED.
WAR IS IMPERATIVE FOR PEOPLE TO EVOLVE.
AND THAT IS WHY AKATSUKI EXISTS.
...
YOU'RE AN EVEN BIGGER FOOL THAN OROCHI-MARU!
IT'S LIKE YOU...
...DON'T UNDERSTAND AT ALL WHAT SHOULD BE IMPORTANT AS A PARENT!
COME ON, STOP THAT.
I DON'T WANT TO BE CALLED "CAPTAIN" BY THE HOKAGE!

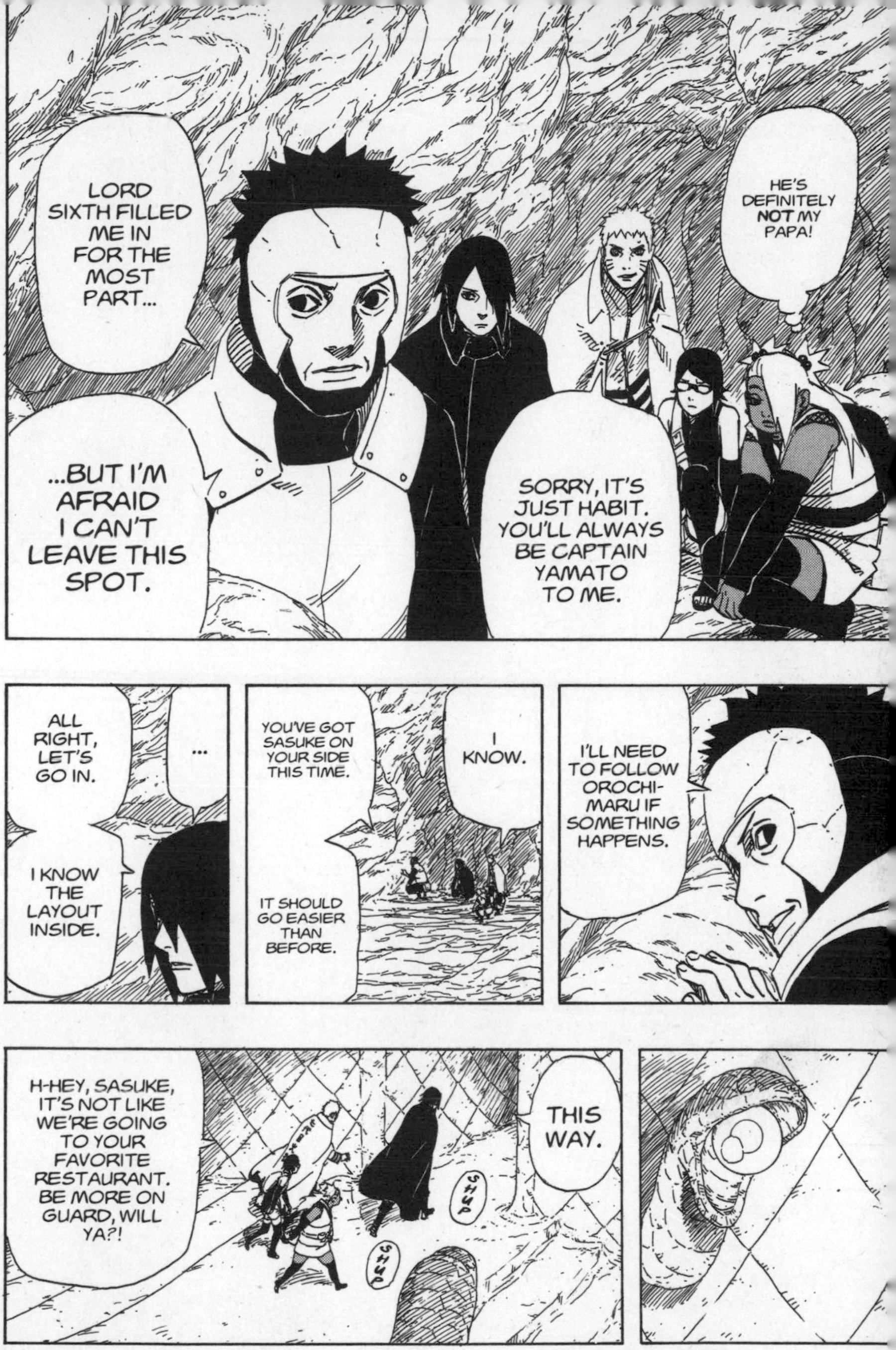
HE'S DEFINITELY **NOT** MY PAPA!
SORRY, IT'S JUST HABIT. YOU'LL ALWAYS BE CAPTAIN YAMATO TO ME.
LORD SIXTH FILLED ME IN FOR THE MOST PART...
...BUT I'M AFRAID I CAN'T LEAVE THIS SPOT.
I'LL NEED TO FOLLOW OROCHI-MARU IF SOMETHING HAPPENS.
I KNOW.
YOU'VE GOT SASUKE ON YOUR SIDE THIS TIME.
IT SHOULD GO EASIER THAN BEFORE.
...
ALL RIGHT, LET'S GO IN.
I KNOW THE LAYOUT INSIDE.
THIS WAY.
SHUP
SHUP
H-HEY, SASUKE, IT'S NOT LIKE WE'RE GOING TO YOUR FAVORITE RESTAURANT. BE MORE ON GUARD, WILL YA?!

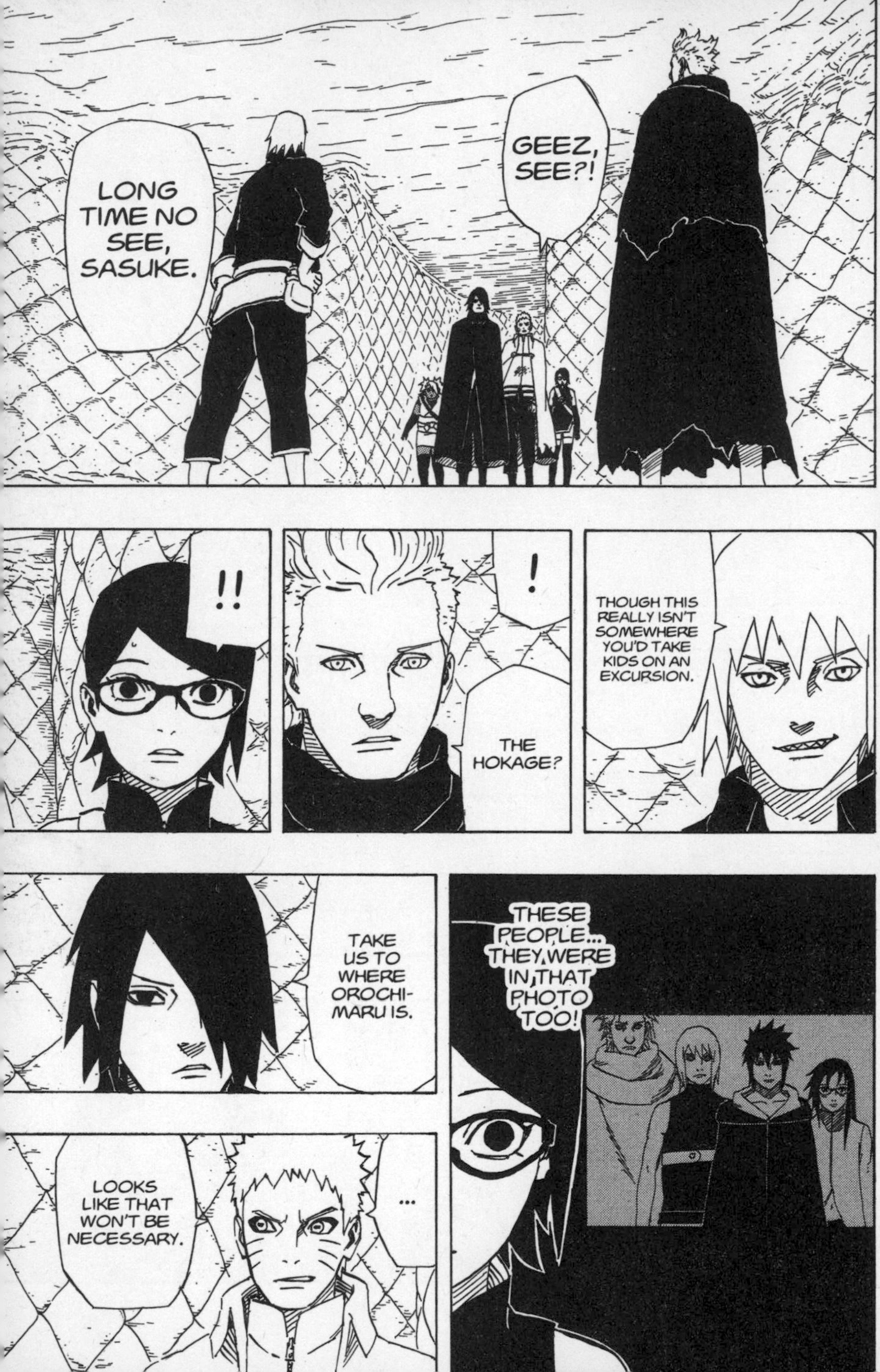
GEEZ, SEE?!
LONG TIME NO SEE, SASUKE.
THOUGH THIS REALLY ISN'T SOMEWHERE YOU'D TAKE KIDS ON AN EXCURSION.
!
THE HOKAGE?
!!
THESE PEOPLE... THEY WERE IN THAT PHOTO TOO!
TAKE US TO WHERE OROCHI-MARU IS.
...
LOOKS LIKE THAT WON'T BE NECESSARY.

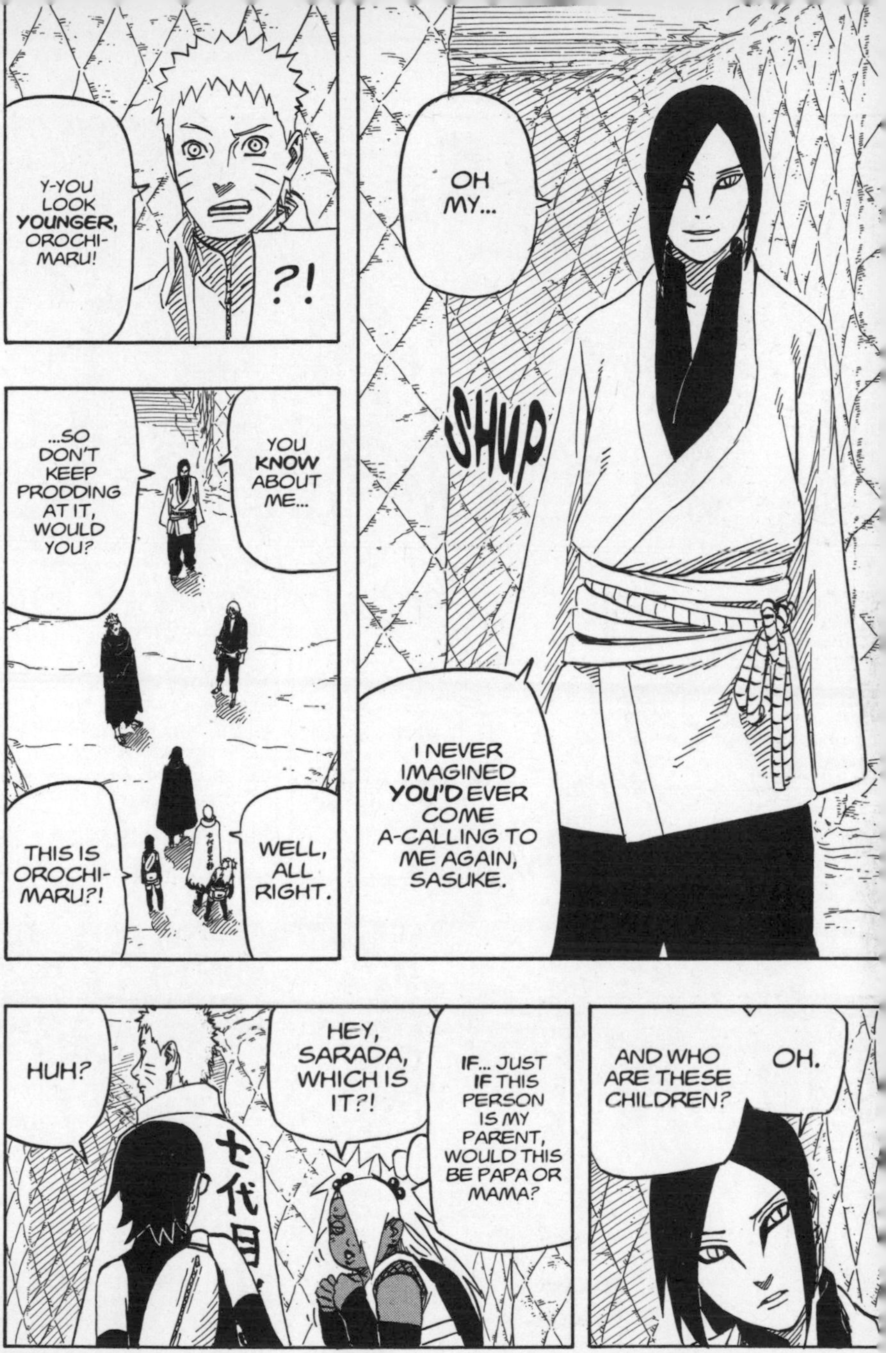
OH MY...
SHUP
I NEVER IMAGINED YOU'D EVER COME A-CALLING TO ME AGAIN, SASUKE.
Y-YOU LOOK YOUNGER, OROCHI-MARU!
?!
YOU KNOW ABOUT ME...
...SO DON'T KEEP PRODDING AT IT, WOULD YOU?
WELL, ALL RIGHT.
THIS IS OROCHI-MARU?!
OH.
AND WHO ARE THESE CHILDREN?
IF... JUST IF THIS PERSON IS MY PARENT, WOULD THIS BE PAPA OR MAMA?
HEY, SARADA, WHICH IS IT?!
HUH?
七代目

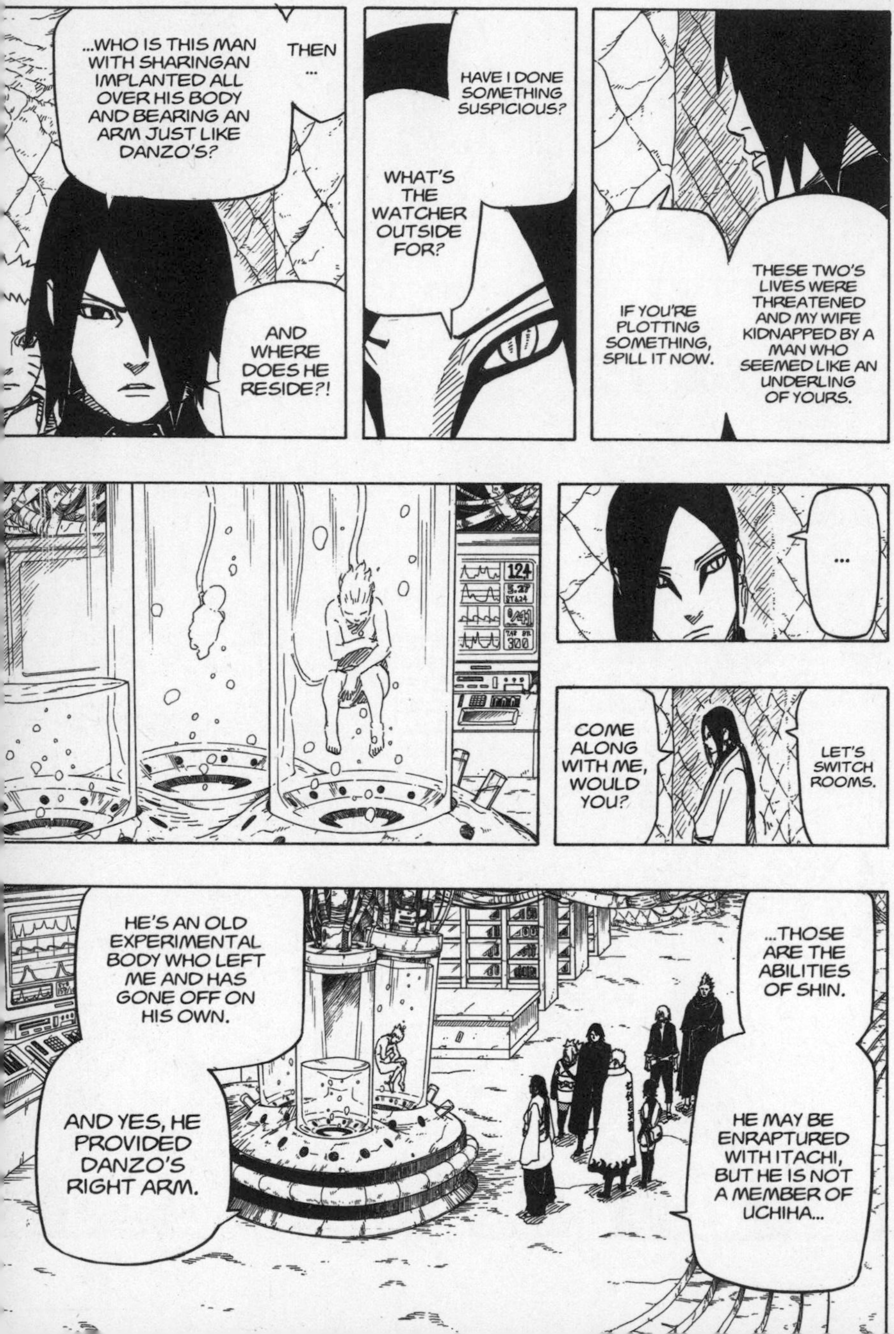
THESE TWO'S LIVES WERE THREATENED AND MY WIFE KIDNAPPED BY A MAN WHO SEEMED LIKE AN UNDERLING OF YOURS.
IF YOU'RE PLOTTING SOMETHING, SPILL IT NOW.
HAVE I DONE SOMETHING SUSPICIOUS?
WHAT'S THE WATCHER OUTSIDE FOR?
THEN ...
...WHO IS THIS MAN WITH SHARINGAN IMPLANTED ALL OVER HIS BODY AND BEARING AN ARM JUST LIKE DANZO'S?
AND WHERE DOES HE RESIDE?!
...
LET'S SWITCH ROOMS.
COME ALONG WITH ME, WOULD YOU?
...THOSE ARE THE ABILITIES OF SHIN.
HE MAY BE ENRAPTURED WITH ITACHI, BUT HE IS NOT A MEMBER OF UCHIHA...
HE'S AN OLD EXPERIMENTAL BODY WHO LEFT ME AND HAS GONE OFF ON HIS OWN.
AND YES, HE PROVIDED DANZO'S RIGHT ARM.

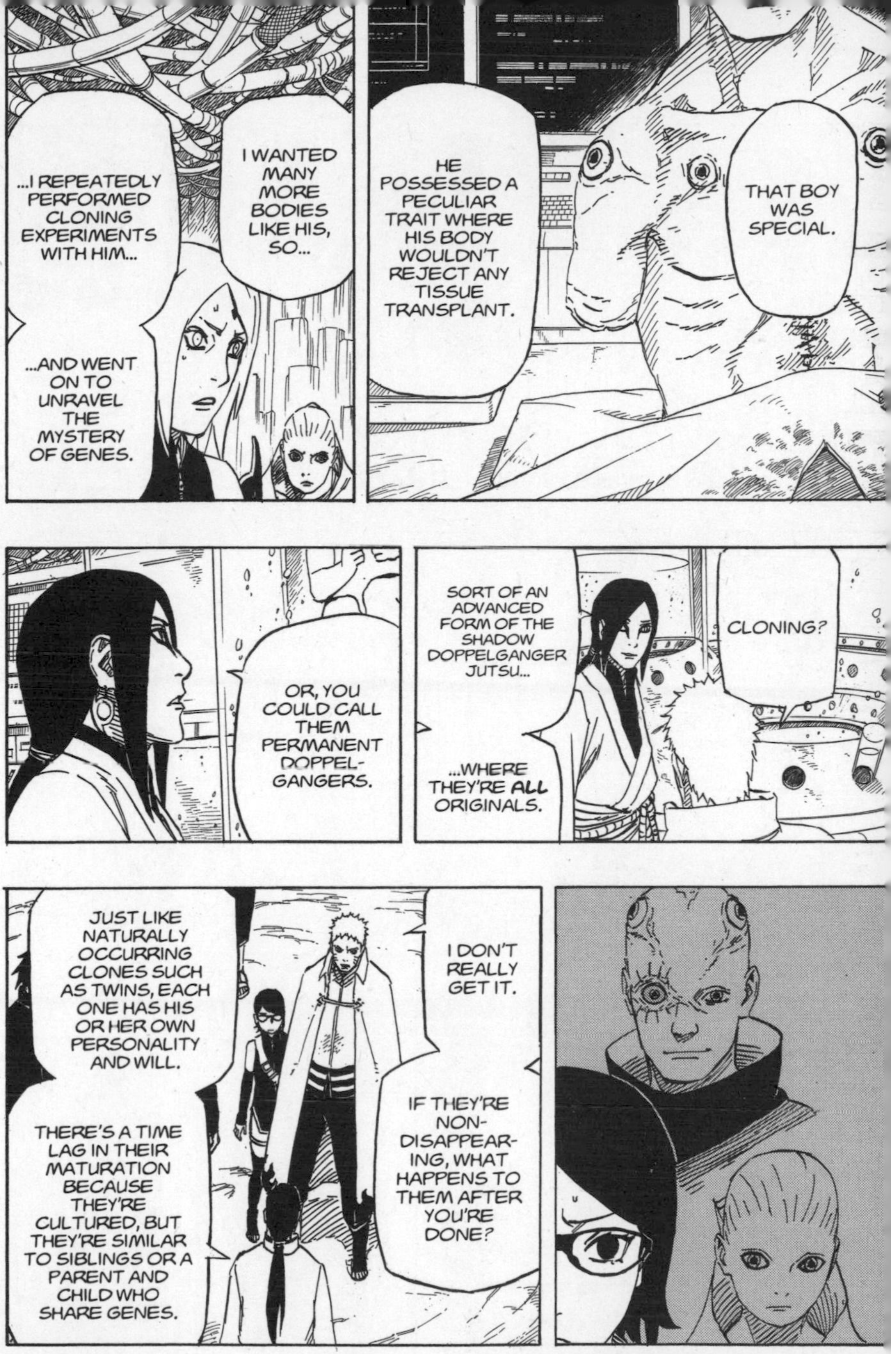
THAT BOY WAS SPECIAL.
HE POSSESSED A PECULIAR TRAIT WHERE HIS BODY WOULDN'T REJECT ANY TISSUE TRANSPLANT.
I WANTED MANY MORE BODIES LIKE HIS, SO...
...I REPEATEDLY PERFORMED CLONING EXPERIMENTS WITH HIM...
...AND WENT ON TO UNRAVEL THE MYSTERY OF GENES.
CLONING?
SORT OF AN ADVANCED FORM OF THE SHADOW DOPPELGANGER JUTSU...
...WHERE THEY'RE **ALL** ORIGINALS.
OR, YOU COULD CALL THEM PERMANENT DOPPEL-GANGERS.
I DON'T REALLY GET IT.
IF THEY'RE NON-DISAPPEAR-ING, WHAT HAPPENS TO THEM AFTER YOU'RE DONE?
JUST LIKE NATURALLY OCCURRING CLONES SUCH AS TWINS, EACH ONE HAS HIS OR HER OWN PERSONALITY AND WILL.
THERE'S A TIME LAG IN THEIR MATURATION BECAUSE THEY'RE CULTURED, BUT THEY'RE SIMILAR TO SIBLINGS OR A PARENT AND CHILD WHO SHARE GENES.

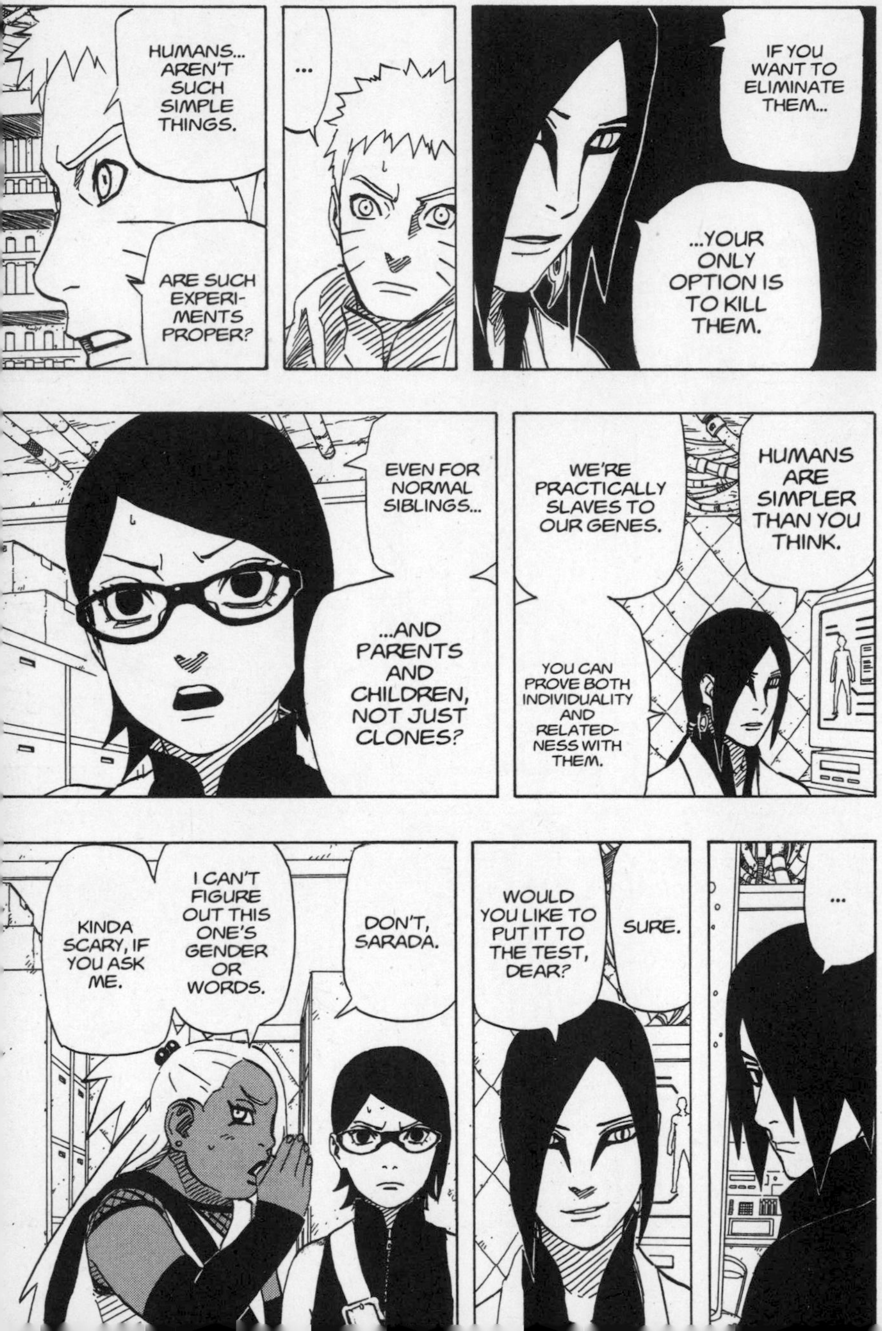
IF YOU WANT TO ELIMINATE THEM...
...YOUR ONLY OPTION IS TO KILL THEM.
...
HUMANS... AREN'T SUCH SIMPLE THINGS.
ARE SUCH EXPERIMENTS PROPER?
HUMANS ARE SIMPLER THAN YOU THINK.
WE'RE PRACTICALLY SLAVES TO OUR GENES.
YOU CAN PROVE BOTH INDIVIDUALITY AND RELATEDNESS WITH THEM.
EVEN FOR NORMAL SIBLINGS...
...AND PARENTS AND CHILDREN, NOT JUST CLONES?
...
WOULD YOU LIKE TO PUT IT TO THE TEST, DEAR?
SURE.
DON'T, SARADA.
I CAN'T FIGURE OUT THIS ONE'S GENDER OR WORDS.
KINDA SCARY, IF YOU ASK ME.

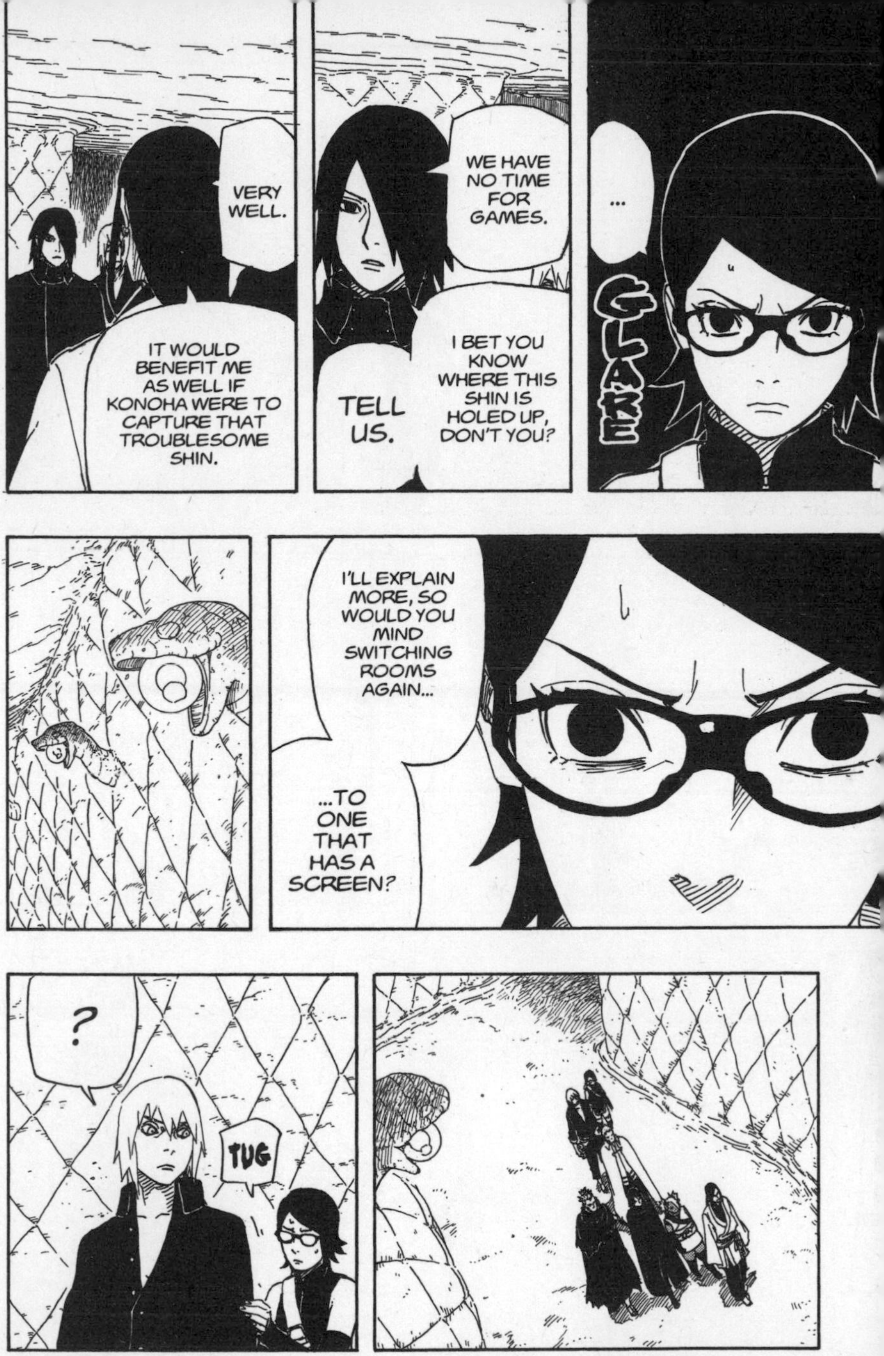
...
GLARE
WE HAVE NO TIME FOR GAMES.
I BET YOU KNOW WHERE THIS SHIN IS HOLED UP, DON'T YOU?
TELL US.
VERY WELL.
IT WOULD BENEFIT ME AS WELL IF KONOHA WERE TO CAPTURE THAT TROUBLESOME SHIN.
I'LL EXPLAIN MORE, SO WOULD YOU MIND SWITCHING ROOMS AGAIN...
...TO ONE THAT HAS A SCREEN?
?
TUG

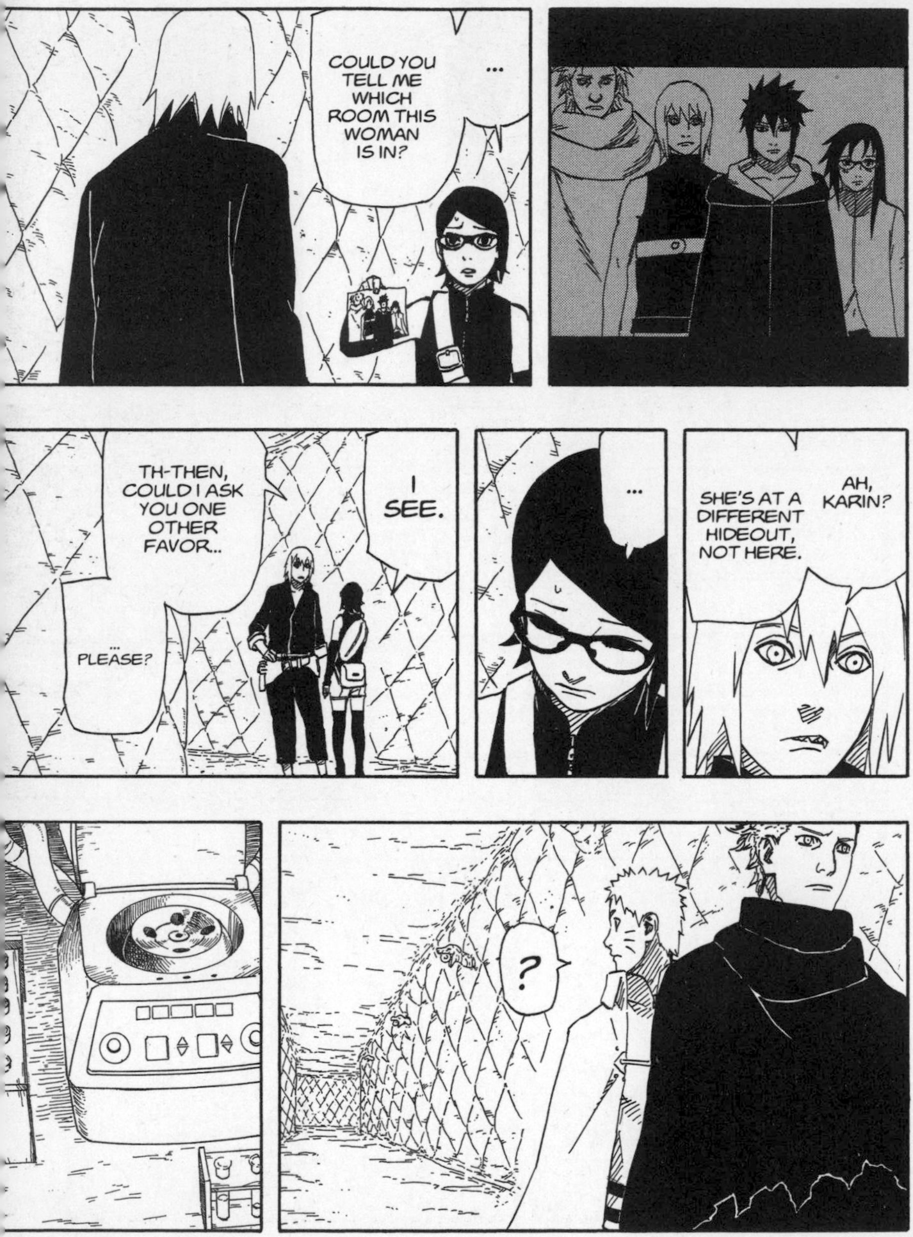
...
COULD YOU TELL ME WHICH ROOM THIS WOMAN IS IN?
AH, KARIN?
SHE'S AT A DIFFERENT HIDEOUT, NOT HERE.
...
I SEE.
TH-THEN, COULD I ASK YOU ONE OTHER FAVOR...
... PLEASE?
?

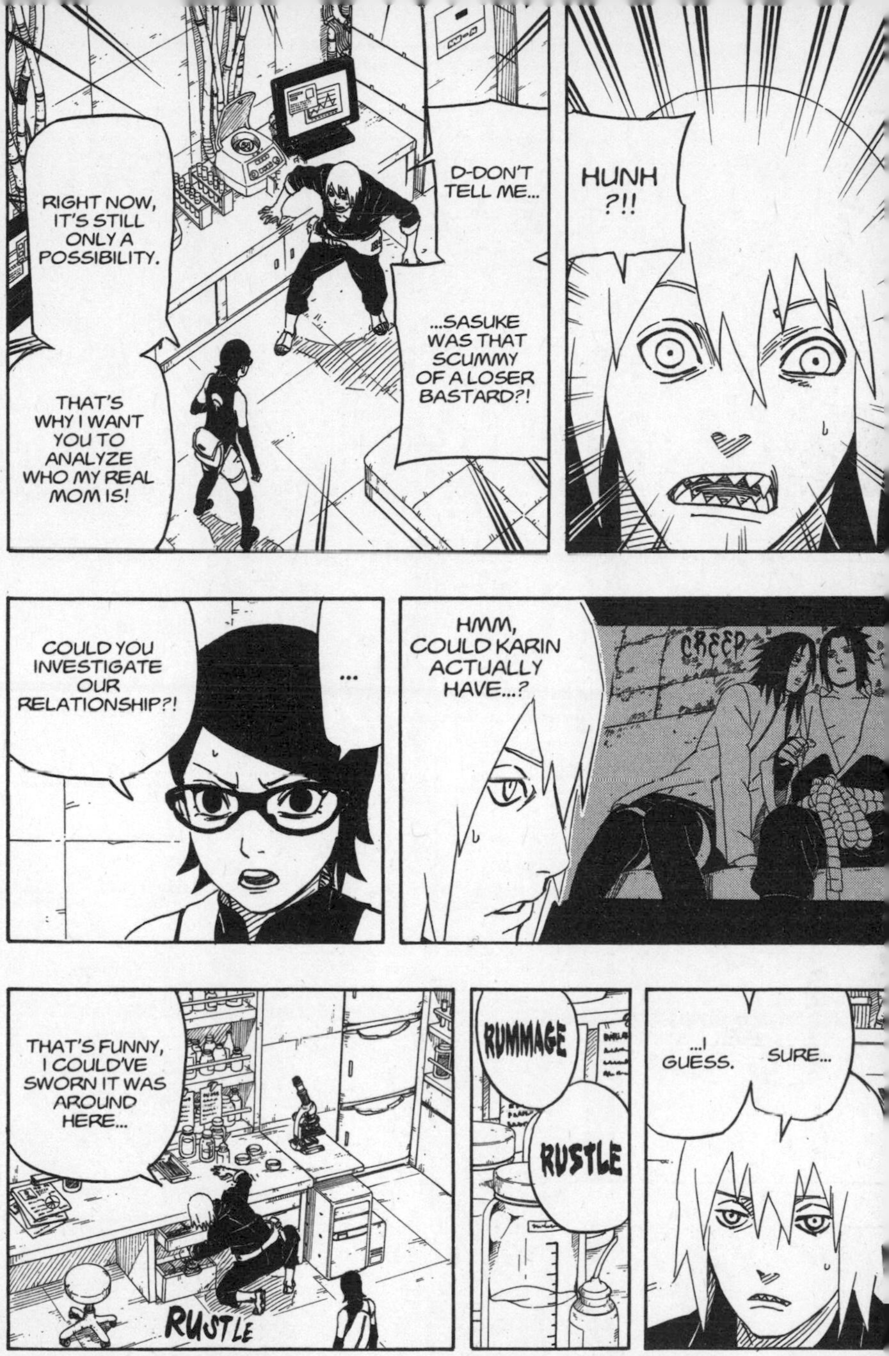
HUNH ?!!
D-DON'T TELL ME...
...SASUKE WAS THAT SCUMMY OF A LOSER BASTARD?!
RIGHT NOW, IT'S STILL ONLY A POSSIBILITY.
THAT'S WHY I WANT YOU TO ANALYZE WHO MY REAL MOM IS!
HMM, COULD KARIN ACTUALLY HAVE...?
CREEP
...
COULD YOU INVESTIGATE OUR RELATIONSHIP?!
SURE...
...I GUESS.
RUMMAGE
RUSTLE
THAT'S FUNNY, I COULD'VE SWORN IT WAS AROUND HERE...
RUSTLE

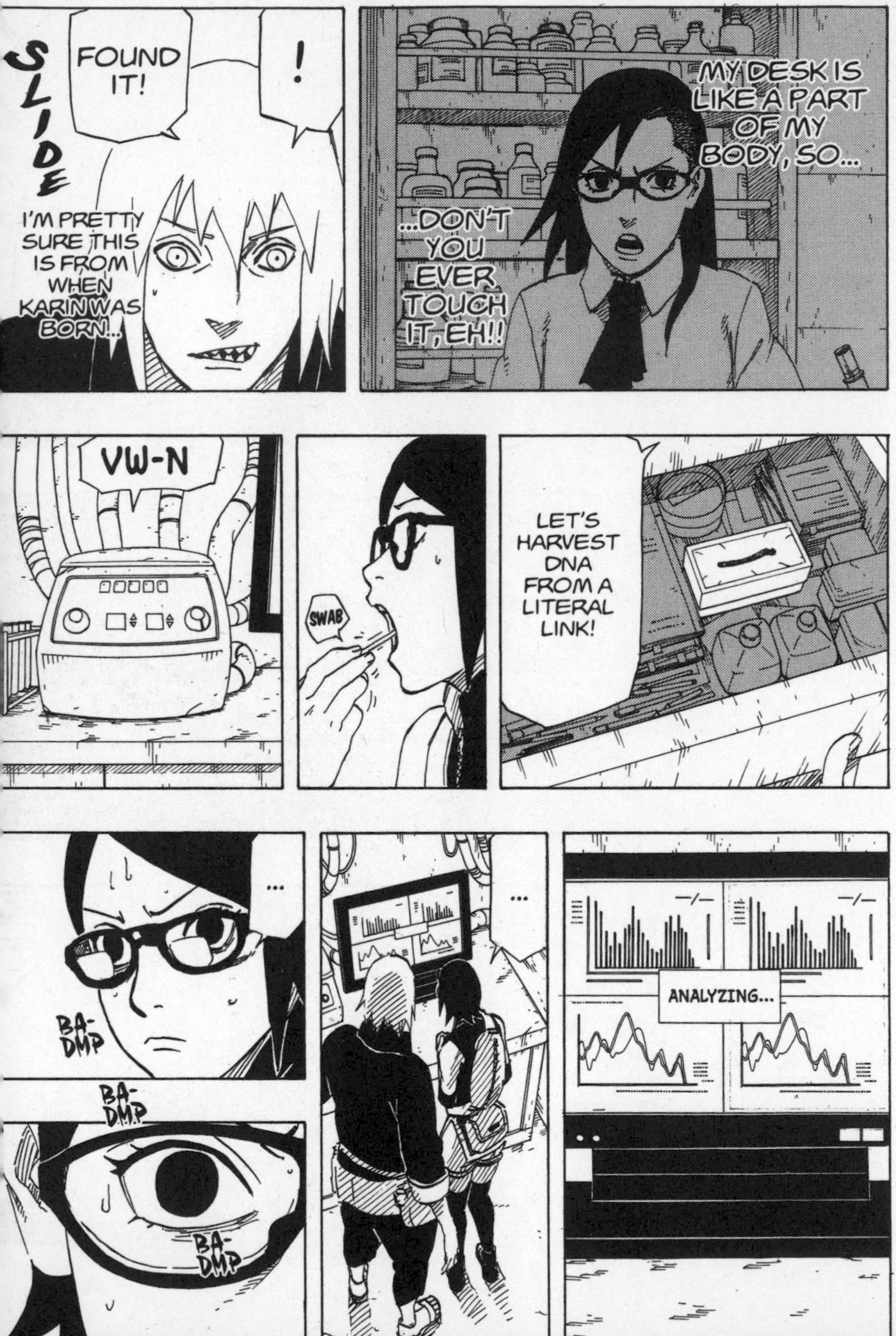

MY DESK IS LIKE A PART OF MY BODY, SO...
...DON'T YOU EVER TOUCH IT, EH!!
!
FOUND IT!
SLIDE
I'M PRETTY SURE THIS IS FROM WHEN KARIN WAS BORN...
LET'S HARVEST DNA FROM A LITERAL LINK!
SWAB
VW-N
ANALYZING...
...
...
BA-DMP
BA-DMP
BA-DMP

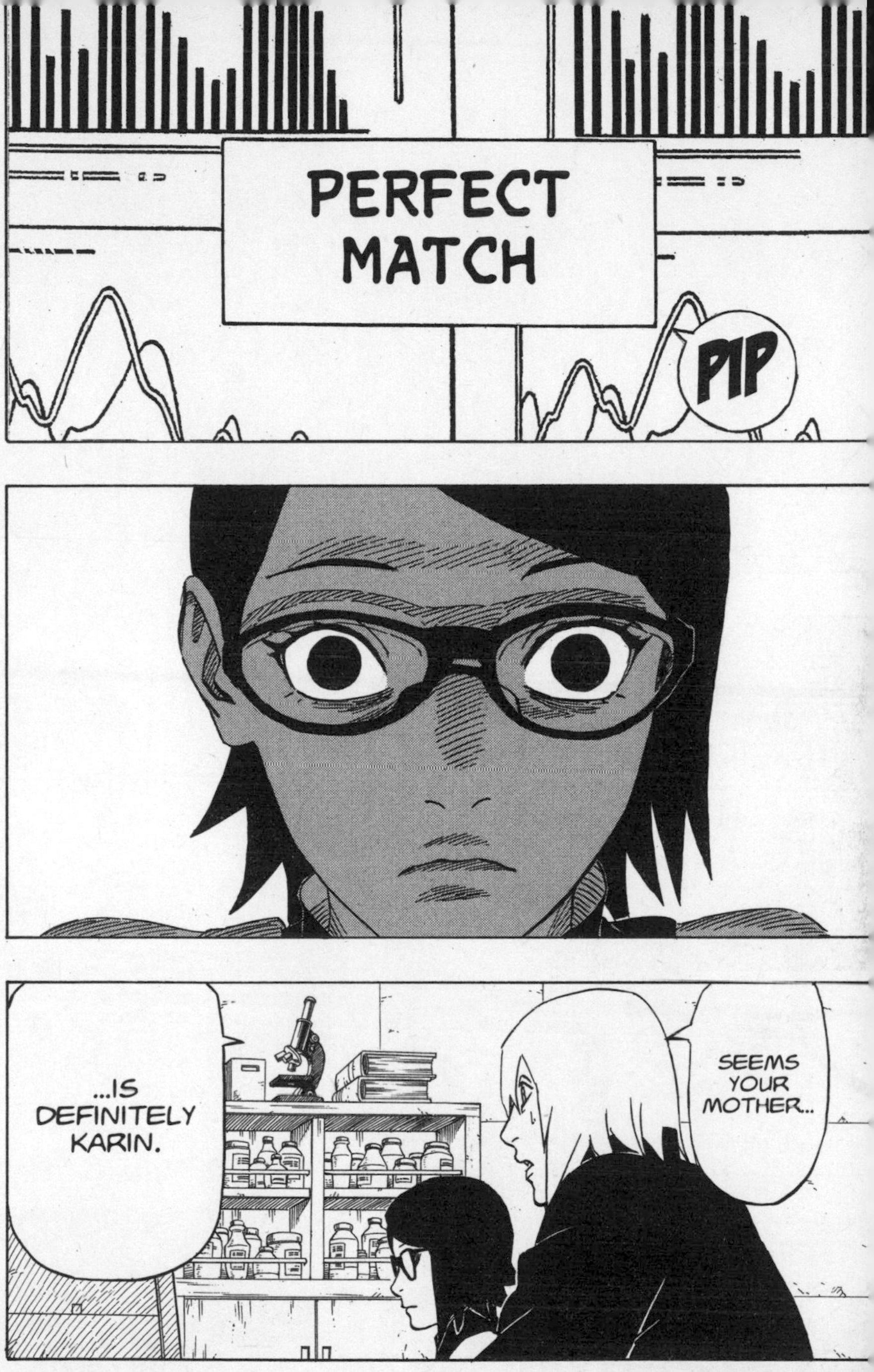
PERFECT MATCH
PIP
SEEMS YOUR MOTHER...
...IS DEFINITELY KARIN.

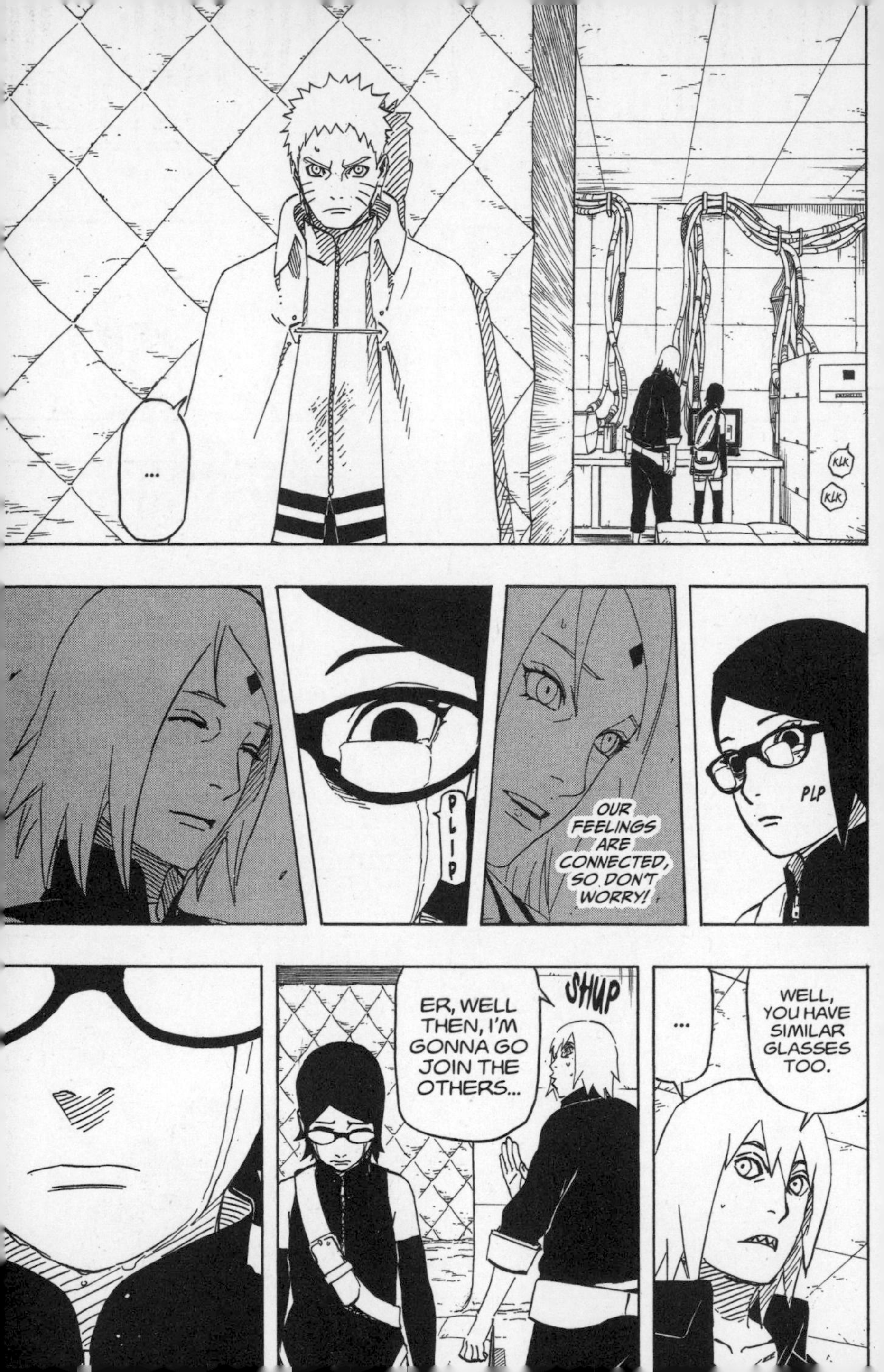

KLK
KLK
...
PLP
OUR FEELINGS ARE CONNECTED, SO DON'T WORRY!
PLIP
WELL, YOU HAVE SIMILAR GLASSES TOO.
...
SHUP
ER, WELL THEN, I'M GONNA GO JOIN THE OTHERS...

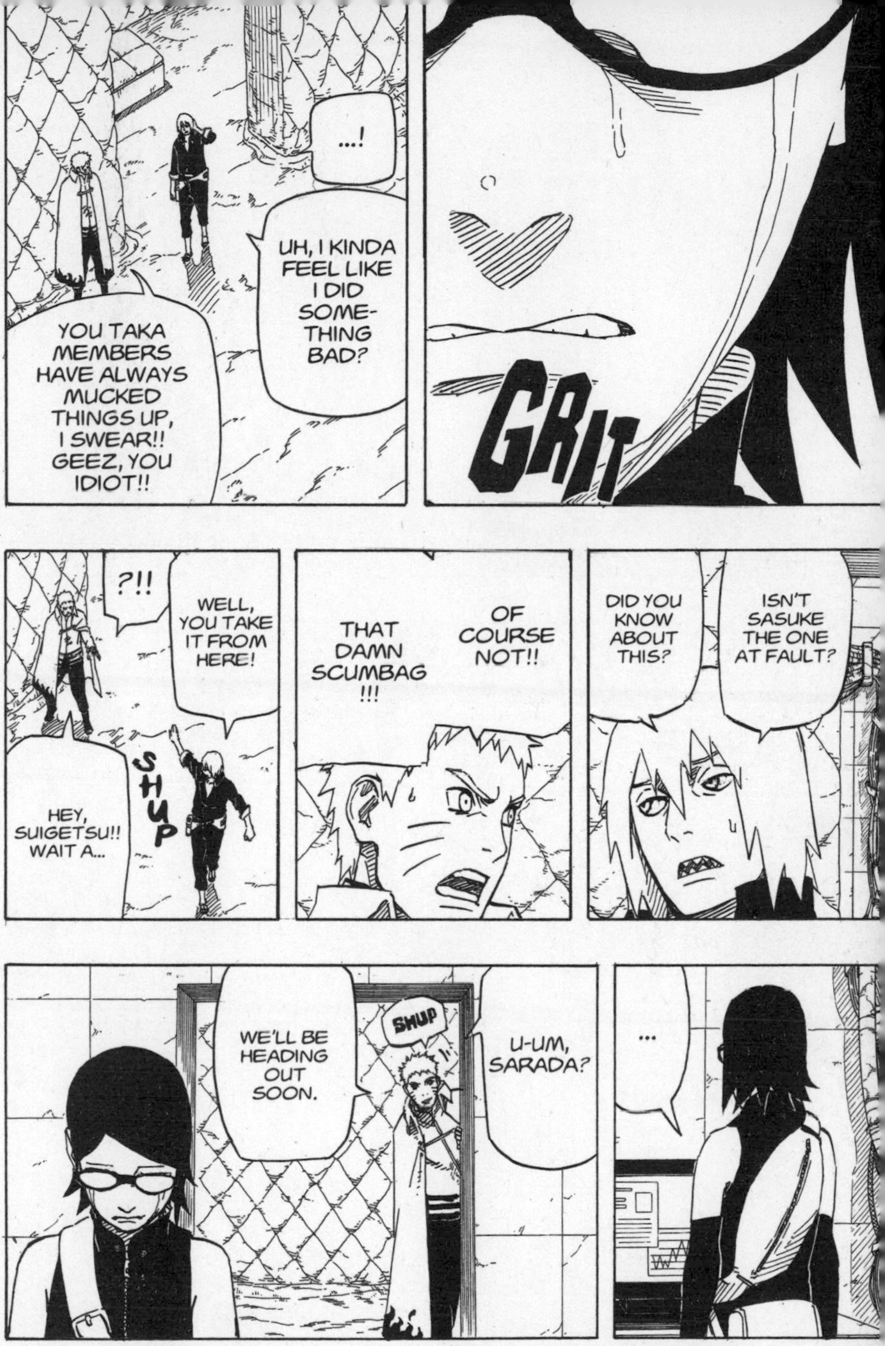
GRIT
...!
UH, I KINDA FEEL LIKE I DID SOME-THING BAD?
YOU TAKA MEMBERS HAVE ALWAYS MUCKED THINGS UP, I SWEAR!! GEEZ, YOU IDIOT!!
ISN'T SASUKE THE ONE AT FAULT?
DID YOU KNOW ABOUT THIS?
OF COURSE NOT!!
THAT DAMN SCUMBAG!!!
WELL, YOU TAKE IT FROM HERE!
?!!
SHUP
HEY, SUIGETSU!! WAIT A...
...
U-UM, SARADA?
SHUP
WE'LL BE HEADING OUT SOON.

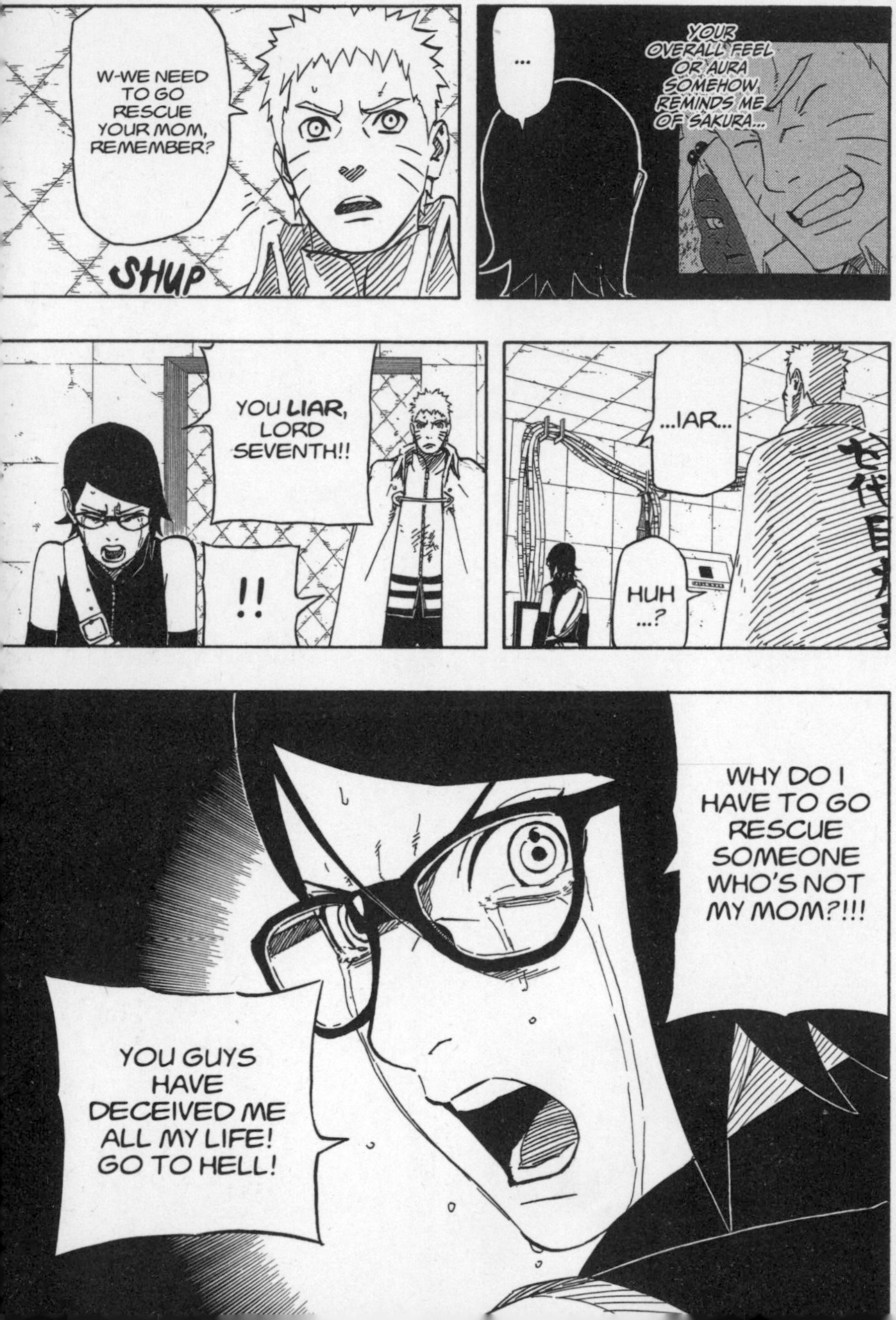
YOUR OVERALL FEEL OR AURA SOMEHOW REMINDS ME OF SAKURA...
...
W-WE NEED TO GO RESCUE YOUR MOM, REMEMBER?
SHUP
...IAR...
HUH ...?
YOU LIAR, LORD SEVENTH!!
!!
WHY DO I HAVE TO GO RESCUE SOMEONE WHO'S NOT MY MOM?!!!
YOU GUYS HAVE DECEIVED ME ALL MY LIFE! GO TO HELL!

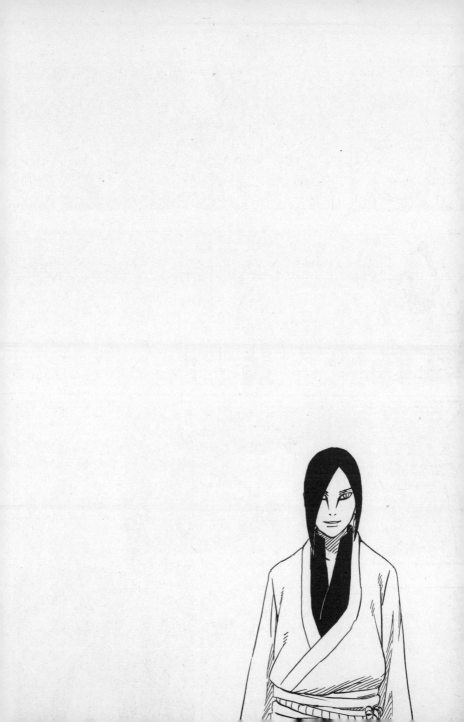

Number 700+8: The Real Thing

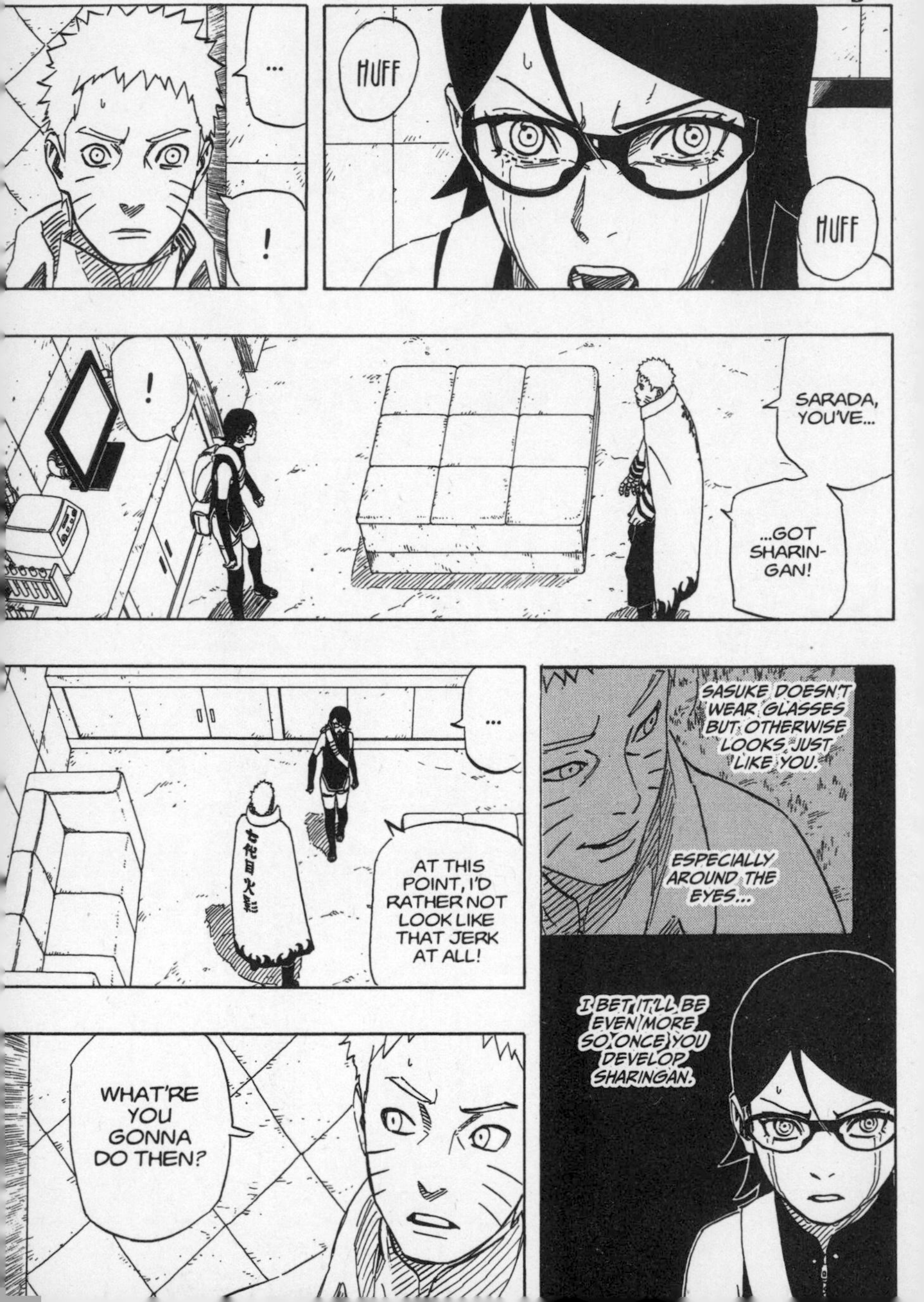
HUFF
HUFF
...
!
SARADA, YOU'VE...
...GOT SHARINGAN!
!
SASUKE DOESN'T WEAR GLASSES BUT OTHERWISE LOOKS JUST LIKE YOU.
ESPECIALLY AROUND THE EYES...
I BET IT'LL BE EVEN MORE SO ONCE YOU DEVELOP SHARINGAN.
...
七代目火影
AT THIS POINT, I'D RATHER NOT LOOK LIKE THAT JERK AT ALL!
WHAT'RE YOU GONNA DO THEN?

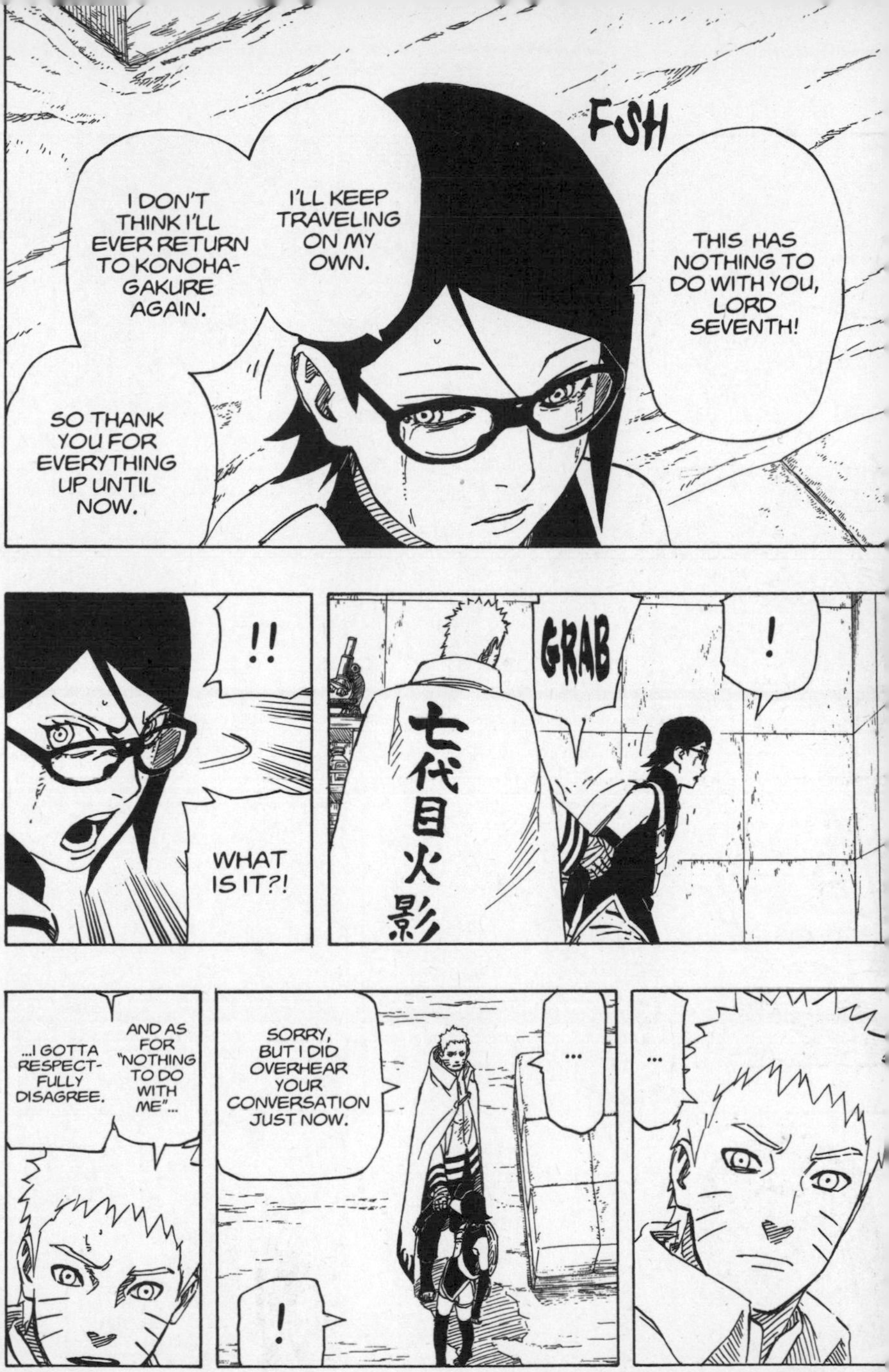
FSH
THIS HAS NOTHING TO DO WITH YOU, LORD SEVENTH!
I'LL KEEP TRAVELING ON MY OWN.
I DON'T THINK I'LL EVER RETURN TO KONOHA-GAKURE AGAIN.
SO THANK YOU FOR EVERYTHING UP UNTIL NOW.
!
GRAB
七代目火影
!!
WHAT IS IT?!
...
...
SORRY, BUT I DID OVERHEAR YOUR CONVERSATION JUST NOW.
!
AND AS FOR "NOTHING TO DO WITH ME"...
...I GOTTA RESPECT-FULLY DISAGREE.

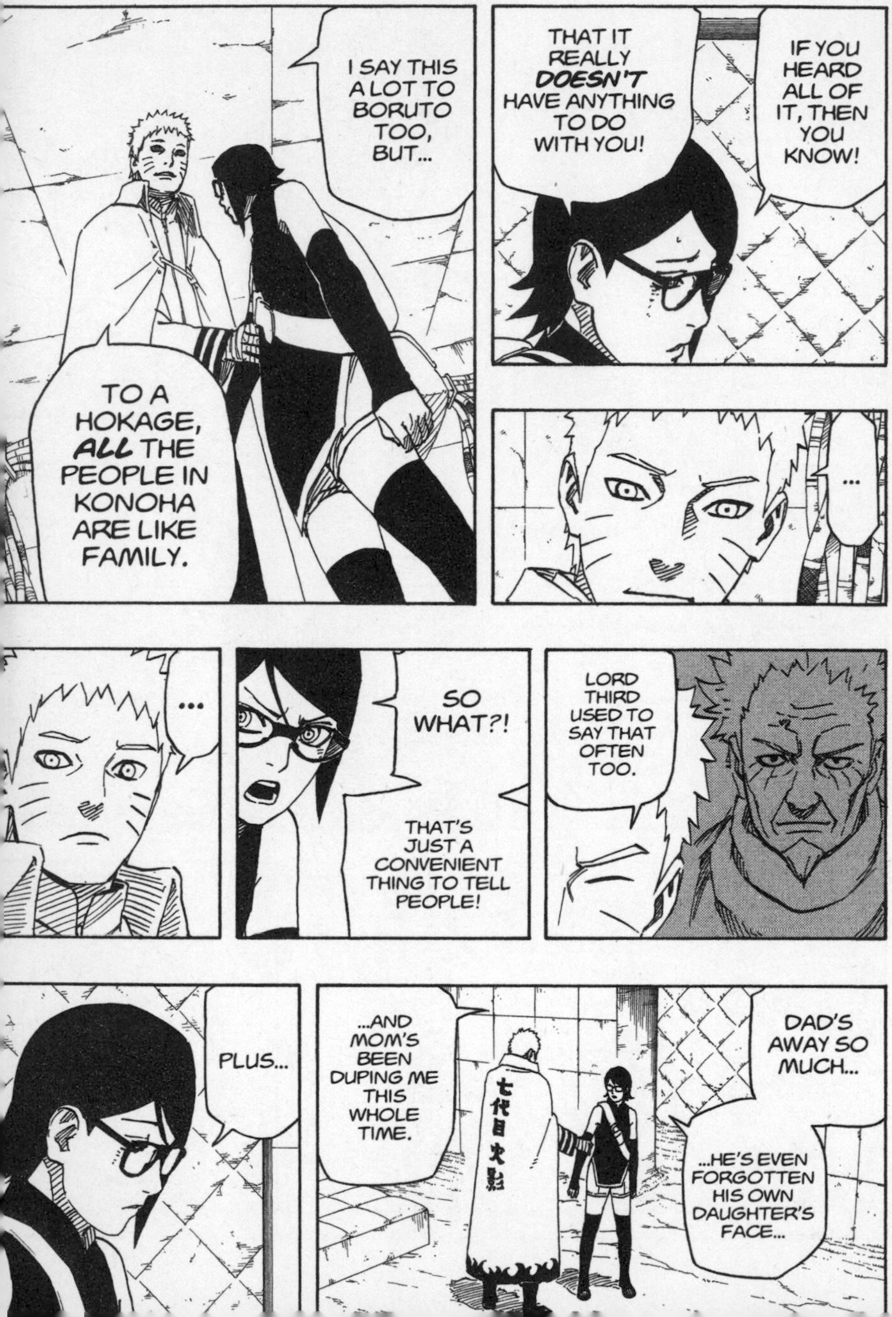
IF YOU HEARD ALL OF IT, THEN YOU KNOW!
THAT IT REALLY DOESN'T HAVE ANYTHING TO DO WITH YOU!
...
I SAY THIS A LOT TO BORUTO TOO, BUT...
TO A HOKAGE, ALL THE PEOPLE IN KONOHA ARE LIKE FAMILY.
LORD THIRD USED TO SAY THAT OFTEN TOO.
SO WHAT?!
THAT'S JUST A CONVENIENT THING TO TELL PEOPLE!
...
DAD'S AWAY SO MUCH...
...HE'S EVEN FORGOTTEN HIS OWN DAUGHTER'S FACE...
七代目火影
...AND MOM'S BEEN DUPING ME THIS WHOLE TIME.
PLUS...

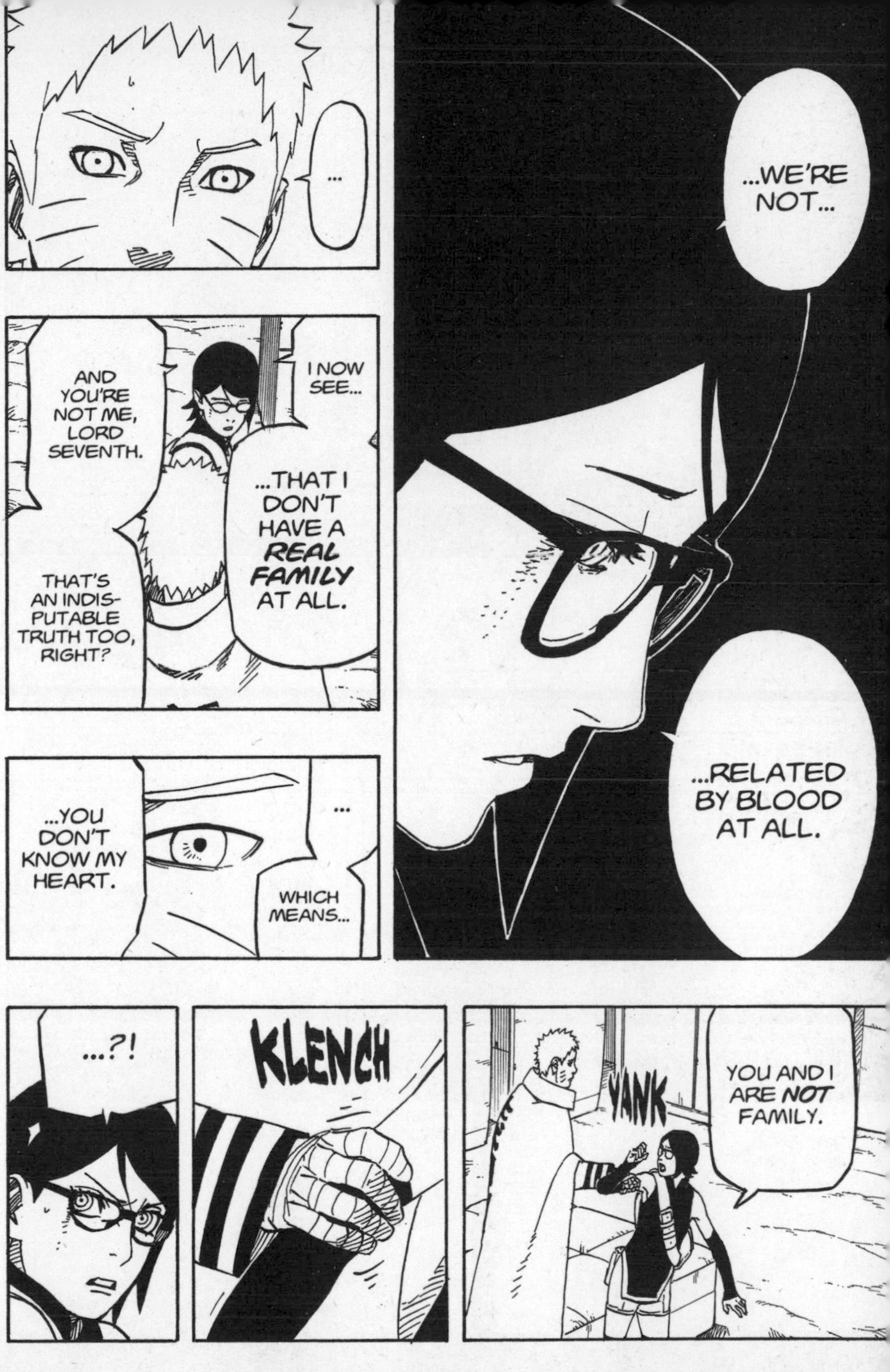
...WE'RE NOT...
...RELATED BY BLOOD AT ALL.
...
I NOW SEE...
...THAT I DON'T HAVE A REAL FAMILY AT ALL.
AND YOU'RE NOT ME, LORD SEVENTH.
THAT'S AN INDIS-PUTABLE TRUTH TOO, RIGHT?
...
WHICH MEANS...
...YOU DON'T KNOW MY HEART.
YOU AND I ARE NOT FAMILY.
YANK
KLENCH
...?!

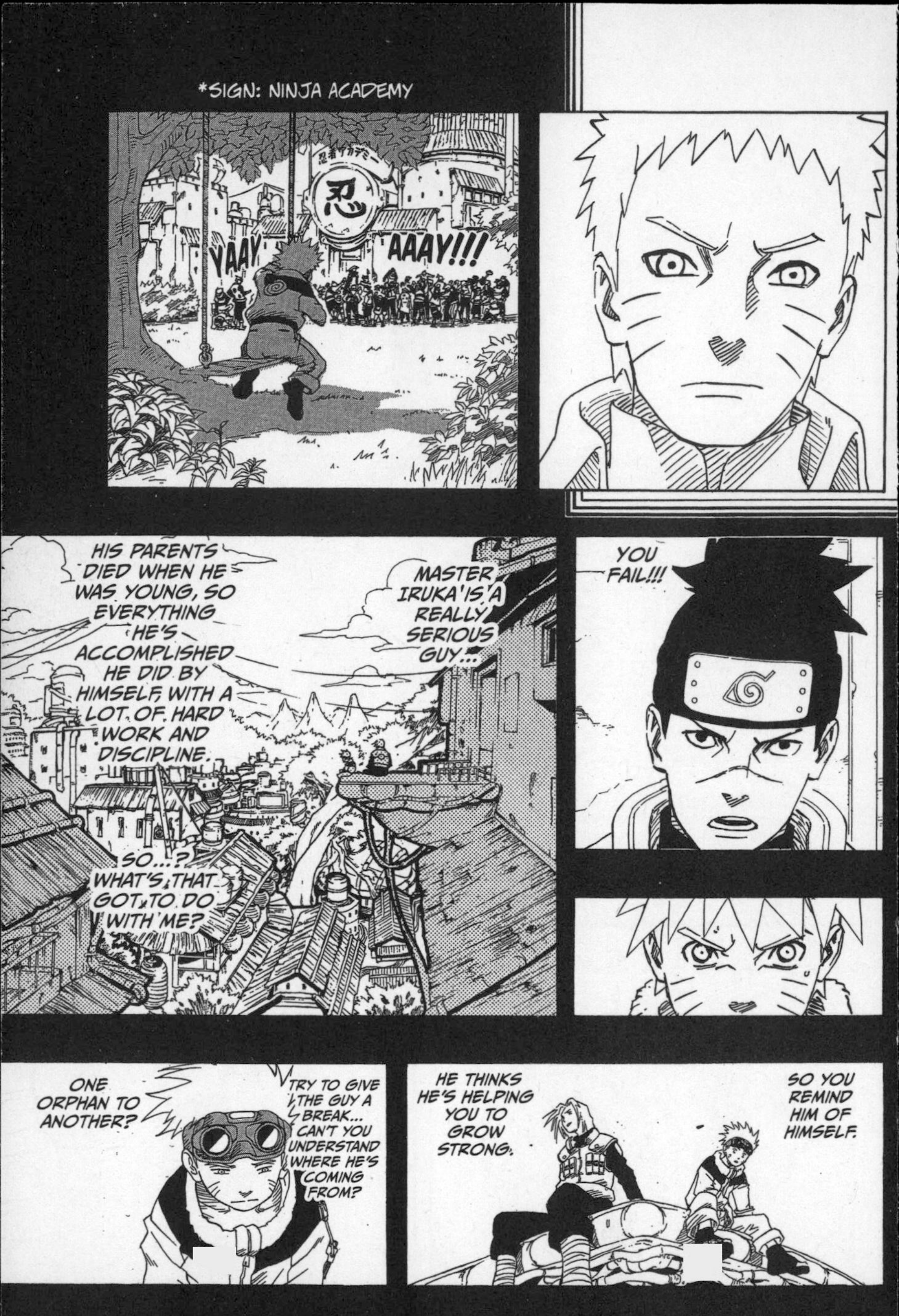
*SIGN: NINJA ACADEMY
忍者アカデミー
忍
YAAY
AAAY!!!
YOU FAIL!!!
MASTER IRUKA'S A REALLY SERIOUS GUY...
HIS PARENTS DIED WHEN HE WAS YOUNG, SO EVERYTHING HE'S ACCOMPLISHED HE DID BY HIMSELF, WITH A LOT OF HARD WORK AND DISCIPLINE.
SO...? WHAT'S THAT GOT TO DO WITH ME?
SO YOU REMIND HIM OF HIMSELF.
HE THINKS HE'S HELPING YOU TO GROW STRONG.
TRY TO GIVE THE GUY A BREAK... CAN'T YOU UNDERSTAND WHERE HE'S COMING FROM?
ONE ORPHAN TO ANOTHER?

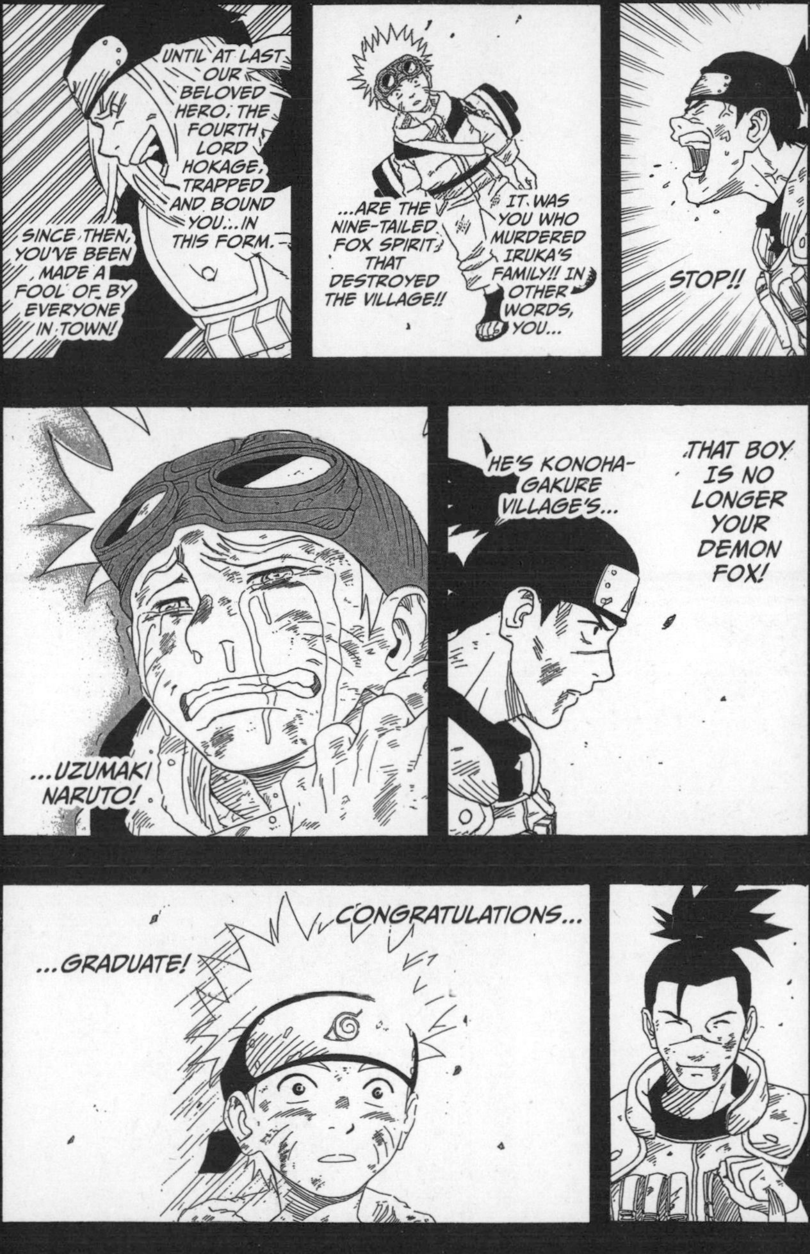
STOP!!
IT WAS YOU WHO MURDERED IRUKA'S FAMILY!! IN OTHER WORDS, YOU...
...ARE THE NINE-TAILED FOX SPIRIT THAT DESTROYED THE VILLAGE!!
UNTIL AT LAST OUR BELOVED HERO, THE FOURTH LORD HOKAGE, TRAPPED AND BOUND YOU... IN THIS FORM.
SINCE THEN, YOU'VE BEEN MADE A FOOL OF BY EVERYONE IN TOWN!
THAT BOY IS NO LONGER YOUR DEMON FOX!
HE'S KONOHAGAKURE VILLAGE'S...
...UZUMAKI NARUTO!
CONGRATULATIONS...
...GRADUATE!

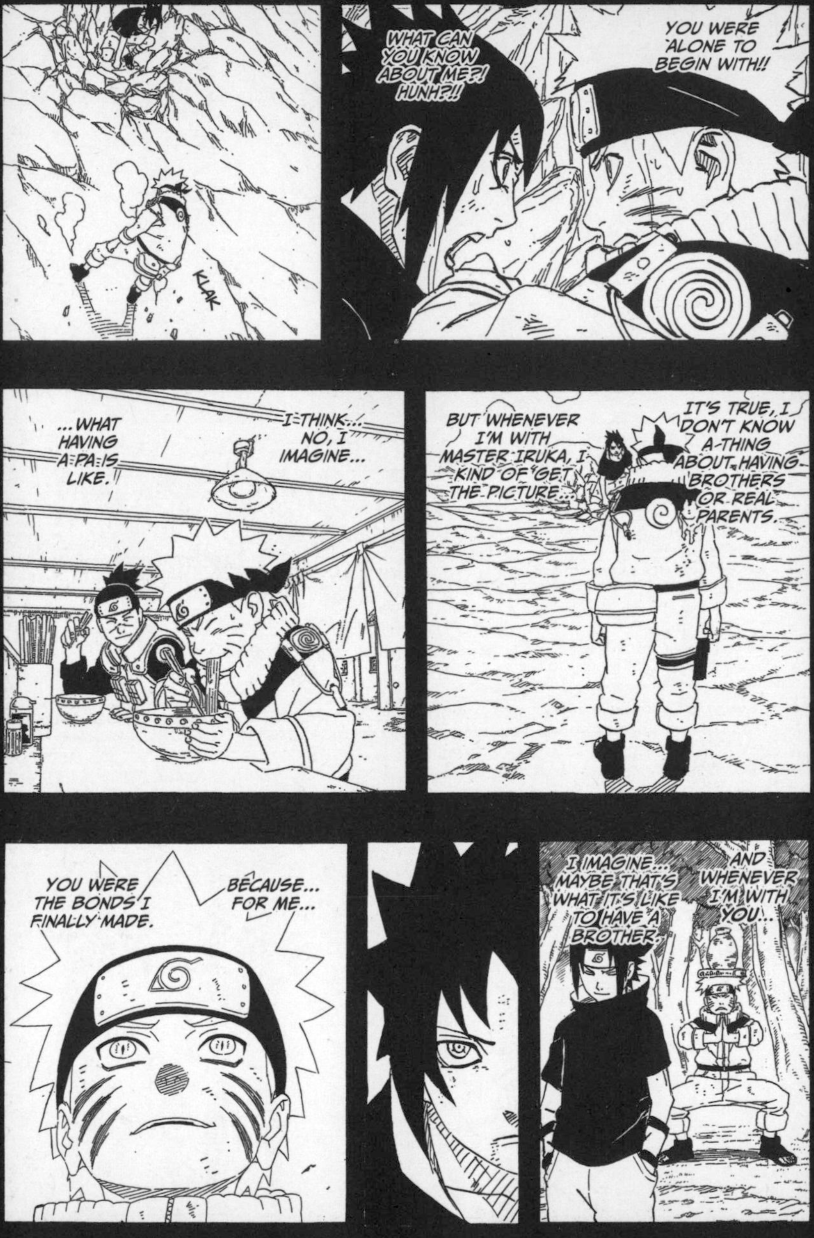
YOU WERE ALONE TO BEGIN WITH!!
WHAT CAN YOU KNOW ABOUT ME?! HUNH?!
KLAK
IT'S TRUE, I DON'T KNOW A THING ABOUT HAVING BROTHERS OR REAL PARENTS.
BUT WHENEVER I'M WITH MASTER IRUKA, I KIND OF GET THE PICTURE...
I THINK... NO, I IMAGINE...
...WHAT HAVING A PA IS LIKE.
AND WHENEVER I'M WITH YOU...
I IMAGINE... MAYBE THAT'S WHAT IT'S LIKE TO HAVE A BROTHER.
BECAUSE... FOR ME...
YOU WERE THE BONDS I FINALLY MADE.

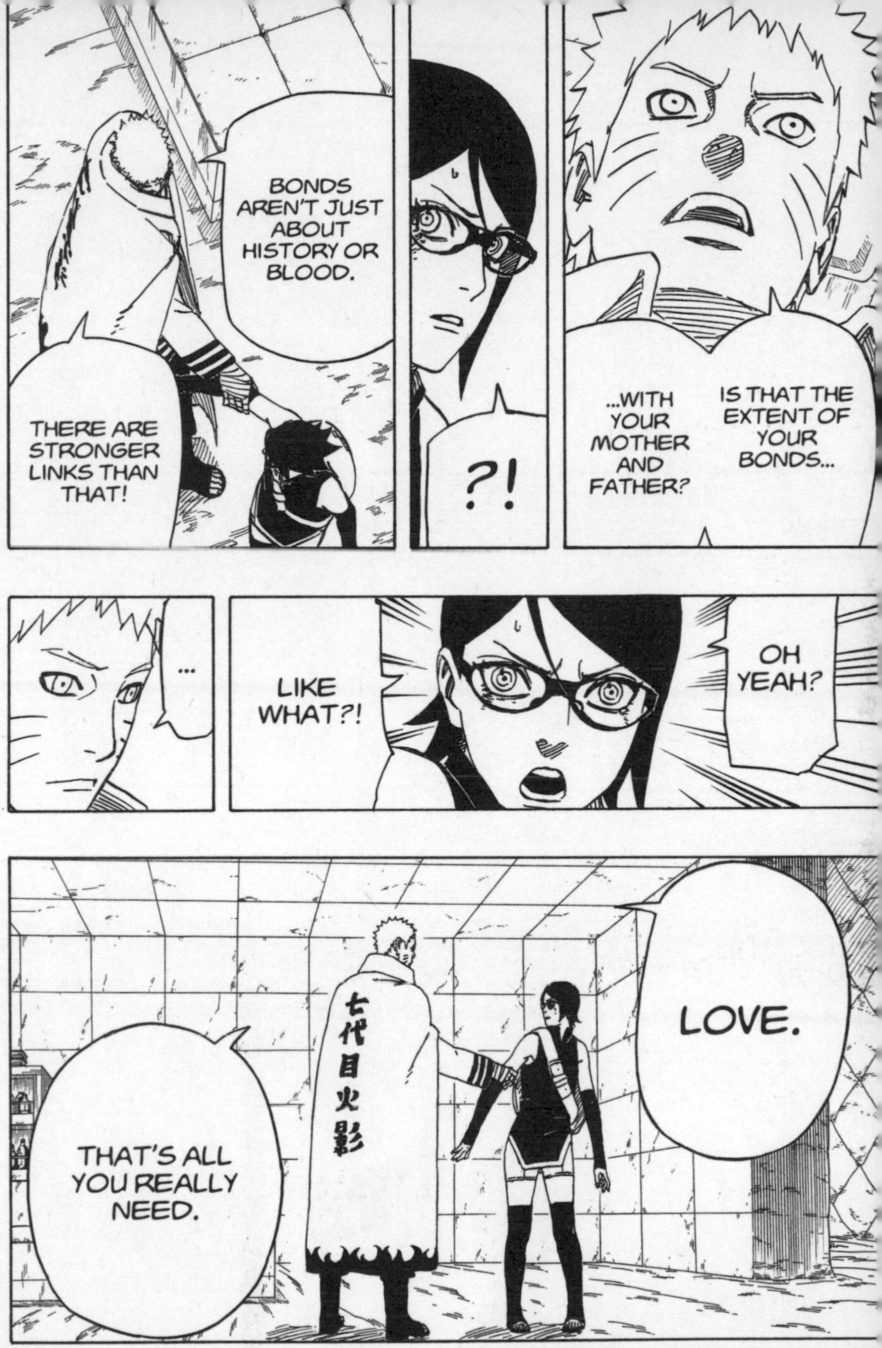
IS THAT THE EXTENT OF YOUR BONDS...
...WITH YOUR MOTHER AND FATHER?
?!
BONDS AREN'T JUST ABOUT HISTORY OR BLOOD.
THERE ARE STRONGER LINKS THAN THAT!
OH YEAH?
LIKE WHAT?!
...
LOVE.
七代目火影
THAT'S ALL YOU REALLY NEED.

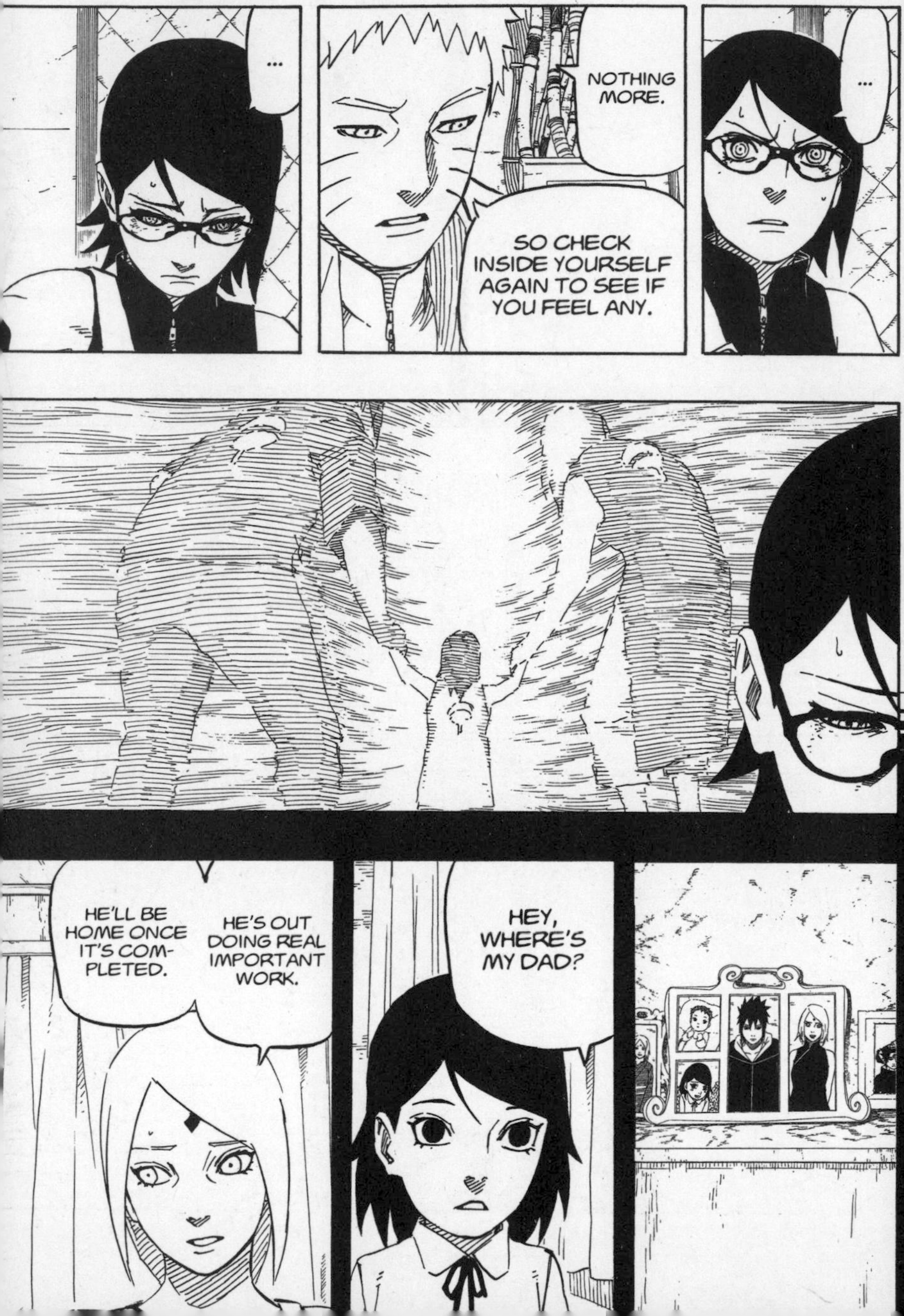
...
NOTHING MORE.
SO CHECK INSIDE YOURSELF AGAIN TO SEE IF YOU FEEL ANY.
...
HEY, WHERE'S MY DAD?
HE'S OUT DOING REAL IMPORTANT WORK.
HE'LL BE HOME ONCE IT'S COM-PLETED.

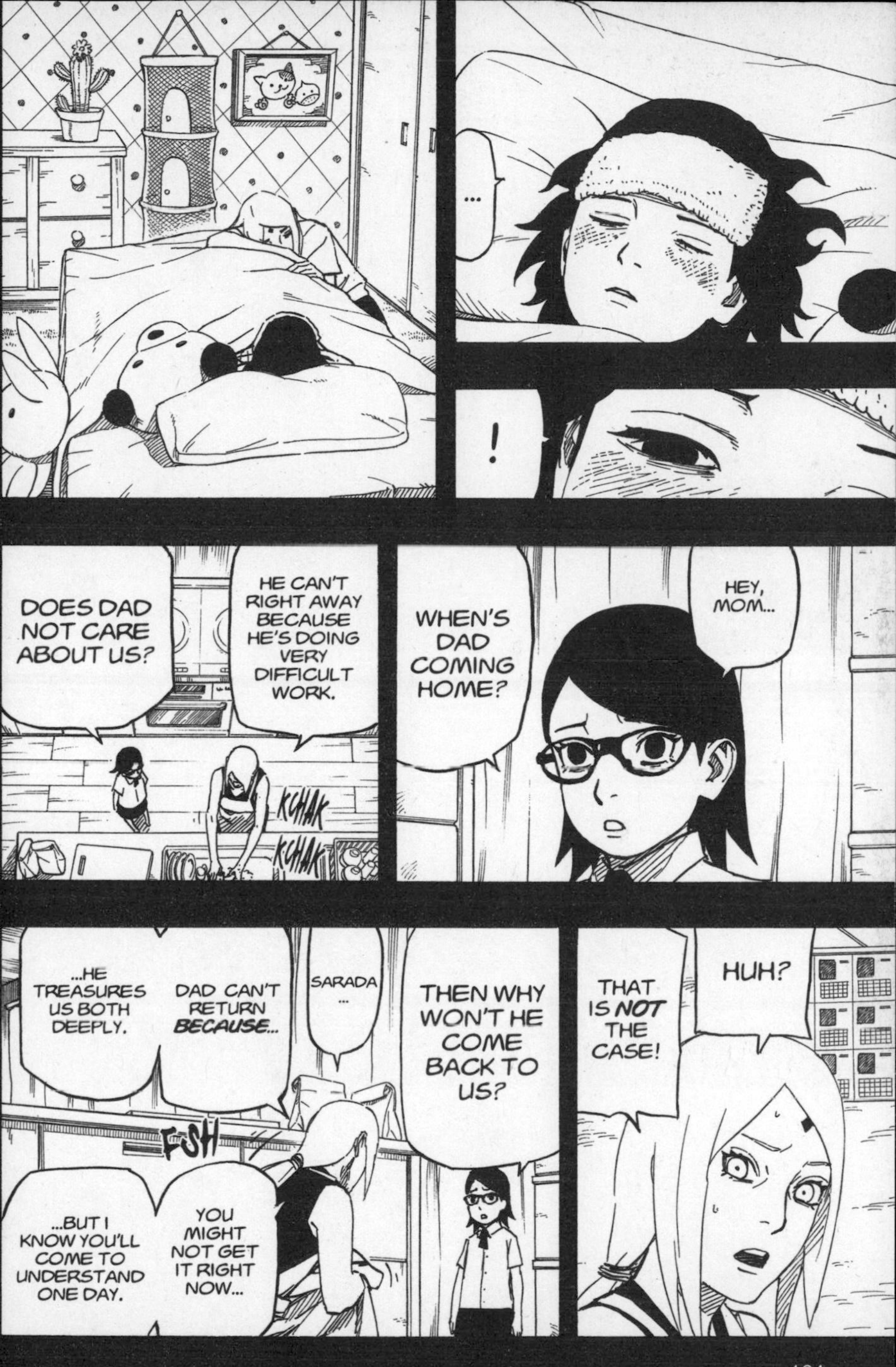
...
!
HEY, MOM...
WHEN'S DAD COMING HOME?
HE CAN'T RIGHT AWAY BECAUSE HE'S DOING VERY DIFFICULT WORK.
DOES DAD NOT CARE ABOUT US?
KCHAK
KCHAK
HUH?
THAT IS *NOT* THE CASE!
THEN WHY WON'T HE COME BACK TO US?
SARADA...
DAD CAN'T RETURN *BECAUSE*...
...HE TREASURES US BOTH DEEPLY.
FSH
YOU MIGHT NOT GET IT RIGHT NOW...
...BUT I KNOW YOU'LL COME TO UNDERSTAND ONE DAY.

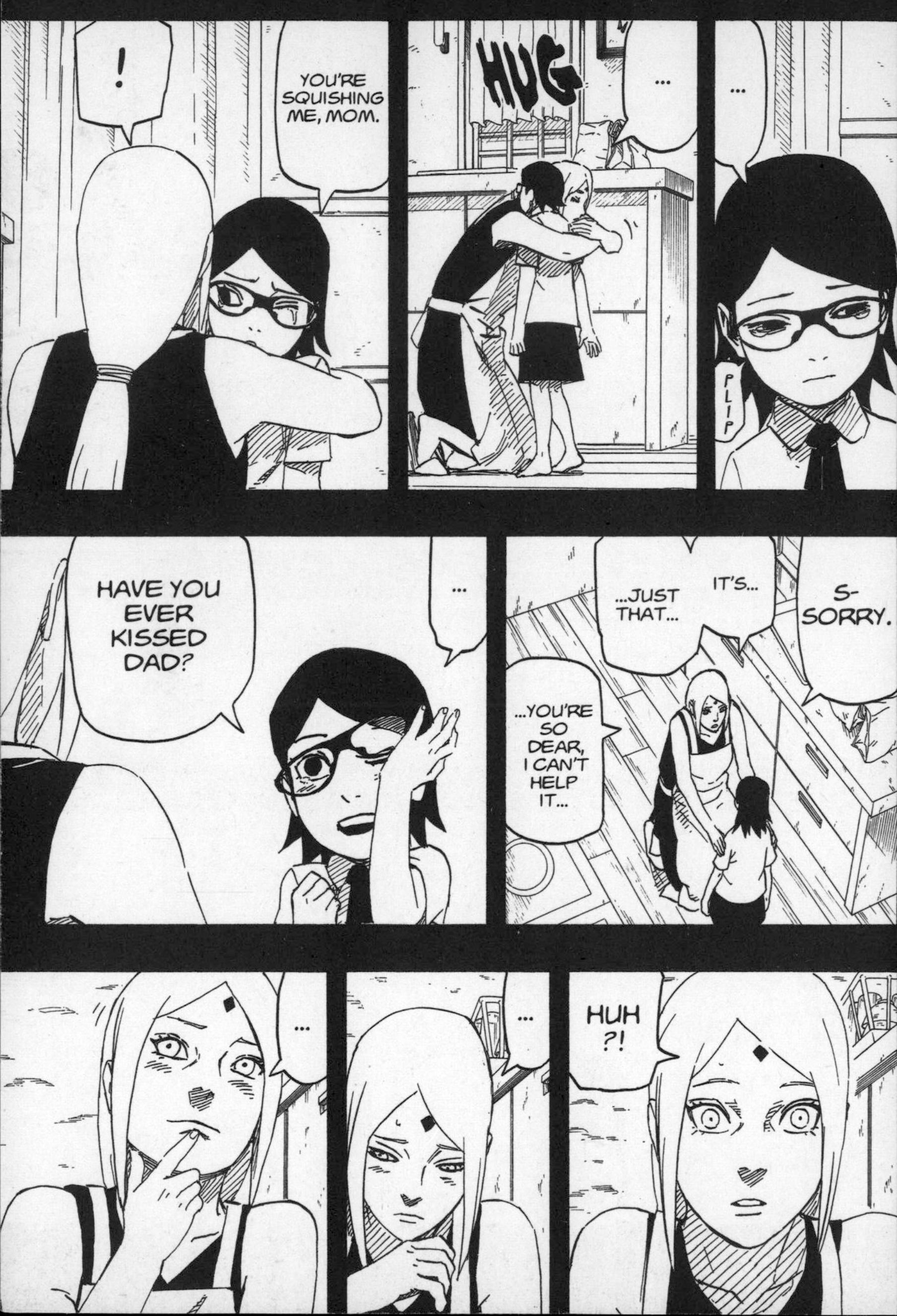
...
PLIP
...
HUG
YOU'RE SQUISHING ME, MOM.
!
S-SORRY.
IT'S...
...JUST THAT...
...YOU'RE SO DEAR, I CAN'T HELP IT...
...
HAVE YOU EVER KISSED DAD?
HUH ?!
...
...

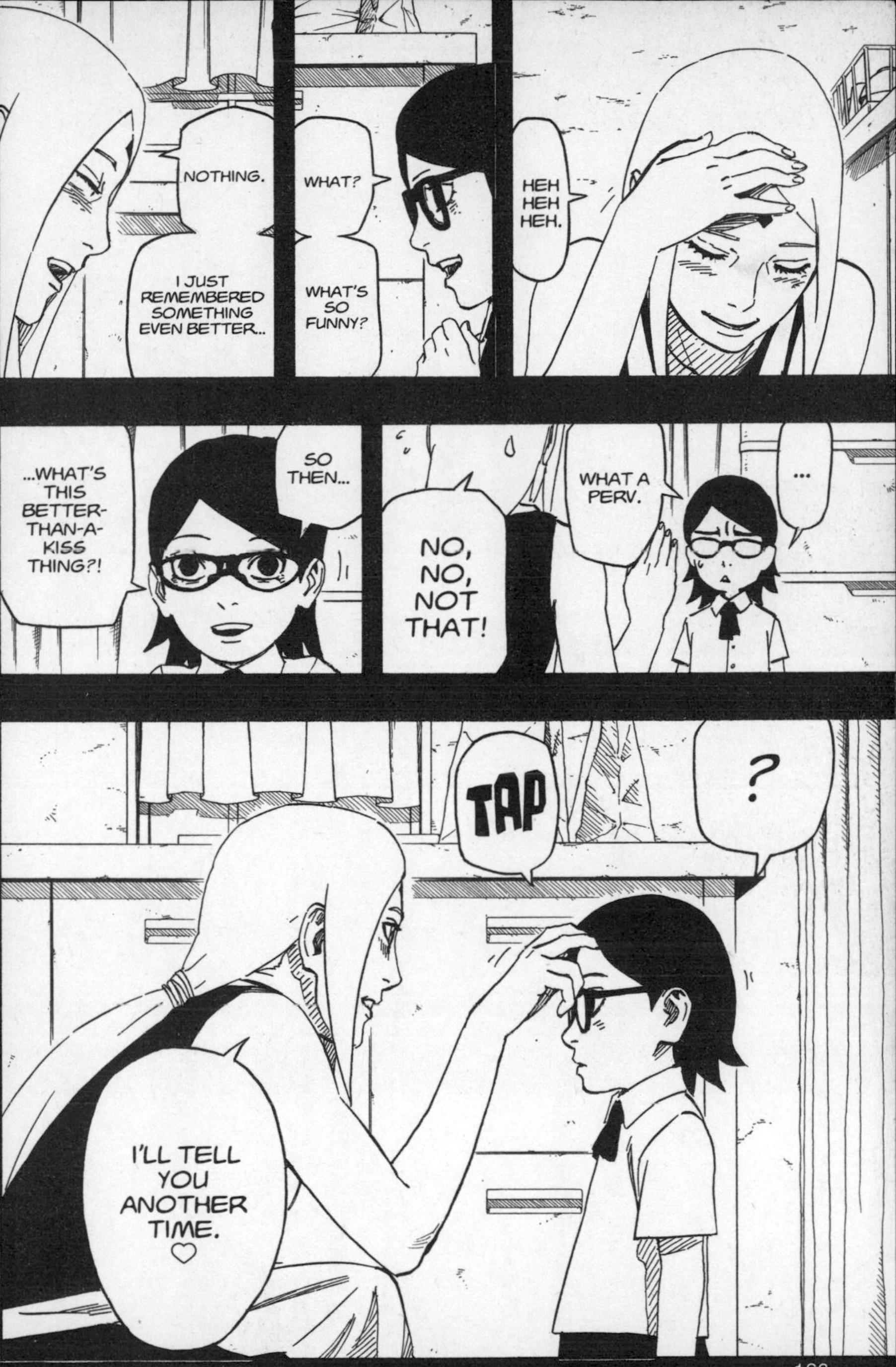
HEH HEH HEH.
WHAT?
WHAT'S SO FUNNY?
NOTHING.
I JUST REMEMBERED SOMETHING EVEN BETTER...
...
WHAT A PERV.
NO, NO, NOT THAT!
SO THEN...
...WHAT'S THIS BETTER-THAN-A-KISS THING?!
?
TAP
I'LL TELL YOU ANOTHER TIME. ♡

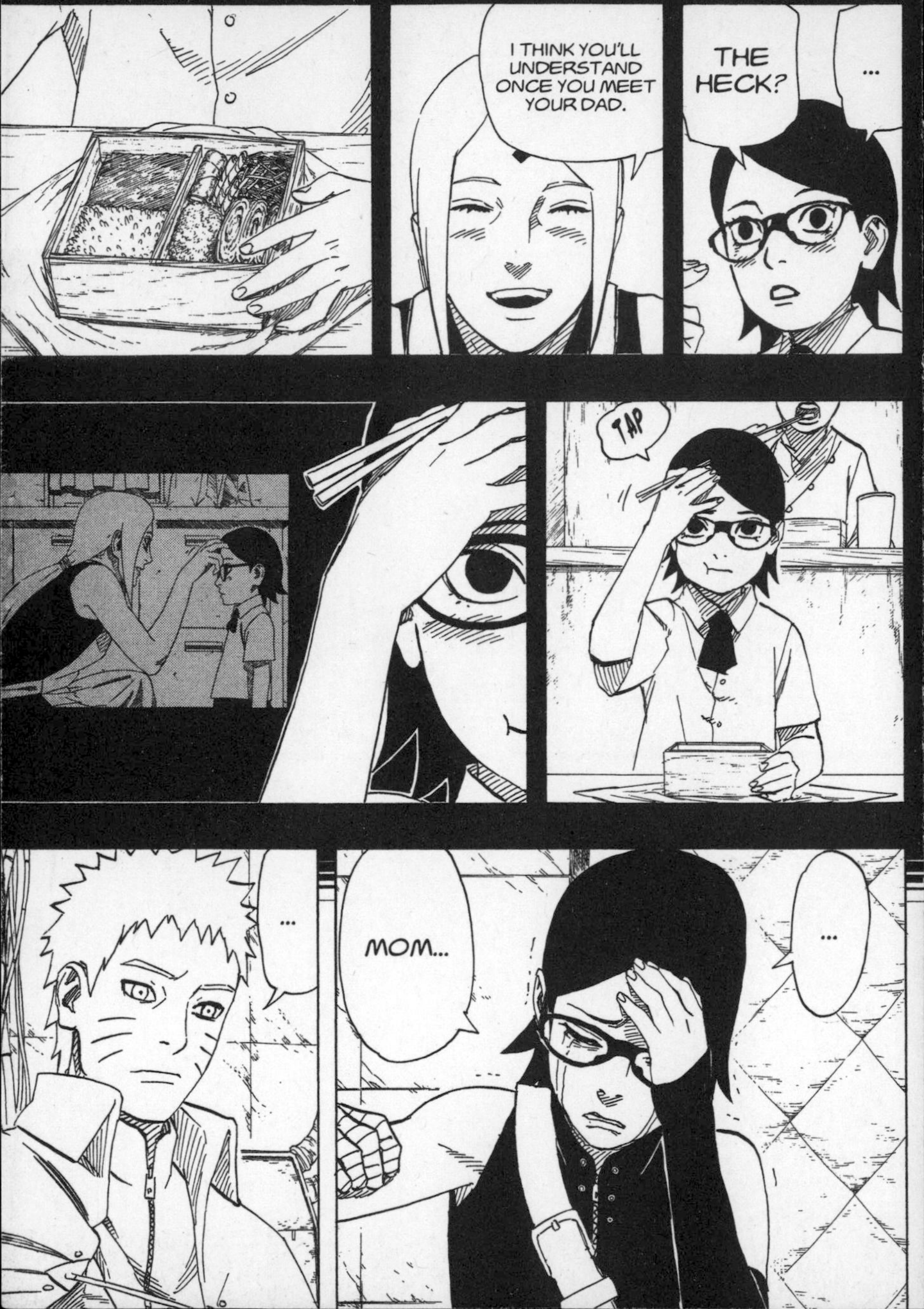
...
THE HECK?
I THINK YOU'LL UNDERSTAND ONCE YOU MEET YOUR DAD.
TAP
...
MOM...
...

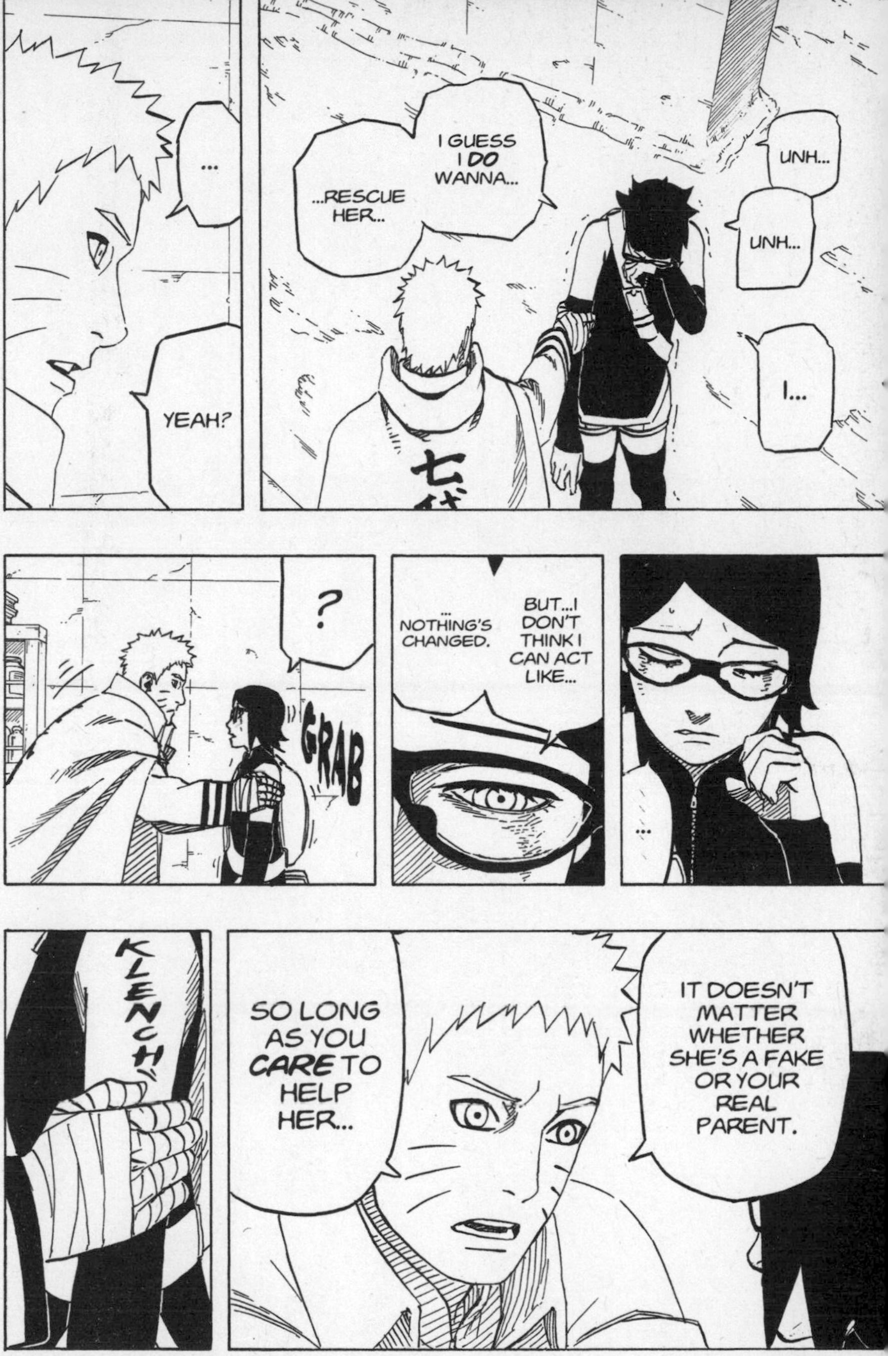
UNH...
UNH...
I...
I GUESS I DO WANNA...
...RESCUE HER...
...
YEAH?
...
BUT...I DON'T THINK I CAN ACT LIKE...
...NOTHING'S CHANGED.
?
GRAB
IT DOESN'T MATTER WHETHER SHE'S A FAKE OR YOUR REAL PARENT.
SO LONG AS YOU CARE TO HELP HER...
KLENCH!

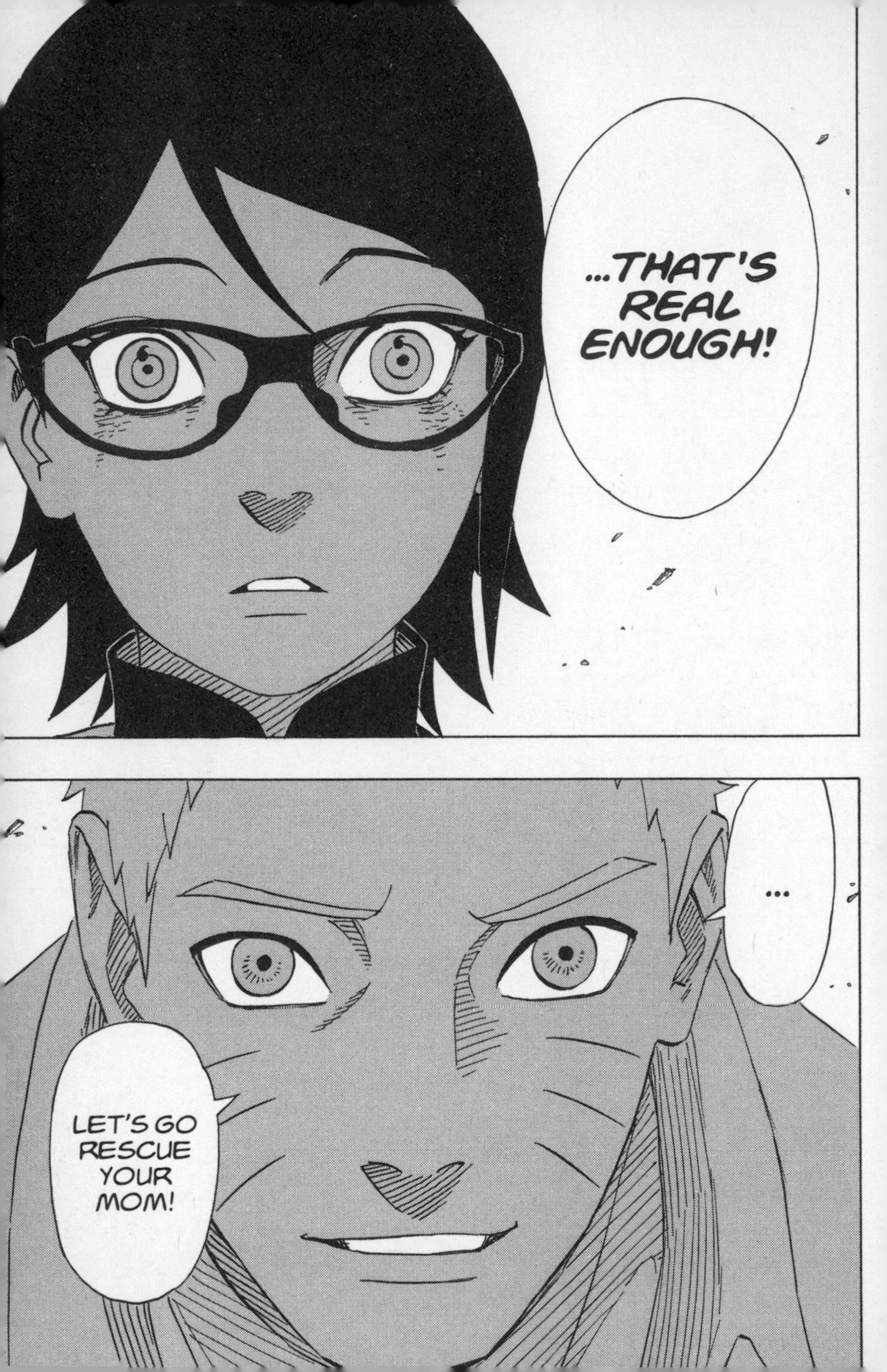
...THAT'S REAL ENOUGH!
...
LET'S GO RESCUE YOUR MOM!

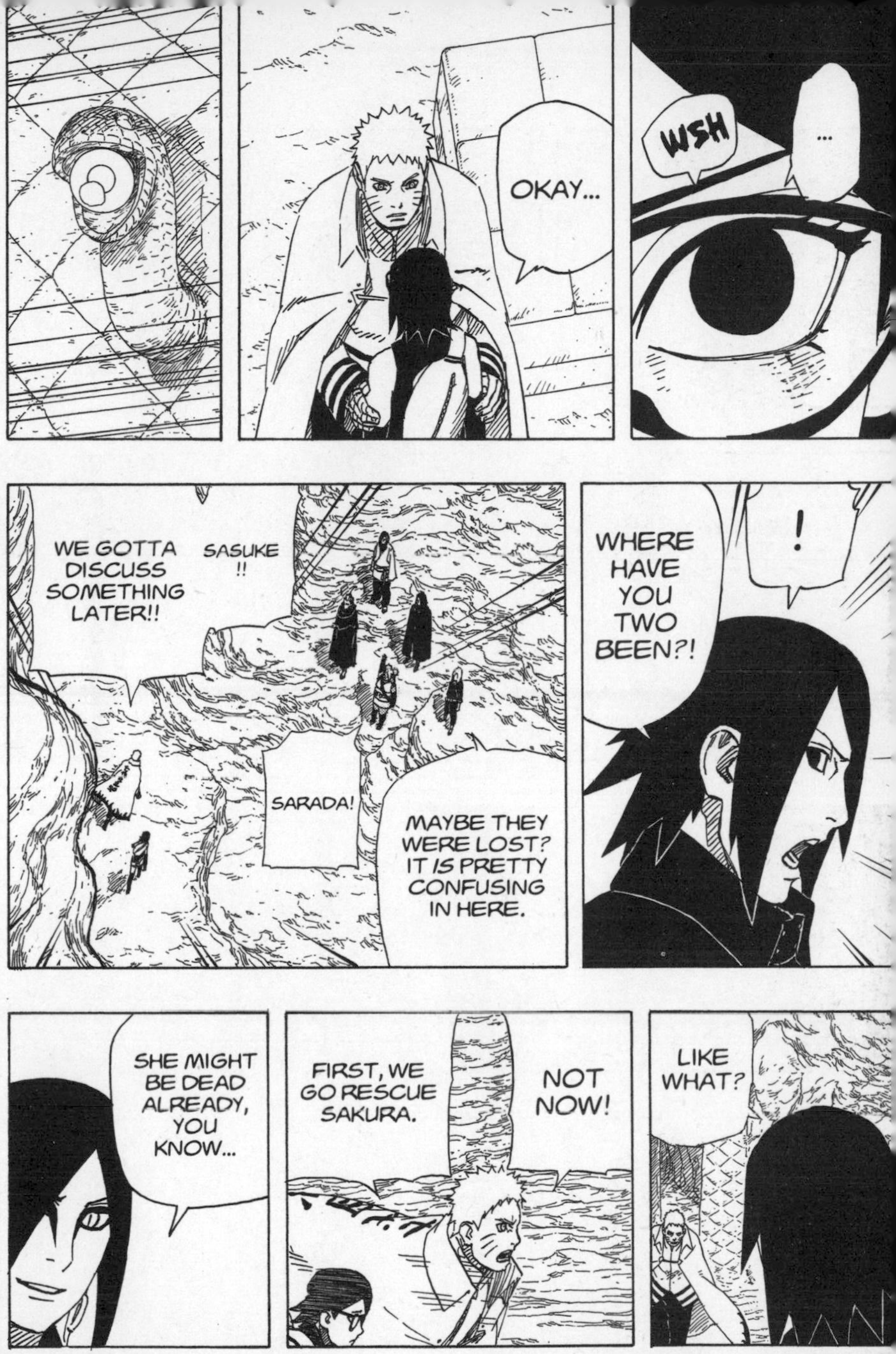
WSH
...
OKAY...
!
WHERE HAVE YOU TWO BEEN?!
SASUKE!!
WE GOTTA DISCUSS SOMETHING LATER!!
MAYBE THEY WERE LOST? IT IS PRETTY CONFUSING IN HERE.
SARADA!
LIKE WHAT?
NOT NOW!
FIRST, WE GO RESCUE SAKURA.
SHE MIGHT BE DEAD ALREADY, YOU KNOW...

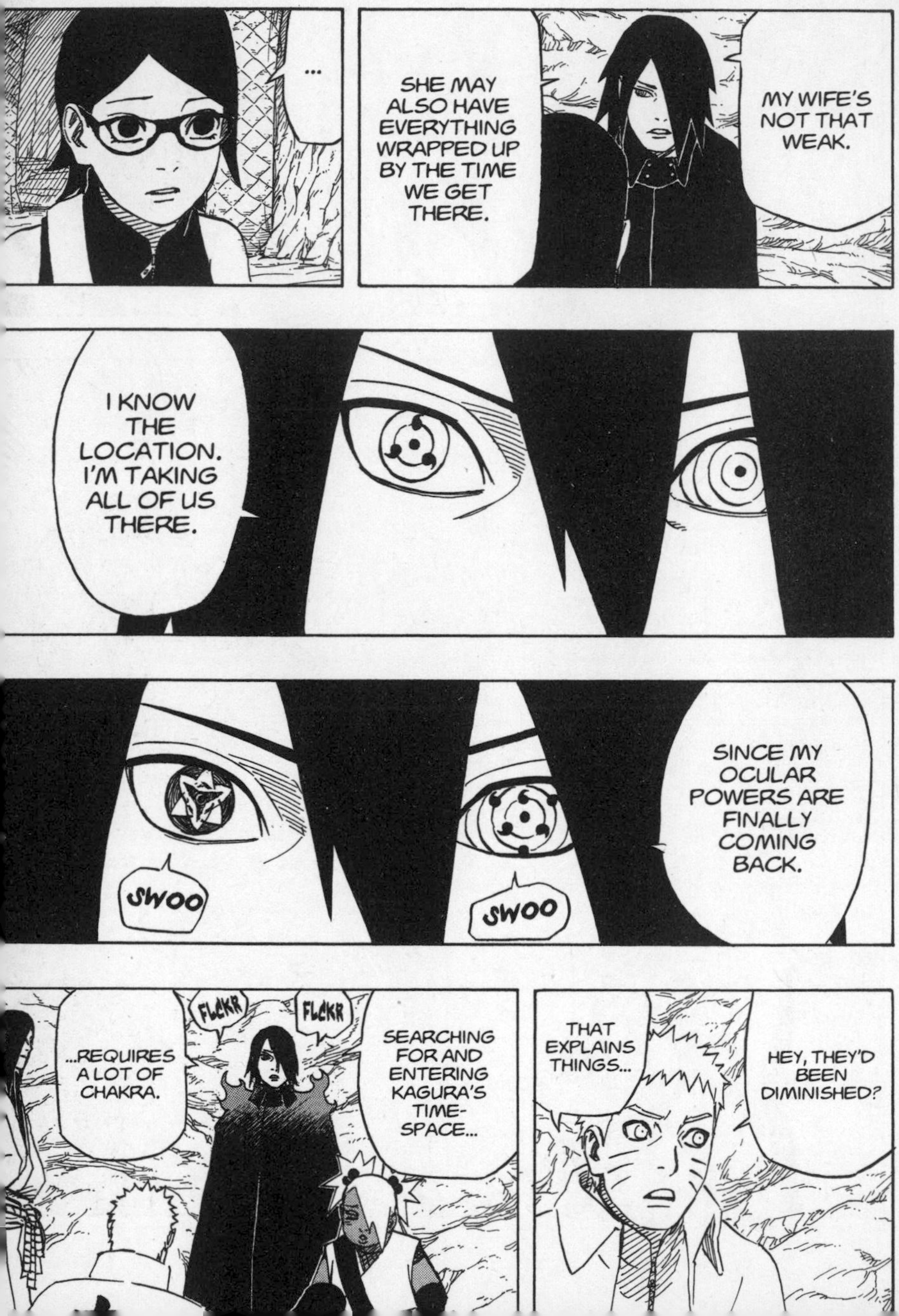
MY WIFE'S NOT THAT WEAK.
SHE MAY ALSO HAVE EVERYTHING WRAPPED UP BY THE TIME WE GET THERE.
...
I KNOW THE LOCATION. I'M TAKING ALL OF US THERE.
SINCE MY OCULAR POWERS ARE FINALLY COMING BACK.
SWOO
SWOO
HEY, THEY'D BEEN DIMINISHED?
THAT EXPLAINS THINGS...
FLCKR
FLCKR
SEARCHING FOR AND ENTERING KAGURA'S TIME-SPACE...
...REQUIRES A LOT OF CHAKRA.

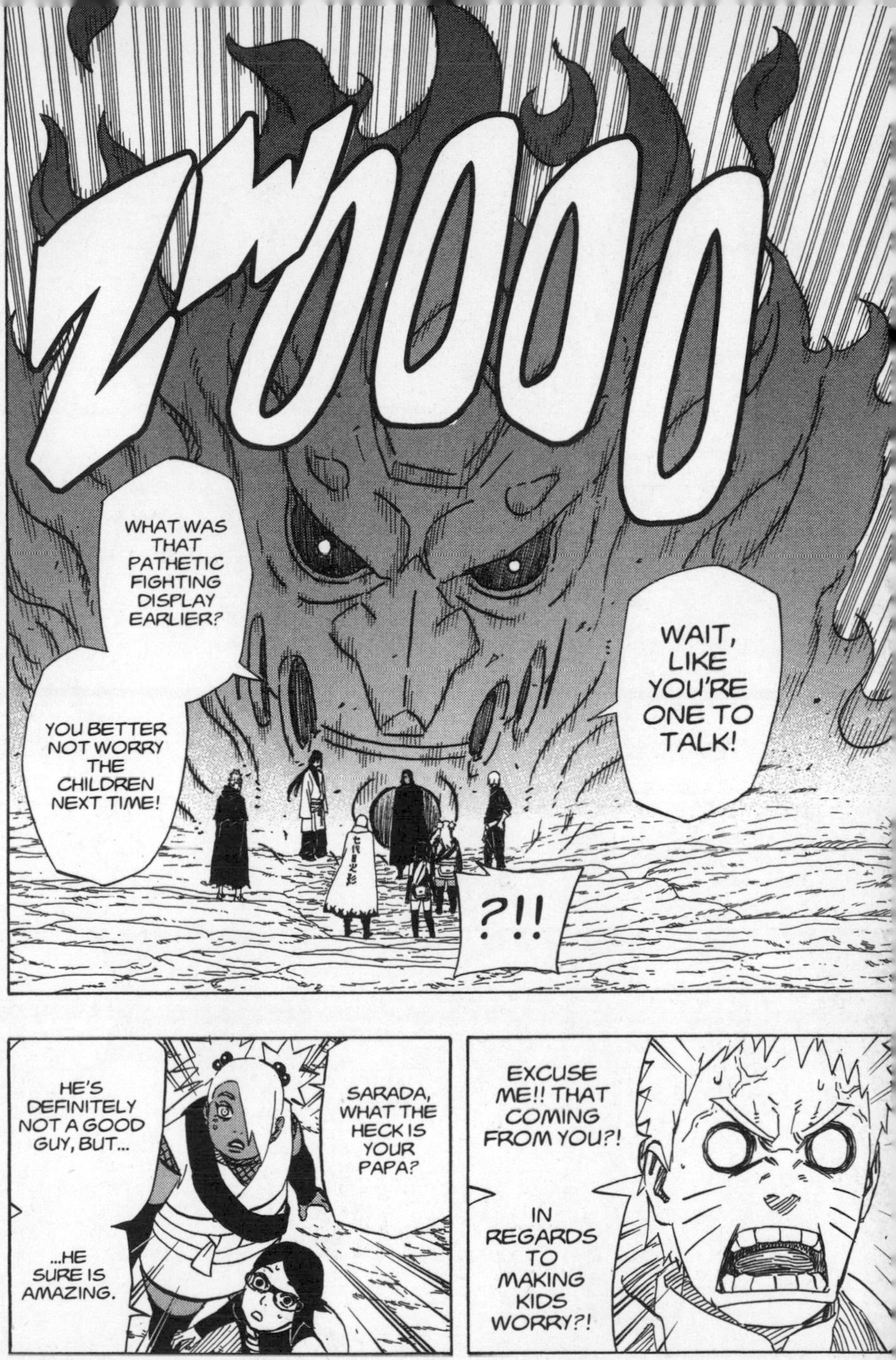
Z-OOOO
WHAT WAS THAT PATHETIC FIGHTING DISPLAY EARLIER?
YOU BETTER NOT WORRY THE CHILDREN NEXT TIME!
WAIT, LIKE YOU'RE ONE TO TALK!
?!!
EXCUSE ME!! THAT COMING FROM YOU?!
IN REGARDS TO MAKING KIDS WORRY?!
SARADA, WHAT THE HECK IS YOUR PAPA?
HE'S DEFINITELY NOT A GOOD GUY, BUT...
...HE SURE IS AMAZING.

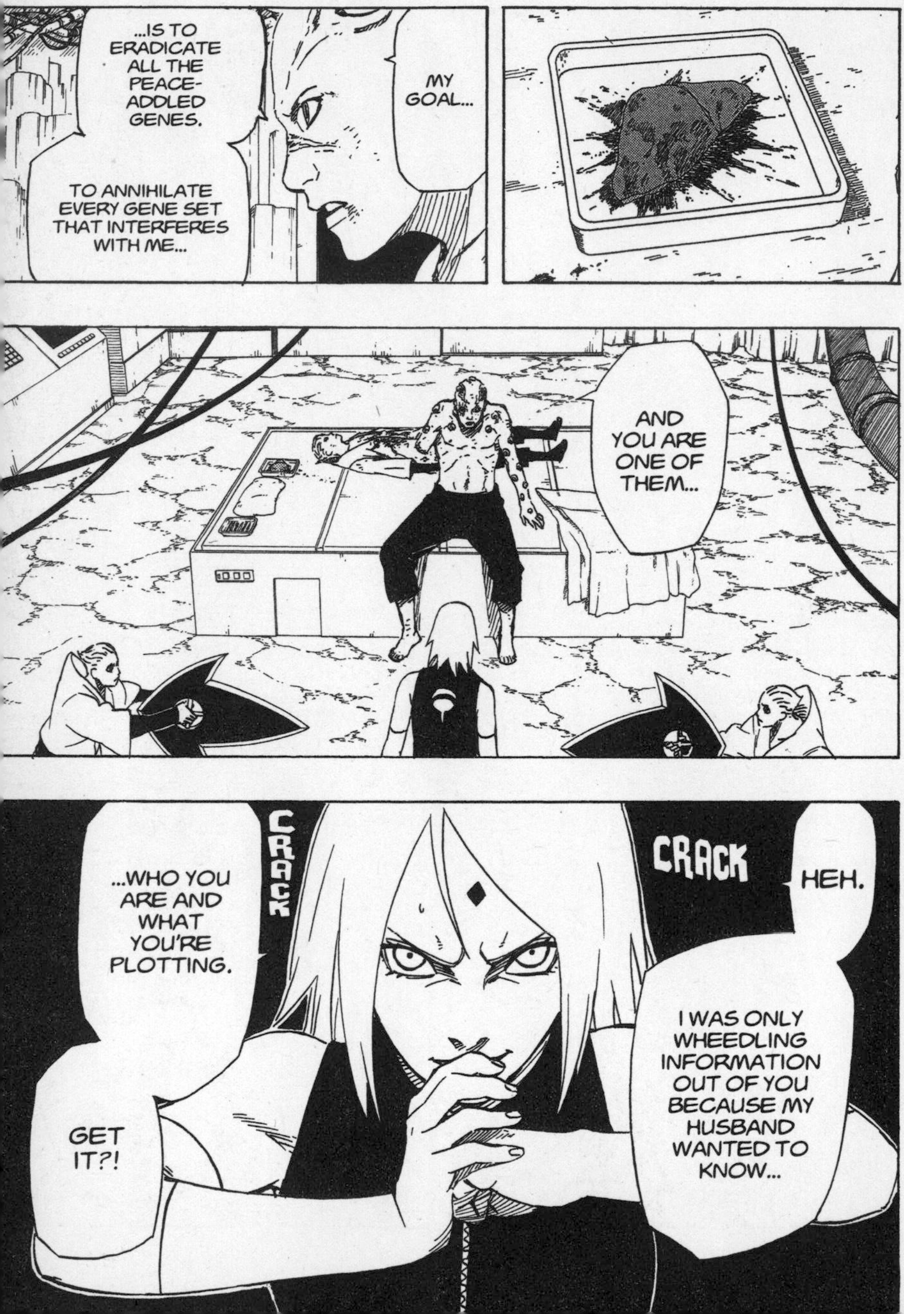
MY GOAL...
...IS TO ERADICATE ALL THE PEACE-ADDLED GENES.
TO ANNIHILATE EVERY GENE SET THAT INTERFERES WITH ME...
AND YOU ARE ONE OF THEM...
HEH.
CRACK
CRACK
I WAS ONLY WHEEDLING INFORMATION OUT OF YOU BECAUSE MY HUSBAND WANTED TO KNOW...
...WHO YOU ARE AND WHAT YOU'RE PLOTTING.
GET IT?!

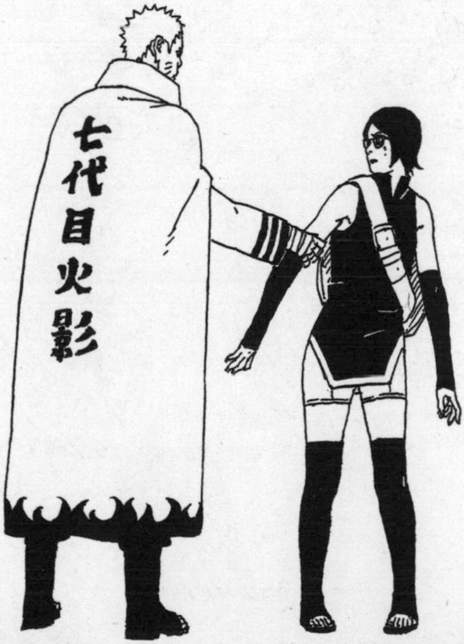
七代目火影

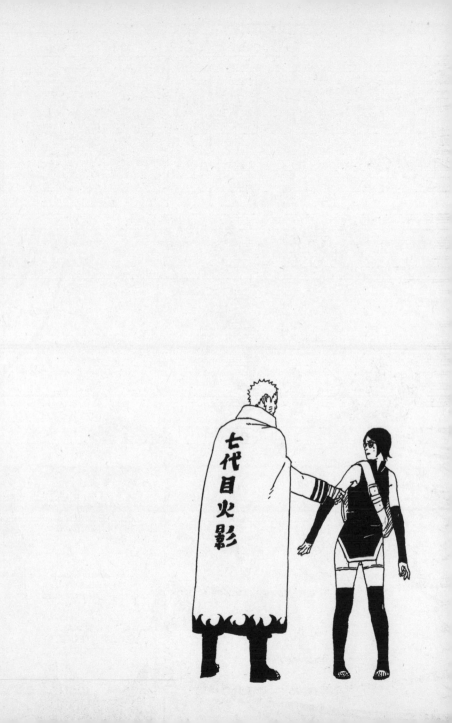

Number 700+9: I'll Protect You

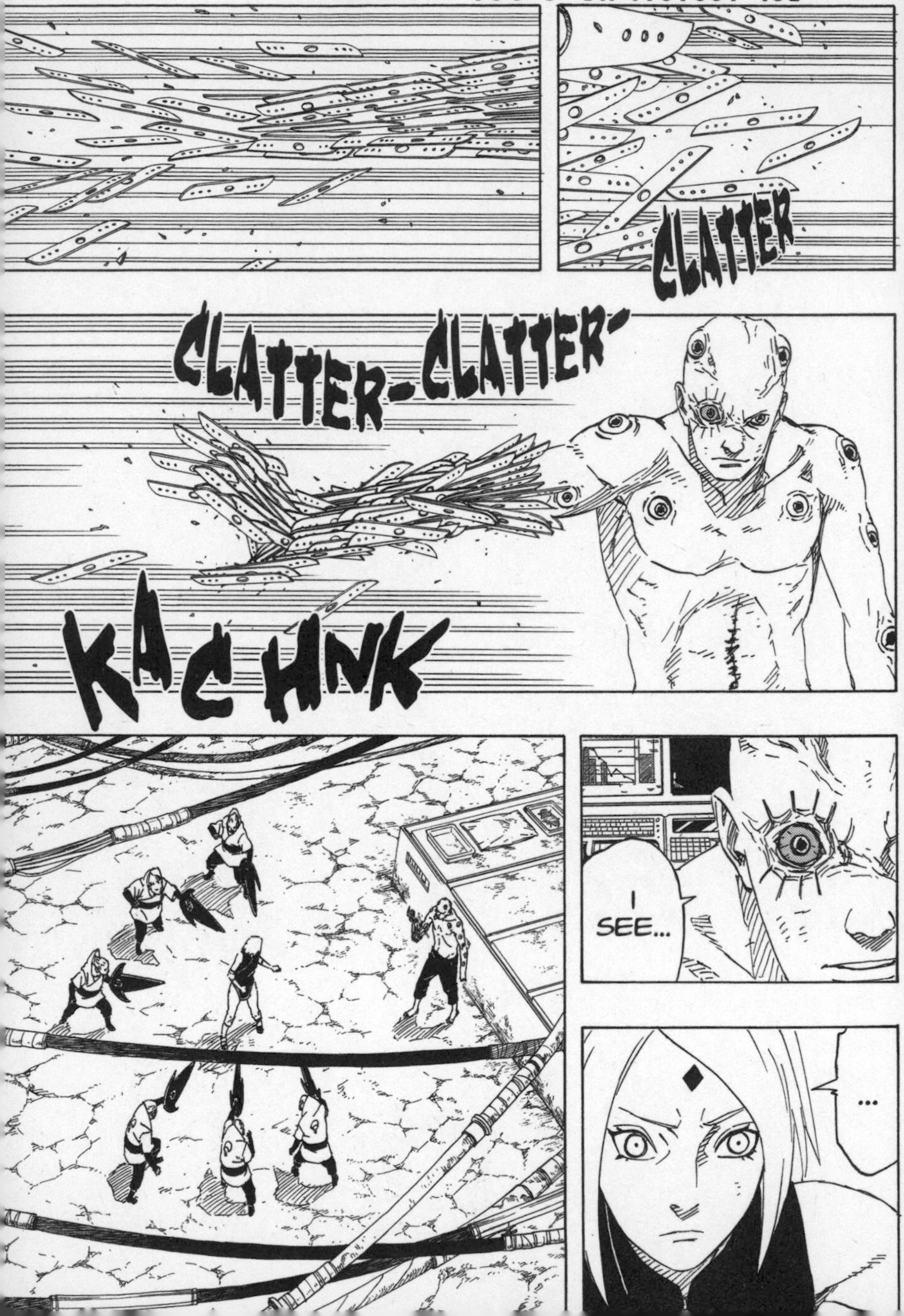
CLATTER
CLATTER-CLATTER-
KACHNK
I SEE...
...

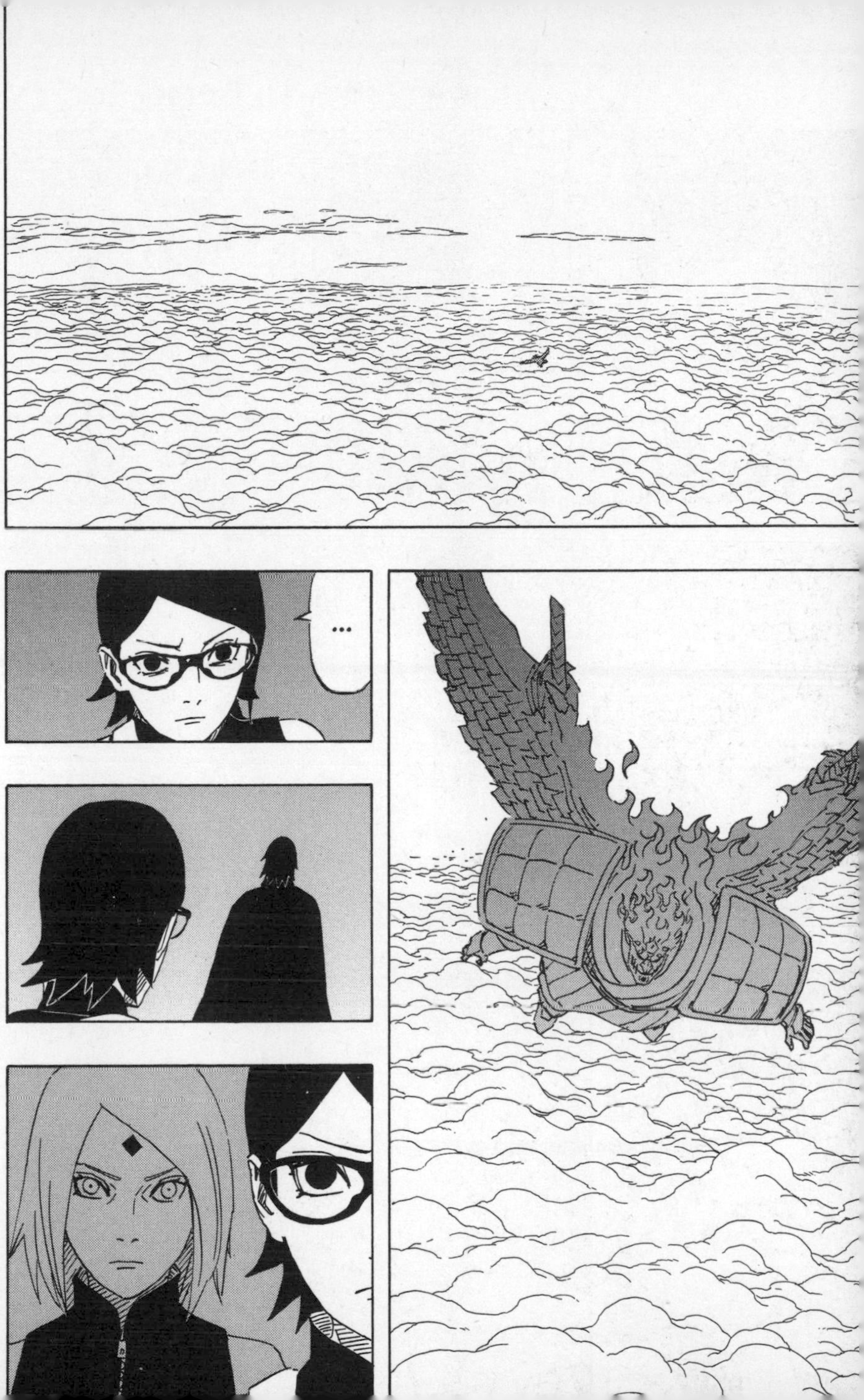
...

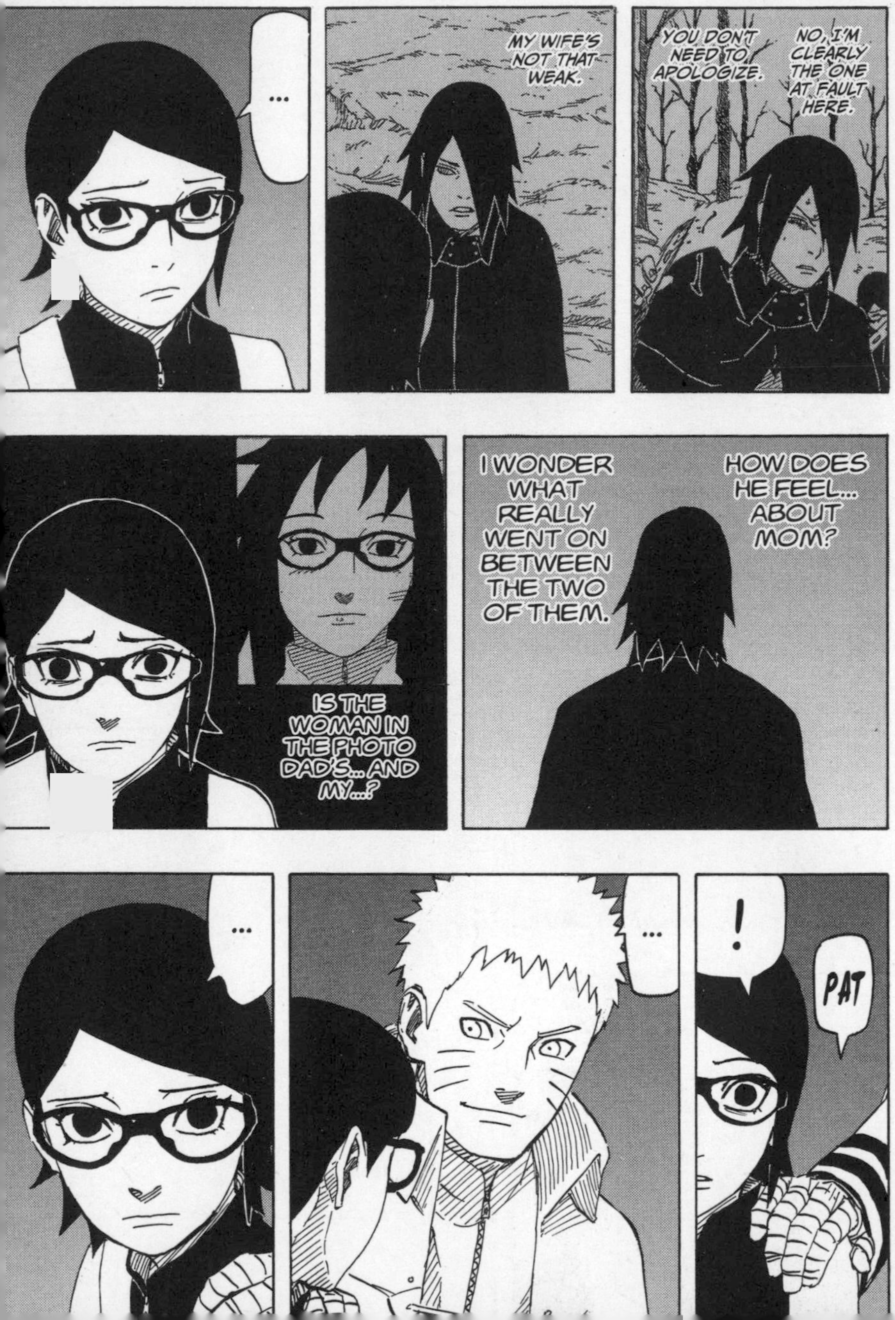
NO, I'M CLEARLY THE ONE AT FAULT HERE.
YOU DON'T NEED TO APOLOGIZE.
MY WIFE'S NOT THAT WEAK.
...
HOW DOES HE FEEL... ABOUT MOM?
I WONDER WHAT REALLY WENT ON BETWEEN THE TWO OF THEM.
IS THE WOMAN IN THE PHOTO DAD'S... AND MY...?
!
PAT
...
...

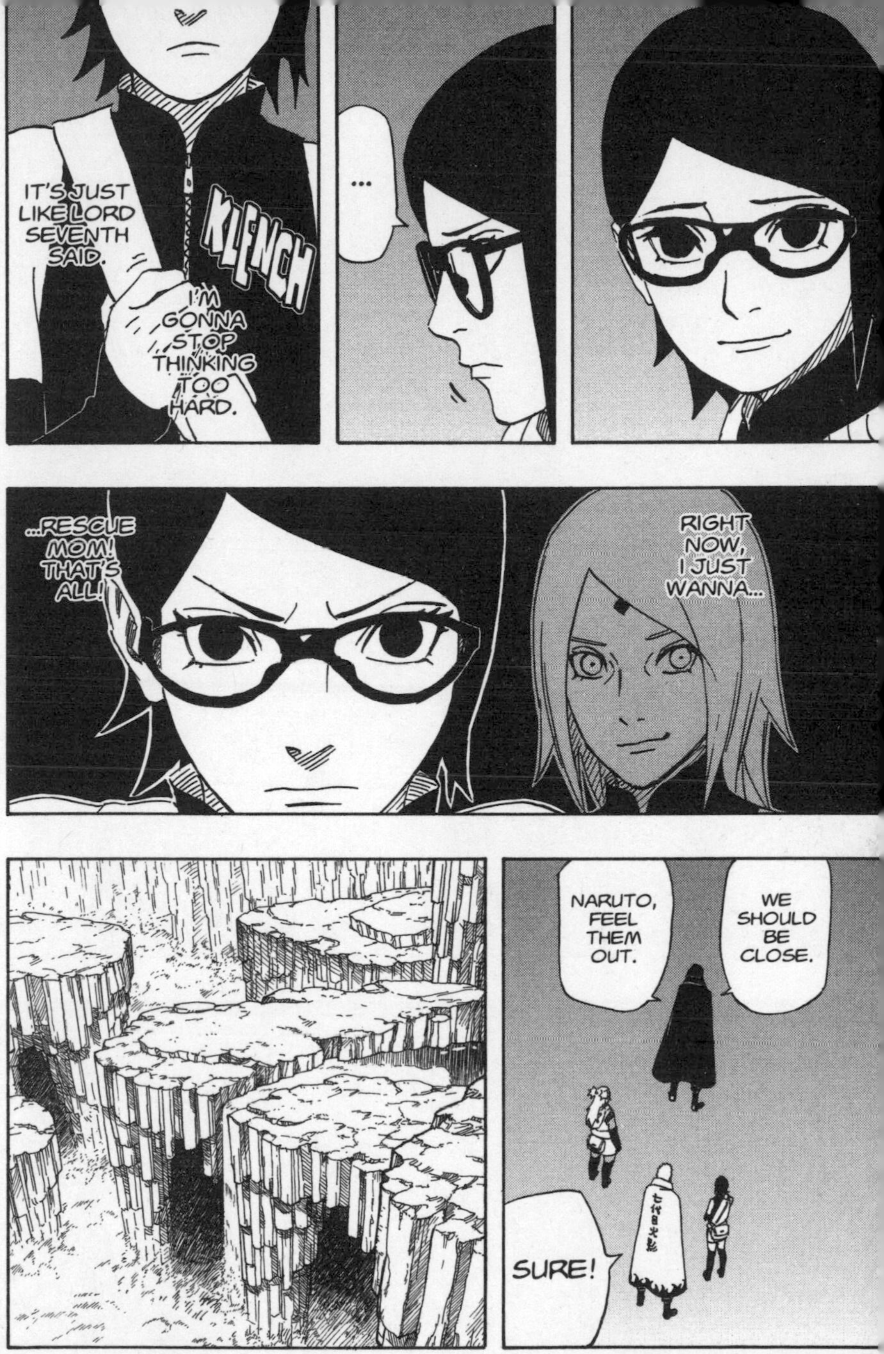
...
IT'S JUST LIKE LORD SEVENTH SAID.
KLENCH
I'M GONNA STOP THINKING TOO HARD.
RIGHT NOW, I JUST WANNA...
...RESCUE MOM! THAT'S ALL!
WE SHOULD BE CLOSE.
NARUTO, FEEL THEM OUT.
SURE!

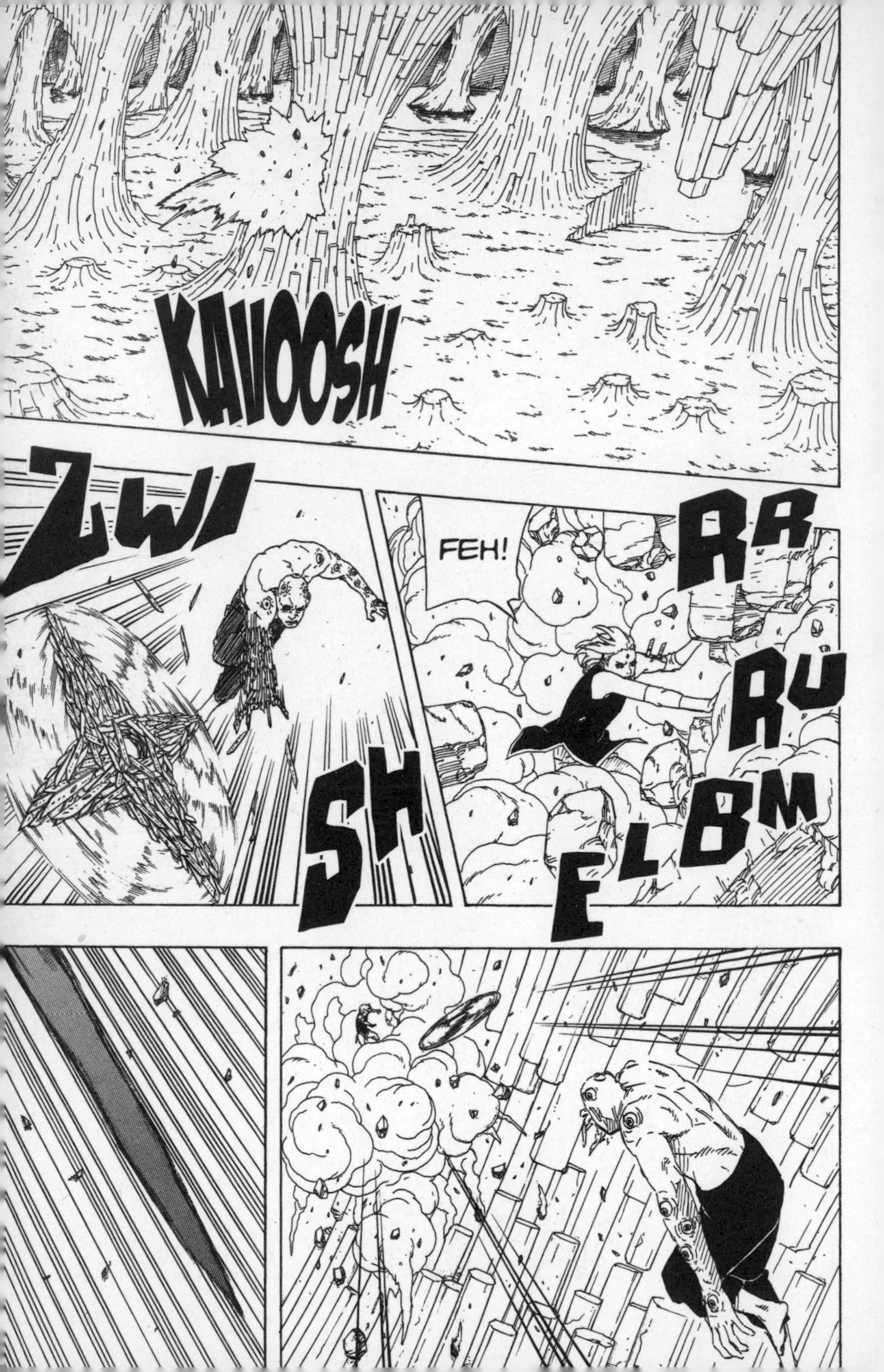
KAVOOSH
FEH!
RR
RU
R
ELBM
ZWI
SH

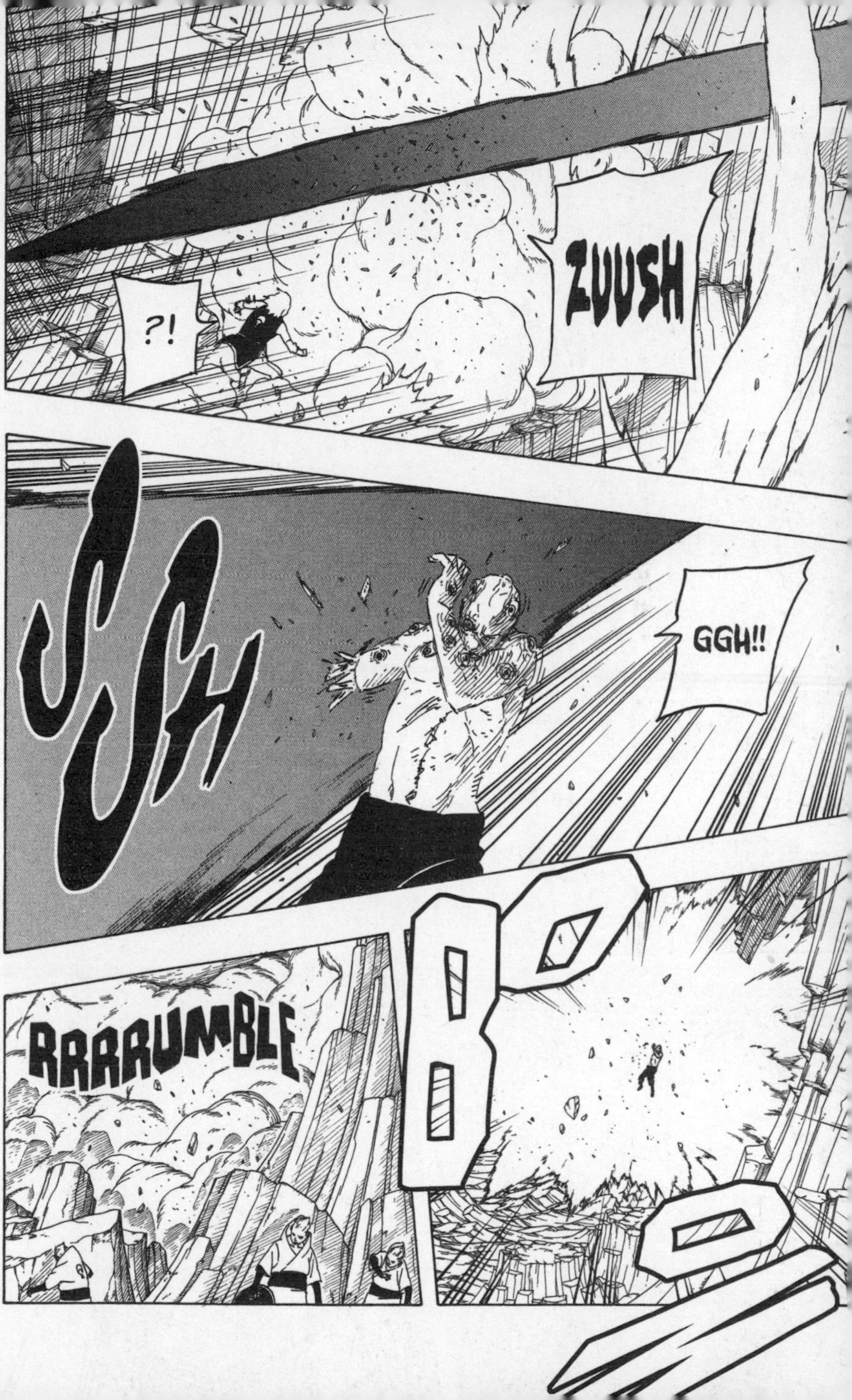
ZUUSH
?!
GGH!!
RRRRUMBLE

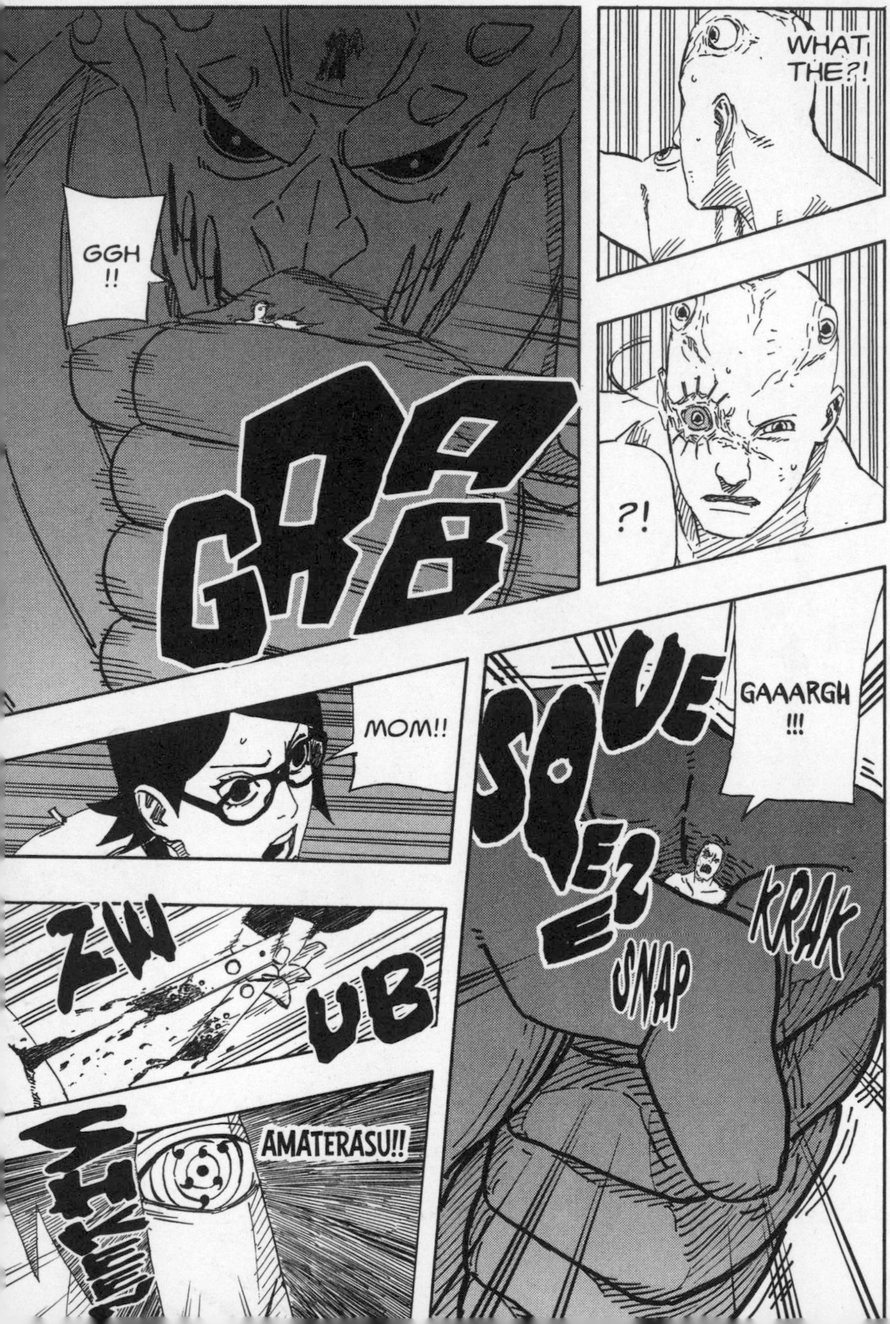
WHAT THE?!
?!
GGH !!
GRAB
SQUEEZE
GAAARGH !!!
KRAK
SNAP
MOM!!
ZWUB
AMATERASU!!

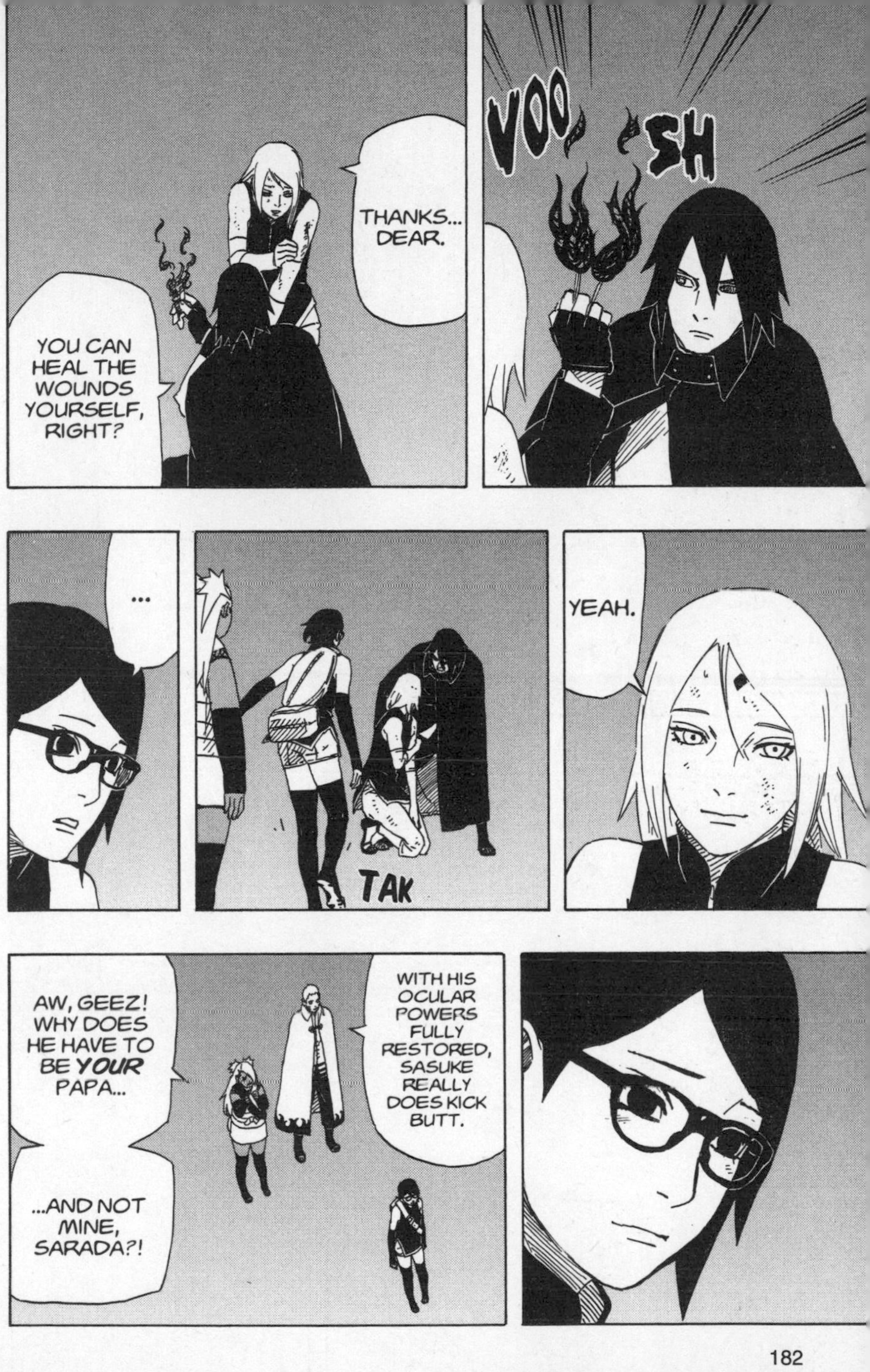
VOOSH
THANKS... DEAR.
YOU CAN HEAL THE WOUNDS YOURSELF, RIGHT?
YEAH.
TAK
...
WITH HIS OCULAR POWERS FULLY RESTORED, SASUKE REALLY DOES KICK BUTT.
AW, GEEZ! WHY DOES HE HAVE TO BE ***YOUR*** PAPA...
...AND NOT MINE, SARADA?!

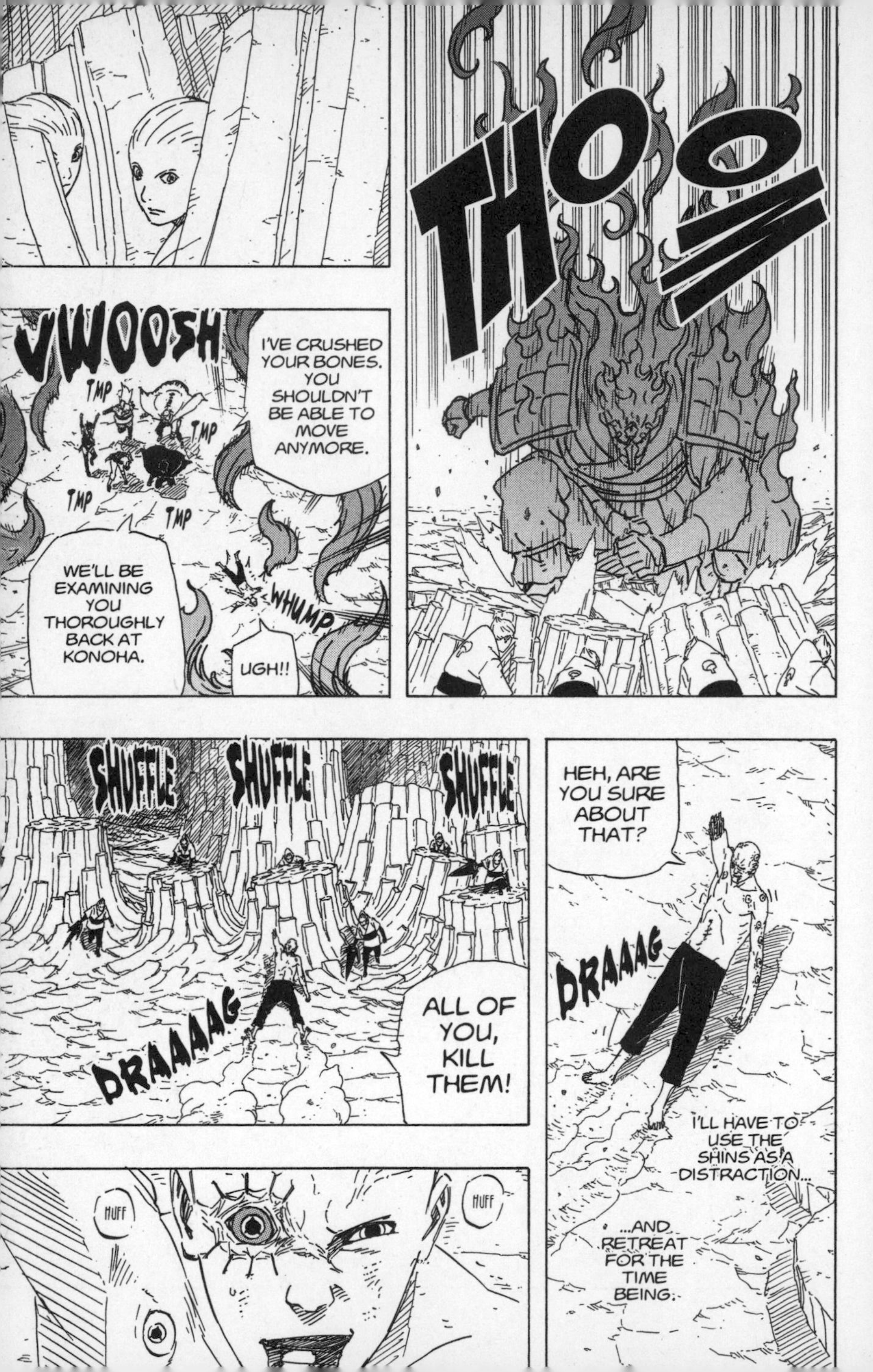
THOOM
I'VE CRUSHED YOUR BONES. YOU SHOULDN'T BE ABLE TO MOVE ANYMORE.
VWOOSH
TMP
TMP
TMP
TMP
WHUMP
WE'LL BE EXAMINING YOU THOROUGHLY BACK AT KONOHA.
UGH!!
HEH, ARE YOU SURE ABOUT THAT?
DRAAAG
I'LL HAVE TO USE THE SHINS AS A DISTRACTION...
...AND RETREAT FOR THE TIME BEING.
SHUFFLE
SHUFFLE
SHUFFLE
ALL OF YOU, KILL THEM!
DRAAAAG
HUFF
HUFF

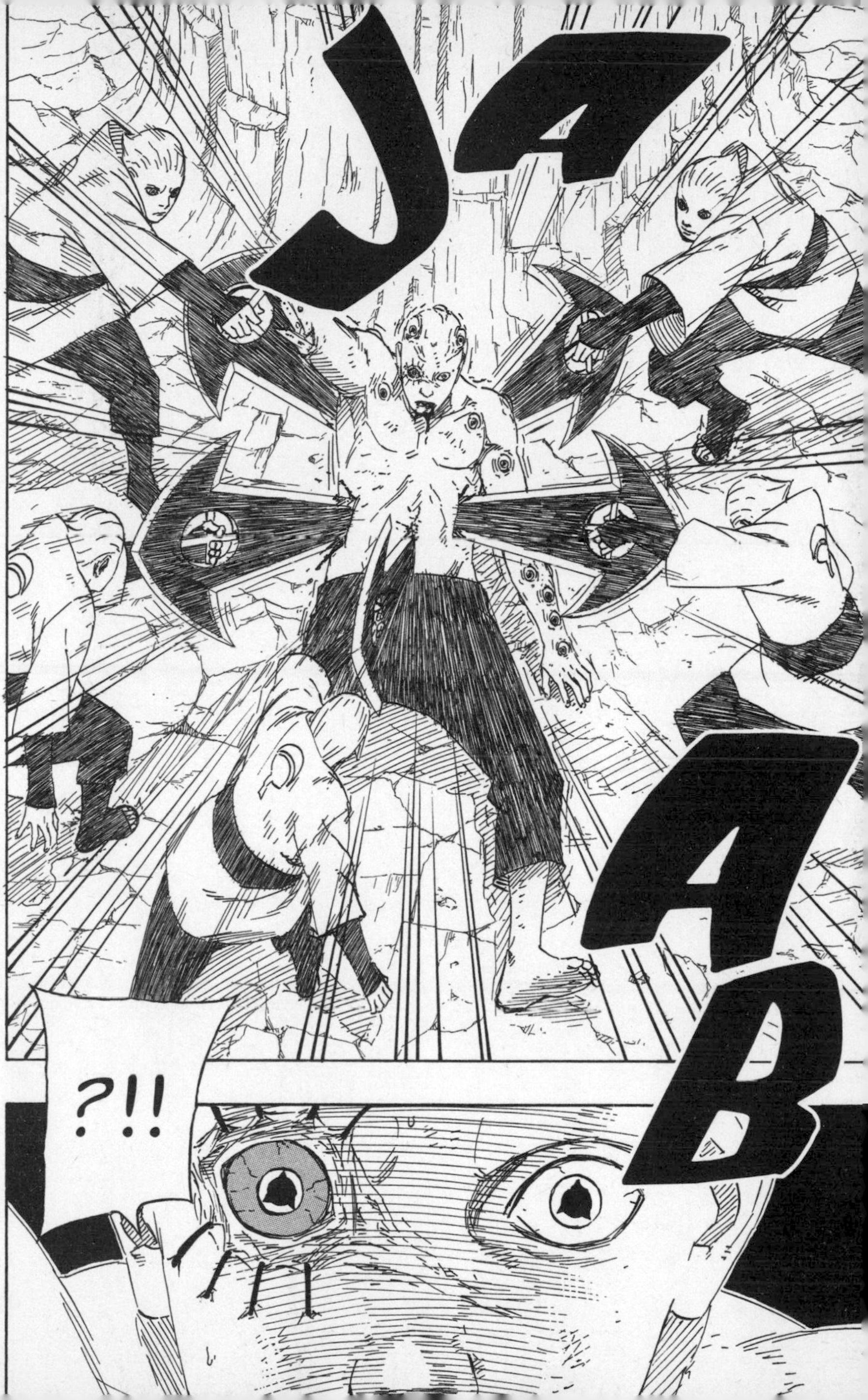
JAAB
?!!

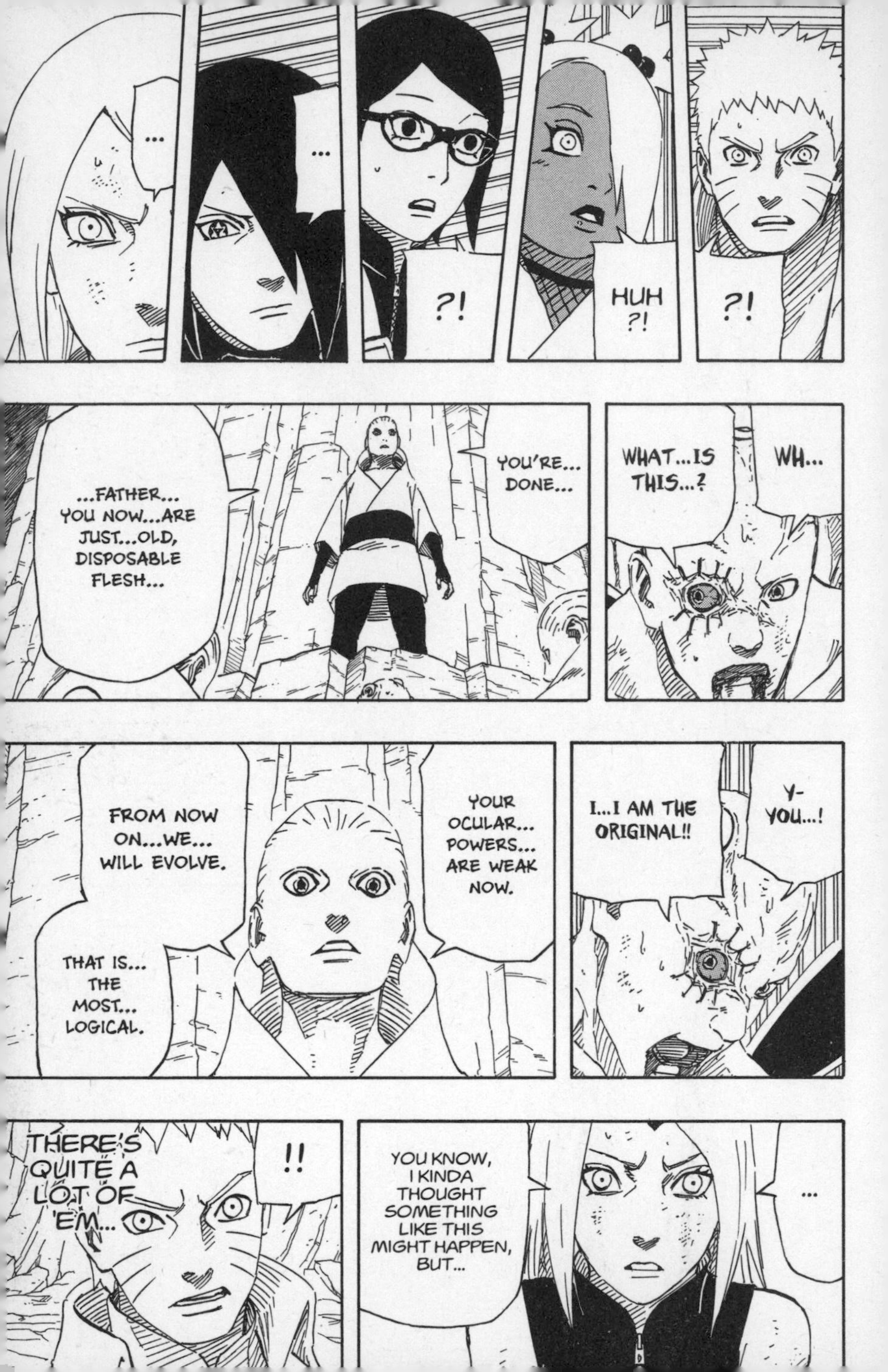
?!
HUH ?!
?!
...
...
WH...
WHAT...IS THIS...?
YOU'RE... DONE...
...FATHER... YOU NOW...ARE JUST...OLD, DISPOSABLE FLESH...
Y-YOU...!
I...I AM THE ORIGINAL!!
YOUR OCULAR... POWERS... ARE WEAK NOW.
FROM NOW ON...WE... WILL EVOLVE.
THAT IS... THE MOST... LOGICAL.
...
YOU KNOW, I KINDA THOUGHT SOMETHING LIKE THIS MIGHT HAPPEN, BUT...
!!
THERE'S QUITE A LOT OF 'EM...

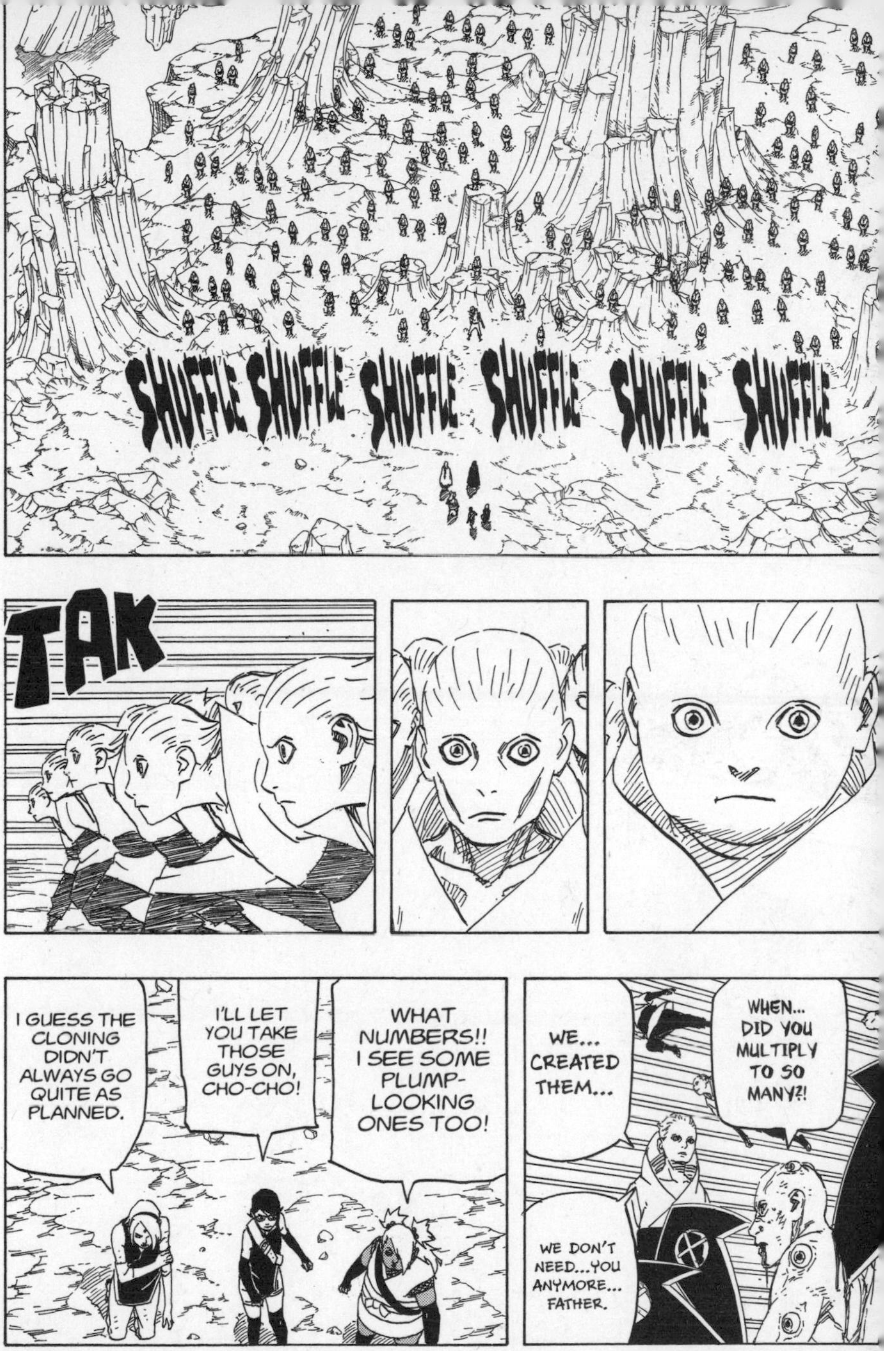
SHUFFLE SHUFFLE SHUFFLE SHUFFLE SHUFFLE SHUFFLE
TAK
WHEN... DID YOU MULTIPLY TO SO MANY?!
WE... CREATED THEM...
WE DON'T NEED...YOU ANYMORE... FATHER.
WHAT NUMBERS!! I SEE SOME PLUMP-LOOKING ONES TOO!
I'LL LET YOU TAKE THOSE GUYS ON, CHO-CHO!
I GUESS THE CLONING DIDN'T ALWAYS GO QUITE AS PLANNED.

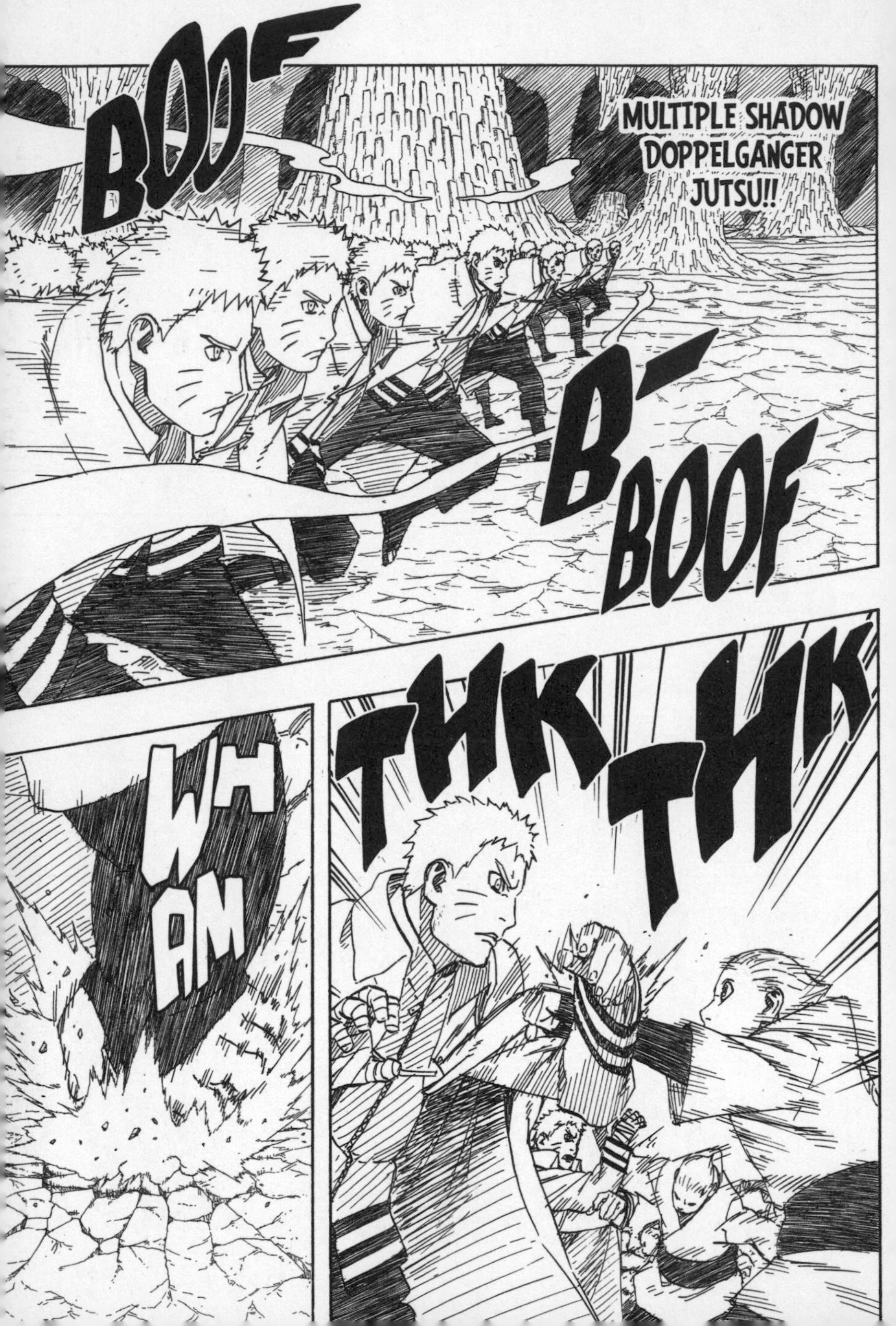
MULTIPLE SHADOW DOPPELGANGER JUTSU!!
BOOF
B-BOOF
THK
THK
WHAM

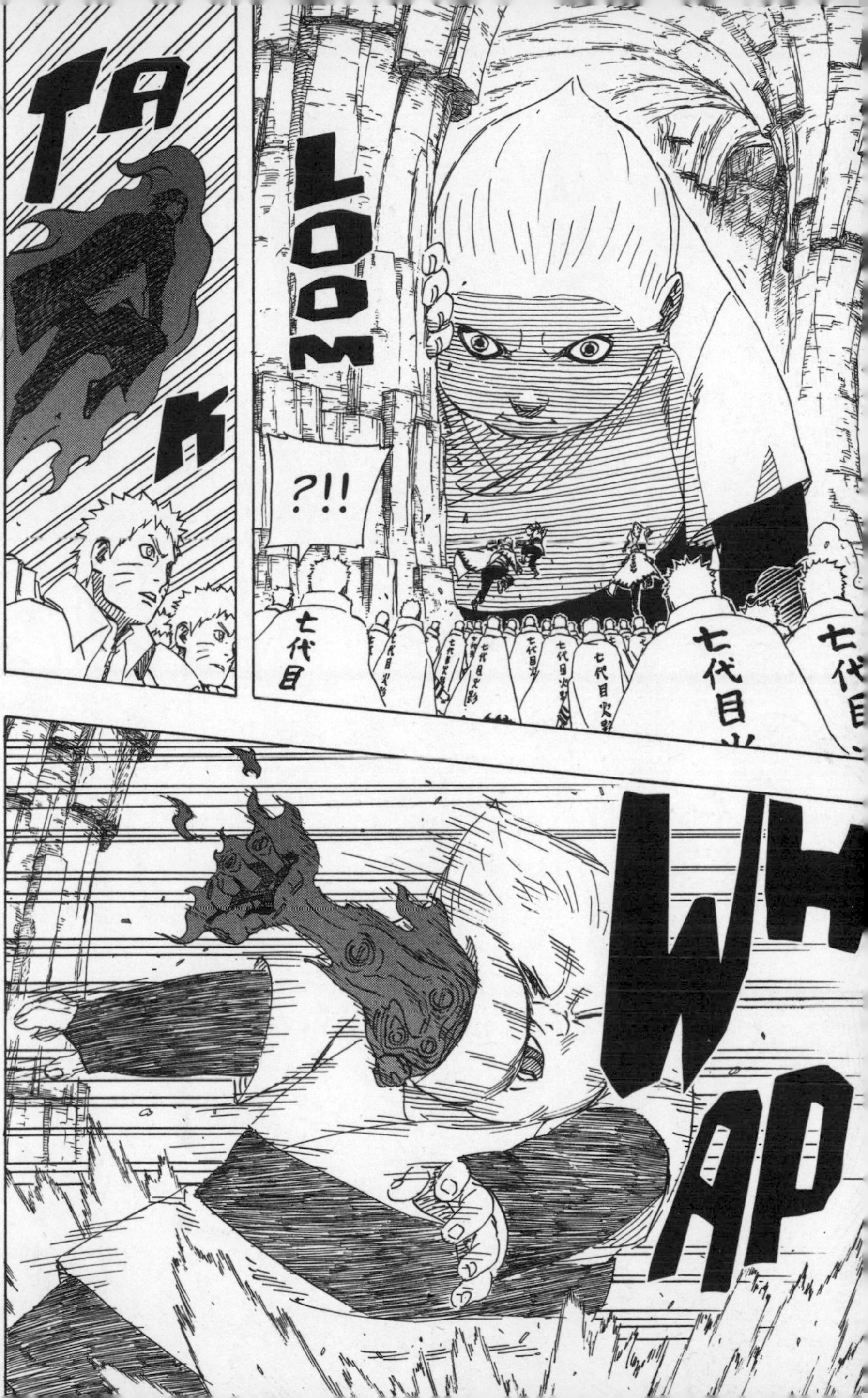
LOOM
?!!
七代目
七代目
七代目
TAK
WHAP

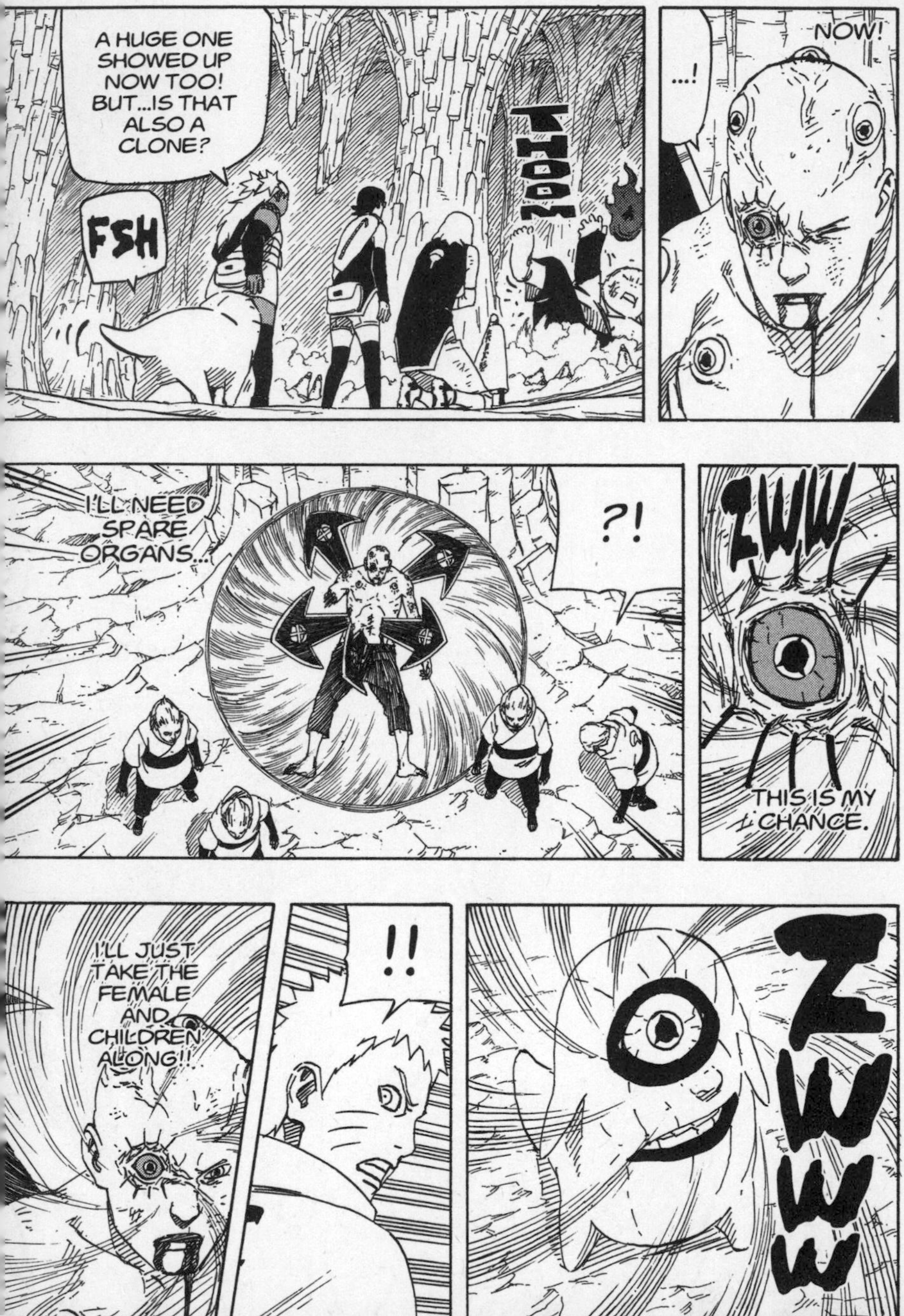
NOW!
...!
THOOM
A HUGE ONE SHOWED UP NOW TOO! BUT...IS THAT ALSO A CLONE?
FSH
ZWW
THIS IS MY CHANCE.
?!
I'LL NEED SPARE ORGANS...
ZWWW
!!
I'LL JUST TAKE THE FEMALE AND CHILDREN ALONG!!

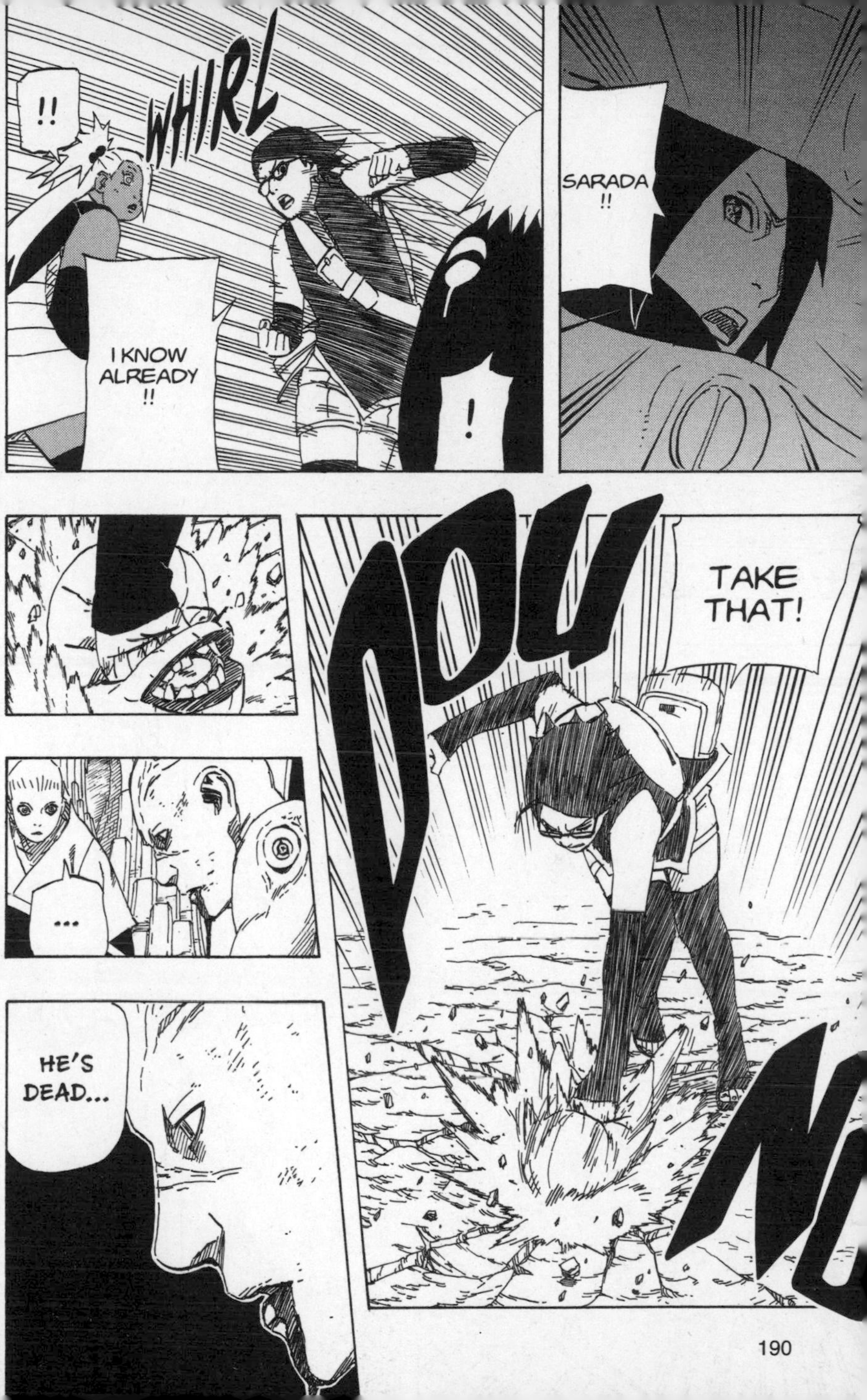
SARADA!!
WHIRL
!!
I KNOW ALREADY!!
!
TAKE THAT!
...
HE'S DEAD...

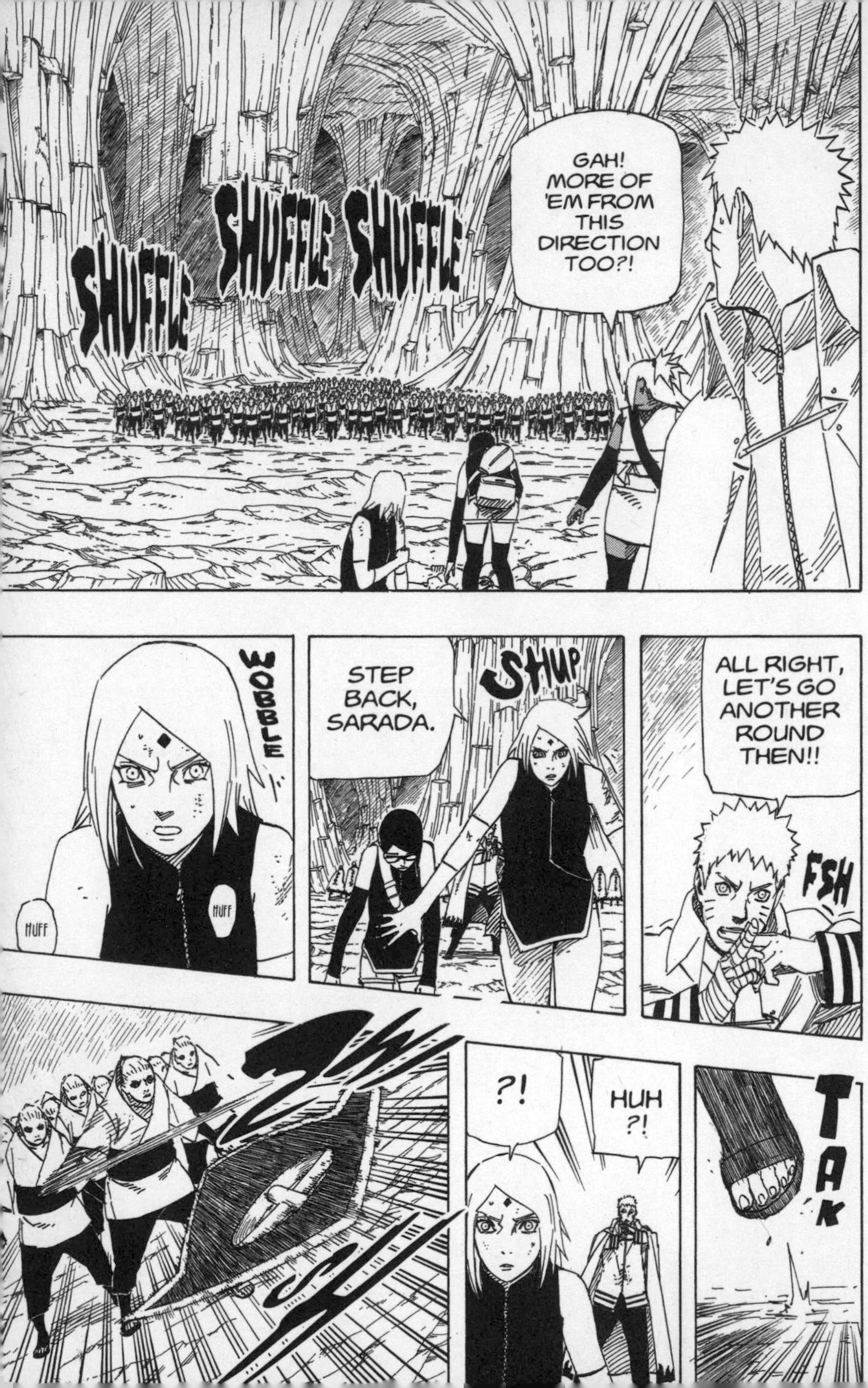
GAH! MORE OF 'EM FROM THIS DIRECTION TOO?!
SHUFFLE
SHUFFLE
SHUFFLE
ALL RIGHT, LET'S GO ANOTHER ROUND THEN!!
FSH
STEP BACK, SARADA.
SHUP
WOBBLE
HUFF
HUFF
TAK
HUH ?!
?!

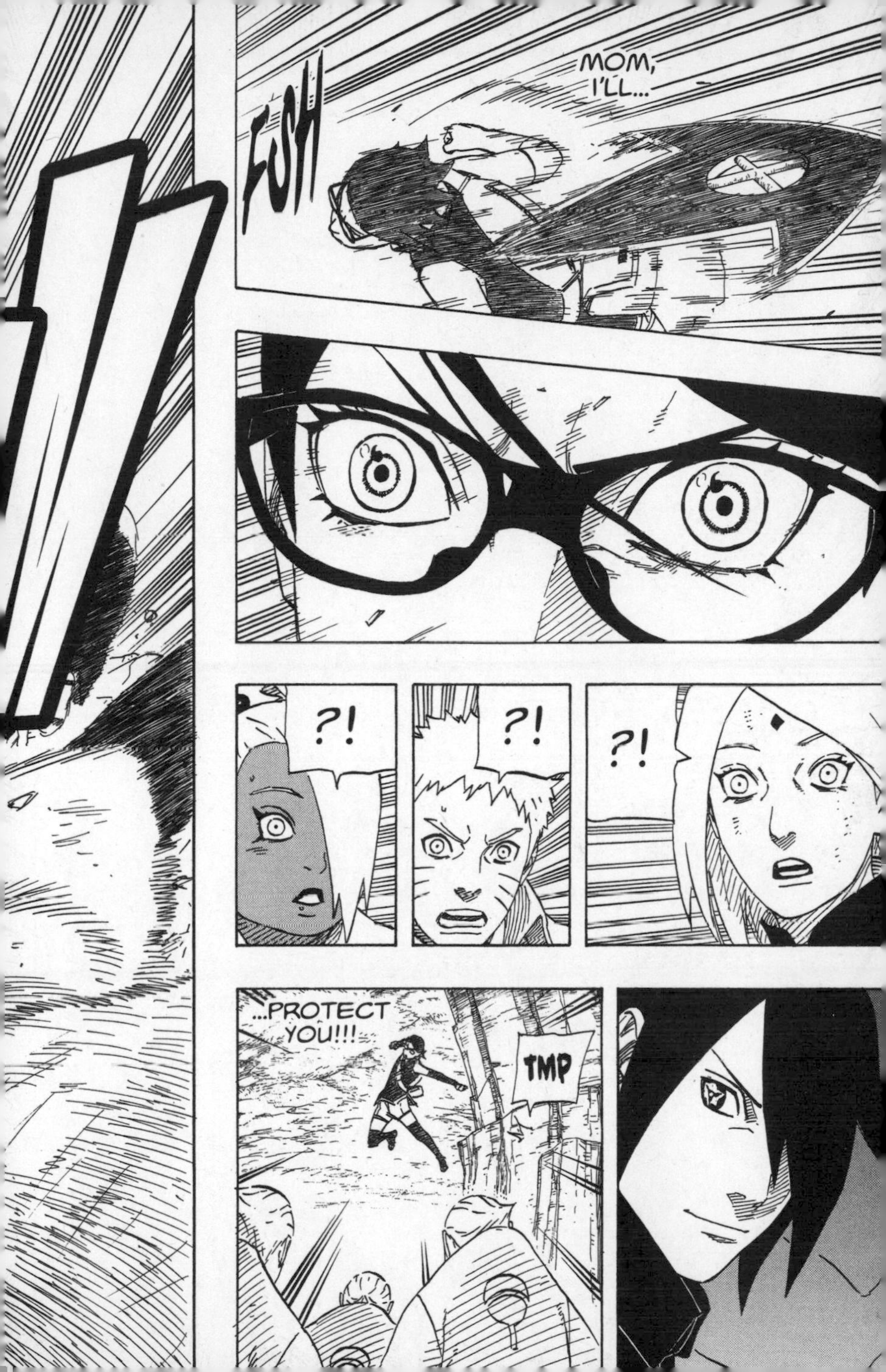
MOM, I'LL...
FSH
?!
?!
?!
...PROTECT YOU!!!
TMP
!!

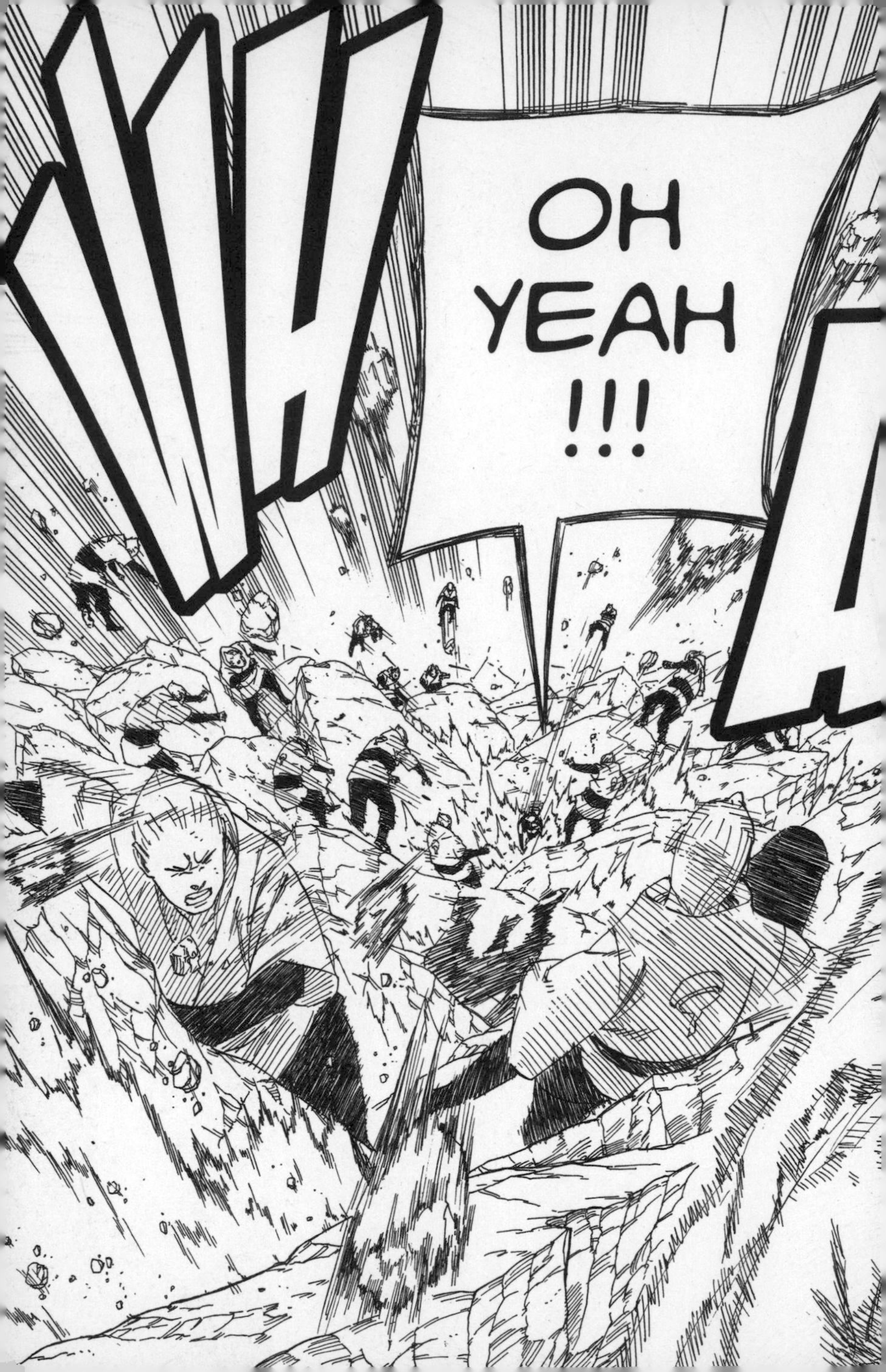
OH YEAH !!!

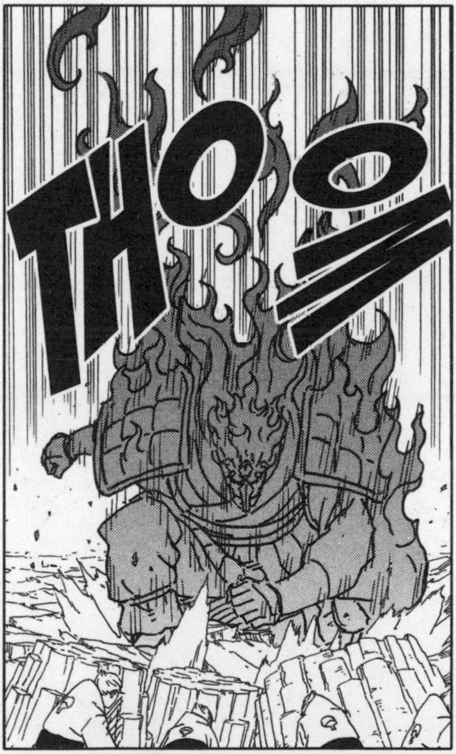
THOOM

Number 700+10: Reflected in Those Eyes

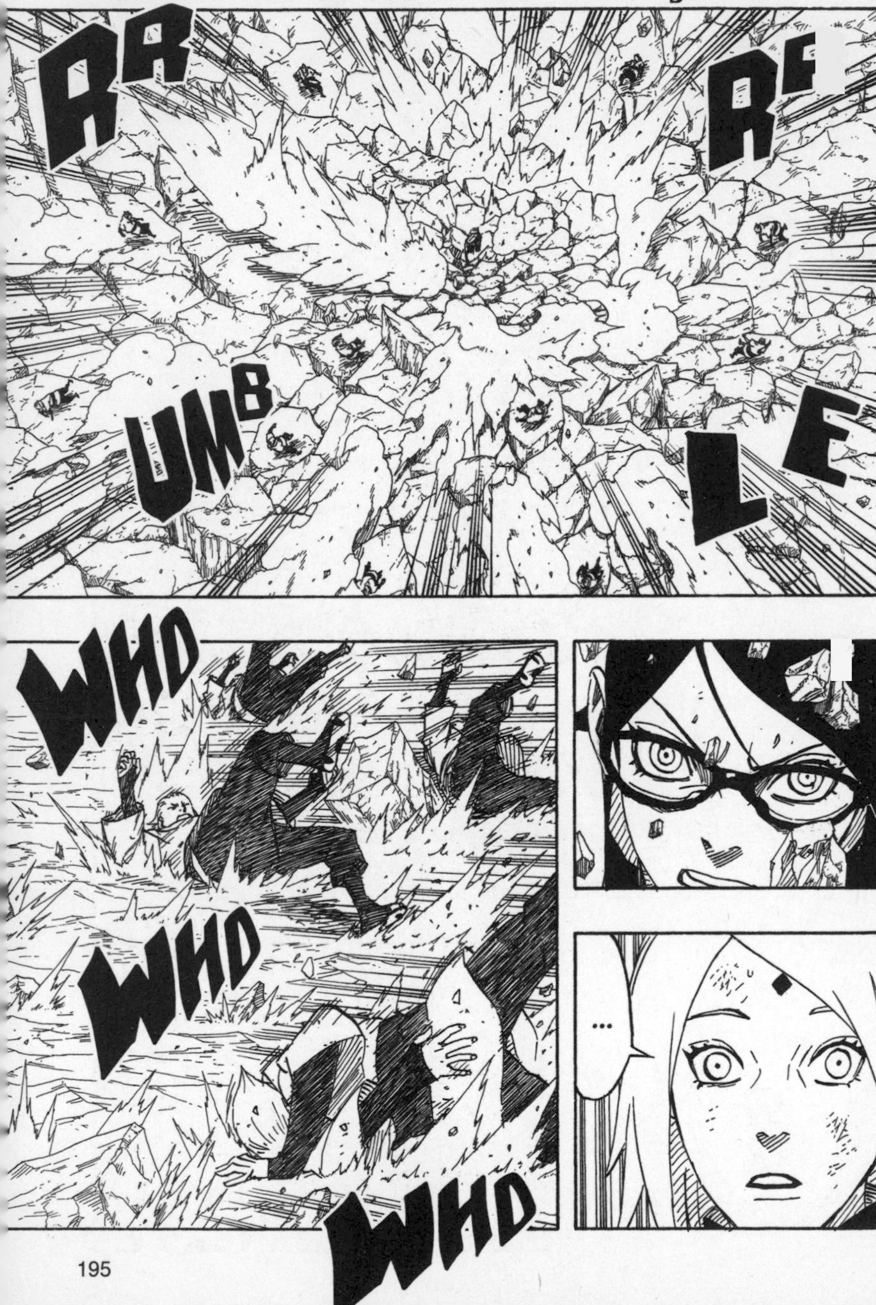
RR
RR
UMB
LE
...
WHD
WHD
WHD

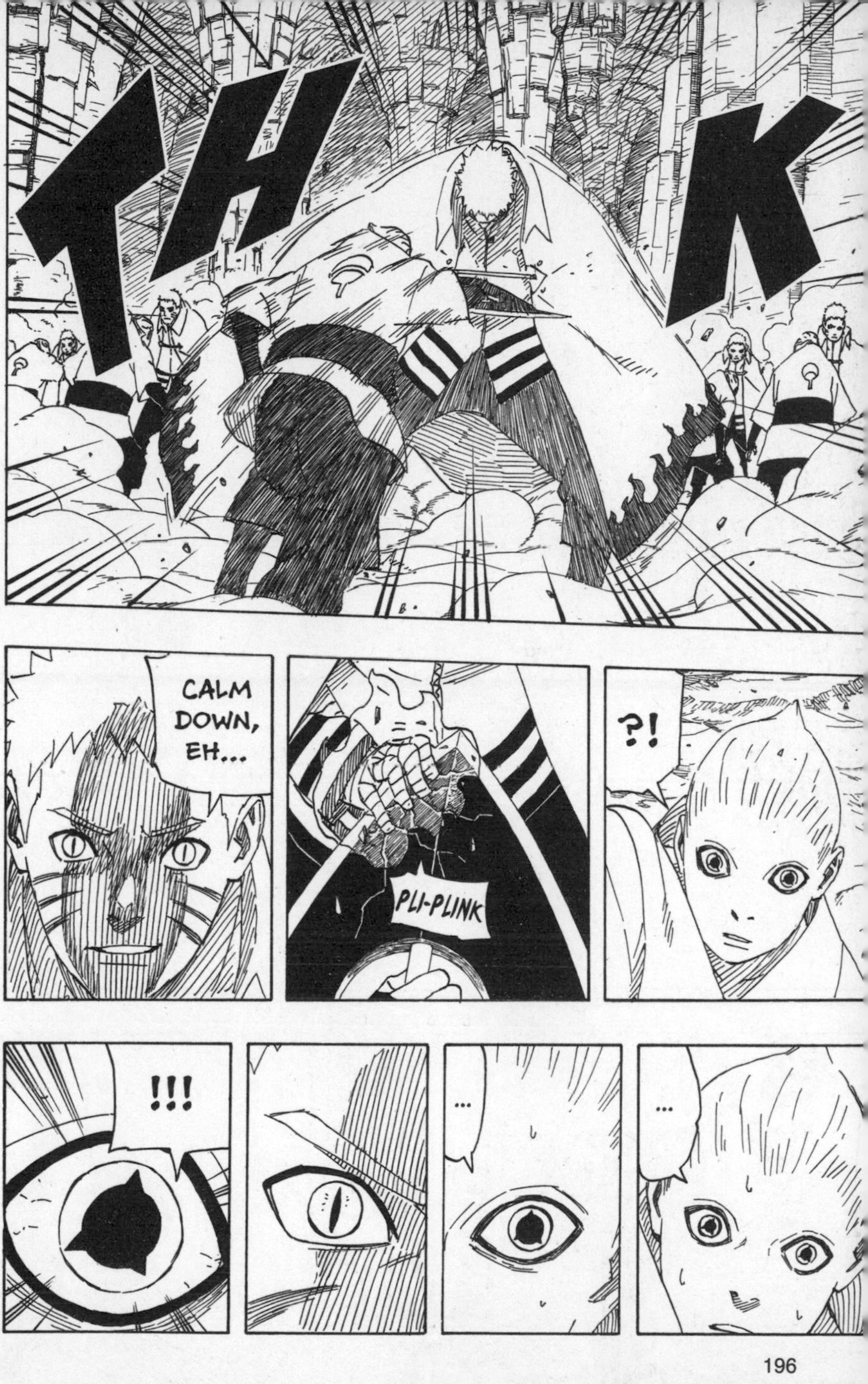
THK
?!
PLI-PLINK
CALM DOWN, EH...
...
...
!!!

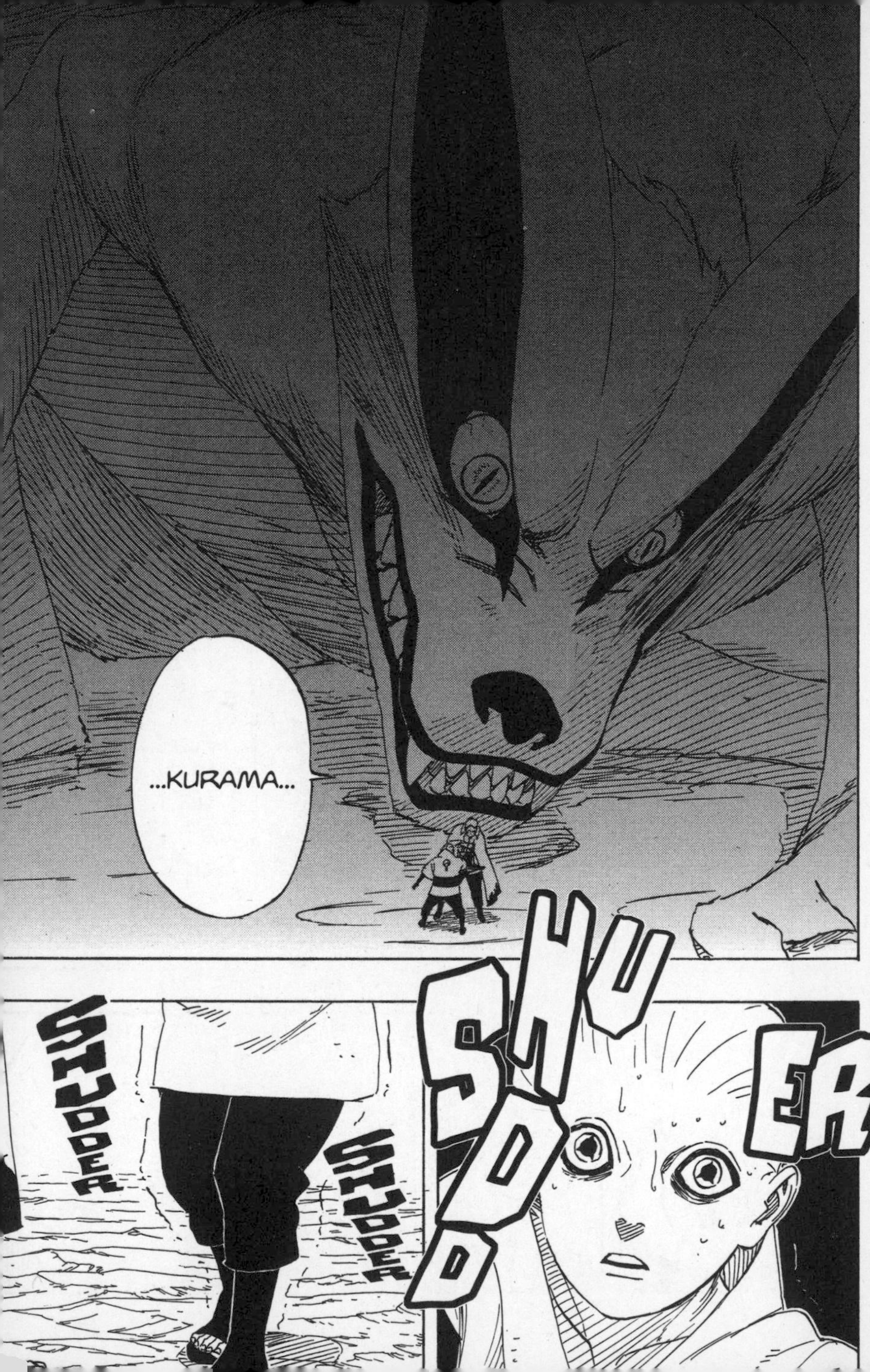
...KURAMA...
SHUDDER
SHUDDER
SHUDDER

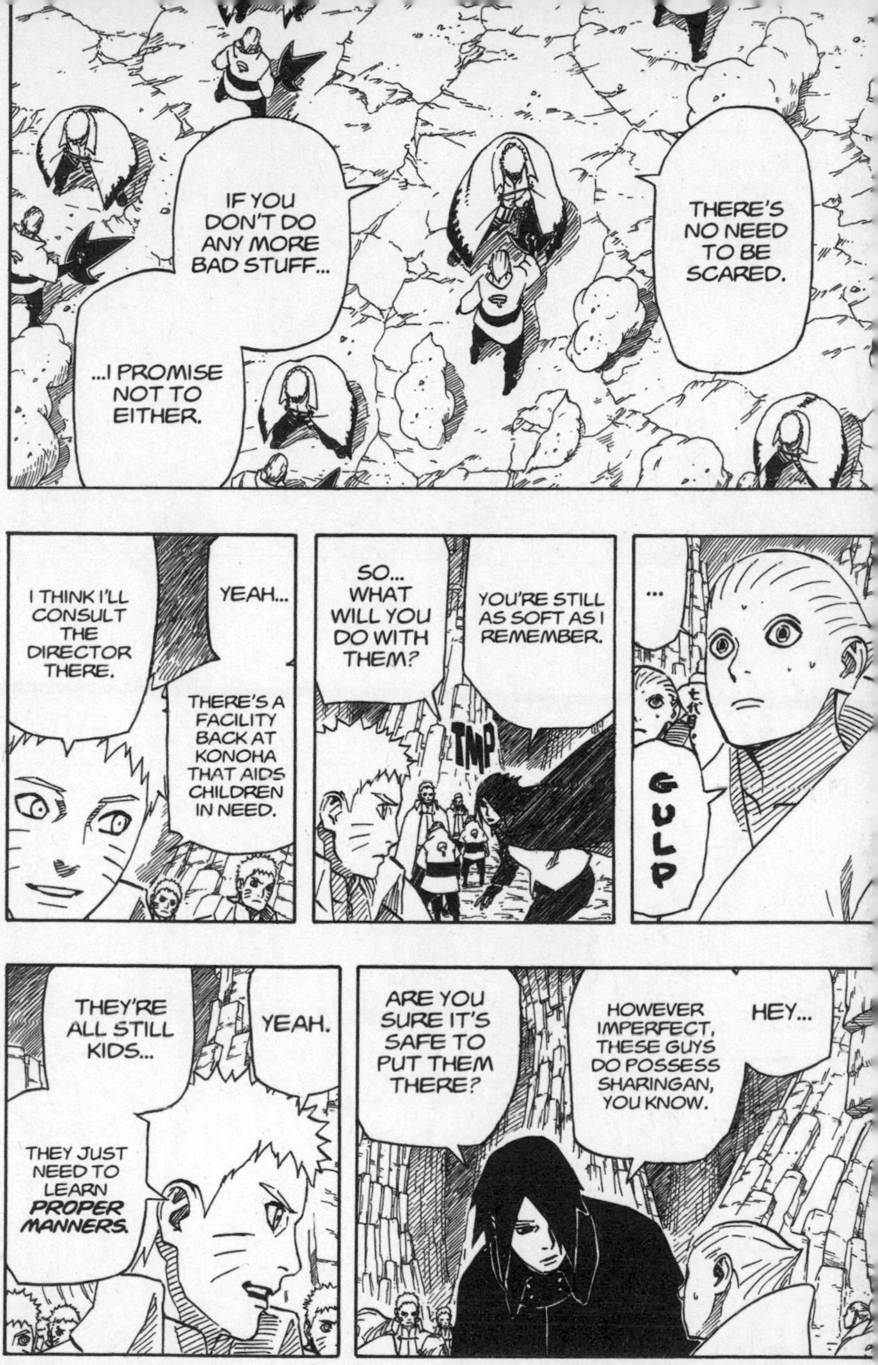
THERE'S NO NEED TO BE SCARED.
IF YOU DON'T DO ANY MORE BAD STUFF...
...I PROMISE NOT TO EITHER.
...
GULP
YOU'RE STILL AS SOFT AS I REMEMBER.
TMP
SO... WHAT WILL YOU DO WITH THEM?
YEAH...
THERE'S A FACILITY BACK AT KONOHA THAT AIDS CHILDREN IN NEED.
I THINK I'LL CONSULT THE DIRECTOR THERE.
HEY...
HOWEVER IMPERFECT, THESE GUYS DO POSSESS SHARINGAN, YOU KNOW.
ARE YOU SURE IT'S SAFE TO PUT THEM THERE?
YEAH.
THEY'RE ALL STILL KIDS...
THEY JUST NEED TO LEARN ***PROPER MANNERS.***

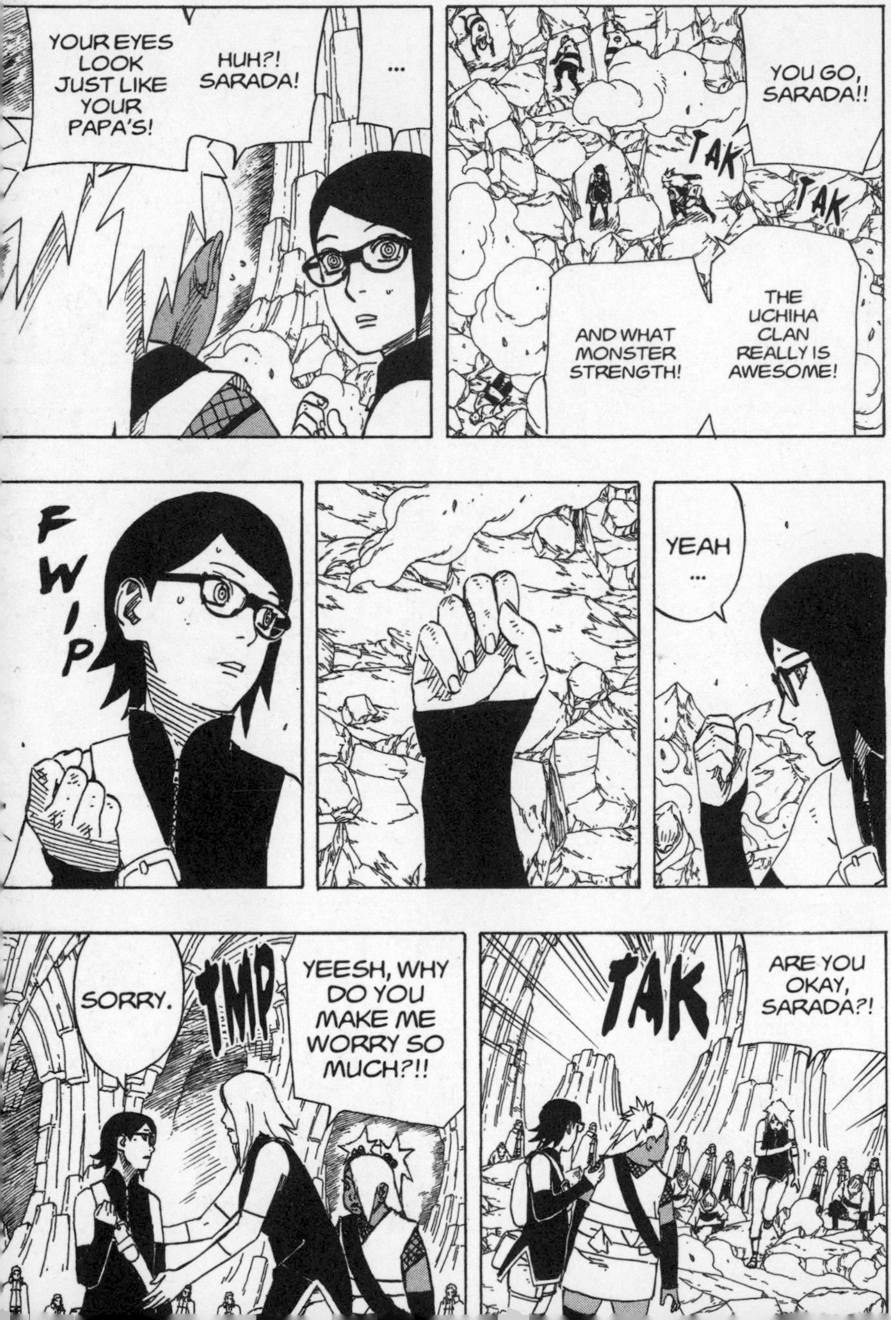
YOU GO, SARADA!!
TAK
TAK
THE UCHIHA CLAN REALLY IS AWESOME!
AND WHAT MONSTER STRENGTH!
...
HUH?! SARADA!
YOUR EYES LOOK JUST LIKE YOUR PAPA'S!
YEAH ...
FWIP
ARE YOU OKAY, SARADA?!
TAK
YEESH, WHY DO YOU MAKE ME WORRY SO MUCH?!!
TMP
SORRY.

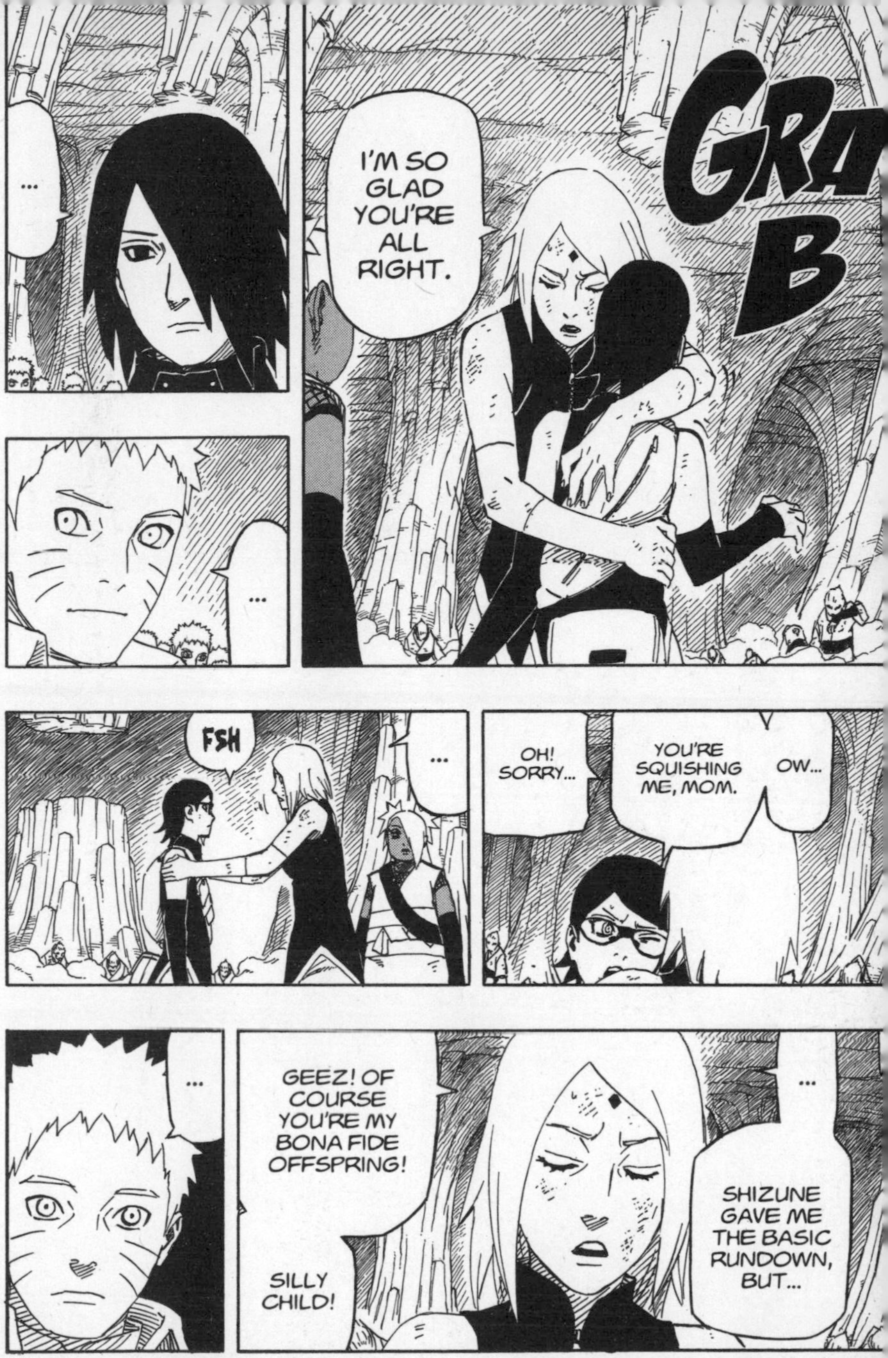
GRA
B
I'M SO GLAD YOU'RE ALL RIGHT.
...
...
OW...
YOU'RE SQUISHING ME, MOM.
OH! SORRY...
...
FSH
...
SHIZUNE GAVE ME THE BASIC RUNDOWN, BUT...
GEEZ! OF COURSE YOU'RE MY BONA FIDE OFFSPRING!
SILLY CHILD!
...

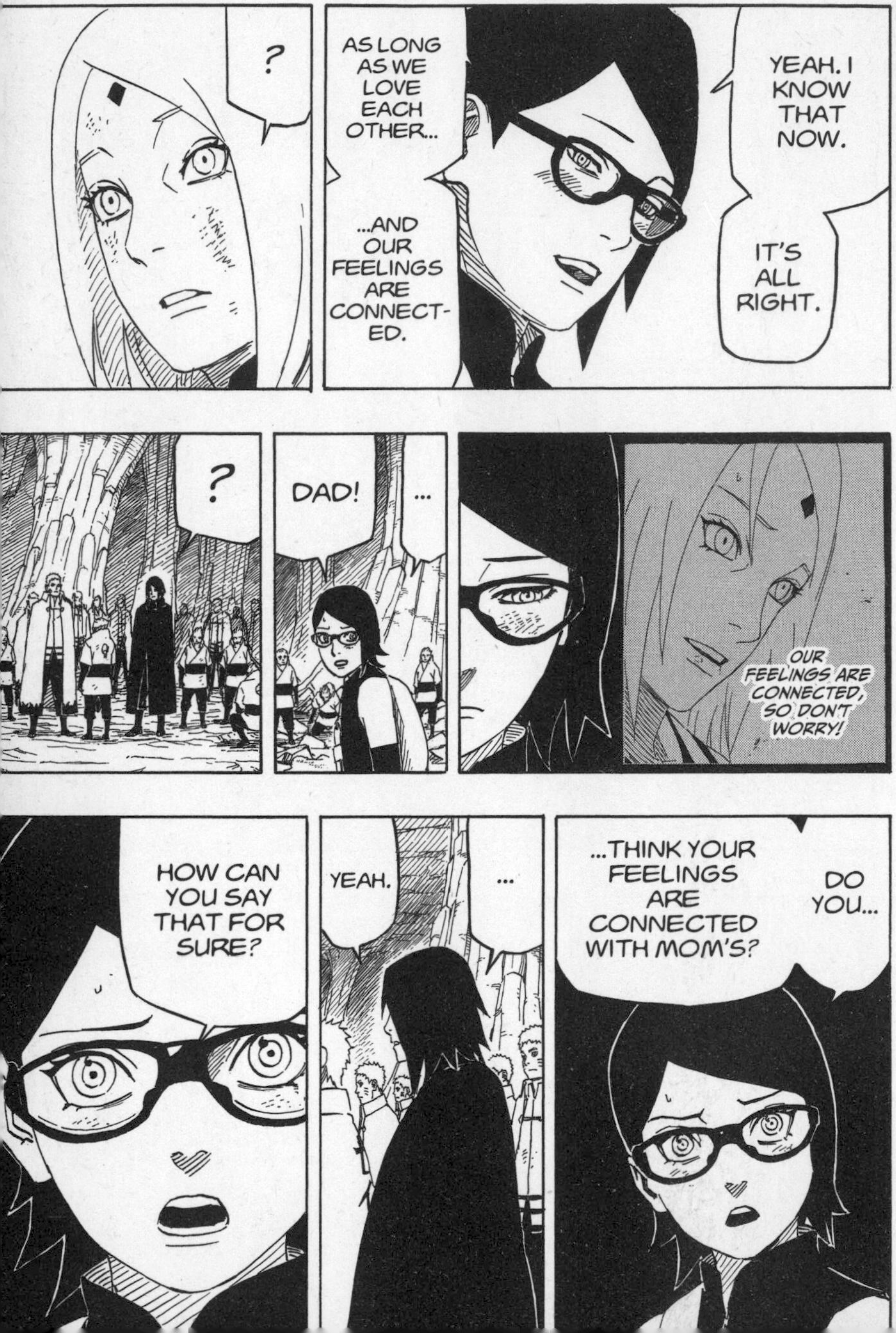

YEAH. I KNOW THAT NOW.
IT'S ALL RIGHT.
AS LONG AS WE LOVE EACH OTHER...
...AND OUR FEELINGS ARE CONNECT-ED.
?
OUR FEELINGS ARE CONNECTED, SO DON'T WORRY!
...
DAD!
?
DO YOU...
...THINK YOUR FEELINGS ARE CONNECTED WITH MOM'S?
...
YEAH.
HOW CAN YOU SAY THAT FOR SURE?

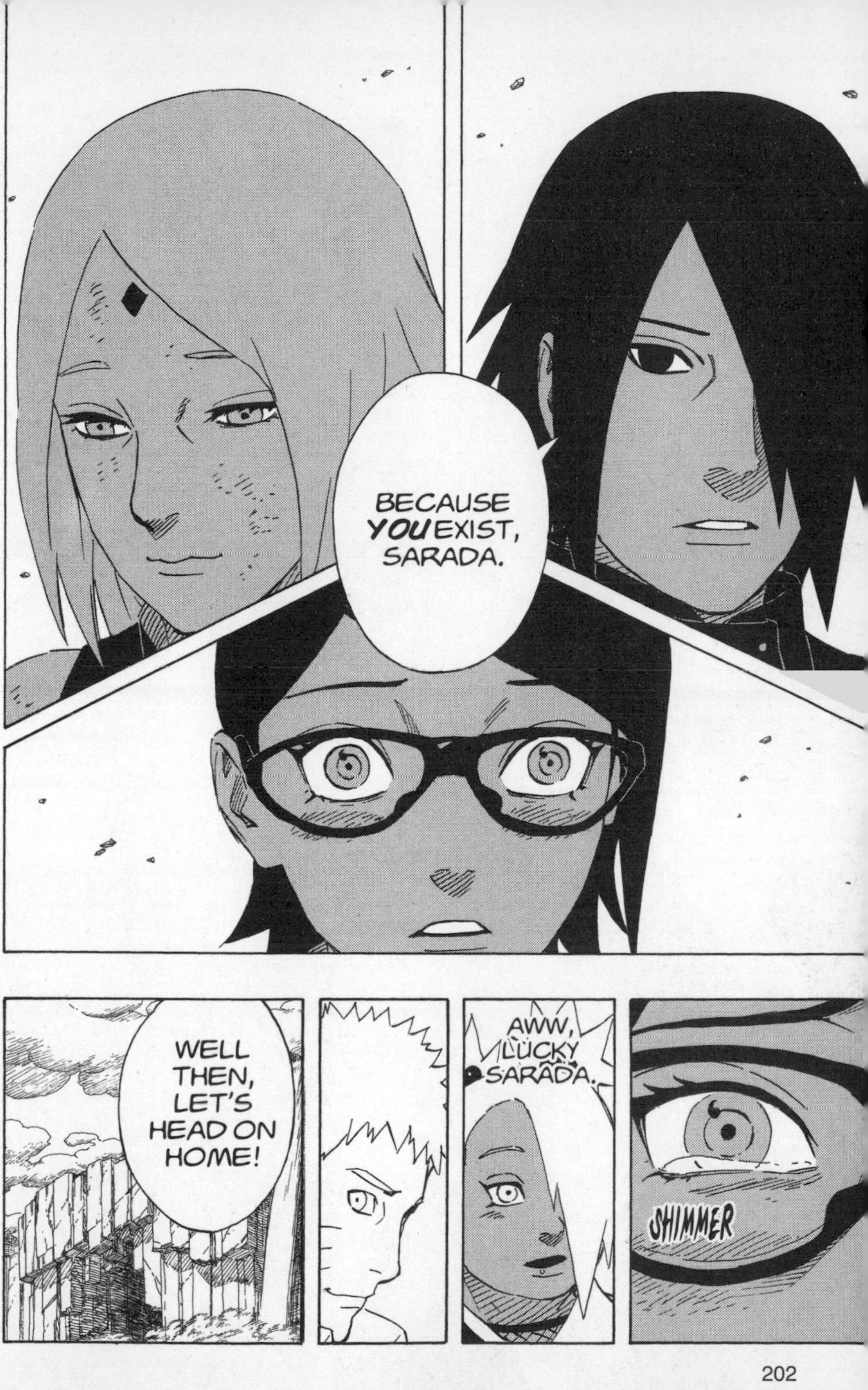
BECAUSE YOU EXIST, SARADA.
SHIMMER
AWW, LUCKY SARADA.
WELL THEN, LET'S HEAD ON HOME!

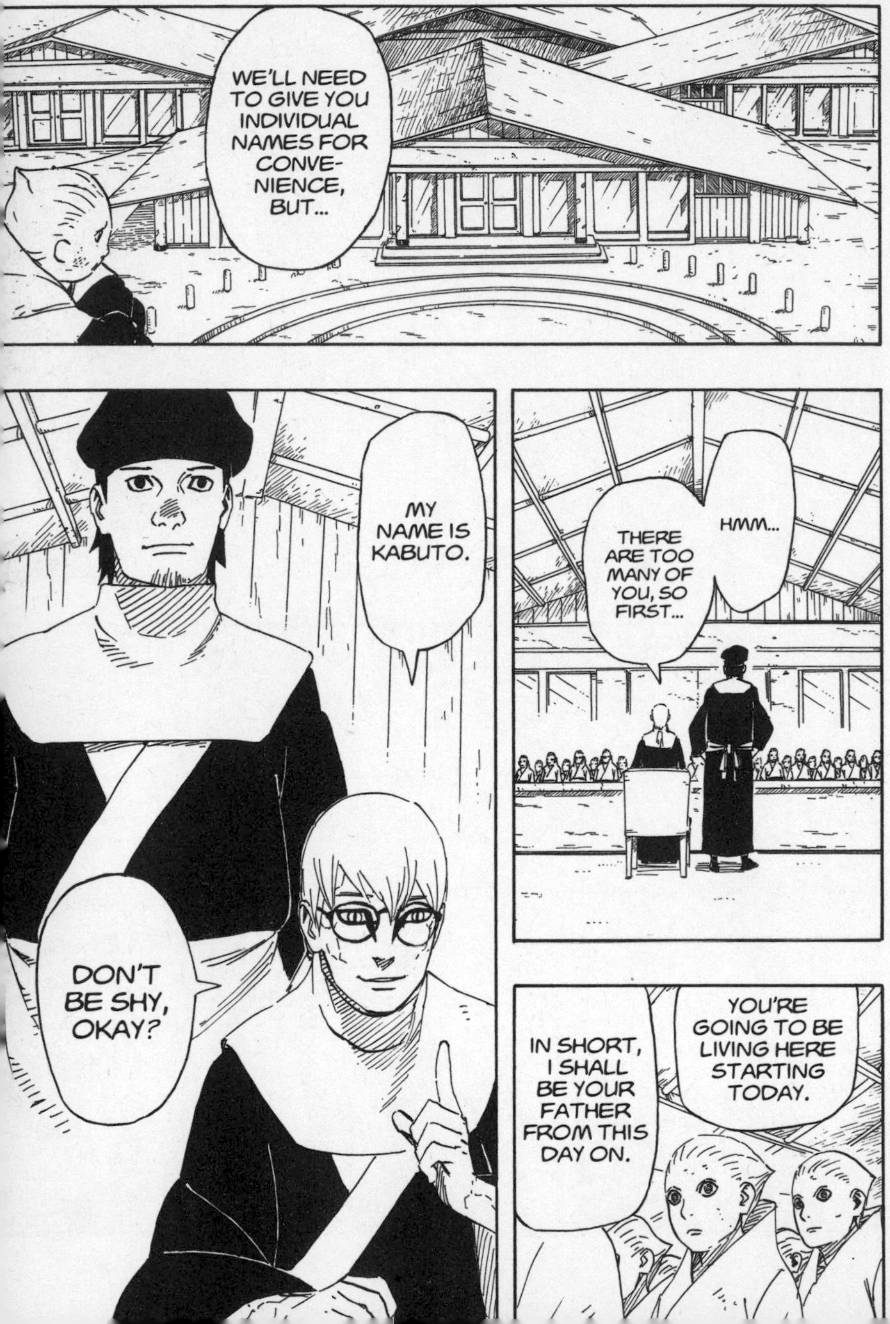
WE'LL NEED TO GIVE YOU INDIVIDUAL NAMES FOR CONVE-NIENCE, BUT...
HMM...
THERE ARE TOO MANY OF YOU, SO FIRST...
YOU'RE GOING TO BE LIVING HERE STARTING TODAY.
IN SHORT, I SHALL BE YOUR FATHER FROM THIS DAY ON.
MY NAME IS KABUTO.
DON'T BE SHY, OKAY?

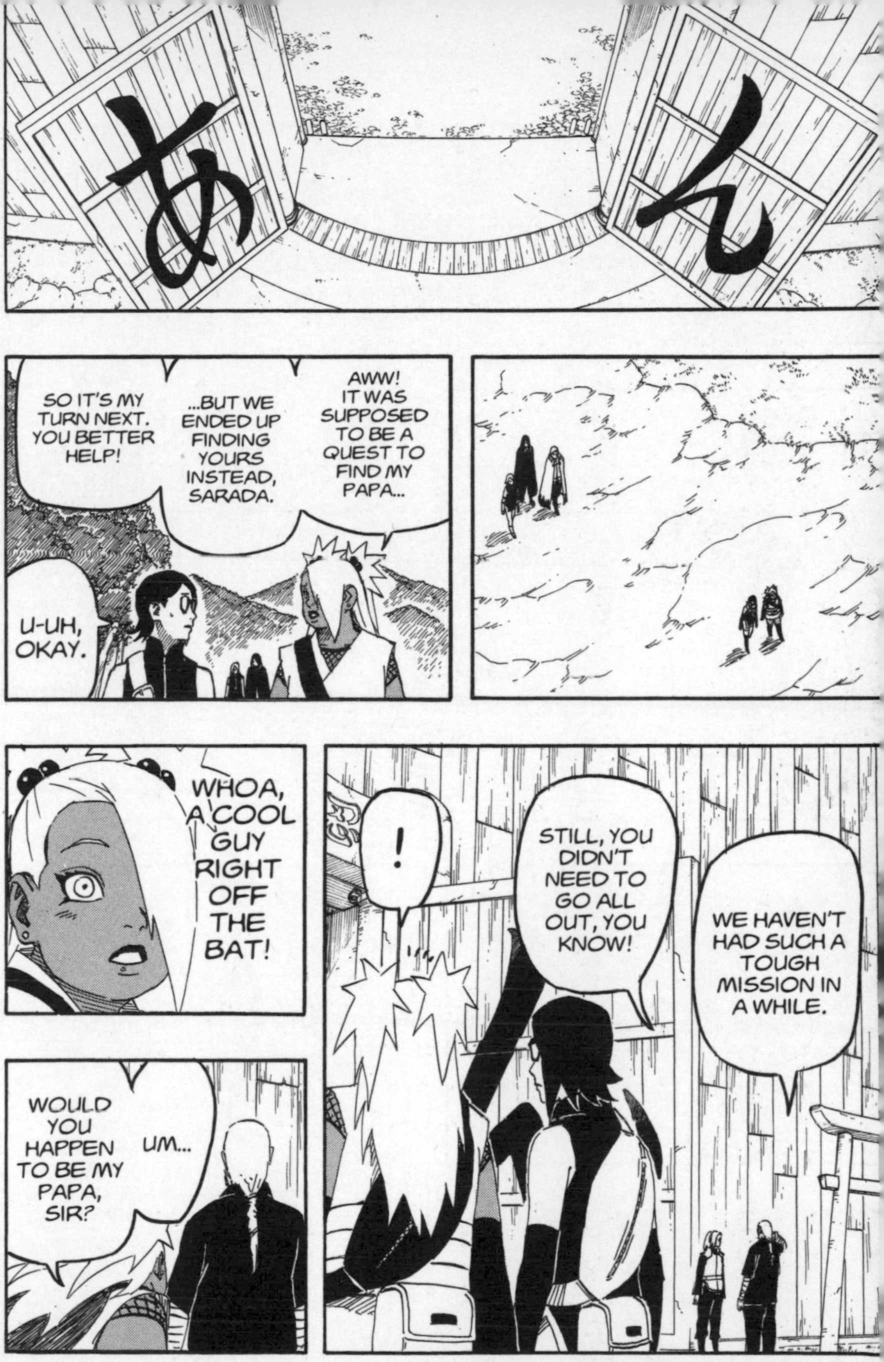
あん
AWW! IT WAS SUPPOSED TO BE A QUEST TO FIND MY PAPA...
...BUT WE ENDED UP FINDING YOURS INSTEAD, SARADA.
SO IT'S MY TURN NEXT. YOU BETTER HELP!
U-UH, OKAY.
WE HAVEN'T HAD SUCH A TOUGH MISSION IN A WHILE.
STILL, YOU DIDN'T NEED TO GO ALL OUT, YOU KNOW!
!
WHOA, A COOL GUY RIGHT OFF THE BAT!
UM...
WOULD YOU HAPPEN TO BE MY PAPA, SIR?

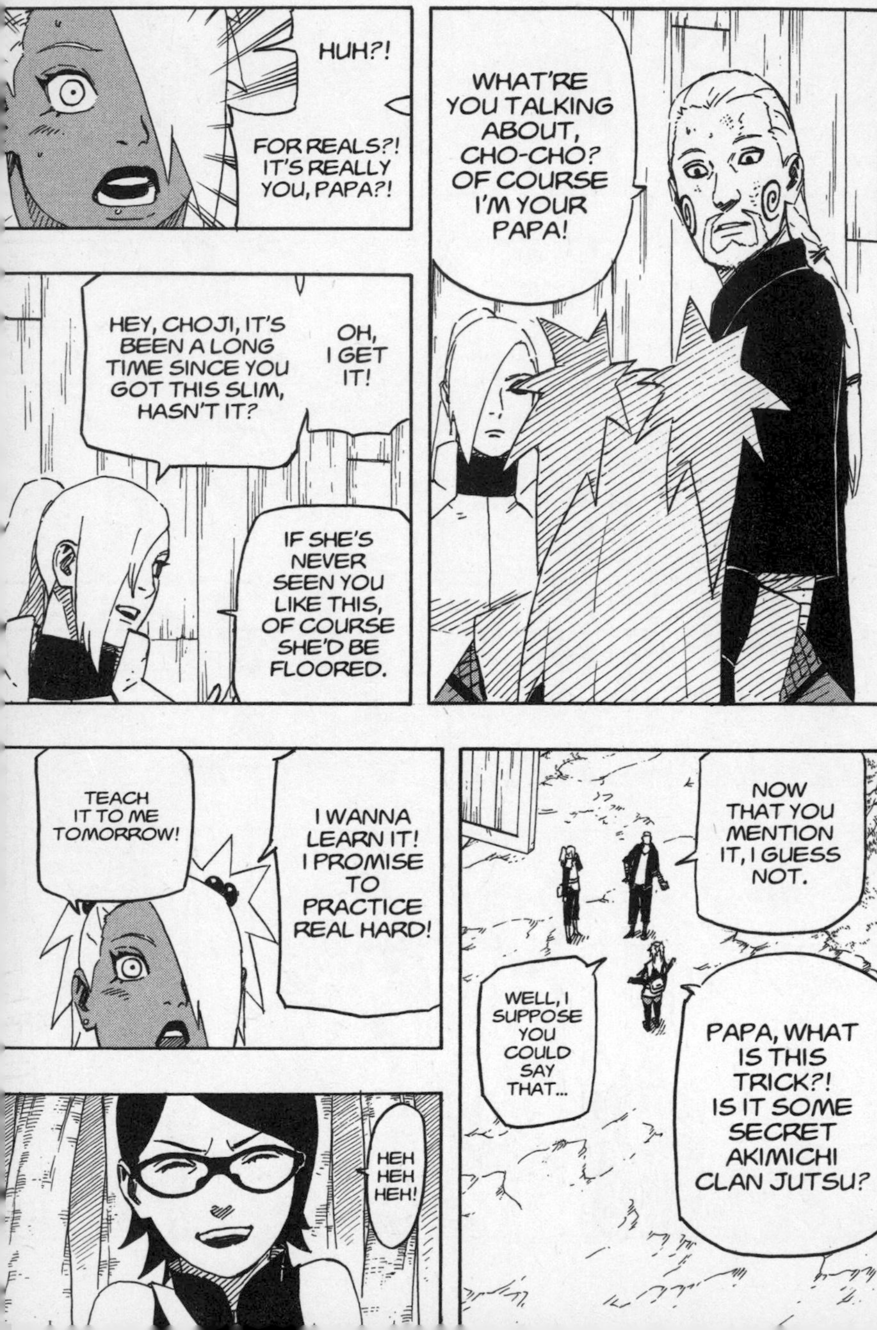
WHAT'RE YOU TALKING ABOUT, CHO-CHO? OF COURSE I'M YOUR PAPA!
HUH?!
FOR REALS?! IT'S REALLY YOU, PAPA?!
OH, I GET IT!
HEY, CHOJI, IT'S BEEN A LONG TIME SINCE YOU GOT THIS SLIM, HASN'T IT?
IF SHE'S NEVER SEEN YOU LIKE THIS, OF COURSE SHE'D BE FLOORED.
NOW THAT YOU MENTION IT, I GUESS NOT.
PAPA, WHAT IS THIS TRICK?! IS IT SOME SECRET AKIMICHI CLAN JUTSU?
WELL, I SUPPOSE YOU COULD SAY THAT...
I WANNA LEARN IT! I PROMISE TO PRACTICE REAL HARD!
TEACH IT TO ME TOMORROW!
HEH HEH HEH!

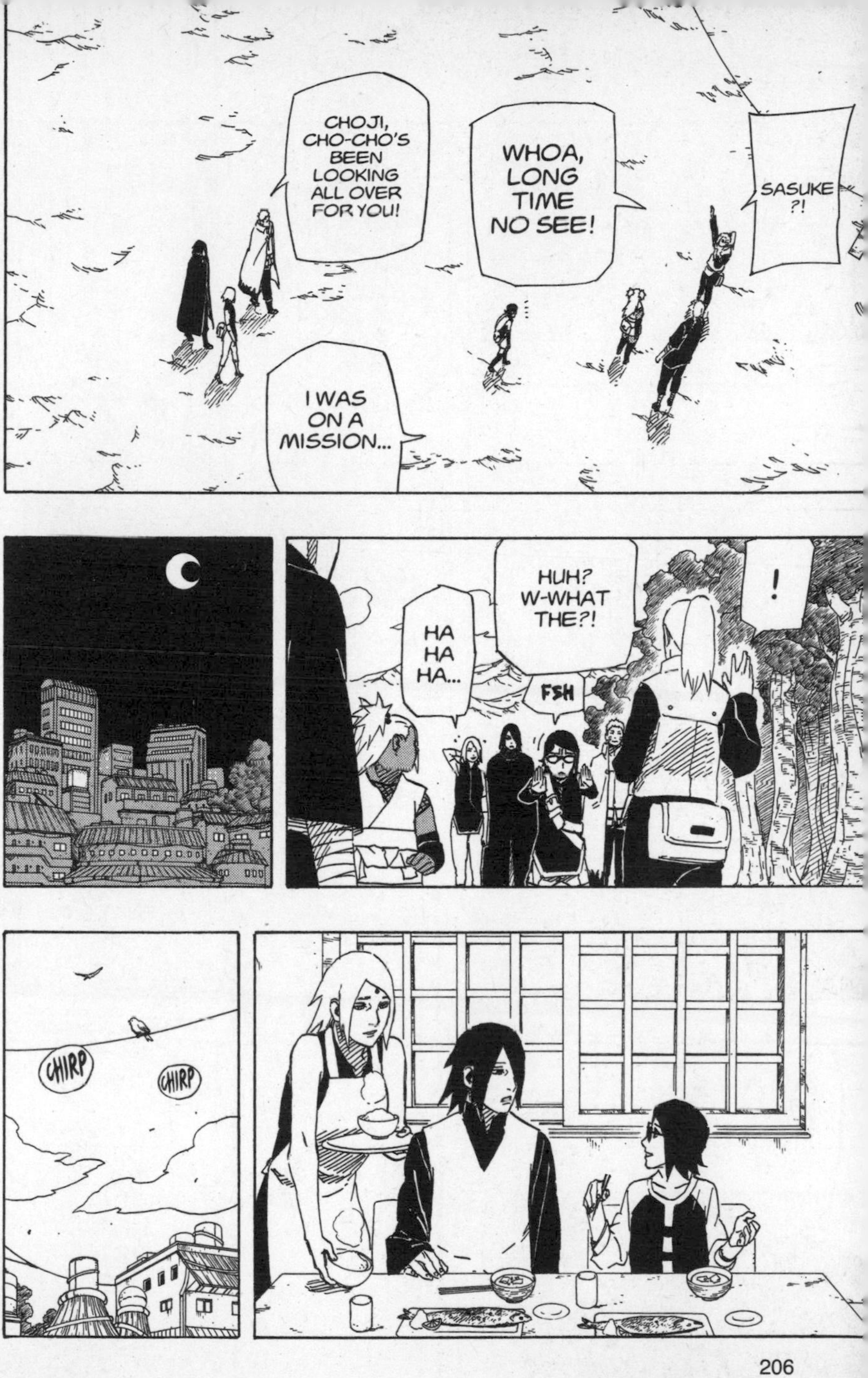
SASUKE ?!
WHOA, LONG TIME NO SEE!
CHOJI, CHO-CHO'S BEEN LOOKING ALL OVER FOR YOU!
I WAS ON A MISSION...
!
HUH? W-WHAT THE?!
FSH
HA HA HA...
CHIRP
CHIRP

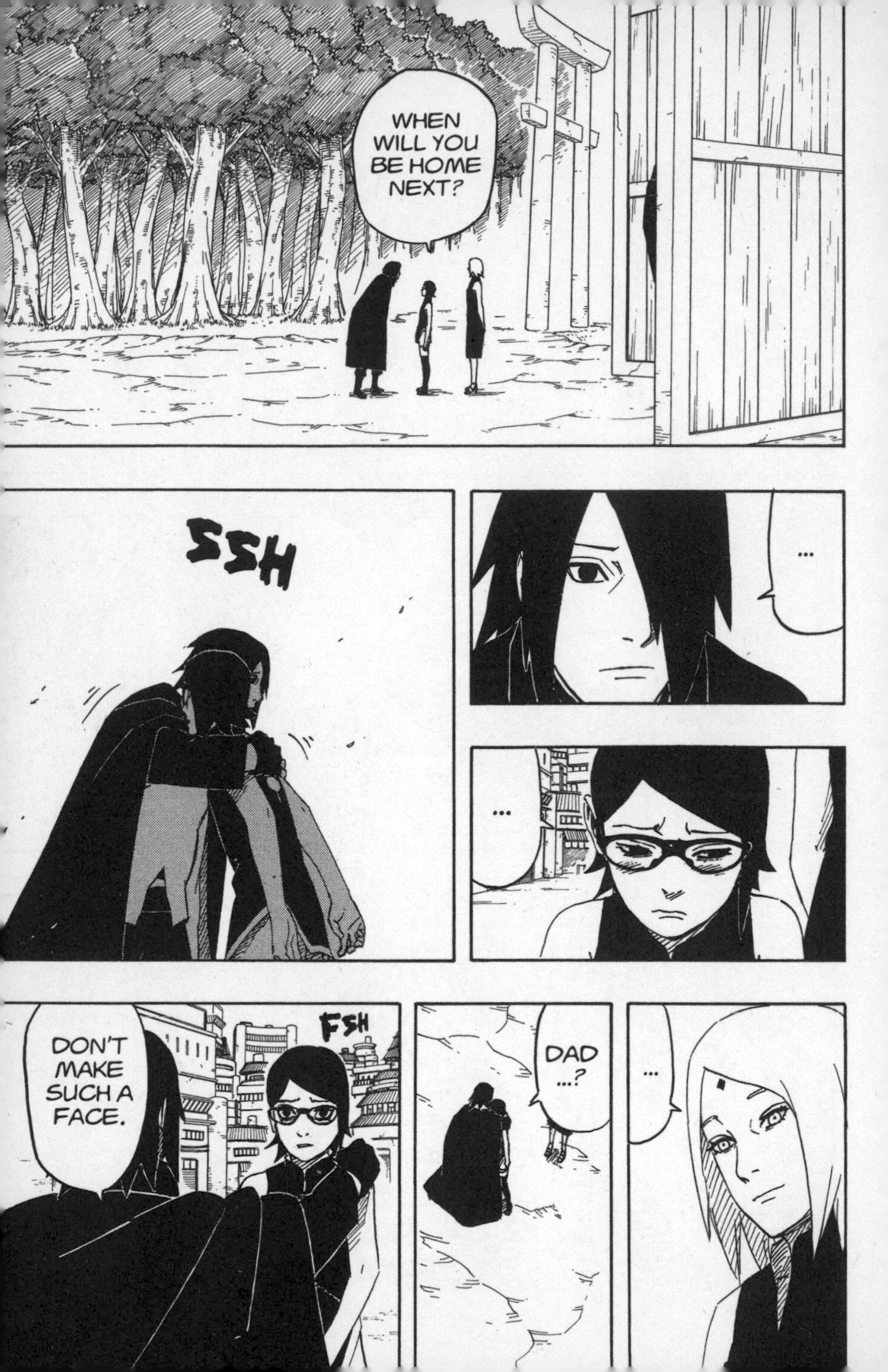
WHEN WILL YOU BE HOME NEXT?
...
...
SSH
...
DAD ...?
FSH
DON'T MAKE SUCH A FACE.

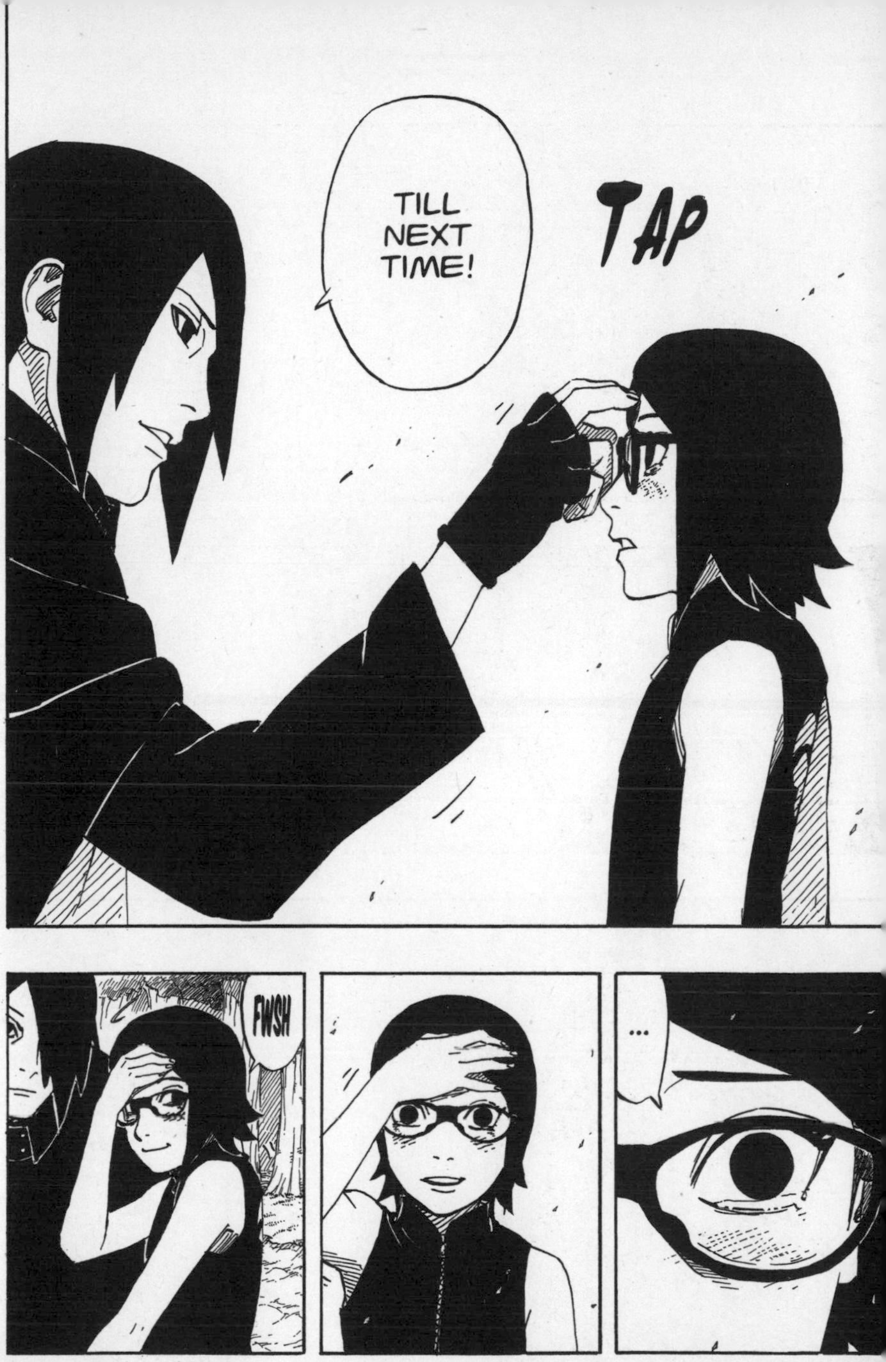
TILL NEXT TIME!
TAP
...
FWSH

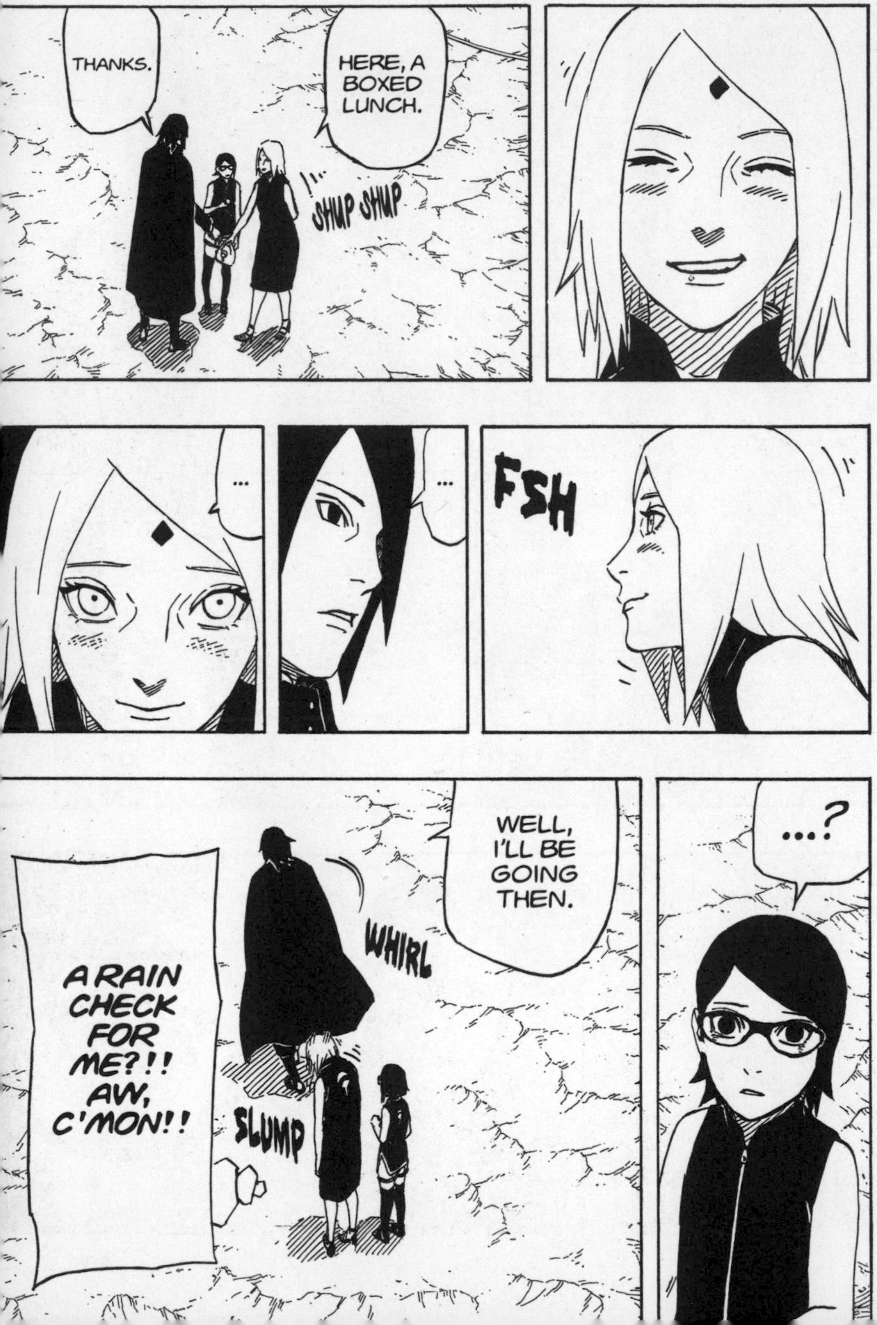
HERE, A BOXED LUNCH.
THANKS.
SHUP SHUP
FSH
...
...
...?
WELL, I'LL BE GOING THEN.
WHIRL
A RAIN CHECK FOR ME?!! AW, C'MON!!
SLUMP

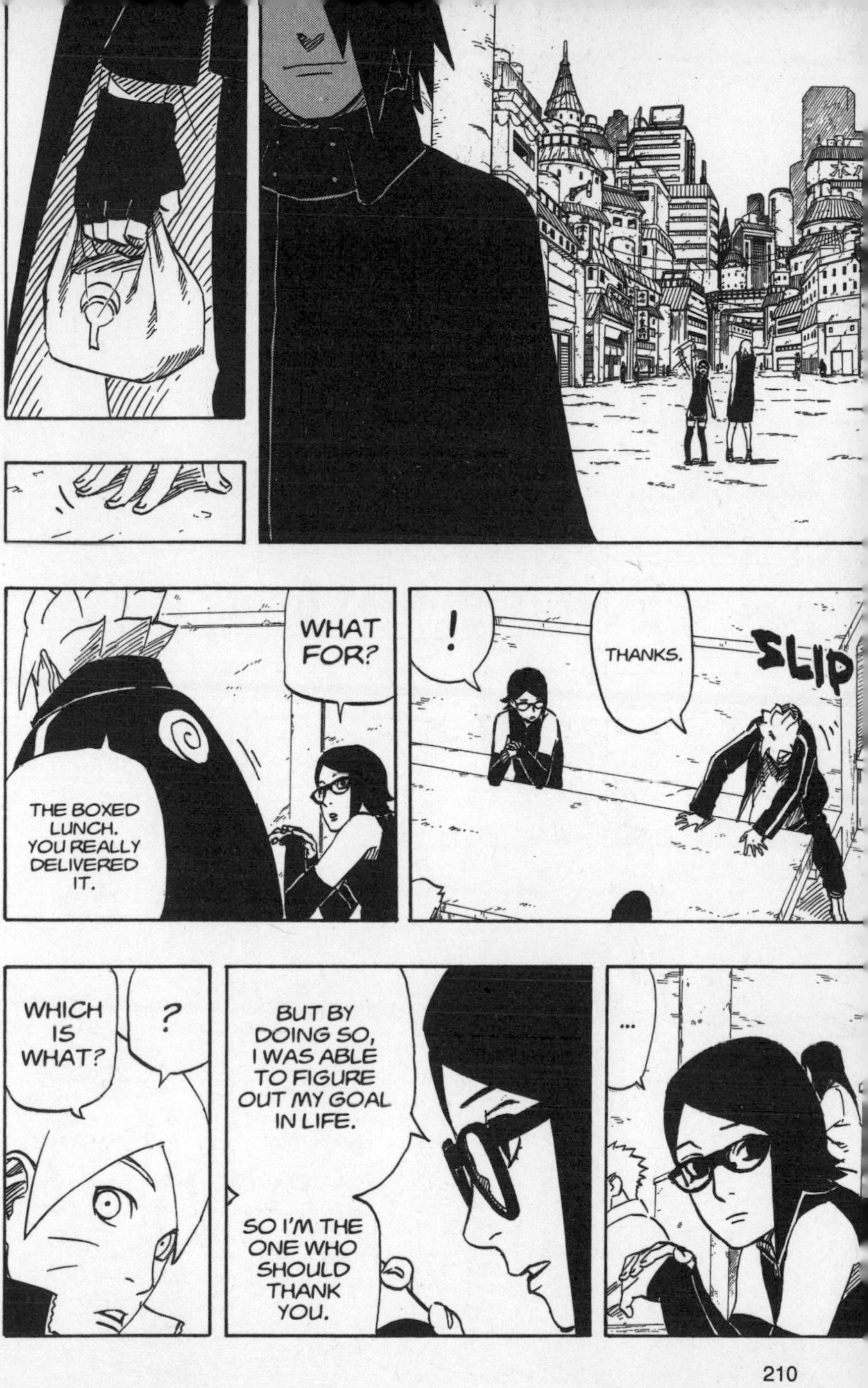
SLIP
THANKS.
!
WHAT FOR?
THE BOXED LUNCH. YOU REALLY DELIVERED IT.
...
BUT BY DOING SO, I WAS ABLE TO FIGURE OUT MY GOAL IN LIFE.
SO I'M THE ONE WHO SHOULD THANK YOU.
?
WHICH IS WHAT?

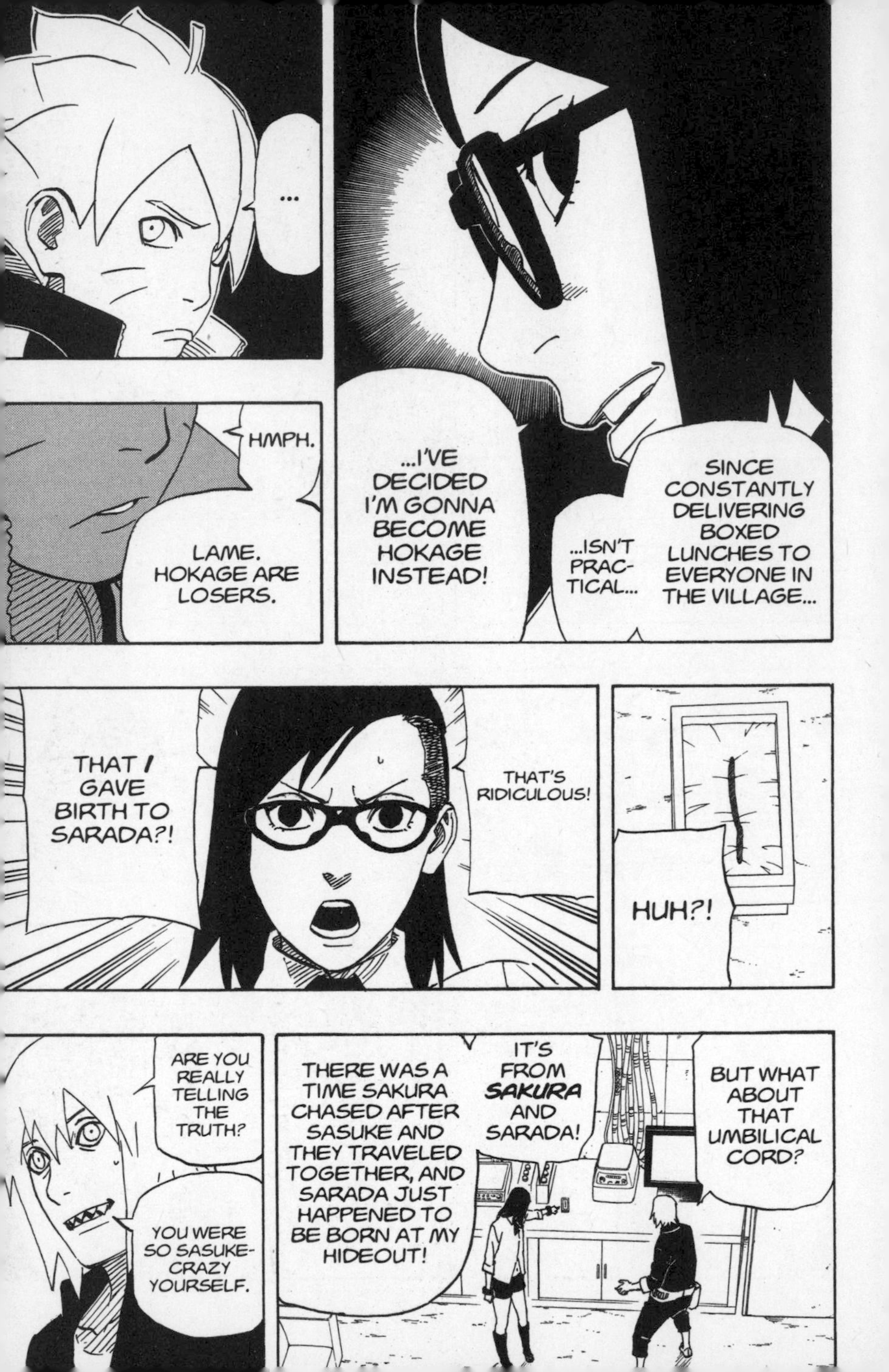
SINCE CONSTANTLY DELIVERING BOXED LUNCHES TO EVERYONE IN THE VILLAGE...
...ISN'T PRAC-TICAL...
...I'VE DECIDED I'M GONNA BECOME HOKAGE INSTEAD!
...
HMPH.
LAME. HOKAGE ARE LOSERS.
HUH?!
THAT'S RIDICULOUS!
THAT *I* GAVE BIRTH TO SARADA?!
BUT WHAT ABOUT THAT UMBILICAL CORD?
IT'S FROM **SAKURA** AND SARADA!
THERE WAS A TIME SAKURA CHASED AFTER SASUKE AND THEY TRAVELED TOGETHER, AND SARADA JUST HAPPENED TO BE BORN AT MY HIDEOUT!
ARE YOU REALLY TELLING THE TRUTH?
YOU WERE SO SASUKE-CRAZY YOURSELF.

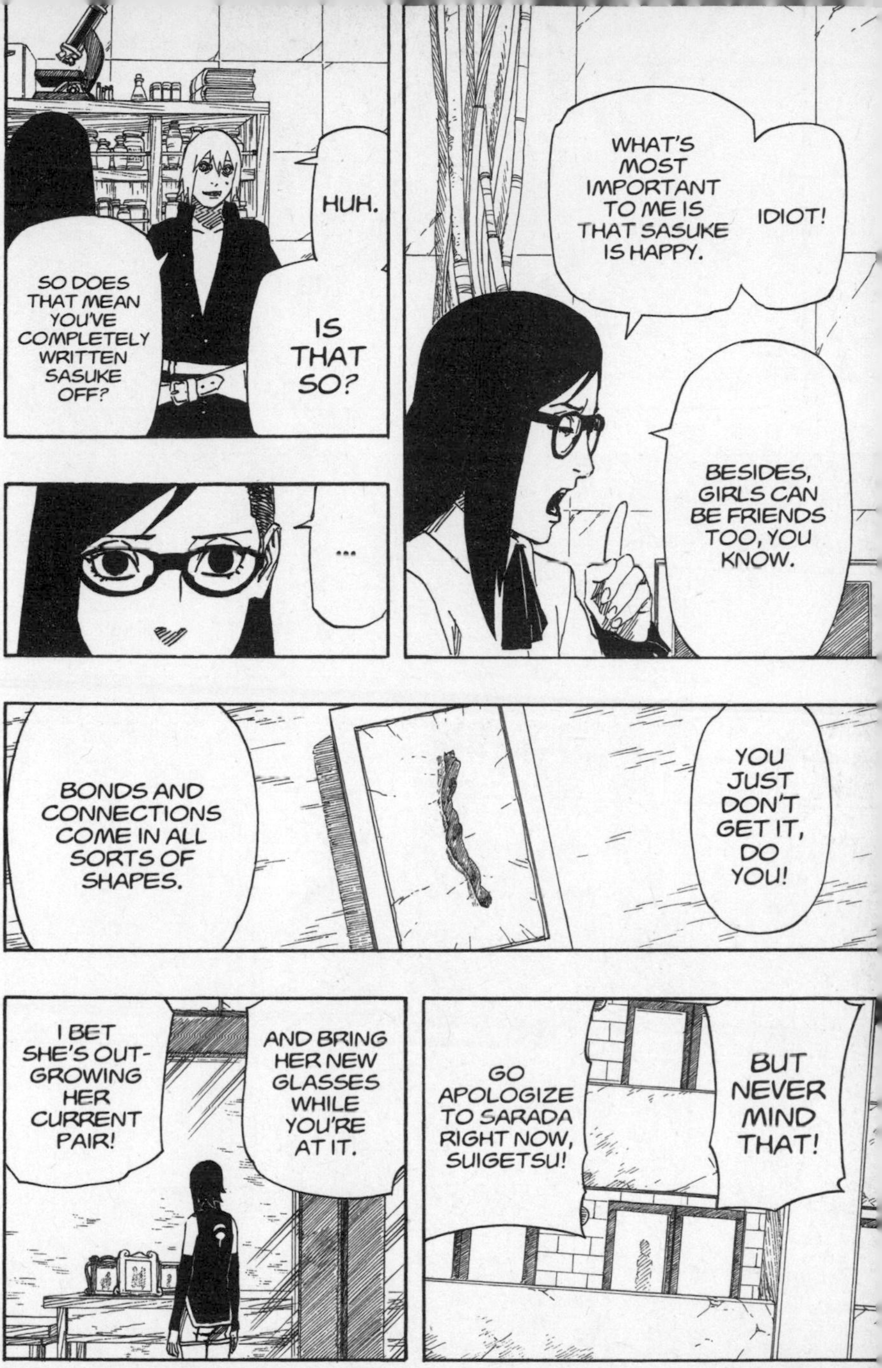
IDIOT!
WHAT'S MOST IMPORTANT TO ME IS THAT SASUKE IS HAPPY.
BESIDES, GIRLS CAN BE FRIENDS TOO, YOU KNOW.
HUH.
IS THAT SO?
SO DOES THAT MEAN YOU'VE COMPLETELY WRITTEN SASUKE OFF?
...
YOU JUST DON'T GET IT, DO YOU!
BONDS AND CONNECTIONS COME IN ALL SORTS OF SHAPES.
BUT NEVER MIND THAT!
GO APOLOGIZE TO SARADA RIGHT NOW, SUIGETSU!
AND BRING HER NEW GLASSES WHILE YOU'RE AT IT.
I BET SHE'S OUT-GROWING HER CURRENT PAIR!

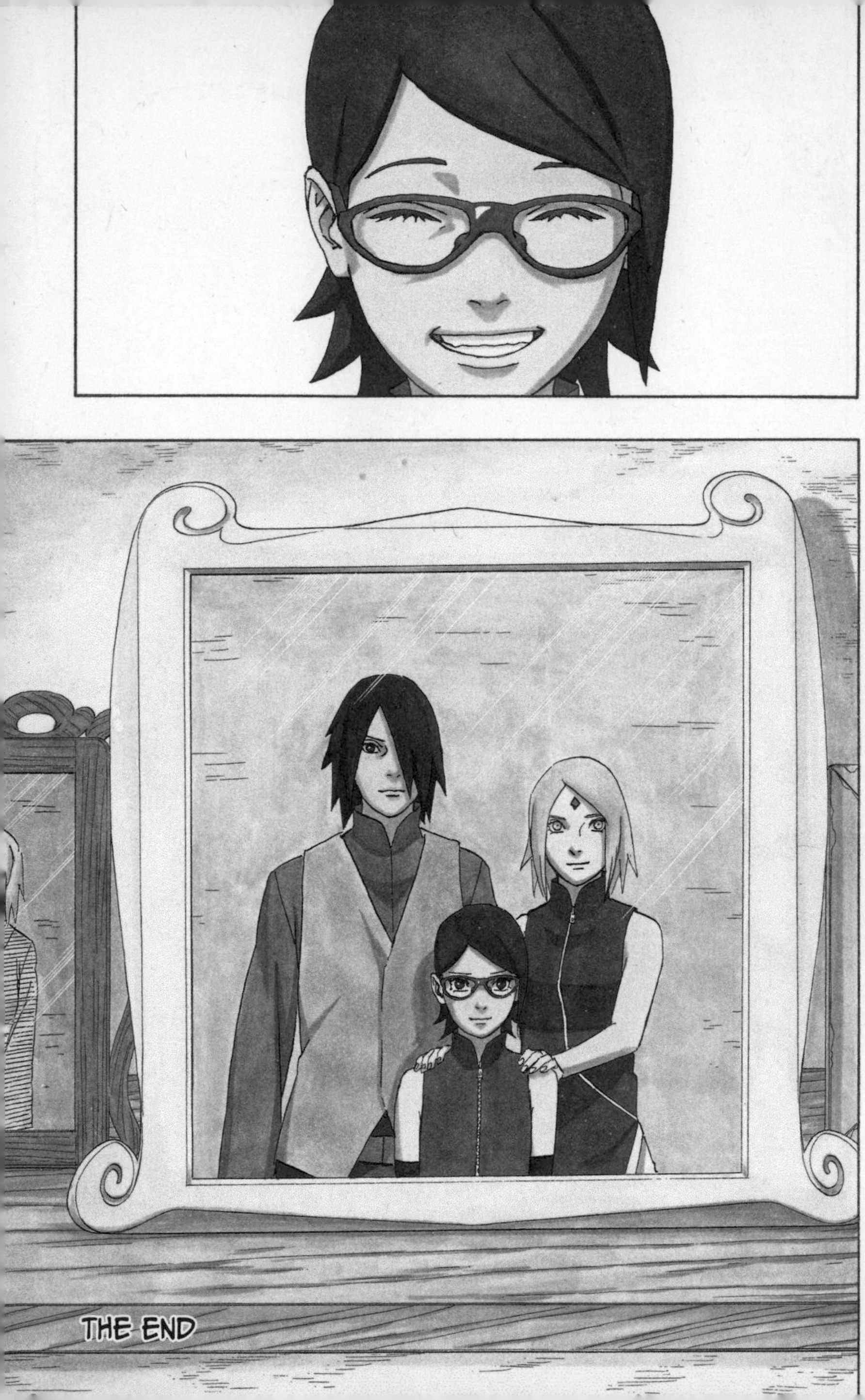
THE END

NARUTO: The Seventh Hokage and the Scarlet Spring
SHONEN JUMP Manga Edition

STORY AND ART BY MASASHI KISHIMOTO

Translation/Mari Morimoto
Touch-up Art & Lettering/John Hunt
Design/Yukiko Whitley, Brianna Depue
Editor/Alexis Kirsch

Printed in the U.S.A.

Published by VIZ Media, LLC
P.O. Box 77010
San Francisco, CA 94107

10 9 8 7 6 5 4 3 2
First printing, January 2016
Second printing, February 2016

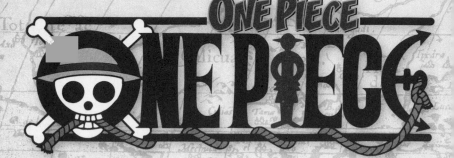
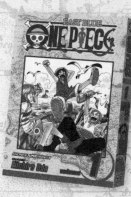
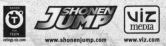

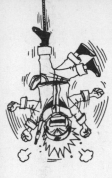

You're Reading in the Wrong Direction!!

Whoops! Guess what? You're starting at the wrong end of the comic!

...It's true! In keeping with the original Japanese format, **Naruto** is meant to be read from right to left, starting in the upper-right corner.

Unlike English, which is read from left to right, Japanese is read from right to left, meaning that action, sound effects and word-balloon order are completely reversed... something which can make readers unfamiliar with Japanese feel pretty backwards themselves. For this reason, manga or Japanese comics published in the U.S. in English have sometimes been published "flopped"—that is, printed in exact reverse order, as though seen from the other side of a mirror.

By flopping pages, U.S. publishers can avoid confusing readers, but the compromise is not without its downside. For one thing, a character in a flopped manga series who once wore in the original Japanese version a T-shirt emblazoned with "M A Y" (as in "the merry month of") now wears one which reads "Y A M"! Additionally, many manga creators in Japan are themselves unhappy with the process, as some feel the mirror-imaging of their art alters their original intentions.

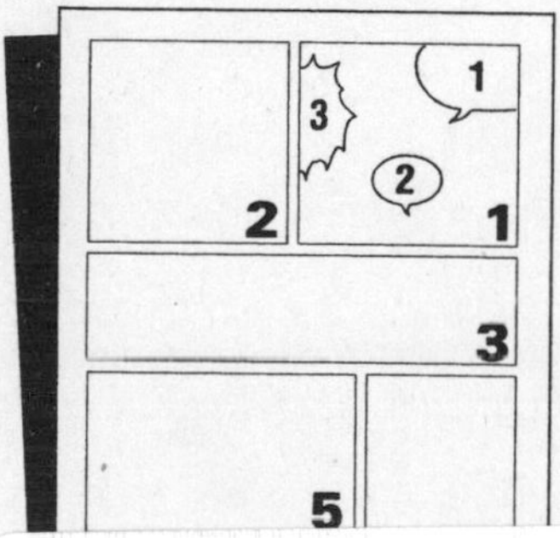

We are proud to bring you Masashi Kishimoto's **Naruto** in the original unflopped format. For now, though, turn to the other side of the book and let the ninjutsu begin...!

—Editor

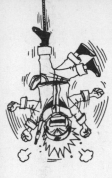